"With *NoMeansNo: From Obscurity to Oblivion*, Jason has documented every part big and small associated with the story of NoMeansNo, isolating them into a book filled with an explosion of posters, clippings, and interviews. This is it! The definitive tome! *From Obscurity to Oblivion* has so many subplots and stories, I don't know how Jason edited it! A fascinating read and look (did I mention all the tidbits and pictures?) into the legendary Victoria, BC, band."
—Nardwuar the Human Serviette

"Out of the blue, NoMeansNo showed up in San Francisco. Playing to a tiny crowd at a tiny dive bar. Blew the roof off several buildings in a matter of minutes. The drums and the bass were so tight and so intense, it was almost like they were one person. Could they be brothers? Ruth Schwartz of Mordam and I smiled warily at each other, thinking, 'Okay, which one of us gets this one?' And that wonderful era we will always treasure began."
—Jello Biafra

"I don't understand how the hell all these punks remember everything that made them the legends they are, but after reading *NoMeansNo: From Obscurity to Oblivion*, I'm grateful they do! The often-forgotten third point of the Canadian trifecta (Rush, Voivod, and NoMeansNo), this incredibly thorough oral history is a necessary read for any punk."
—Shawna Potter, singer for War on Women and author of *Making Spaces Safer: A Guide to Giving Harassment the Boot Wherever You Work, Play, and Gather*

"NoMeansNo mashed all the best in hard rock, metal, punk, and the art of politics in throughout their eleven albums, and Jason Lamb's book is just as important to the understanding of Canadian music and the band's astonishing place in it. We might not have the band around anymore, but this book will make you wish they were."
—Eric Alper, ThatEricAlper.com

"Jason Lamb has birthed into the world a stunning work of punk rock scholarship. Mirroring the complexity of the NoMeansNo story and the array of bands Rob and John inspired and influenced, there could be no other way to present the tale than oral history. It reads like a panoramic—but at each stop, reverent—a celebration of this Canadian progressive punk treasure, and one feels the love with every speaker. But Lamb also interjects with necessary action points just to make sure we understand the near indescribable. Along the way as well, elucidating pictures help tell the story. The end effect is saga told in granular detail, yet made swiftly readable due to the format."
—Martin Popoff, author of *The Clash: All the Albums, All the Songs* and *Ramones at 40*

"If you've never heard NoMeansNo, shame on you. If you have, then you're in the know. Either way, they're one of the most important underground bands of all time, and this book is for you."

—Sam Dunn, Banger Films

"NoMeansNo were the greatest punk rock group that ever existed; of that I am absolutely sure. In this snappy, fabulously readable oral history, writer Jason Lamb has done an admirable job in tracking down all the main players plus a gratifying array of musicians from bands such as Fugazi, Soundgarden, Faith No More, Foo Fighters, and Black Flag, who turn out to be staunch fans. Their incredible back catalogue is just waiting to be discovered by a younger audience, and hopefully this book will be picked up by young souls who will be inspired to do something unique and audacious themselves. Probably the greatest gift NoMeansNo have left us fans is the idea that we have to work it out for ourselves—to do it for ourselves."

—John Doran, *The Quietus*

"As a broadcaster, Lamb's style is fundamentally interviews and context. What makes *NoMeansNo: From Obscurity to Oblivion* crucially important is that the voices provide the context. Lamb has masterfully curated these voices and captured what is arguably the most important Canadian band to emerge from the post-punk Eighties scene. I personally saw NoMeansNo perform as a two-piece, then a three-piece, and then morphing into a four-piece, and then back to a three-piece. The talent of the Wrights can't be overstated, nor that of their guitarists Tom and Andy. Their mammoth catalogue rises among some of the greatest music ever created by a so-called independent punk band. The fact that it's taken this long to assess the environment that led to their creation is alarming to me. If you are a fan of music, hardcore punk, jazz, rock, and counterculture, this book is for you."

—Phil Saunders, author of *No Flash, Please! Underground Music in Toronto, 1987–92*

# NOMEANSNO
## From Obscurity to Oblivion
### An Oral History

**Jason Lamb**

Edited with Paul Prescott
Foreword by Fred Armisen

*NoMeansNo: From Obscurity to Oblivion; An Oral History*


ISBN: 979–888–744–014–9 (paperback)
ISBN: 979–888–744–018–7 (hardcover)
ISBN: 979–888–744–015–6 (ebook)
Library of Congress Control Number: 2023930617

Cover design by John Yates / stealworks.com
Cover illustration by John Wright
Interior design by briandesign

10 9 8 7 6 5 4 3 2 1

PM Press
PO Box 23912
Oakland, CA 94623
www.pmpress.org

Printed in the USA.

# CONTENTS

# FOREWORD

When I first heard NoMeansNo in the early '90s, I thought, "This is how everything should sound! How isn't every band going for this?" I realize it's not logical, the word "should." It was just my immediate reaction to that heavy and clearly defined sound of their bass and drums.

I loved that guitar. Rob's vocals were so gripping that I wanted to join up with whatever he was singing about. Do you know that feeling? The intensity of their music was unlike anything I had known before. It wasn't just simple intensity through volume and speed. It was balanced out by a subtle sense of humor. I don't mean that as in jokey lyrics. There was something in the complete sound itself that felt fun. It was a great new way for punk to exist. *Wrong* is one of my favorite albums ever.

My band, Trenchmouth, opened for NoMeansNo at Rice University in Houston, Texas. This was when they had two drummers. I felt so lucky that I had a chance to see them live. When my band watched them, it was like a celebration of everything we loved.

In that moment, I wanted the whole world to experience them.

I learned more about them throughout the years in that way we used to learn about bands, just from hearing stories from other musicians. Every new bit of information seemed improbable and funny to me—where they were from, that two of them were brothers, and that they had all of these interesting side projects going. It made sense to me that they had the support of Alternative Tentacles.

The song that keeps jumping out to me is "It's Catching Up." Might it be one of the heaviest and greatest songs ever? I'm not exaggerating. What is that intro part? That repeated thud? How does that exist? Every one of those parts, I can't imagine having the energy to play the drums that intensely.

When I listen to NoMeansNo now, it still feels new to me. Like they found the key to sounding urgent and timeless at the same time.

**Fred Armisen**

# INTRODUCTION

## "They lived und laughed ant loved end left."
## —James Joyce, *Finnegans Wake*

Being a NoMeansNo fan has never been easy. We know that this band is the most insanely talented, deepest-thinking, hardest-working, and most influential band in the world. Yet most of our friends have never heard of them.

Their albums are incredible, but somehow they were ten times better live. We think the whole wide world deserves to love them too, yet we want to hold on to them ourselves. It's like a kid not wanting to share his rarest hockey cards. We also secretly feel that some people just don't *deserve* to like NoMeansNo.

They were a punk band that challenged everyone's perception of what punk could be, and they did so on their own terms the whole way through. They didn't sing about Reagan or Thatcher or the politics of the day. They sang about *human* politics and the suffering and joy just in being alive.

They always seemed older and wiser, and they never really *looked* punk. They would show up to some grotty venue looking more like television repairmen than musicians. Punk elitists in the crowd would scoff, until the band got onstage and played.

One of the most appealing things about NoMeansNo is the way they balance deep, insightful lyrics with powerful music, often with a wink of humour and mystery. You're in on the joke, but only so far.

I hope to honour that dynamic in this book, while presenting for the first time the whole story of NoMeansNo and their remarkable and unconventional career.

I was born and raised in Victoria, British Columbia, the same hometown as NoMeansNo. I started going to see punk shows as a teenager around 1986, as NMN was hitting their stride. This was just before they signed with Alternative Tentacles and were about to go international. They were still playing often in Victoria and were widely considered to be the best band in the city. I saw every NoMeansNo show I could, maybe twenty-five times over the years. They became my favourite band.

The process of researching, interviewing, and collecting material for this book has been a massive undertaking, but I've loved every minute of it. I hope the finished product reflects that.

I spoke to hundreds of people in gathering the content for this book, from childhood buddies to big-time rock stars. From fans and family to the band members themselves. I've had middle-aged men break down weeping as they recounted how important NoMeansNo's music is to them. Women have told me how the band made them feel safer in a male-dominated scene.

I want this to be an introduction to NoMeansNo for the uninitiated. More importantly, though, I want this to be a celebration of the band for those who already adore them. A love letter from their many thousands of fans around the world. The folks who *know.*

**Julie Moore and Scott Henderson at Richard's Records, Victoria**

When we played the song, I was fucking nervous as fuck. I couldn't stop my foot from shaking. I'm like, "Ah! I'm not going to be able to play if my foot doesn't settle down. I'm gonna fall flat on my face." It was right then that I decided being nervous is stupid. I'm never going to be nervous again, because being nervous before you go onstage is a nightmare. I just made that conscious decision: "This is stupid. You can't play if you're feeling this way." I never got nervous again.

**Karl Johanson** There's an argument some people have about whether talent is innate or learned. I'm of the opinion that it's both. There are clearly some people who have a better genetic gift. Without hard work, it's nothing, and John seemed to work very hard.

**Randy Strobl** We would hang out in John's basement, and that's where I met his brother. Rob started coming home with bags full of records: the Specials, the Selecter, Madness. Weird bands too, like Hawaiian Pups and the Residents. Every couple days he'd have new records; he spent all his money on them. He'd take the bus downtown and buy records and show them to us: Ramones, the first Clash record. We were like fifteen- or sixteen-year-old kids going, "Wow, what is this?" He would read *NME* [*New Musical Express*] magazine. It felt like we got jump-started into all this music, ahead of everybody else around us.

**Doug Burgess** Rob started buying records and bringing them home. John maybe had fifteen to twenty records, but Rob already had a couple hundred in his collection. This was the impetus for us when it came to punk rock. Rob started bringing home new-wave and punk records, stuff he got at A&B Sound and Kelly's but also stuff he found at Richard's Records. Cool, first-issue stuff from the UK and such. We were gobsmacked by a lot of it.

**John Wright** I didn't really like punk rock when I first heard it, because I thought, "Oh, this sounds kind of crappy, and it's not played very well. It's all rough and weird." I was still of the mentality that there should be some musicianship, and, "Is it serious?" All that bullshit.

**Rob Wright** Getting John to actually listen to punk rock and breaking through to him was a job. I alienated everyone with the Ramones because I would play this record for people and they'd go, "Huh?" No one wanted to hear that. No one. I thought it was just the best thing I'd ever heard. That was a big divide right there.

I saw the Ramones in Vancouver. I came out of the show and was like, "What time is it?" The show was forty-three minutes long. They played twenty songs in forty-three minutes. They were unbelievably good in their own way, which was not like anybody else.

**Doug Burgess** Right around that time, Rob started working at the dining room at the Commons Block at the University of Victoria, where they feed all the resident students. One day he came home with a four-track TEAC recorder. The two brothers started collaborating on stuff. At first, it was kind of quiet, jazz-inflected stuff, because at that time Rob only had an acoustic guitar.

**Rob Wright** I had plucked on a guitar since I was in grade four or five. I learned just on my own. I learned a few songs from a couple of books, and I would just strum chords and play little runs. I learned the minor blues scale, so I played that over and over, which you can tell if you listen to my songs.

I don't really know what motivated me, but the only thing I was interested in was music. The punk rock thing was just kind of starting, and things were changing. I'd been listening to fusion jazz and whatever. It wasn't until I started listening to the Ramones that I realized, "God, what the heck have I been doing? This is the stuff!" That was really the motivator that got me started. I realized that all I do is listen to music, all I'm interested in is music, so I might as well make music.

I came back home from Alberta and bought a four-track recorder and a couple of semiprofessional microphones with the money I'd saved. I had no idea what I was getting into. I had some knowledge of music, so I bought this four-track because I knew it could overlay tracks. It was the first one that did that. It's still sitting in my living room. It weighs a ton.

John was in high school at that time. He was a drummer, and he played piano. I said, "Let's do some stuff," which we did: first in the living room, and then we moved down to the basement. We made a studio/practice space down there. Drove our parents crazy. I still don't understand how they managed to survive.

**Rob's TEAC four-track recorder**

**John's high school yearbook photo**

**Randy Strobl** I was kind of a witness to that time when John went from being an annoying little brother to Rob saying, "Hey, wait, you're actually pretty cool and creative," and they started doing stuff together. Rob slept in a tent in the backyard of their parents' house at that time, and he got a good union job washing dishes at the university. His dad was a campus security officer there as well.

John lived at home until he was thirty, and we'd tease him about that sometimes. His nickname at that time was "Johnny Ass Dragger," because he was so patient and talented. He would work on just one part of a song for days. Sometimes we'd have plans to see a movie or something, and we'd be waiting for him, saying, "C'mon John! Let's go!" and he'd say, "Yeah, yeah. I just gotta work this thing out." Two hours later, he'd come out and say, "Okay, let's go, man," and we'd say, "John, we missed the movie."

**John Wright** I was smoking pot and hanging out. The band leader in grades eleven and twelve, Mr. Michaux, didn't like me, because he was a real straight-edged guy. I wasn't in trouble or anything. I just didn't conform to that high school thing. I didn't want to have anything to do with it, except playing in the band. I loved playing music. He didn't like me, but he did tell me, "Look, you're not the best drummer

Castle Music store, Victoria

here, but you're the only one who knows how to swing."

Thedor was a keyboard player, and Robbie and I played briefly with him in a cover band that never played any shows. We just jammed a bit together. I remember having to learn a Rush song. The one time in my life I ever learned a Rush song. I'm sure I didn't play it very well.

**Shelley Wright** Early on, Rob and John were in a band called Castle. It was a cover band and really schlocky, but they did a kick-ass version of "My Sharona"!

**Nancy Lipsett (formerly Castle)—Castle** I opened a music store called Castle Music with my husband, Rob. We were the first ones to sell computer-generated music and synthesizers. We used to have a lot of nice guitars and had music lessons. Rob and John Wright were in the same neighbourhood in the Cedar Hill area. They used to come in, and that's how we met.

**Rob Wright** We were making these recordings, but we realized that you can't be a band unless you play somewhere. We'd never been onstage playing music in our lives, what were we going to do? Well, we gotta join a band.

Castle Music was just down the street from us, at this little mall. The owner contacted us through Thedor, who was in our crummy little cover band. He said, "There's this guy Rob Castle, and he's looking for a rhythm section because he's got gigs on Salt Spring Island. He just wants to do a bunch of covers." I said, "John, let's go down and talk to him, because whatever it is, it's more than what we're doing, which is just nothing."

Within two or three weeks, we learned forty songs. Motown and all this classic rock. Whatever he could think of, because we were just going to a little bar on Salt Spring to play. That was the first time we played live. Then we played all sorts of places, Campbell River, Cumberland. The biggest gig was a New Year's dance in Port Hardy.

**John Wright** The one and only time I've actually been to Port Hardy. We were booked for a New Year's Eve gig, and it paid really well. We got paid a couple of thousand bucks, and I was, "Whoa, I got paid something, holy shit!" We had to do four sets. We only had three, so we played our first set again.

**Scott Henderson—Shovlhed, Show Business Giants, Swell Prod., Hissanol, producer, engineer** In the late '70s, I lived across the street from Castle Music, and I would hang out there quite a bit. One fine day I went in, and there's a guy there with

Castle: Rob Wright, Nancy Castle, Dean Strickland, Rob Castle, and John Wright

WAVERLEY BONO'S FASTBALL CLUB

Invite you to
Boogie with "Special Guests"

CASTLE

at the CRI hall in Cumberland
Saturday, October 27, 1979

TICKETS $5.00 EACH

JAN. 27, 1980
7:30 - 12:00
OAP HALL
1600 GOVERNMENT ST

ZYLUS
&
CASTLE
*Two Band Rock & Roll*

$4.00 - ADVANCE SALE
$5.00 - AT THE DOOR

a Tascam 33-4 four-track reel-to-reel tape deck. The first song he played was "You're So Blind." I'm just like, "Wow, that's great! You guys are good. You got anything else?" So he played me a bunch more. He said, "Yeah, it's just me and my brother. We also play with Rob and Nancy in Castle."

**Rob Wright** We did three or four sets a night, and eventually we became sort of like a rock band, doing mostly covers. We did "My Sharona" and stuff that was starting to cross over. I remember "Sultans of Swing" was my first singing gig. It was a job for me, because I had to sing and play at the same time, which I hadn't done before. That was always a challenge.

**John Wright** It was a great experience. The music was fun to play. "Honky Tonk Women," what's there to hate? You played the song and people danced. It was a really good experience for Robbie and me to be actually performing.

**Rob Wright** It didn't last long. We did a lot of work, though, and we learned a lot of stuff. We bought a lot of equipment from Rob Castle at wholesale prices, and we kept recording. Eventually, Rob got kind of mad at us. He didn't like punk rock at all. He was a flower child. He didn't like this nastiness, aggression, and "life is shit" attitude.

**John Wright** I remember we were building a practice studio out in the Castles' house, and around then their marriage fell apart. And that was the end of that.

## THE D.O.A. SHOW THAT CHANGED EVERYTHING

The following is from an essay that Rob wrote for a planned project about D.O.A. by manager Laurie Mercer that never came to fruition:

**D.O.A. Live at the Commons Block**
by Rob Wright
March 23, 1979

D.O.A. were scary.

I had been into punk rock for a while, but it was something that was going on far away, in London or New York. Hardcore hadn't been invented yet, and no hint of what was happening in California had filtered this far north. I was right into the Ramones, Sex Pistols, the Clash, the Jam, the Stranglers, Talking Heads. But I only knew them from their records and what I'd read about them, which was mostly disparaging. They were legendary figures to me, patron saints of damage and hopelessness who played music with such primitive, savage joy that it basically wiped the slate clean for many people.

SICK! SICK! SICK!!!

| FRI. MAY 12, 1978 | SAT. MAY 13, 1978 |
|---|---|
| DOMINION HALL | GLENWOOD CENTRE |
| 802 ESQUIMALT | PORT ALBERNI |
| 8:00 P.M. | 8:00 P.M. |
| D.O.A. AV STIFFS AND THE DISHRAGS | AV D.O.A. AND THE STIFFS |

But these were cool people in some cool scene that would never reach sleepy Victoria. Then, suddenly, here were these posters showing some guy with a crew cut and shades looking arrogant and angry and stupid and all that other real cool, punk rock stuff. They were for a band from Vancouver called D.O.A. Unfortunately, when I saw the posters it was two days after the show had happened. But that was kind of a relief. I would have been very nervous about going down to see them. These guys looked like the real thing, and that was dangerous. (Remember when music was dangerous?)

There were no punks in Victoria. Some people were listening to punk music, but there were no short haircuts, or torn jeans, or safety pins, or green hair dye—these things were still beyond the pale. No one yet had the guts or gall to be that weird. I was still listening to a lot of mainstream music at the time; punk rock was my secret vice.

I had played the first Ramones album to family and friends, with me basically frothing at the mouth about how great it was. But I had seen their looks of horror and disgust. Looks that clearly said: "Are you joking or have you simply lost your mind? What is this garbage?" I realized that my generation and I had parted ways forever.

I began hanging out with my brother, John, and his friends, people who were seven or eight years younger than I was: high school students whose main preoccupations were still booze and drugs and sex and all other forms of having fun. Their minds were a little more open, although it took a while before the wider ramifications of this crude and radical noise began to sink in. I'd slip a little Wire or Clash onto a tape in between Boston or Van Halen or the Cars. It would go down all right at a party. "Hey, it's loud and obnoxious, it's okay, but that Eddie Van Halen, now there's a guitar player!" They could relate to stuff done by people who still played reasonably proficiently, like the Stranglers; or stuff that was still rooted pretty recognizably in rock, like the Jam; or stuff that was just downright undeniably savage, like Sex Pistols. But the Ramones were generally still too hard to swallow, even for John: "They can't play; they're just dumb." But whether they thought the music was okay, or bizarre and interesting, or just dumb, it still didn't mean anything to them. I was one step ahead on that score.

I knew it meant something more, but I didn't know what. I was still just a listener.

I was working in the residence kitchen of the University of Victoria, washing pots. This job supported my music habit for six years or so. The students ate in the Commons Block, about a thousand at a time, and this large room was also the place where student dances and socials were held. One Friday, at coffee break, the janitors began to move away the tables at the far corner of the room and push together the segments of a low portable stage. Some PA equipment began to arrive, and I asked one of my fellow galley slaves if he knew what was going on. "They're having some kind of dance tonight. Some band from Vancouver is playing. It's a punk rock band. They're called D.O.A."

Oh, really? I remember sneaking out of the kitchen later and standing behind a pillar, listening to the sound check. I couldn't fucking believe it. Those cool people from that cool scene were coming right into my own personal little sweatshop to play. This I could not miss. I went home, and I had to convince my brother, John, that this was a must-see event. He was reluctant to go, but I insisted. I put on my oldest jeans and wore my dad's brown leather jacket, complete with fake fur collar. I was unshaven, unwashed, and, all in all, felt pretty hip—as hip as anyone who had never done anything more than stand at a safe distance and watch.

The place was crowded. I didn't know anyone there. There were no punks at that time, and gigs at the Commons Block were only open to students and university employees. The majority were jocks who had come to get drunk and heckle the punk rock freak show.

The room was charged with hostility. Somebody dressed in a cheap blazer and wearing sharp-looking shades got up onstage. He was obviously one of "them." He approached the microphone and sneered at the crowd. "So, are you ready to rock?" he asked, his expression implying that he doubted anyone there had any idea just what they were letting themselves in for. "Are you ready to fucking rock!" he repeated; this time it was clearly a threat. Some of the jocks replied with catcalls, but you could tell they were already beginning to feel unsure of themselves. They had come to bully and ridicule, not to be bullied and ridiculed. The first band up was the Wasted Lives. I had never heard of them. John and I were standing at the far right of the stage, on the fringes of the crowd. The sound was horrible; what we heard was a solid mass of painfully loud, indistinguishable noise. Later, after I'd done this sort of thing myself a few times, I realized I hadn't seen any monitors onstage: the bands must have heard fuck-all of what they were doing. Even so, I was impressed by one song which had a section with hard stops and starts: "No more pain, there's a wire in my brain!" It was about getting shock treatment! The lead singer obviously didn't give a damn about what anyone thought of him and made no bones about his contempt for the audience, so he was all right by me.

Two or three jocks moved to the front of the stage and began hassling the guitar player, who responded by taking a lunge at one of them during a song. Eventually a big guy with a prickly short crew cut, something of a gut under his dirty T-shirt, tattered jeans, and big boots stepped out from the back of the stage and planted himself directly in front of the guitar player. He had the look of a semi-deranged redneck, or a recently escaped inmate from a work farm for the criminally insane. Later, when D.O.A. came on, I realized he was Joey Shithead, their guitar player and singer. He stood right in the midst of the jocks and began to dance to the music, jumping heavily up and down in one spot, his lips slack and jiggling with every hop, his eyes glazed over. He looked grim. Within seconds, the jocks had melted away into the crowd and the guitar player was no longer being hassled. It occurred to me that perhaps these jocks were not the tough, dangerous men they appeared to be; perhaps they were just chickenshits.

John and I moved up closer after the Wasted Lives finished their set. We eased our way around the back of the stage and managed finally to seat ourselves right on the table holding up the left PA column. There was no stage security. We were basically on the stage. Unfortunately, some of the jocks got the same idea, and three of them came up and sat down with us.

The next band was the Dishrags: three young women, none of whom looked over sixteen. The bass player had a Fender Precision, which I swear was as big as she was. They gave new depth and meaning to the word *cacophony*. Their lead singer and guitar player, a small woman called Jade Blade, would periodically lunge at the microphone and scream something incomprehensible while looking deadly serious. The bass player just stood and tried to grapple with her unwieldy instrument. Judging by the glazed expression on her face, she had no idea what the hell she was doing there. The jocks immediately started to scream insults at them. They were a definite nonthreatening target; the big men could indulge themselves without trepidation. But the band kept playing, ignoring the assholes; ignoring their own fear and complete musical ineptness; intent on screaming and blasting out their violent little tunes. I thought they were great, and I started to get really pissed off with the guys beside me, especially one guy, the loudest, who was always looking to his friends for encouragement and braying with laughter at his own stupid remarks. At one point, I reached over and took his beer out of his hand with a big smile on my face, downed a good portion of it, and handed it back. His sneer evaporated, and he became suddenly very studious of the band. It was true! They were just a bunch of chickenshits! I began to enjoy myself immensely.

When D.O.A. finally got onstage, John and I sat alone, right beside Randy Rampage. His arms were covered with tattoos, and his face was set in an expression of studied vacancy. Joey was stage right. Chuck Biscuits was on a small drum riser behind the other two. The overriding elements of speed and violence in his drumming were somewhat of a revelation to John, whose own playing has never strayed far from those prerequisites to this day. They all played with considerably more musical expertise than the other bands, but straight-ahead, angry energy was still the basic and most important ingredient. Songs like "Nazi Training Camp," "Disco Sucks," and "The Prisoner," besides being loud, lean, powerful little pop songs, were direct attacks on the mindless complacency in both music and society, represented typically by the people in the audience that night. They knew they were being insulted, and I think they also knew that all the bloated bullshit about rock 'n' roll that they had cherished for the last ten years was being rendered irrelevant and obsolete right before their eyes.

A lot of them were mad. Then an empty beer bottle sailed out of nowhere and hit Randy's bass dead centre, shattering on his pick hand. Chuck came off the drum riser like a shot, wielding his high-hat stand like a battle axe. I don't know who he thought he was going to brain; the bottle had come from some anonymous hero in the middle of the crowd. He just stood on the edge of the stage and threatened everyone. Randy wiped a swath of blood across his T-shirt, playing up the drama of the situation. He grabbed his microphone and began to curse the entire audience in the most graphically obscene terms possible.

They played for a while longer, till Chuck got so pissed off he kicked his drum set apart. The bass drum rolled off the riser onto the stage. Thank you, good night. They got more cheers than boos, and Joey came back to say that there would be no encore due to things being broken. That was the end of the show.

I sat there feeling, if not born again, at least several inches taller. You could be real, you could force other people to be real, you could even get away with it: these were novel concepts which I now had to entertain seriously, and with which I have been experimenting ever since. I went up to Randy as he was packing away his gear and told him how great I thought the show was. He said that they would have liked to play more but that people were just being too rowdy to go on. I said, "No, man, it was great . . . like, I fucking work here, man! I work in this place!" I couldn't say anything more. I couldn't describe to him what it meant to me. He looked at me like I was some kind of dweeb and walked away to talk to some girls.

John and I hung around after most of the crowd had left. We were sharing a last beer when some yob wandered over to us. I asked him if he'd had a good time. He said that it was the worst shit he had ever seen. I then did something I had never done to anybody in my life up to that point; I told him quite plainly, even pleasantly, to fuck right off. And after some grumbling, that's exactly what he did.

**John Wright** Robbie dragged me to that D.O.A. show at the Commons Block. I was just blown away. That night is basically what started everything rolling with my brother and me. He was already listening to all those punk rock bands coming out in the latter half of the '70s. But I was still pretty cold on a lot of them. He said, "D.O.A.'s coming. We gotta go." I'm like, "Oh, I don't know." So he played me "The Prisoner" and "Thirteen." I thought it was kind of cool, so I agreed to go check it out, and oh my god, I'd never seen anything like it.

It was this insane amount of energy and Chuck Biscuits's foot just going so fast on that kick drum. It was just so basic. Everything he did was about pounding those drums. I loved that. The whole thing, the rugby players and Joe, the whole tension in the room. Literally, I'm sitting on a table, there's the stage, there's the crowd, there's the band, and Randy Rampage is standing right there and this bottle comes—*smash*—and he's cut. He's flicking blood on all the people. I'd never experienced anything like that. It was just so aggressive and so intense. It was all new to me. I just was observing and going, "Holy fuck . . . wow." This band just was so powerful. That was it!

I had been listening to everything at that point: punk rock, any new music, even the fluffy, poppy stuff. It didn't really matter. But now it was more about, "What are they saying?" They're not just singing, "Love me, baby," or some fantasy lyrics about fighting dragons or something. It was real. I quickly got into the scene, listening to all this independent stuff that was coming out.

**Doug Burgess** We were having a beach party the night that John and Rob went to see D.O.A. They came down to the party afterwards and were just raving about it. John had seen Chuck Biscuits for the first time and was completely blown away by them. The UVic rugby team had apparently shown up and were trying to provoke them. A few months later, D.O.A. played again with the Sikphux opening at the Da Vinci Hall, and that gig was a bit of a revelation as well. A lot of the Mount Doug kids went to that show.

**Rob Wright** This punk rock thing, it swept people up. Punk rock said to people, "It doesn't matter if

you don't know how to play guitar. Just form a band and learn whatever instrument you manage to make sounds with."

A lot of people consider punk rock as a style of music, a way of playing, a way of looking. A fashion thing. It was none of those things. To me, it was people admitting they were little monkeys who weren't that smart and weren't that happy and were kind of afraid of everything. The answer to that was to look at other people and go, "Fuck you. You don't like it? Lump it. I don't give a shit."

I thought the politics were superfluous as well. It was this attitude and this angst and this anger and this fear. I fit totally into that. When I saw the Ramones, that was it. It wasn't that I suddenly thought this was a great little pop band, with an edge. No. The edge was everything. The edge was completely what that band was about. Dee Dee's fucked-up life and personality, on display for anyone who wanted to watch it. There was no bullshit at all about that band. It was a perfect band.

**John Wright** It seemed that Victoria suddenly had this scene starting up, with everyone just doing it themselves. No one else was going to do it. No one in Victoria would put on a show for a punk rock band at all. You had to go rent a hall and do it yourself. No club in town would ever have any local band play, unless it was a cover band playing Trooper songs.

**Rob Wright** Victoria was always the weak sister to Vancouver, and that was one of the reasons it was very nourishing for us, and very sheltered. I don't know what we would have done if we'd been in Vancouver. Being in Victoria at that time, in the little sheltered punk rock community, was a very safe and pleasant place to be.

Later, when we got to Vancouver, it was great, because we were outsiders. We weren't part of any of the cliques, any of the gang. We weren't part of any of the lifestyle things that were going on. For bands that started in Vancouver, it was all very competitive and hard, and tons of heroin. It was just an entirely different feel. The scene in Victoria was always more open, comfy, homey. I never really made any friends or got close to anybody in Vancouver the way I did in Victoria.

CHAPTER TWO

# WELCOME TO VICTORIA

## "From Oak Bay to the Gorge. All the geeks at the Forge. Victoria, what a bore!"

It's impossible to fully appreciate the origins of NoMeansNo without knowing a little bit about Victoria. Although neither of the Wright brothers was born here, Victoria was the closest thing to a hometown they had, and it played an important role in defining what made NoMeansNo initially tick.

Victoria, the westernmost city in Canada, is the capital of the province of British Columbia and is located on the southern tip of Vancouver Island, which is a couple of hours away on an overpriced ferry from the city of Vancouver. The island is about three times the size of Jamaica but has less than a third of that country's population.

These days, Victoria is a beautiful, vibrant city with a mild climate and sky-high real estate prices. The Garden City is often voted one of the friendliest cities in the world. Victoria in the 1970s and 1980s was a completely different place: a sleepy town, known to outsiders as a quaint tourist trap, a parody of an Olde England village.

For the local kids, Victoria was a place where they had to make their own fun or die from boredom. House parties were constantly being busted by overzealous and equally bored cops. Booze, pot, acid, and magic mushrooms were the intoxicants of choice, and getting beaten up for being different was a very real possibility. "Newlyweds and Nearly Deads" was the popular catchphrase for Victoria at the time, and that was certainly not meant in a favourable way. But sometimes boredom and oppression can be the soil to grow the seeds of creativity or even a microcultural movement. That's what happened in Victoria in the early 1980s.

**Kev Smith—NEOs, Mission of Christ**
Geographic isolation back in pre-internet days meant that trends in music or popular culture took an extra couple of years to arrive here. This explains why punk had already happened years before in other places, even as close by as Vancouver. Punk barely reared its head in Victoria until around 1980. The pace of life was generally slower, and in some ways the town kind of went to sleep over the winter.

There was a kind of inherent, historic lameness too: fallout from the general mindset and civic influence of generations of British immigrants who came here to retire. Victoria used to be known as "Lotus Land," the sleepiest, most pleasant, most conservative place in the former British Empire that wasn't in the tropics. The place had an implicit "You kids better not even think about having any fun" mentality that kind of hung over everything.

**Craig Else—Twisted Minds** Victoria's kind of strange. It's got this veneer of cordiality, but it's a thin veneer, and underneath is the basic structure of its discontent: boredom and mistrust. I guess it's because it's on an island.

There's a strong desire for conformity. If some guy is walking down the street with his hair cut funny

NOMEANSNO's
VICTORIA
S.O.S
AUSFAHRT
YOU KILL ME
N
Saanich
Cedar Hill
UVic
Cadboro Bay
Uplands
Esquimalt
VicWest
Fernwood
Oak Bay
Downtown
James Bay
Fairfield
1. Wright Family Home
2. UVic Commons Block
3. Mount Doug High
4. Cedar Hill Middle School
5. Reynolds Secondary
6. Rats Nest
7. Norway House
8. MOC House
9. Day Glos House
10. OAP Hall
11. Keye Studios
12. FOE Hall
13. Piss Alley
14. Vancouver House
15. Ad Lib Café
16. Oak Bay High
17. Armadillo Café
18. Dollhouse Studios
19. Fernwood Community Centre
20. Balmoral House
21. Castle Music
22. Lee & Sons Market
23. Union Hall
24. Holliston Family Home
25. Kerr Family Home
26. Richard's Records
27. Douglas & Yates
28. Random House
29. Beaver Pub & Purple City
30. Gordon Head House

Pink Steel at OAP Hall

or dyed, people don't like it. They want in-group cohesion. But where there is a strong expectation of conformity, there is a backlash effect.

Victoria bands ended up being really independent, because they just figured that since they're not going to conform, they might as well be as weird as they want. Victoria bands have always had a really good streak of individuality.

**Pete Campbell—Pink Steel** There was an iconic Vancouver *sound*, which there definitely wasn't in Victoria. I think the isolation led to Victoria bands being distinct from one another, and also very original.

**Eric Lowe—Ryvals, Automatic Shock** I do think it's because we are on the island. Victoria did, and still does, have a unique music scene. I was a new kid from Oak Bay. I've been asked if I felt like a visible minority back then, and I never did. And neither did Tim Chan or Kev Lee. It's mad, actually. Whoever wanted to get up onstage and put themselves out there and be vulnerable and play would get support. Maybe not everyone would love you, but certainly you wouldn't be hated.

You could be really shitty, or brand new, or shy, or you could be incredibly awesome, and everyone would nurture you. Your creativity was able to grow simply from the fact that your confidence grew because you were putting yourself out there. You could barely play your instrument, but people kept saying, "Keep on going! Do your thing and we will keep on coming down to see you and we will keep putting you on bills." There were jocks that picked on punks, but they ended up coming around and liking this music eventually. If you went to shows, people would accept you there.

**Jacqueline McLaughlin—musician, artist** It took a long time for heroin to get here. I think that played into it. I remember going to Vancouver and going to a party with my punk rock friends who were originally from Calgary, and people were shooting up in the bathtub. I was probably sixteen. I was shocked. In Victoria, there was lots of booze, and lots of mushrooms, and quite a bit of acid, and a shit-ton of speed. But those kinds of heavier drugs, like coke and heroin, were really rare. Victoria didn't have the kind of drugs that would really fuck up your life. I also think that most of those people in Victoria were middle class or higher. We're not talking the punks of West London.

OAP Hall, Victoria

Steve McBean outside "Piss Alley"

**Stefan "Scream" Niemann—friend, photographer** We were standing outside the OAP Hall and it must have been probably one of the Subhumans (Canada) shows. This van drove up to the traffic light, and this woman casually leaned over and locked the door on her side. We started laughing, because we're not the LA hardcore scene. We're just a bunch of suburban Canadian kids. We weren't looking for violence.

**Rob Wright** To become a punk rocker was not an improvement. A lot of people went downhill in a hurry and were gone. It's one of those movements that just swept people up and then either threw them away or made them do things that were amazing and wonderful. It was a strange time for sure.

**Steve McBean—Jerk Ward, Black Mountain** There was a while where a bunch of us did the whole "down 'n' out" thing. We'd hang out in what we used to call "Piss Alley," which is Maynard Court. But just down at Yates and Douglas, that's where all the rockers hung out. They'd be selling hash, weed, acid, or whatever. I think there's definitely a pretty nasty underside of Victoria, with the drugs market.

**Andrew Molloy—Bed Spins, BUM** I went to Oak Bay High in grades eleven and twelve, and there were only a few punk rockers there. Kev Smith from the NEOs was one, and a really great artist named Tara Miller. I remember at a Halloween dance in grade eleven, all the rugby players dressed up like the Blues Brothers and called themselves PES, the Punk Extermination Squad. They went around being dicks and intimidating people they thought were punk rockers. Ridiculous. That was the milieu back then. I remember getting punched in the face a couple of times because of the way I dressed. I'm sure I'm one of many with that kind of story.

**Steve McBean** Once in a while, you'd hear rumours of a "Fuckin' punk hunt tonight!"

**Greg Graham—House of Commons** I mean, there were only so many punks around back then, right? It's the old joke: I was punk rock back when it used to be called, "Hey, faggot!"

**Tara Miller—artist** The thing that I liked most about the people I was hanging out with then is that they were aware of what was going on in the world around them. It wasn't just Victoria-centric. They knew what was happening everywhere and were putting on shows to help other people, benefits and such. Creating a scene to give us something to do.

**Kev Smith** I think that young people in Victoria did more or less the same things for fun that I imagine they still do. Same as they have for the past fifty years: test their mortality by doing stupid shit in cars, messing around with drugs and alcohol, trying to get laid. All that small-town stuff. We had to go out to find anything fun to do. Us old-time punk rock folks like to be proud that we at least got off our ass and tried to make something happen.

For myself at that age, playing in bands was something I was compelled to do, and I'm sure many others would say the same. There was really nothing else that interested me, so I got very involved with the scene, playing in various bands, doing a fanzine, and going to every show.

The very beginnings of the scene are documented pretty well in the *All Your Ears Can Hear* book [see Recommended Reading, p. 312]. Basically, it was very scattered and minimal until around 1980 and then started to take off in early 1981. More and more out-of-town bands started to play here, and we saw a lot of the great underground bands of the time: Black Flag, D.O.A., Dead Kennedys, Subhumans (Canada), Hüsker Dü, X, Angelic Upstarts, Meat Puppets. It's a pretty long list.

Dead Kennedys at OAP Hall, 1983: D.H. Peligro, Jello Biafra, and East Bay Ray

A Benefit for the Vancouver Five
DEAD KENNEDYS
THE NEOS
RED TIDE
MORAL LEPERS
Monday, April 25
The O.A.P. Hall
1600 Government
$6 advance
$7 door
minors welcome
FREE THE FIVE
PROTECT THE EARTH

In the 1980s, there was a real sense of discovery that was very exciting. There was no feeling that everything had been done already. There was a new sense that you could do anything you wanted.

**Tolan McNeil—Mission of Christ, Gus** There was a weird recession back then. A lot of my friends left home really early. Real estate was different. You could rent a house for $500 and load it up with ten friends. Welfare was $310 a month. There were a lot of basement gigs too. That basement culture was a big part of Victoria. People would just do shows in their basements, then the cops would come. It was kinda fun.

**Owen Atkins—Seaweed** Growing up down here in Washington state, Victoria was known as a tourist destination, this fantasy land. My memories of Victoria as a kid were the double-decker buses and all the Britishness of it. You could go to England without going to England.

Then, when I was fifteen, I went there with my parents on vacation and wandered around the actual city and found some cool record stores. There was one downtown that had a really good independent metal and punk section, much better than anything we had down here, actually.

That gave me a whole other impression that Victoria is a real city and not just a facade of crumpets and tea. It was really cool to find out that this stuff was happening up in BC.

The New Wave Cave, a basement venue in Victoria

**Ford Pier—Roots Roundup, D.O.A., Show Business Giants** I'm from Edmonton, and I think there were some similarities to the music scene in Victoria in the 1980s. We were just a little bit off the beaten path. It was a smaller core of like-minded people who were going to make something—*anything*—happen. One of the best consequences of that arrangement, although an unintended one, is that if there's going to be a show, then all of the bands are going to be on the bill. You aren't going to be able to have a lineup of *just* hardcore bands, or *just* metal bands, or *just* pop bands. It's going to have to appeal to everybody; otherwise, there isn't going to be enough resources to make any kind of show happen. People were exposed to things that they wouldn't have sought out on their own.

**Doug Burgess** One of the things that happened, which I think happens in smaller towns, is that everyone sort of converged on the scene. The scene was too small for things to become tribal. The same venues would have the hardcore kids, the slightly older punks, and others. There would be gay men and women there; it was a safe place to drink and hang out and hear good music.

**Rob Wright** The uniqueness was accepted. A guy like Marcus Pollard, who was a stalwart of the scene, was nothing like the punkies. We didn't have hardcore, rigorously regimented kinds of people. They were all just oddball, weird guys playing every different kind of music. The scene in Victoria was

Hanging out inside the FOE Hall, Victoria

always sort of funny and laughable. The tribe was full of goofballs.

**Kev Smith** It's surprising, actually, that when people started putting on gigs, the cops didn't just quash it immediately. We're talking about a city where before the vagrancy laws were reformed, they'd round up all the homeless at the beginning of tourist season every year and drop them off over on the mainland!

**Tim Crow—Suburban Menace, Red Tide** There was a place called the FOE Hall, for Fraternal Order of Eagles. It was a legion for war vets. Some punks had convinced them to issue memberships to a bunch of us, so the FOE Hall started serving liquor to fifteen- and sixteen-year-olds. It was a huge hangout spot. Later, they put on punk shows there too. The whole scene would go to the FOE.

**Trevor "Spud" Hagen—Dayglo Abortions** We'd go down to the FOE Hall and someone would sign

Dayglo Abortions: The Cretin, Spud, and Jesus Bonehead

Rob Wright and Andy Kerr inside the FOE Hall

us in, and we'd drink really cheap beer and play pool. They had this big hall in the back, so we asked them about it. They told us they only rent it out to members, for something like fifty bucks a night—dirt cheap. We became members and started putting on shows there. We put on Dayglos shows, we put on NoMeansNo shows, SNFU played there. It was great for the longest time; unfortunately, they never asked anybody for ID. One time when a show had ended, a cop saw these young punks coming out of the FOE, and he freaked out and called the riot squad. Just like that, it was over.

**Doug Burgess** At some point, Marcus Pollard and Scott Henderson convinced the bar manager at the FOE Hall to give them access to the jukebox, so

Assorted Victoria fanzines

they put a bunch of cool music on there. We were listening to all kinds of stuff, not just punk rock: reggae, ska, stuff like Gang of Four, New Order, and club music. I'd say that's a reason why NoMeansNo's music soon started to be funk-tinged quite quickly.

**Brian "Jesus Bonehead" Whitehead—Dayglo Abortions**
The Dayglos had a house in Esquimalt in those early years. It was at 567 Head Street. It's now a children's music school, which is just fucking insane.

**Matthew Mallon—*Random Thought* magazine** I went to a boarding school north of Victoria called Brentwood College. My introduction to the Victoria punk scene was, bizarrely enough, when our grade twelve class took a field trip to see the band X play at the OAP Hall with Infamous Scientists and Subhumans (Canada). Suddenly, one day there was this sign-up sheet for a field trip to go to see X! I was, "What the fuck? Are you kidding me?" I was a huge fan, so I signed up and got on the bus.

It was 1980: people just didn't know what was going on at all. I think it was just this young, naive teacher who wanted the kids to like her. A big yellow bus from up-island, delivering twelve little private school kids to the OAP Hall.

We walked in, and right away the first thing we saw was at least one dude with a swastika, like an arm band or something. That was really freaky. We were little private school kids huddled up in the corner going, "What's going to happen here? When's the anarchy going to start?" It was a great show, and everybody was really friendly. We had an amazing time. Obviously, X were great, but I was really blown away by Infamous Scientists. I just thought they were the coolest thing. Then we got back on the bus and went back to school.

**Doug Burgess** At the end of September 1980, a few of us pooled our money together and rented this house at 306 Vancouver Street, which soon became known as Vancouver House. We had some notorious parties there. One of the first big parties that stands out was the one after the seminal X show at the OAP Hall. I remember there was a guy in the crowd who was wearing a Nazi armband, and Infamous Scientists did an impromptu cover of "Nazi Punks Fuck Off" while giving the finger to that guy. A bit later, Randy Strobl and I were watching Subhumans (Canada) play, and we met Exene near the side of the stage. We pointed out the Nazi guy, and she said, "Oh, that's gross." Later, when X went on, she dedicated a song to us. She said, "This is for Doug and Randy, who don't like Nazis, and neither do we!" During Subhumans' set, Randy did a stage dive, but the crowd parted, and Randy hit the floor and broke his collarbone. He walked around the rest of the gig with one shoulder lower than the other.

After the show, we all went back to Vancouver House, where we had a ripping party until about four in the morning, at which point we finally convinced Randy to go to the hospital. X put us on the guest list for their show the next night in Vancouver at the Commodore Ballroom, so we took a bus over and saw them again.

Vancouver House was a steady stream of people moving in and out. Eventually Bruno moved in. Bruno was a really nice guy, a bit of a party animal. Years later, NoMeansNo wrote a song about him. He was such a character that I can see why. We hung out a lot at the Beaver Pub at the Empress Hotel, playing darts and drinking. Bruno was always there. If you sat by the window at the Beaver, sometimes you could look out and see people at the floodlights in front of the Empress Hotel doing the "Purple City" thing.

T-shirt for the Beaver Pub, a favourite hangout

**Scott Henderson** Ah, yes, the Purple City phenomenon. In those days, the front of the Empress was illuminated by these yellow mercury vapour lights. These lights were on the ground, shooting up the walls, and they were high intensity. The idea was you'd get kind of *altered*, and then you'd go and stare into these lights as long as you could stand it. Then you'd turn away and look around, and the whole city would be purple. "Let's go do Purple City!" meant "Let's go and stare into the huge lights." It's probably why so many of us wear glasses now. I named my first band Purple City.

**Tom Holliston—Show Business Giants, Hanson Brothers, NoMeansNo** The Beaver Pub was probably the closest Victoria ever got to the vibrancy and excitement of early punk rock London, where there were specific places to hang out. That was the Beaver. I mean, *everybody* went there, all different parts of society. It was the place in Victoria I think that nurtured the so-called punk or alternative scene.

Bruno was at the Beaver a lot, playing darts with Johnny and Rob. Rob was a very good dart player. He's also a really good pool player. I think that's sort of the "twenty for two, thirty for six" in "Oh No! Bruno!" That was a little reference to being at the Beaver Pub.

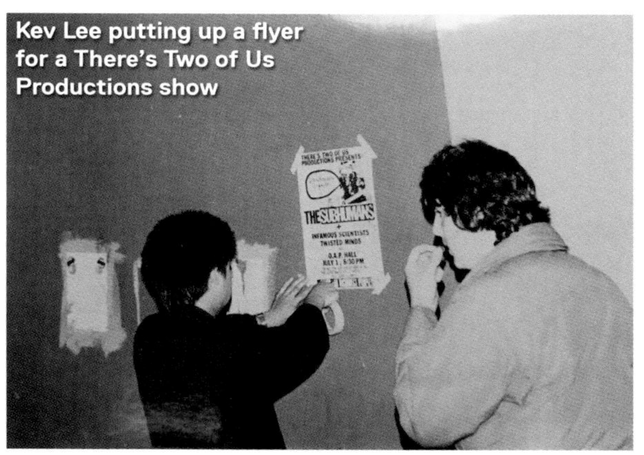
Kev Lee putting up a flyer for a There's Two of Us Productions show

**Bruno St. Martin—friend** I didn't really dress like a punk, but I hung out with everybody in that scene. I kinda dressed more with army fatigues, but once I got into NoMeansNo, I would wear their T-shirts all the time. I ended up living in Vancouver House for a while. Everybody was friends with everybody. It was very unique. I wasn't from Victoria originally, but I met people from the punk scene, and everybody was just really nice. It wasn't people with attitudes. It was a really fun time to be in Victoria: the music was happening, and there were gigs going on everywhere.

Province photo by John Thompson

From left: Andrew, 14, Dave, 15, and Rob, 17. Storekeepers, police express concern.

PUNKS 'GROSSING OUT' VICTORIA

By BARBARA McLINTOCK
Victoria Bureau

They dye their hair fire-engine red or royal purple.

Their talk is laced with four-letter words.

They "gross out" each other and passersby with spitting contests.

They're Victoria's punks and they're driving a group of downtown merchants crazy.

They hang out at a small shopping mall and shopowners say they're keeping customers away. They also blame them for a recent rash of vandalism — a charge the punks hotly deny.

"That's really unfair," says Karl, 21. "Because we're very noticeable and around here, we get blamed for a lot, even for what happens when we're not here."

But merchants' spokesman Jason Austin says he's seen punks hassling police and terrifying elderly customers.

"They have these spitting contests," says Austin. "They spit on each other, into each other's mouths, on the windows. It's disgusting. People take one look at that and walk away."

There's little police can do. Sgt. Doug Potentier, head of the police community services division, says they can only respond to specific complaints.

Austin fears merchants may take matters into their own hands. "We don't want that. That's the breakdown of law and order."

Karl and his friends say they don't want to hurt anyone and just use the area as a meeting-place.

"I'm a pacifist myself," says Karl.

An article in the *Province*, March 31, 1985

**Steve Sandve—friend, promoter** I started getting into punk music and alternative music in the late '70s when I was still in high school. I graduated in 1980, and I saw all these people putting on shows in Vancouver. I met Kev Lee drunk at a bar when we were both underage, and we figured out we wanted to put on a show. I found a hall; it was a dance studio downtown. Basically, we lied and said we were a Christian dance group and we were gonna play some music. They were like, "Sure, no problem," and they handed over the keys and left. John Wright did the sound. From there, we continued to put on lots of shows with different bands. We called ourselves There's Two of Us Productions.

**Marcus Pollard, Jeremy Deighton, Kev Lee, and Steve Sandve**

**Kev Lee—Infamous Scientists** It was just a matter of, "Well, if we want to play shows, I guess we just have to put them on." We'd just go around to different places and rent the halls. It was mostly just local shows, and we'd put ourselves on the bill when we could.

**Tim Crow** Guys like Steve Sandve and Kev Lee made the scene happen on their backs. It enabled shit-disturbers like me to come along and start doing gigs. They had already forged relationships with the owners of the halls: the OAP Hall, Fernwood, the Da Vinci Centre. That was Steve Sandve, Rob Wright, and Kev Lee convincing them that it wasn't a losing prospect to deal with us. All these people were saying, "We're not booking punk rock shows. We saw that episode of *Quincy*. You're just gonna smash the bathrooms up and kill each other." But these guys were mature, they were straight shooters, and they were fiscally responsible.

The relationships that these guys forged, the Wright brothers, Two of Us Productions, enabled punk rock to live in Victoria. They were really the first people who opened up all the venues, and even equipment rentals. You couldn't rent equipment from a music place if it was for a punk rock show. They just wouldn't do it. But Steve Sandve dealt with people in such a way that we were able to go in after him and say, "We're doing a show. We're friends with Steve." I can't overstate how the whole thing wouldn't have worked without these guys.

**Rob Wright** We started playing our own organized shows in little public halls. The woman I was living with at the time organized some of our shows. We could dare get up there with bass and drums and do something. That would be very hard to get going in Vancouver. I credit Victoria and the whole scene there with being one of the reasons why we even existed as a band.

We're out there screaming away and making a huge racket, but the context was one of middle-class security. Everyone's fine, no one's in the gutter, no one's OD'd. Vancouver was much, much more hard edged than that, and I don't know if we would have prospered or even existed in that kind of milieu.

**Steve Bailey—NEOs, Show Business Giants** In the early '80s, it was Infamous Scientists and NoMeansNo at the top of the Victoria punk scene. Everybody else was third or fourth tier.

CHAPTER THREE

# INFAMOUS SCIENTISTS

## "I can't get the sounds I want."

Kerr family, Andy on guitar

Around the same time the Wright brothers were getting serious about writing and recording music, another young band had formed in Victoria. Fronted by the charismatic Andy Kerr, Infamous Scientists performed a mix of covers and originals. They quickly became one of the most popular punk bands in town. "I-Sci's" released two records but were together less than three years and only played a few dozen shows while never venturing beyond southern Vancouver Island. However, they made a lasting impression on the burgeoning Victoria punk scene and provided a connection that would later change the dynamic of NoMeansNo.

Young Andy Kerr

### MEET ANDY KERR

**Andy Kerr—Infamous Scientists, NoMeansNo, Hanson Brothers** My brother, Doug, wanted to play electric guitar, so he took lessons. My sister had an acoustic guitar in her room, and my brother had a songbook of Creedence Clearwater Revival. He also had literally all of their albums, and I knew all their songs just by hearing my brother playing them. I took my sister's guitar and his book and put two and two together: "Okay, this is a chord, how do you do this?" I really just taught myself how to play the guitar from the age of nine. All I wanted to do was just have a way to make music. I started learning the chords: G chord, C chord, A minor, and the difficult ones like C ninth.

Years later, my mother revealed to me that everyone in the house could hear me singing. Although I had my door closed the entire time, they could hear me singing continually in my room for the better part of five or six years. It's probably a good thing I had no idea.

The music that influenced me was my brother's records and AM radio, CKDA. I was a big fan of the Who, also because of Doug. At least until punk rock came around. Then everything changed, in a day, basically.

**Doug Kerr—brother of Andy Kerr** I am four years older than Andy, so I came from a slightly different era. I was into rock music for as long as I can remember. My bedroom was covered with band posters, and I was always playing records in my room. I'd let Andy listen to what I was into: the Beatles, the Stones, Alice Cooper, Led Zep, Sonny Terry. Andy remembers me placing my big padded headphones on him to check out how "cool" stereo records like *The Dark Side of the Moon* sounded real loud and up close!

I got an electric guitar and taught myself some basic skills. I don't remember teaching Andy that much, maybe some simple things like "Smoke on the Water" on one string. Andy kind of taught himself to play. He would just stay in his bedroom and play and sing.

It was a strange time for me musically. Driving around in fast cars listening to Styx, David Bowie, Jethro Tull, and Heart by day, and at night in the clubs only hearing disco like Bee Gees and Donna Summer. Unbeknownst to me, Andy was becoming a full-on punk rocker. Sort of like parallel universes of music going on in Victoria during those years.

Our mom and dad both knew Andy loved music. They were super supportive and often asked what musical things he was up to. I think they paid for Andy's first guitar and little amp. When he got in his first band, Infamous Scientists, my mom would cut out newspaper clippings about the band and save them. Same with NoMeansNo.

**Andy Kerr** It was Steve Martin who started it. I was in grade ten, 1977. Steve Martin was a big thing, with the *Let's Get Small* record, and he was on *Saturday Night Live*. I thought he was very funny. I was in Woodward's department store, and I saw a copy of *Rolling Stone* magazine with Steve Martin on the cover. I thought, "Wow, cool. I'll buy this!"

I took it home, and there was all this stuff about music in it as well, along with pictures of these albums coming out. There was a Random Notes thing about the Sex Pistols, and there was a thing about the Jam and Dead Boys. I think there was a full-page ad for *My Aim Is True* by Elvis Costello. I thought, "What the fuck is this?" just by how it looked. I bought the next issue of *Rolling Stone*, and the one after, and I started reading about all this stuff.

At some point, I saw this tedious entertainment program on American TV. It had this completely trashy '70s crap pop music. Then they said, "Later in the program, we'll have from Britain, the new sensation, the Sex Pistols!" I thought, "Okay, I've read about these guys." They played a shortened, edited version of the "God Save the Queen" video, and I thought, "Wow, that's really weird."

A few months later, I bought a *Rolling Stone* and it said that the Sex Pistols had split up. In the same magazine was this article about their tour in America with all these pictures by Annie Leibovitz. I was just completely blown away by how they looked.

I went on a class trip to France in the spring with the French Club at school. I was in a record store there, and I saw a copy of *My Aim Is True*. I thought, "Oh, I know this record!" because I saw it in *Rolling Stone*. When I got home, I put it on and thought, "Wow, this is kind of like the pop music I listen to, but the lyrics really sound new and modern." For the very first time, I really, really related to what the singer was saying. The lyrics were different, and there was so much anger being spat out. The songs were different because they were short, and they weren't bloated.

Within weeks, I thought, "Okay, I've got to go buy the Sex Pistols album, obviously." It took me three times to actually buy it. I was fourteen or fifteen, and the thought about coming home to my folks with an album with "Sex Pistols" on the front of it was embarrassing. So the third time I went down to Kelly's Records, I bought it and came home. I'd never heard anything like it. It sounds like such hyperbole, but that was my punk moment. For me, the Sex Pistols were like ground zero. Within a day, all of that music that my brother was into seemed totally irrelevant to me.

Andy Kerr in the I-Sci's practice space, 1980

## INFAMOUS SCIENTISTS

Andy Kerr—guitar and vocals
Kev Lee—bass
Murray Jackson—drums (1980–81)
John Wright—drums (1981–82)

**Andy Kerr** Kev Lee and I met at Reynolds High. He was a year younger. Pete Campbell, who sang for Pink Steel, introduced me to Kevin in the gym during lunch hour. He said, "Hey, Andy, this is Kevin Lee. He likes the same kind of music as you." At a certain point, Kevin walked up to me in the hall outside my homeroom and said, "I was thinking about maybe buying a bass." I said, "Do it! We're forming a band!" We practised in the garage of Kevin's parents' store, Lee & Sons.

**Kev Lee** After seeing the Clash at the PNE Gardens in Vancouver in October '79 with D.O.A. opening, I was like, "Okay, well, I want to be in a band now." I knew Andy had the same kind of musical tastes. The first wave of punk was kind of over then, so now it's like new wave, post-punk. I bought a P-Bass copy, and so that is basically where it started. We did a lot of covers back then: the first Clash album, Gang of Four. Andy was quite into theatre and drama, so that kind of translated well to being lead singer/front man. He was very into Johnny Rotten and Elvis Costello and kinda mixed them up together.

Kev Lee at I-Sci's practice, 1980

**Andy Kerr** I took drama in high school and enjoyed doing it. I just basically liked showing off. People would say, "You make really funny faces, and you seem to be enjoying what you're doing."

**Steve Bailey** The first time I ever met Andy and Kev Lee, I was sitting behind them at the Vic movie theatre. It was Don Letts's *The Punk Rock Movie*. That was the first time being in a room and thinking, "Wow, there's other punk rockers in Victoria!" Andy and Kev were having this whole conversation about starting their band. They were joking about calling the band Brussel Sprout and the Veggies. I told my mom, and she repeated it to me for the next thirty years: "Whatever happened to those guys in Brussel Sprout and the Veggies?"

**Andy Kerr** Eventually, we put an ad in the paper, and this guy even younger than Kevin showed up. He kinda looked like a rocker but was very soft-spoken. He could keep a beat, but he knew nothing about punk rock at all. We thought, "Sure, why not this guy?" That was Murray Jackson. That's when we started making music as an actual band.

**Murray Jackson—Infamous Scientists** I would have been fifteen or sixteen. I'd been taking drum lessons at the Tempo Trend Music store for a few

Murray Jackson and Kev Lee, 1980

months, and I saw an ad for a drummer. Something like, "Local bassist and guitarist looking for a drummer to start an original punk band into the likes of Elvis Costello, Sex Pistols, the Clash." Well, I'd heard of the Clash; "London Calling" was one of the very few punk songs that was played on CKDA. I called, and they auditioned me in the garage of Kevin's family's corner store.

I think I was the last out of two or three tryouts. We seemed to click, but I was pretty green when it came to punk rock. I don't think I understood the whole thing. I remember seeing Andy and Kevin for the first time. I'd never seen hair standing straight up. What? How's that work? Andy was an odd-looking fellow, but both were charming and made me feel at ease. We played through a few songs, and I believe they made their choice when I was there. We went up to Kevin's bedroom, where he had mountains of bootleg records, bands I'd never heard of. The walls were plastered with all sorts of punk band posters and album covers. Way too much to take in. They played some of their favourites for me. I liked the music but didn't really understand the screaming and the yelling, but it sounded like fun to play. I was a major Rush fan and definitely a Neil Peart wannabe. I was a rocker in a punk band. But I wasn't mad at anyone.

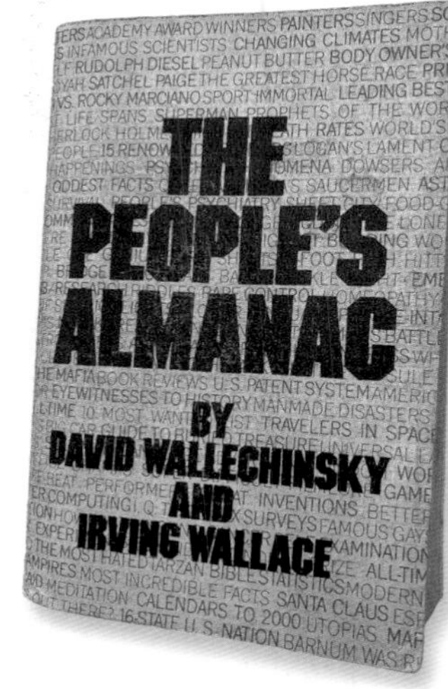


**Andy Kerr** We were looking for a band name. There was this book in the '70s of just trivia and information called *The People's Almanac*. It covered a zillion subjects. On the front cover was a series of words attached to each other, of all the subjects covered. One of them was "Infamous Scientists," so we just thought that sounded pretty cool. "I-Sci's" came later as just a short thing people would call us.

Pete Campbell lived at this house just off the highway where some people had been squatting. We called it the Destruction House because it was due for demolition. They had a final party there, and Pete said, "Do you guys want to play?" We had never played a show before but said, "Okay." We just played covers. That was our first show, and we were really thrilled with that! Our second show was at High Rollers, a roller-skating rink.

Then we played Norway House with Pink Steel. That was the game changer, because people actually showed up. They put out posters. A few people walked in who we had never seen before! It could well be that I met Rob Wright at that show.

**Michael Carter—friend** I first saw them at Reynolds High School in the fall of 1980 when I was a young thirteen-year-old punk rocker. They played a five-song lunchtime concert. I also saw them during gym class, since they were doing a sound check. I think that they were playing Stiff Little Fingers' "Wasted Life" during gym. Amazing.

**Andrew Molloy** In 1981, I was in grade ten at Glenlyon School when I first started to get into punk rock.

Infamous Scientists at the Reynolds High lunchtime gig

LIVE IN THE GYM
Lunch Hour
OCT 30
The Infamous Scientist's
&
The Find
$.50 at the door
Proceeds go to er 12

A couple friends and I went to a dance at Norfolk House, the girls' school. We had heard there was going to be a live band playing, and we thought, "Oh, that is different!" because it was usually always just canned music.

We were walking up the block toward the school and heard a band playing "(What's So Funny 'Bout) Peace, Love, and Understanding." Then they finished and went into "Slave to My Dick" by Subhumans (Canada), and we were like, "Holy shit!" We had just discovered Subhumans maybe a few months before. We were like, "Wow, this is going to be really fun, and who are these guys?"

We got into the gym, and it was Infamous Scientists, who are probably still my favourite Victoria band of all time. That was my first glimpse at Andy Kerr playing live. I think they finished with "No Feelings." That was kind of a seminal night for me.

**Steve Bailey** I met this guy Graham Littler in a record store. He said, "There's this band that had nowhere to rehearse, so I let them rehearse in my basement. You can come by next weekend and watch them." I don't know if they were called Infamous Scientists yet, but it was Kevin, Andy, and Murray, and they were playing covers and some of their early songs. I was taking pictures and recording it. I thought it was the greatest thing.

I told them I had this band too, and they came to see us, the NEOs, rehearse. That was the very beginning of 1981, and there was a show that was going to happen at the Ray Ellis Dance Studio. A big early local punk show and the first show we ever played. I-Sci's were headlining, and I got to be friends with Kev and Andy after that.

**Jeff Carter—Pink Steel** At CKDA, there was a DJ called BJ Bennett who played a small but vital role in supporting the local scene back then. He had a half-hour show that featured local Victoria bands of all stripes. He would interview band members and usually play a couple of their songs. He even had Infamous Scientists on after they wrote their song slamming his radio station. He also hosted a similar show on TV for the local cable access network, and NoMeansNo ended up appearing on that.

**Pete Campbell** There was a memorable show at the Norway House. They wouldn't rent the hall to us because we were so young, so my older brother rented it. He was perceived as a bit of a tough guy, and his nickname was Spinebreaker. Then he became a born-again Christian and was known as the Reverend Spinebreaker. So if you see any of the posters for that show, it says, "The Reverend Spinebreaker Presents." That was the pivotal moment in the formation of the scene. All the cool kids from high school were there. I remember walking into the Norway House while Infamous Scientists were playing and the whole place was jam-packed with kids pogoing.

**Kev Lee** The first seven-inch, *Noise 'n' Rhythm*, was basically recorded at Rob and John Wright's place. Rob had seen us play, maybe at the roller rink show. He said, "Well, I got this four-track Tascam

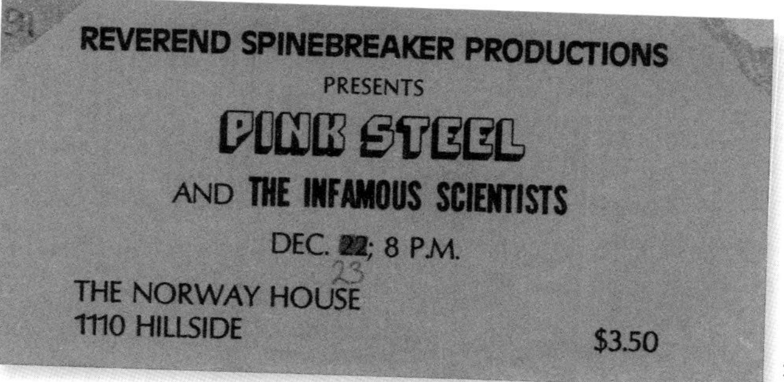

reel-to-reel that we have been recording on. Do you guys want to come record?" Rob just let us play, and would maybe say, "You could probably play that better," but that was really the extent of the producing.

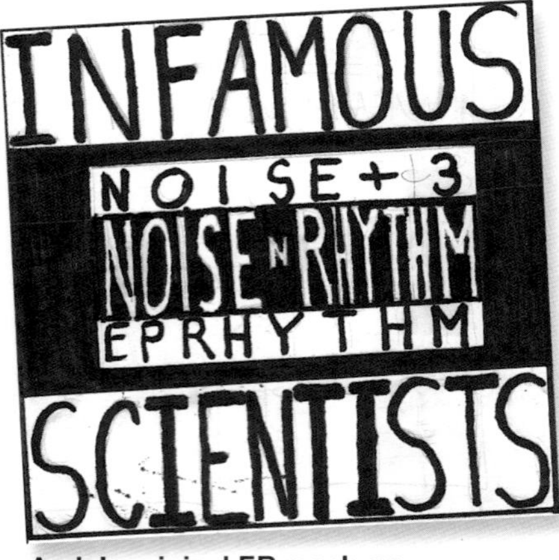

Andy's original EP mock-up

**Murray Jackson** I think we recorded a total of seven songs, all done in the Wrights' basement. That was a little stressful but fun. I don't recall much of this, only extra overdubs on the snare and a bunch of people coming out of nowhere to sing "Baldwang Must Die."

**Andy Kerr** Baldwang was a schoolmate named Mark Beaudoin. A very funny, sweet, eccentric guy who was pals with the Pink Steel guys but also knew Kev and me. No idea where he is now, but the "must die" thing was meant as an exasperated response to the sometimes odd things he would say.

**Doug Kerr** I checked out a couple of I-Sci's shows. It wasn't really my scene, but it was cool to see my bro up there onstage doing his thing. It was obvious he was really into it, and the crowd even more so! Andy gave me a copy of *Noise 'n' Rhythm* for Christmas one year, and I remember thinking what a cool song "CKDA" was. At that time, very few people in Victoria even had access to FM radio, so that AM station was what we were all stuck listening to.

**Stefan "Scream" Niemann** On Halloween one year, Kev Lee ran out of candy to give the kids who were coming to his door, so he started handing out copies of the first I-Sci's single! Who knows? Maybe they got turned on to punk rock, or maybe they got thrown in the garbage?

**Rick Andrews—*Random Thought* magazine** The band that got everyone going in Victoria at that time was Infamous Scientists. They were the kind of band where you could bring your friends along who weren't necessarily into punk rock, and they'd be blown away.

**Andy Kerr** Murray played on the seven-inch and played a bunch of shows. At one point, Kevin and I were hanging out with John Wright, and we said, "How about if you come and play keyboard on a few songs?" So, at a show at the Norway House, we did three or four songs together. John leaped up onstage with the same keyboard he played on the NoMeansNo song "Forget Your Life" and a number of those old four-track songs. It sounded great, because suddenly Infamous Scientists were a four-piece!

**Murray Jackson** I remember I had a problem with bad timing issues, which used to drive Andy and Kevin a little crazy. I could rarely remember the songs we were playing. No drugs or alcohol that I recall—maybe that would have helped! My common question to the band at the start of almost every song was, "How does this one go?" I think it wore on me just as much as it wore on them. I recall Andy getting quite pissed off to the point of almost walking off. I was super shy, and I used to shake like a leaf going onstage, always hiding behind my cymbals. I had this outfit I would wear, kind of my "band attire," if you will. It helped me prepare. I had found an old black dancer top of my sister's, and it was super tight. I tore the arms off, and it made for a really nice muscle shirt. That, along with some high-waisted white bell-bottoms, and I was ready to go!

I do remember playing a place in Chinatown, and that could have been our last show together. We were

I-Sci's live: Andy Kerr and Kev Lee

Infamous Scientists: John Wright, Andy Kerr, and Kev Lee

headlining, and when we got up to play, the place was just stuffed. I recall coming out onstage to a sweaty, smoke-filled room. I could barely make out the crowd, but the energy was intense and exciting. It was like a dream state. The audience was ready for us, and the whole crowd bounced to our beat. It was a great feeling that I don't think I'll get to experience again, so cool. Maybe it scared me.

**Andy Kerr** We had a show coming up, and we just said to Murray that we'd like to go further with John as our drummer. Looking back, there's no nice way to do that. It's just an awful thing to say to somebody who had put in so much time. I can imagine he would have been angry and upset. We probably could've done it better. Anyway, we did that without making a big drama out of it. We said to John, "Do you wanna drum for us?" He said, "Yeah, sure." Then we went to a practice, and he knew all of our songs anyway. John played and Kevin and I just walked out thinking, "Oh my god, he's good." Suddenly, he made us sound about ten times better. That was our inspiration to keep on going. That's how Murray got out and John got in.

**Murray Jackson** I wasn't really hanging out with the guys, so that didn't help. I used to blame it on the girlfriend getting more and more annoyed with the band schedule. John started showing up at the practices, playing keyboards, I recall. Realistically, though, have you seen the guy play drums? I just felt the writing was on the wall. I wasn't practising and was no match for that talent. I also was not into touring. I had a job, I may have just dropped out of school, and there was no time to be a rock star. I think I called them or told them after a show. I was a working man, and although I loved to play, getting popular and touring wasn't my cup of tea. I was more into just making music and jamming.

**John Wright** I remember seeing them and thinking, "Wow, this is great." I think I joined and played one show on keyboards. I can't remember why Murray left, but I quickly went onto the drums.

That was a lot of fun. Now I was playing straighter music, not so weird, and with guitar and bass. Andy was such a great front man. He was so animated and such a great vocalist. Great guitar player, great sense of rhythm. For me, it was like playing in a real band, a real punk rock band. Of course, I was still also playing music with Rob.

**Kev Lee** John joined the group, and we gigged a fair amount; unfortunately, we didn't really gig out of town. There was talk of maybe going to Calgary to play a few shows, but that never developed.

I-Sci's live, with John on drums

The second record, *Trouble*, was done at a real studio, Keye Studios. There was an engineer there. It was very rushed because we only had so much time and so much money. I remember the mixing session went really late. I think it might suffer a bit because of that.

**Rob Wright** Infamous Scientists ended up practising in our basement for a while, which seemed natural after John had joined them. I helped produce their second album.

**John Wright** I think eventually Kev got kind of bored with it. There was no bad blood or anything weird like that. Andy had started doing a couple songs at NoMeansNo shows with us, and that's around the time that Infamous Scientists folded.

**Rob Wright** Infamous Scientists were a much more prominent band than we were in the local scene, but they kinda ran out of steam.

**Andy Kerr** We did a one-time reunion in 1985 at La Hacienda. We said to Marcus Pollard, "We'll play it, but we're going to do it as a benefit for prisoners' rights." Rob was at the door, and he made sure everyone paid to get in. We played our set, and we were gonna do an encore, but Murray was there. He said, "Well, I think I should be able to play." We just kinda went, "Yeah, you're right." For two or three songs during the encore, Murray played the drums. John just danced at the side, and when all was said and done, Bruno brought us all champagne. There you go. That's the happy end of Infamous Scientists.

**Kev Lee** After Infamous Scientists, I sold my bass and used that money to buy an Intellivision gaming console. That bass actually made it around to a few people. The Dayglos I think had it for a while. I think it might be resting in Marcus Pollard's basement right now.

**Marcus Pollard—Show Business Giants, promoter** It is. Thanks.

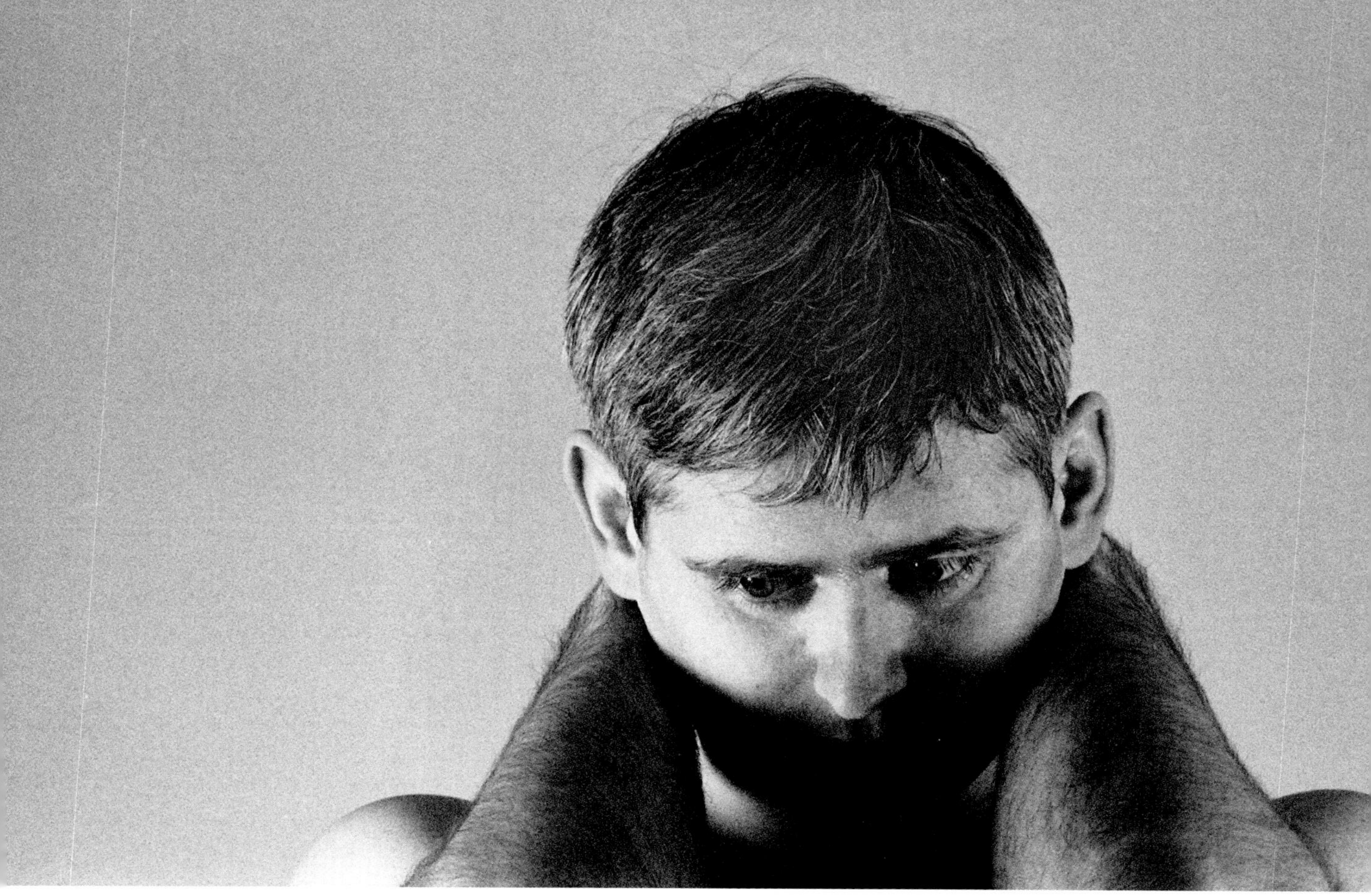

CHAPTER FOUR

# APPROACHING ZERO

## "If you see nothing and no one, forget your life."

At the very least, being a rhythm section and playing cover tunes with Castle had given the Wright brothers a taste of performing live and the desire to write more original music. They began tinkering in their parents' basement, which they later dubbed "Subterranean Studios," messing around and recording on Rob's newly acquired four-track. By late 1979, they were starting to get serious about releasing their own music. A friendship struck up by Rob would set those wheels in motion and change other aspects of their lives as well.

**Rob Wright** The first things we started playing and recording were really just a lot of bad pop rock. John would come up with something on the piano, and I'd come up with something on the guitar. I wasn't playing bass at that time. We just recorded it and put vocals on it, because it was cool. I switched to bass when we started to write bona fide rock and punk rock songs. The bass took over, of course, when we decided to play live and there was just the two of us.

**Shelley Wright** By the time they really got going with the music, I was out of the house with my own life. Our parents may not have been the biggest fans of the early stages of punk rock, but they were very tolerant of everything. Rob and John would practise in the basement all the time, and it was very loud.

**Doug Burgess** When I first met Rob in the late '70s, he had a vintage Rex Aragon acoustic, with an arch-top, f-holes, and a crack in the body. His father, Bob, won it in a poker game. Rob pulled it from the attic as a teen, put strings on it, and the rest is history. When I first saw him play, he'd been at it long enough that he knew his fretboard inside out. No wonder bass came easily to him.

**Rob Wright** At that time in the punk scene, it was all about making a record and having a single out. D.O.A., Pointed Sticks, all these people made their own records and released them. What do we do now? Well, we had to put a record out. We used one of John's new-wave catchy pop songs.

**Doug Burgess** Our friend Randy Strobl had a 1969 Pontiac Parisienne. It was a big boat; you could fit six people in it. We would often hang out in his car in the back parking lot of Mount Doug, which was also the smoke pit. One day John had been to a biology class on phylum Annelida, which is worms. We were sitting and smoking in the car, and he took out a piece of paper and started writing, "Look here come the wormies." It literally just came to him because he had been in class, learning all these terms. There was one worm called Oligochaeta, which is collared earthworms. So he ended up with the lines "anarchaic Annelid" and "Oligochaeta revolt." I didn't think much of it, because John was always writing and composing shit. It was around that time that he bought a keyboard, which he ended up using on the song "Look Here Come the Wormies."

They had met a guy named Ray Carter through Rob Castle and the music store. Ray was a lot more into the punk stuff that was going on, and Robbie and he connected over that.

**Ray Carter—Mass Appeal** I honestly can't remember how I met Rob, but we became really tight friends just talking about music. I was not a musician, but he was. We both immediately realized that we loved a lot of the same bands. I think I turned him on to some of the more British political bands like the Sex Pistols, whereas he was a big Ramones fan at the time. We were definitely best friends. I hung out with him during 1980 as much if not more than I did with my family.

Rob Wright and Emma Lee, 1984

He was playing in Castle, and he thought it was a pretty square situation, in terms of what he wanted to do, and so did I. We started talking about recording, and he wanted to record with his brother. He had written some things. I said I was interested, even though I wasn't a musician.

**Emma Lee—friend** Ray Carter was my husband at that time, and it was him who encouraged them to do something, which became the *Look Here Come the Wormies/SS Social Service* single. His side was "SS Social Service" and their side was "Wormies," which John wrote. It was kind of a silly throwaway song, but they wanted to do something. Ray later became an artist called Mandad. And that's who I left for Rob.

**Ray Carter** Not only did that destroy my marriage, but it was my whole social life, because all of my friends were also friends of Emma and Rob. I felt like I had to get out of town. I ran away for a couple of weeks, and when I came back to my house I thought I would confront Rob. He wasn't there, so that's when I carved the word *Betrayal* into his bass. It sounds so weird now. I had no intention of violence—I've never been violent—but I think I scared Emma, who was there at the time. NoMeansNo's next release was *Betrayal Fear Anger Hatred*, and I'm pretty sure the guy drawn on the cover with the knife is me. I mean, who else could it be?

**Emma Lee** There's some hurt feelings out there, but they're not big hurt feelings because everybody has gotten on with their lives. I think Ray and Rob actually patched things up a bit from what I've heard. You can hold on to an emotion if you want, and you

Rob in his priest collar and clerical shirt

can let it eat away at you, or you can remove yourself from that. NoMeansNo would never have happened without the help of their friends as a support system. They didn't have a manager; they had nothing.

**Ray Carter** It was eighteen years later, and I was with my son at a NoMeansNo gig at the Roberts Creek Hall. I literally just went up to Rob and said, "Hello." We shook hands, said a few pleasantries, and that was it.

**Emma Lee** Rob was very introverted and kind of insecure, but he was very well read. I'm a huge reader myself, and he was the only person I've ever met who was better read than I was. It's because he'd spent his life hiding and reading. Of course, unfortunately it didn't serve him well in the end, but he was sweet. He was different.

**Rob Wright** The things that I went through personally and musically are the same. There was never any sort of objectivity to any of it, and I already had the fears, the anger, the hatred, and the betrayal. By that time, it was firmly entrenched in my persona, in my thinking, and in my genes. It was only in a way of breaking out of that prison that the music happened, and by expressing it. Music, in that sense, was being free of it.

**Steve Bailey** I think Emma Lee, and probably Ray too, had a big influence on Rob. They are slightly older than Rob, and they were part of his introduction to certain thinking and ideas. Emma Lee was a feminist and sex positive. Rob, in particular, started dealing with sexuality, and it's not in small part due to her influence and that whole scene.

**Andy Kerr** Emma was right there at the scene's beginning. When I was first introduced to her, she thought I looked like a narc. Along with Rob and their roommate, Deborah, they were kind of the older sages of the scene to us.

**Deborah Ritchie (née Mitchell)—friend** I met Emma first because her kid was at Sundance school, where I was a teacher's aide. Then we met Rob because Ray was connected with him. The band was just starting out. We lived in several places together, and I put up some of the money for the first single, and then I think I did some financing with *Mama* as well. Emma Lee was one of the main organizers for pulling all that together.

**John Wright** We were trying to figure out a name, because we wanted to release the "Wormies" single. We were going through stupid names. I remember there was a place near Victoria called Iron Mine Bay. I said, "Why don't we call ourselves Iron Mine Bay? Like, who the fuck cares? We've gotta call ourselves something." Thank god we didn't. That's the only one I remember, but there were a bunch, and they were all terrible, for sure.

**Rob Wright** We had no name. At one point we were thinking Null and Void. John Null and Rob Void. And there was Iron Mine Bay. Oh my god. There was no focus at all. We hadn't got any grasp of what we were gonna do. We were just doing whatever we heard, or saw, or thought we'd try. But then I saw that graffiti.

**Ray Carter** Rob and I were in Vancouver when he came up with "No Means No." I'm sure he remembers this. We just saw some classic feminist anti-rape-type graffiti, and he just loved the name.

**Rob Wright** I think we were just over in Vancouver on a jaunt. Just going over there, smoking some dope, and going around Granville Island and Gastown. I saw this graffiti, and it struck me as being appropriate. It was about the message, but it was also "No Means No." It was catchy. It was what your mother always told you, and it had this significance of ending rape. But as I thought about it, it's the right to refuse. The right to say no. No means no, that's it. My form, or our form, of rebelliousness was not political. It was personal, and it was, "Nope, I ain't gonna be that, ain't gonna do that. I ain't gonna say that. I ain't gonna think that." It was negative, yes, but it was negative hopefully in an empowering way. In terms of not having your voice quenched and being forced to be what everyone expects you to be.

**Emma Lee** I was always involved in feminist politics. I didn't even like the name of the band. I remember saying to Rob, "You know, that's a women's anti-rape slogan. Do you think you really should be using that?" He said, "That's the very reason I want to use it." So I left it there: "Okay, it's your choice."

**John Wright** Rob had seen the graffiti scrawled. It made sense. He was getting involved with Emma at that time and then was starting to write the first album. A lot of personal politics and sexual politics. There was a real eye-opening feminist perspective for all of us at that time, and Emma was a big influence in that respect. The name just seemed to suit the direction that the writing was heading.

**Doug Burgess** I remember sitting with John at his kitchen table and they had a list of band names they were considering. One of the names was "No Means No," which Rob had suggested. Once they decided on the name, they went to Island Blueprint and got that NOMEANSNO logo put onto a rubber stamp. I remember sitting around the table with a bunch of people one day, folding and gluing the *Look Here Come the Wormies* covers and stamping each of the inserts with the NMN logo.

**Ray Carter** When we were recording "SS," we would book a time when I would come over to their house, and every time I showed up, John would still be in bed. We'd have to wake him up to record. In the liner notes of *Social Service*, on drums I put "Sleepy John Wright." At the beginning of the song, there's a door slam. We turned on the recorder and the door slammed, and it was an accident, but I loved it for some reason, and we left it in. If you look at the recording, it says, "Bass, Vocals, and Door."

**John Wright** Oh yeah. My hours of awakeness. After I got out of school, I was often going to bed at four or five in the morning and getting up about three or four in the afternoon, because I was a total night owl.

**Ray Carter** After we recorded "SS," and before all the chaos, the next thing we recorded was something called "White Man's Burden." It was a NoMeansNo song, but Rob asked me to do the vocals, which were just *screaming*, just screaming in agony the entire time, while the drumming and Rob's guitar was going on. I thought it was brilliant, and so did they at the time, or at least Rob did.

Many, many years later, I talked to John about this, and he claimed that the masters were at the pressing plant when it went out of business and they were thrown away. I don't believe him, honestly. I just think there was so much negativity around that time that either they have it somewhere or they destroyed it. But I think it's great that there's a lost track.

**John Wright** *Look Here Come the Wormies* came out in March of 1980. That was the first time we used the name NoMeansNo, and I'd say that's the start point.

**Mark Blaseckie** On the cover for *Wormies*, there's a telephone sitting on a stand. You can see a pad of paper with a number on it: that was *my* telephone number! I feel sorry for the person who has that number now: 721-0414. I actually looked it up a while ago and found someone in the attorney general's office. I keep meaning to send her a note to say sorry for all the calls she might be getting from old punks who want to reconnect with their youth!

**Andy Kerr** I bought *Wormies* when it came out, and I thought it was okay, but it wasn't really what I was into at the time. I didn't know who these guys were, and it was just a song about worms.

**Greg Graham** I had just bought the *Wormies* single, and Andrew from HOC and I were walking downtown and all of a sudden we see Phyllis Diller walking with her bodyguard. In Victoria! We asked for an autograph and the only thing I had was the record, so Phyllis Diller signed my NoMeansNo single. Then I lost it. If you ever come across a *Wormies* single with Phyllis Diller's autograph on it, that's mine!

**Rob Wright** At one point, two bands were practising in our basement, Infamous Scientists and NoMeansNo, and all at ear-splitting volume. My dad would be up in the TV room with maximum volume just so he could hear the fucking TV, but they put up with it. That was amazing. He never understood the music, though. Neither of them did.

**John Wright** Our mom initially thought Robbie and I were just going through a phase, and eventually I needed to figure out what I was going to do with my life. I didn't go to university. I didn't want to. I think my parents were pretty happy about that, because they didn't have to pay for it. Everyone else did, but my brother didn't go for long. My sister Shannon ended up going to nursing school and getting a job in the States. Shelley went to university and never left. She eventually became a professor and retired.

It wasn't until we were on the cover of *Monday Magazine*.

I remember it was a picture of me, and Mom was, "Wow, ooh, maybe there's something to this." Eventually, she came to see some shows, and she was thrilled, of course. Her kids were up there playing, with the crowd of people going crazy. She was perfectly happy that we didn't end up in jail.

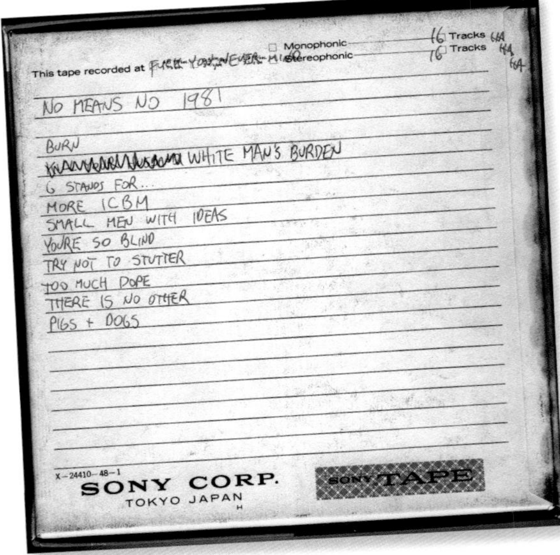


**Rob Wright** Our family was interesting because the two girls became professionals and we became vagabond musicians. It was kind of funny: there was a role reversal for the genders there, especially at that time. Shelley did the professorship and Shannon's a nurse, both highly professional and successful. Whereas we're out there screaming and running around the country playing punk rock.

**Doug Burgess** There are a few songs on *Betrayal Fear Anger Hatred* that were actually recorded before the *Wormies* single. "Try Not to Stutter" is definitely older. I remember that because when I was in English 12, for the second time, the teacher asked us to bring in a song and talk about the lyrics. I brought in a cassette of "Try Not to Stutter" and talked about the words. It was Rob's take on a guy who was trying to be a big-shot drug dealer, I think.

**John Wright** Most of the stuff on the *Betrayal* EP was all recorded before *Wormies*. They were already done in around 1979–80, on Rob's TEAC four-track. There was a whole batch of material we did in our basement. "Approaching Zero" is kind of a typical piano pop song that I wrote, and Rob put his lyrics on it. It was all about us learning to write and arrange original music. You can see some of the early genesis of what was to come. I am a bit more of a pop writer, a melodic writer, and Robbie is more riff driven. Rob was also getting into his lyric writing, with songs like "Try Not to Stutter" and even "Approaching Zero." We'd done "Living in Detente" at that time too, which ended up on *Mama*. That was from those original batches of four-track recordings.

You can see those ideas starting to form, but we were pretending to be a band. We realized that if we wanted to perform, it's just gonna be the two of us. We said, "Okay, if we're gonna play, it's going to be just bass and drums." Robbie proceeded to start writing on bass, and not so much on guitar. We started forming those two-piece songs, and that's what got us off on a bit of an odd footing, which led to us being kind of an odd band later. Writing for bass and drums became a whole new approach.

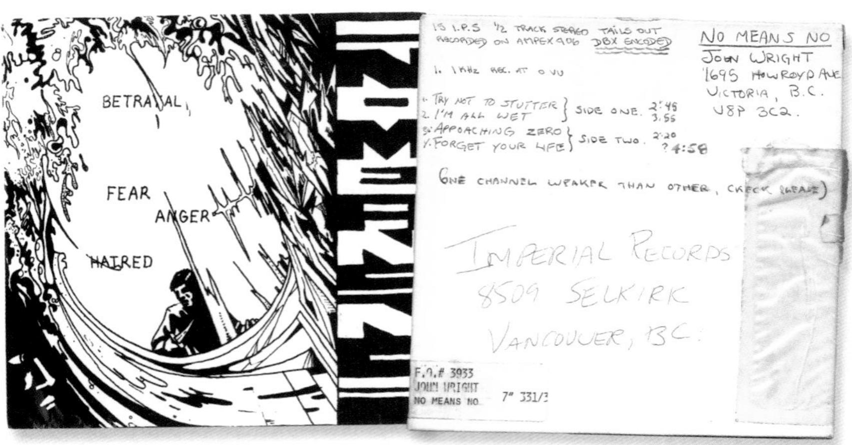


**Rob Wright** That's when we had the idea that really made the band happen and made it work. We started playing just bass and drums. In doing so, I could not just sit there playing the bass notes of every chord and providing a bottom to the music. I had to be right up front, doing stuff that was demanding attention, not just supporting something else. Then I had to sing at the same

Rob at Dallas Road beach, Victoria

time. John also sang, because we both had to do as much as we could. Fortunately, I took to that like a duck to water, and I enjoyed it, and John's always been a very good drummer. He could write music and notation.

**Craig Else** The amazing thing with Rob's bass playing even back then was how he'd play a complicated looping figure and then sing on top of that. It's a whole other discipline. Rob was appealing to my musician side, not just my rebellious punk rock side. Now I was listening to a guy who could really play. He could do what Sting was doing in those days, which was sing a completely independent phrasing over the top of a locked-in bass line. And that bass line didn't move. It was still groovin', but he managed to improvise and float over the top with his vocals. He was very, very skilled.

**Rob Wright** There was a firm bond that gave John and I the time to really, really connect musically. That's why the brother thing is always good. It's a permanent relationship. Your brother is never *not* going to be your brother, whereas if you work with someone else and he pisses you off, you go, "That's it, screw you!" and you never see them again. You can't do that when you're brothers. We also both had a great deal of testosterone and energy to throw out there. That was why it was a good pairing. We're both players who love to play hard and loud and aggressively. John was a full-on maniac on the drums, and I was a full-on maniac on the bass. Because we were brothers, and because we kept at it for so long, we got to be a pretty tight rhythm section.

John with a beach find, Dallas Road, Victoria

Later, people would ask me about the way I play, but it's not about the way I play. It's the volume and the aggression, and if I've got any technique whatsoever, fine. But it's subservient to the original impetus: motivation, energy, and a lot of anger.

**Sam Dunn—founder of Banger Films** One of my best friends still to this day is Jade Carter. Jade's mother, Emma Lee, lived with Rob Wright. So I was aware of NoMeansNo at a very young age. The band used to rehearse in the basement. I must have been around twelve years old. Jade's bedroom was next to the rehearsal room, and he didn't have a door. We used to put up a four-by-eight piece of plywood and sit in his bedroom and listen to NoMeansNo rehearse. I'm telling you, it was like a fucking Boeing 767 was landing in the building. I'd never heard anything so heavy, so loud, so menacing before.

**Jade Carter—son of Emma Lee and Ray Carter** When I was maybe nine or ten, there was a NMN show at UVic. I was at the front of the stage jumping

John Wright

Rob Wright

around. Sure enough, things got a little moshy and a sudden surge from behind threw me into the stage, which was about two feet high. I was bawling. Robbie stopped everything, pointed into the crowd and hollered, "Get that fucker out of here!" My mom grabbed this large guy by the hair and ejected him out the door. Spent the rest of the set sitting on the pop table, drinking cans of Orange Crush. "Living in Detente," indeed.

**Dory Carter—daughter of Emma Lee and Ray Carter** Rob was "Uncle Rob" to me and my brother, Jade. I actually found out my parents were separating at my fifth birthday party. They arranged an odd custody arrangement where they would trade us every year in August. We lived with my dad for a year, in this very stable, kind of nurturing environment. The next August we would go back to where there was a gig space in the basement and people partying all the time.

We had a drum kit in our dining room; we didn't have a dining-room table. A totally different environment. A lot of travelling bands would float through and stay on our floor. There was a lot of what I would describe as an "alternative family." The Foul Bay House was an infamous house in the Victoria punk rock scene. I remember waking up and walking downstairs and seeing Bruno passed out on the stairwell a couple of times. Ultimately, though, our home life was at times chaotic but also immensely creative. There was a sense of community that was very different from a traditional family home.

My mom and Rob split up after a few years, just before they put out *The Day Everything Became Nothing*. I think that song might have a little bit to do with that time, actually. My mom was getting tired of him being away on tour so much.

**Rob Wright** It is part of my personal history that led me to be in a band, but to be successful, I had to leave it all behind. It all blew up. My relationship with Emma Lee blew up because of my touring. But that relationship was part and parcel with my relationship with punk rock and the whole burgeoning attitude in myself that allowed me to do *anything*. I hadn't done much of anything up to that point. That's what inspired me to get going, and Victoria was the place to do it. The irony is that, in the end, it was all completely left behind. Once I started actually *doing* it, it was gone. It's funny how these things work out.

CHAPTER FIVE

# MAMA

## "She said, 'Son, don't hide everything inside or someday it will turn and eat you alive.'"

NoMeansNo had released two seven-inch records that were making the rounds locally in Victoria. Then, the time arrived to get out and play live, ideally to an attentive audience. Rob and John were writing a lot of new material, and a thematic "sound" was starting to emerge. The keyboards and guitars were mostly set aside, and the Wrights concentrated on bass and drums. Lyrically, Rob was beginning to explore darker themes of sexuality and the human condition, something that would carry through in his songwriting for years to come. In 1982, NoMeansNo released their first full-length album, *Mama*.

**Steve Bailey** The NEOs' second show ever was at the Fernwood Community Centre with Infamous Scientists. That was also NoMeansNo's first time playing live, as a two-piece. Of course, they blew everybody's minds. They basically came out and played the whole *Mama* record.

**Kev Smith** I certainly remember that night. It was the first time I ever got up onstage. It was August 1, 1981, and there was some kind of strike going on that affected everyone; I think it was Canada Post [Canadian Union of Postal Workers]. That's why the poster John drew said, "Not on Strike." The Fernwood space was a gymnasium, with a basketball hoop above the stage. Our set was a blur, and I was nervous and couldn't hear anything. As usual, there were twelve people we knew who were into it, and everyone else kind of hung back.

Before our set, though, NoMeansNo played their very first gig. They got up on this little half-foot stage with just bass and drums and some kind of keyboard, which was used on their feel-good anthem "Forget Your Life." They were very tight and together. Their

**The door at the Fernwood Community Centre, Victoria: Tim Crow second from left**

sound made me think of a cement mixer, probably because of the bass tone and the way the songs were built with repeating patterns. Rob mentioned to me once that he really liked drones and chants, which I guess is where that circular, repetitive thing came from. I remember when they came on, he said, "We're only half a band, but you're only half an audience," which was true: the place was not exactly packed. They did a version of "Go Mental" by the Ramones, which sounded absolutely nothing like the original, as a sort of performance art piece. Ubiquitous scene-maker Steve Sandve sat in a chair onstage getting his hair cut during that song. It was just good, original shit, and looking back it's obvious that they were already on their own path with their own sound and set of ideas. They were a lot more professional and focused at their first gig than most bands I was in *ever* got!

I recall some time later discussing the song "Forget Your Life" with Rob, where he asserted that far from being the seeming downer statement I interpreted it as, the idea was very positive: a new beginning or even a rebirth. Must have been that heavy, doomy guitar riff that fooled me.

One thing about a lot of those early NoMeansNo gigs here in Victoria is that they often got a way better response than most bands. Typically, the prophet is without honour in his own country, and that goes double for rock bands, but they were such a good rhythm section that they'd have everybody dancing. It usually went down really well. They were somehow accessible and weird at the same time. It's no wonder they were so successful out there in the world.

**Rob Wright** We did our first show at the Fernwood Community Centre with the NEOs. We were thick with them at that point. They were a beautiful band, insane. Jello Biafra loves the NEOs too, and Jello has very good taste in music. Those guys used to go into their basement and shut all the windows, turn the heat on, and then play forty songs in twenty minutes, until they were exhausted, covered in sweat, and falling over. Brilliant pioneers. Their drummer, Mario, was great. He would come out of his seat and attack those drums.

**Mario Kasapi—NEOs** Like a lot of rebellious people, I had some serious issues, so the punk stuff was perfect for me. It was a way of being able to vent, without any judgment. That was the magnet for me to be in a band.

There was one time that NoMeansNo were going to have a gig in Steve Bailey's house, in his basement. John couldn't make it for some reason, so Rob asked me to fill in for him. I was totally surprised and honoured. I got to play a set of their stuff in front of a group of maybe fifty people in Steve's small basement. I actually had the honour of being NMN's drummer for a set!

**Rob Wright** We figured out pretty quickly after that first show to put John and his drums up front. Otherwise, I'm in front of him, and I can't see him. One of the best things about a live show is watching the drummer play. It's a spectacle in itself, especially if he's really good. John was always really good, always really forceful, and always totally into it. There was no laid-back quality in his playing or performing at any point. Not for any of us. It was all basically ten to the tenth degree of aggression.

**John Wright** With the jazz groups, the drums were often on the side of the stage. The big bands spread out with the drums over on the side. If you saw a drummer like Buddy Rich, he was right front. He's the leader.

**Steve Bailey** Around that time was when the NEOs decided to start recording. Rob said to us, "If you

**NoMeansNo at OAP Hall, 1982: Rob and John**

guys want to make a recording, I will do it," because Rob had the four-track reel-to-reel and a mixer. NoMeansNo were already recording songs.

We recorded with him September '81, and I'm pretty sure they were working on *Mama*, or it had just come out. He brought his gear over to my parents' basement, and we set up, and he recorded the first NEOs record just off the floor. We didn't do the vocals then; we added them later. Rob took us to Keye Studios to master it and held our hands through the whole thing. It was embarrassing, because the people who ran the studio were horrified. They wrote up the receipt, and it actually said, "You are never to tell anybody that Keye Recording had anything to do with this whatsoever." So, on the inside sleeve of the record, we included the receipt with, "Thank you Keye Recording for making this record sound like this!" Rob wasn't interested in getting paid; he just wanted to do it. That was the NEOs' *End All Discrimination* record.

**NEOs assembling *End All Discrimination*: Steve Bailey and Mario Kasapi**

**Kev Smith** It was done very quickly. We just basically played our set, every song we knew. The setup took about two hours, and recording was done in twenty-five minutes. Rob was a fan of ours, so the whole thing was easy. He really just engineered what amounted to a practice tape on reel-to-reel, and not a very good practice at that!

It's unbelievable to me that anyone finds that record listenable. Personally, I can't stand fifteen seconds of it. But somehow it got out into the world, and a few key people like Jello Biafra heard it, for which we can thank Rob first and foremost. NoMeansNo were always supportive of the NEOs. The second NEOs release, which is a *lot* more together, was recorded by Scott Henderson just over a year later.

**John Wright** To be perfectly honest, I think the NEOs basically created hardcore music. D.O.A. coined the term *hardcore*, but I think it was the NEOs that really spawned the style. The super fucking adrenaline-infused adolescence, just play as fast as you fucking can, and with really short songs. I truly believe that. I don't think anything in that style precedes that first NEOs single that Robbie recorded on our four-track in Steve's basement.

**Shelley Wright** Both of our parents were very tolerant of everything. I think my dad, before he died in November 1981, was a little worried about the two boys, because he wasn't sure where this was all going. After Dad died, my mom continued to be very supportive, and John actually continued to live in the house with Mom for quite a few years after that. Rob moved out around that time to a house on Foul Bay Road.

**Andy Kerr** I met John and Rob's dad a few times before he had a heart attack. My life was essentially staying up late and then going over in the morning to John's house. He worked a late shift at a hotel, and he'd wake up at like eleven a.m. He'd be there in his bathrobe. John and his dad would be smoking cigarettes, drinking coffee, and we'd just hang out. John was the one who got me drinking coffee. His mom was around, and the cats were around. I hung out there tons. Really nice time.

**Steve Bailey** Basically, if you hopped my back fence, crossed the street, and hopped another neighbour's backyard, you were standing in the Wrights' yard. It was a suburban neighbourhood, so you would have to walk around fifteen cul-de-sacs to get there, but if you jumped the fence you were right there.

I have one particularly fond memory. I ended up at the Wrights' house on Christmas Eve with his mom playing the piano and me singing songs from *Jesus Christ Superstar*. It was a very strange, funny moment. I didn't know their father had passed away just before that.

**Emma Lee** Steve Bailey lived around the corner from them in Gordon Head. I remember Rob and John's dad had just died, quite suddenly. He was only in his fifties. It had been tough, because he died within three days of having a heart attack. So the family was sort of still in shock.

Christmas came around, and we had a little get-together, and their mom, Betty, played the piano. She wanted everyone to sing songs, and nobody was really into it. There she is, playing away, and we're drinking gin and tonics, and then Steve Bailey comes over for a visit. He looks at the music and sees *Jesus Christ Superstar* and asks Betty to play it. While Betty is playing the piano, Steve is acting it out for everyone. He's on the cross, he's dying, he's getting rescued by Mary Magdalene. Oh, it was just priceless. I remember Steve more for that than for the NEOs.

**Mario Kasapi** When I was sixteen, I had a bit of an issue at home and I left in the middle of the night. I was riding my bike around, wondering where I was gonna sleep. I knew that the Wrights had kind of an open-door concept, so I went there and knocked on their door in the middle of the night. They said, "Sure, you can stay here." I'll never forget that.

**Steve Bailey** They were a huge part of the community's life. It was imprinted on me. Emma Lee was a huge part of it too. Their house, wherever they lived, would become this kind of mini-cult where all the young punks would come and listen to them.

**Andy Kerr** Around then, Rob moved into a shared house on Foul Bay Road, where most of *Mama* and several future NoMeansNo songs, such as "Body Bag," were written.

**John Wright** We got a bunch of songs together and went to Keye Studios. *Mama* was our first foray into a proper studio.

**Scott Henderson** I was the go-between for the band and the studio. I was buddies with Casey, the main contact at Keye Studios. Keye was really expensive, but we managed to get it for something like thirty-five bucks an hour, which was really cheap in those days. Part of my job was to get the studio to accept recording both these crazy bands, I-Sci's and NoMeansNo, because they were completely frightened of punk rock. They figured they'd come in and trash their nice studio. I had to tell them, "No, no, these guys are normal. Don't worry about them. And can you give them a deal? Because they're poor."

Keye Studios was a proper professional sixteen-track, two-inch, Scully analogue recording studio,

Rob at an early NoMeansNo show

NoMeansNo live as a two-piece: John and Rob

and it was a big step for any kind of band to go there. Sandra Lange was the engineer on *Mama*. Sandra was very professional, and it was rather unusual back then, having a woman who was actually an engineer. She was really good and really nice but very much of the '70s studio crowd, and this whole punk rock thing was all new to her. Every so often, she would roll her eyes; she did not understand. We're talking about the *Rumours* crowd meets NoMeansNo, and it was a clash. It's safe to say that the bass sound on the *Mama* album is Sandra Lange's. It is a bass DI'd into an old analogue mixing board, the antithesis of what Robbie ended up with as his sound. Listen to that bass sound on *Mama*: it's the squeakiest, cleanest compressed bass sound you will ever hear, and it's completely not what Rob sounded like.

**Casey Pechet—engineer** I was working at Keye Studios at the time, and I had already known Scott Henderson. I had also worked at Castle Music, so I had met the NoMeansNo guys briefly before. At Keye, I assisted on the *Mama* sessions. The setup was simply bass and drums, so it wasn't particularly challenging from a technical perspective. If memory serves, we were just trying to capture the energy as much as possible.

**Andy Kerr** I played on a song called "Almost Like Home" during the *Mama* sessions, but it never came out until the *All Your Ears Can Hear* compilation. I was just a friend of NoMeansNo at that point, although John was also in I-Sci's by then. They asked if I felt like joining in on one of John's songs in the studio. I just played some sort of new-wavey guitar.

It's hard to pinpoint when NoMeansNo started in earnest. Rob often said it was when he wrote "Forget Your Life," but to me it was the two-piece songs and the *Mama* album. I really think it's a fantastic record. I loved it. I was a big fan at the time, so much so that when they asked me to contribute things I was not really into it. I just thought, "You guys are a two-piece, you should stay a two-piece. It would be better."

**Doug Burgess** For the song "Rich Guns," John told me he listened to "I hear the rich guns go pop pop" backwards a bunch of times, learned how to sing it that way, then recorded it and flipped it around, resulting in the slurred forward lines you hear at the end of the song.

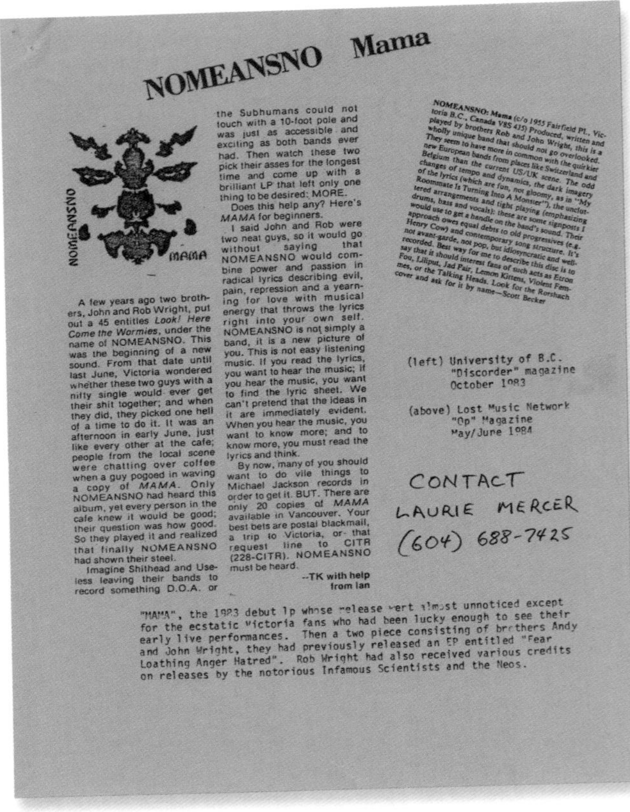

NOMEANSNO Mama

NOMEANSNO
MAMA

A few years ago two brothers, John and Rob Wright, put out a 45 entitles *Look! Here Come the Wormies*, under the name of NOMEANSNO. This was the beginning of a new sound. From that date until last June, Victoria wondered whether these two guys with a nifty single would ever get their shit together; and when they did, they picked one hell of a time to do it. It was an afternoon in early June, just like every other at the cafe; people from the local scene were chatting over coffee when a guy pogoed in waving a copy of *MAMA*. Only NOMEANSNO had heard this album, yet every person in the cafe knew it would be good; their question was how good. So they played it and realized that finally NOMEANSNO had shown their steel.

Imagine Shithead and Useless leaving their bands to record something D.O.A. or the Subhumans could not touch with a 10-foot pole and was just as accessible and exciting as both bands ever had. Then watch these two pick their asses for the longest time and come up with a brilliant LP that left only one thing to be desired: MORE.

Does this help any? Here's *MAMA* for beginners.

I said John and Rob were two neat guys, so it would go without saying that NOMEANSNO would combine power and passion in radical lyrics describing evil, pain, repression and a yearning for love with musical energy that throws the lyrics right into your own self. NOMEANSNO is not simply a band, it is a new picture of you. This is not easy listening music. If you read the lyrics, you want to hear the music; if you hear the music, you want to find the lyric sheet. We can't pretend that the ideas in it are immediately evident. When you hear the music, you want to know more; and to know more, you must read the lyrics and think.

By now, many of you should want to do vile things to Michael Jackson records in order to get it. BUT. There are only 20 copies of *MAMA* available in Vancouver. Your best bets are postal blackmail, a trip to Victoria, or that request line to CITR (228-CITR). NOMEANSNO must be heard.

--TK with help from Ian

**NOMEANSNO: Mama** (c/o 1955 Fairfield Pl., Victoria B.C., Canada V8S 4J5) Produced, written and played by brothers Rob and John Wright, this is a wholly unique band that should not go overlooked. They seem to have more in common with the quirkier new European bands from places like Switzerland and Belgium than the current US/UK scene. The odd changes of tempo and dynamics, the dark imagery of the lyrics (which are fun, not gloomy, as in "My Roommate Is Turning Into A Monster"), the uncluttered arrangements and tight playing (emphasizing drums, bass and vocals): these are some signposts I would use to get a handle on the band's sound. Their approach owes equal debts to old progressives (e.g. Henry Cow) and contemporary song structure. It's not avant-garde, not pop, but idiosyncratic and well-recorded. Best way for me to describe this disc is to say that it should interest fans of such acts as Etron Fou, Lilliput, Jad Fair, Lemon Kittens, Violent Femmes, or the Talking Heads. Look for the Rorshach cover and ask for it by name—Scott Becker

(left) University of B.C. "Discorder" magazine October 1983

(above) Lost Music Network "Op" Magazine May/June 1984

CONTACT
LAURIE MERCER
(604) 688-7425

"MAMA", the 1983 debut lp whose release went almost unnoticed except for the ecstatic Victoria fans who had been lucky enough to see their early live performances. Then a two piece consisting of brothers Andy and John Wright, they had previously released an EP entitled "Fear Loathing Anger Hatred". Rob Wright had also received various credits on releases by the notorious Infamous Scientists and the Neos.

**John Wright** That is correct! David Lynch stole that idea from me years later on *Twin Peaks*. That's how he got the effects for that weird backwards-talking small guy.

**Andy Kerr** Rob made the *Mama* cover. I was hanging around with them by this point, and I did the fake Chinese "Mama" lettering. I looked up Chinese restaurants in the yellow pages. It sounds dodgy now!

**Colin C. Smith—Penn State Department of Philosophy** I've long held that *Mama* is way underrated. It's interesting as a curiosity piece that gestures at what was to come, but it's also a powerful bunch of songs about themes like upper-class decadence ("Rich Guns"), the falsity of the gender binary ("No Sex"), and Freudian psychoanalysis and the internal horrors that it can unearth ("Mama's Little Boy").

**Jeremy Turner—friend** I was best friends with Jade Carter at that time. His mom, Emma Lee, used to sell organic produce door to door, and after *Mama* came out, she'd bring that along to sell too. It was an '80s

NoMeansNo's first show in Vancouver, Carnegie Centre, 1982

thing, like a co-op: you could order custom organic food from her, along with this weird punk record! I remember my parents buying it at my front door and then listening to it with all these pretty demented lyrics.

**Rick Andrews** I'm proud of having lugged the first copies of *Mama* over to Vancouver. I took them over for the guys and put them on consignment at Zulu Records, but nobody was interested. Nobody really paid attention to NoMeansNo in Vancouver until the "Self Pity" single came out a few years later [on the *Undergrowth Vancouver 84* compilation].

**Brad Merritt—54-40** We did a show with them at the Carnegie Centre on Hastings and Main in Vancouver in early 1982. It was just Rob and John. Seeing NoMeansNo as a two-piece, I thought it was a prototype. It was something I had never seen before, and they more than pulled it off. I mean, they had their thing down, and their thing was strange, and it didn't fit into a slot. I dig that kind of stuff. There were effects for the bass, and they had these little stops and starts and little accents and stuff. It was solid.

**John Wright** Our first show off the island was at the Carnegie Hall in East Vancouver and then Kent prison. We went over there in our Dodge Fargo pickup truck with a tarp over all of our gear.

**Emma Lee** They played Kent prison. I was working with families at transitional housing at the time, and through that I met a woman named Claire who was very involved in prisoners' rights. Claire knew Gerry Hannah from the Subhumans (Canada), who was also a member of the Squamish Five. Claire and I got it arranged through the prison entertainment committee. Kent prison was a maximum security prison. I must've been out of my mind to set something like this up. If I recall, it was just the duo: Rob and John. I think Andy came along but didn't play. They were nervous.

There were all these hardened criminals sitting there, and they were not into it. Most of them just got up and left. It wasn't exactly *Johnny Cash at Folsom Prison*. It was a trial by fire early on, and I think it prepared them for some of the tougher punk gigs that would come later.

CHAPTER SIX

# ANDY JOINS NOMEANSNO

## "It's weird being a Bob, but I'll get used to it."

Having played a dozen or so gigs around town as a two-piece, the Wright brothers were now officially part of the flourishing Victoria punk scene. Their self-released *Mama* record was getting attention locally, and their live shows were being heralded as something different and cool. These older, slightly quirky guys were now welcomed into Victoria's unique underground tribe.

Playing in Infamous Scientists, John Wright and Andy Kerr had become fast friends. The brothers decided they wanted a fuller sound for NoMeansNo, and the choice was obvious.

**John Wright** The bass and drums were only going to go so far. We wanted to have a guitar player to add that dimension. As Infamous Scientists had run its course, the obvious choice was to get Andy. He totally was not into it at the beginning. He was a bit of a purist. He'd say, "No, NoMeansNo is you and Rob. It's a two-piece, that's what you are. You don't need a guitar player." We were, "Well, whether we do or we don't, we kinda want one."

We worked at him, and eventually he agreed. We said, "Why don't we just do some songs with guitar?" It's not like we were going to abandon all the two-piece songs or just add guitar to them. It was a bit of a compromise. I presume that he wanted to actually play with us too. When we started, we played four or five songs as a two-piece, then Andy would join and we'd do some more. We started writing a lot of that early *You Kill Me* and *Sex Mad* stuff.

John driving the van on the Oregon trip with the NEOs, 1983

**Andy Kerr** In the summer of 1982, John and I were hanging out all the time. We had no girlfriends, so we would listen to music until late at night. Vancouver House was happening at that point.

In December, there was a show that NoMeansNo played at the FOE Hall. They said, "Do you wanna come up and do a song with us?" I think I did "No Sex," because Rob had just done a demo at home playing guitar along with the recorded version on *Mama*. Then he said, "Could you do 'Stop It' by Pylon?" I said, "Yeah sure, that sounds fun."

I wasn't really in the band per se, but I was an add-on to the band at the end of the sets, which I thought was great. Eventually, they wrote more songs, I added more parts, and it became about half the set as a two-piece and half as a three-piece. It was like that for about six months to a year. Shortly before *You Kill Me*, Rob's voice got blown out. He had nodules on his vocal cords. So I was invited to sing the two-piece stuff temporarily. I ended up being onstage all the time, singing the two-piece songs, and then I'd play guitar and sing the three-piece stuff. John would sing some songs as well, and Rob would just play bass.

I didn't want to join the band. It was nice to be asked, but I still thought, "NoMeansNo are a two-piece. That's what makes it: bass and drums." I thought they could have gone a long time with that and done some really cool stuff. They should be a minimalist band. Alas …

**Rob Wright** When Andy joined, he was totally into doing different things, not just playing three-chord Ramones songs. Of course, he loved that, we all loved that. He wanted to take it over the edge a little bit. He was a great performer and a great presence onstage.

Andy and Kev Lee, Oregon, 1983

He didn't do it by clichéd guitar playing. His playing was always markedly his own and never just run of the mill. With John's drum set on the front side of the stage, we essentially had three front men. One thing about Andy: he was very, very shy and a little uncertain about his writing. He would hesitate to bring stuff to the band. He eventually did, and they were very good songs.

**John Wright** Our first two shows in the States were backing up the NEOs in Oregon. We did a show in somebody's living room in Portland and again in Eugene. We came home, but the NEOs continued down to California. We had borrowed somebody's Volkswagen van, and we were worried about trying to cross the border. No paperwork or nothing, but we had all our musical gear. We brought lots of suitcases and clothes and buried everything and hung the suits up. They said, "Where are you going? What are you doing?" "Oh, we're going to a wedding." "Okay." The border was so much more normal back then. It wasn't nearly as harsh as it is now.

**Andy Kerr** We told the customs guy we were playing a friend's wedding. I don't think he bought it, because

NoMeansNo and NEOs' Oregon trip, 1983: Kev Lee, John, Rob, and Andy

he slyly said, "Uh-huh. Play well, gentlemen, play well."

**Kev Lee** I drove down with NoMeansNo and the NEOs in 1983. I was basically their roadie. Stefan "Scream" Niemann came along too. Steve Bailey's parents drove the NEOs down there.

**Steve Bailey** It was a big sell to get my parents to take us: "Can we have a summer vacation where you take us on tour to play these shows?" My dad emptied out a tent camper, and we put all of our gear into it. When we crossed the border, he told them that we were going on a camping trip. The NoMeansNo guys came down separately.

Portland was a disaster. We drove to some punk house and played very badly in the living room. Thank god NoMeansNo were there to play after us. The police showed up, and a riot started to form. We were scared little boys from Victoria, so we grabbed our stuff and begged for the police to let us through. We stood on the pavement until my parents came to pick us up. Then we went on to Eugene, and it was basically the same story, but better organized.

**Andy Kerr** That "Voodoo Gods of Salvador" promo shot used a headline that was just cut out of a *National Enquirer* or something. That's Rob in the face stocking, me wearing a balaclava, and John as the lizard. The original promo had a James Joyce quote; Rob is mad about him. John and I both have our work name tags on from the Delta Inn. I worked there as a maintenance guy. John worked in banquets.

First promo photo shoot with Andy: "The Voodoo Gods of Salvador" outtake

**Steve Bailey** Around that time, I finished high school and was working. Being inspired by Rob, the first thing I bought was a little Tascam cassette four-track studio. Andy was writing songs he wanted to pitch to NoMeansNo, so he would come over and put down demos. Just him and his guitar, and maybe a drum machine. I recorded him doing his demo version of "Some Bodies" that he took to them. I think that's one of the first songs that he wrote that they played in the band.

A little while after that, they asked me if I could record some demos of NMN stuff. I think they ended up sending it to CiTR, university radio in Vancouver, and it started to get a bit of play. They weren't really ready to make a record yet, but they had a few songs. That was February 1984.

**John Wright** We were writing and rehearsing, and working on songs that ended up on *Sex Mad*. That demo of "Self Pity" ended up being our first big "hit" on CiTR. It was played to death, and it was the song that helped everyone get to know us in Vancouver.

## MEET LAURIE MERCER

**Laurie Mercer—NoMeansNo manager** I was a '60s child, and I had a troubled start. I spent six years in prison for drug-related stuff. After leaving prison, I became a drug rehab counsellor for a few years.

After that, I went to school to become a computer programmer. That got me a job which I hated. It was not what I wanted to be. I was a manic record collector, and I was going to a lot of shows, seeing bands like Pointed Sticks or D.O.A. The whole Vancouver music scene was so exciting to me. I came to the realization that music just filled me, and I decided I was going to go into the music business, even though I knew nothing about it. Nothing.

I just went out to clubs and started talking to musicians, introducing myself and offering help. I met a fellow named Bruce Ployart, and we decided to start promoting concerts. We found a little upstairs Chinese restaurant on Hastings Street called the Tamara. We got them to agree to give us a couple of weeknights, and we started booking this little place.

**Bruce Ployart—promoter** I was an eighteen-year-old kid who loved music, and I started putting on shows around Vancouver. I eventually set up the first tour for House of Commons to go down south through Washington, Oregon, and Nevada. That was all through Ken Lester and D.O.A., who helped me get that all together.

I met Laurie Mercer in September of '83. He was thirty-two, and he knew more about music than anybody I ever came in contact with. I asked him to come along, and he agreed. It grew quite quickly, and we started to gain a lot more credibility with Laurie's maturity. We were doing shows almost daily at that point. Jeff Walker from Collectors RPM record shop came onboard and helped finance some of the stuff we were doing at that time too.

**Laurie Mercer** Bruce and I had started working with a Victoria band called House of Commons. The guitar player asked me if I could help manage them. We put them on at this Tamara Cafe. We did 54-40 and the Animal Slaves. We did all sorts of bands, and we usually lost money.

I really liked House of Commons. I told them, "Wow, you guys must be the best band ever to come out of Victoria," and they said, "Oh no, there's this band NoMeansNo. They're fucking incredible." Well, if HOC says this band is so good, I gotta check them out. I wound up finding a phone number and calling them up and inviting them to come to play the Tamara.

**Bruce Ployart** Jim Laird, the drummer from House of Commons, kept telling me about these brothers in Victoria. He's hounding me about it, these amazing musicians, this crazy punk band called NoMeansNo. I didn't want anything to do with it, because I'd heard the Dayglo Abortions, and it wasn't my thing. HOC were from Victoria too, but they seemed more metal to me.

At one point, the *Mama* record showed up, and I couldn't deny there was something interesting that needed to be seen. So we decided to bring NoMeansNo over. They told us they were gonna do two sets, one with a guitar player.

**Laurie Mercer** We flyered the city like crazy but weren't getting much interest. Braineater, aka Jim Cummins, wanted to do a show, so we added him to the bill, along with Ron Reyes, the former Black Flag singer, who had just moved to Vancouver. That helped garner some interest.

**Ric Arboit—Nettwerk Records** I owned a PA, and from 1982 until Expo 86, I pretty well did every hardcore show in Vancouver. Anybody who put on a DIY show used our PA company. We did a show at the Tamara restaurant. This small room held maybe

**Andy and John at the OAP Hall**

a hundred people if it was jam-packed, and this band that I had never heard of showed up. It was John and Rob, just the two of them. These guys just fucking blew me away at the sound check. I'd never seen a drummer that good and that fast, and then his crazy brother who looked like Phil Donahue.

**Bruce Ployart** The day came and these two old men showed up. They were soft-spoken, gentle, kind, and really cool. I don't think Rob ever took off his woolen parka, and he played the entire set wearing it. He sweated his nuts off! They presented something that had never crossed a punk stage before. Nothing had ever been that progressive and that well executed in the concept of punk.

**Laurie Mercer** Braineater wound up doing an hour-long set, and then NoMeansNo came on. They opened with "Red Devil." Andy was dancing on the floor as the brothers played, and I'm at the back, and I'm fucking blown away. This is as close to King Crimson's *Red* album as anything I've ever heard live. Then we got shut down by the police. Braineater had played too long. NoMeansNo got to maybe their fourth or fifth song.

**Andy Kerr** I remember the first time I went to Vancouver with the guys. Rob and John started their part of the set, and I was coming on for a few songs at the end, and then the cops shut it down because it was too loud. I remember thinking at the time, "Wow, my first show in Vancouver, and I couldn't even really play."

**Laurie Mercer** The cops were there, and I'm dealing with that, and I just walk up to this sweaty fuckin' band saying, "I'm so sorry." Rob is just like keyed out. He said, "Oh, we had a great time! It's only our second time in Vancouver and there's all these people here!" I said, "Who's managing you? You're amazing!" Rob said, "Um, nobody." So I asked if I could take a stab at it. I just wanted them so much. I said, "I'll do everything for 10 percent. I'll book you, I'll manage you, I'll only want 10 percent."

**Bruce Ployart** To me it was just another show, but Laurie was emotionally affected by the performance. He came to me and said, "Bruce, I've never seen anything like this. This is the greatest rock 'n' roll band I've ever seen or heard." Within a very short period of time, Laurie had made an arrangement with them that he was going to be their exclusive representative.

**Laurie Mercer** I was newly married with twin babies, and I took home *Mama* and played it to the wife. She hated it so much and said, "I never wanna hear this band in my house ever again!" So I started managing NoMeansNo, having played *Mama* once at home. Everything else I had to do on headphones. For the next twelve years of my marriage, I wasn't allowed to listen to NoMeansNo at home, while spending my entire energy managing them and trying to make something happen.

I went over to Victoria and visited them at their mom's place. I was there pretending to know my shit. I sat down with them and started listing off the things I planned to do. Everything I threw out got slapped down. Rob would say, "Yeahhh, no. We want to be on Alternative Tentacles. That's the label we wanna go

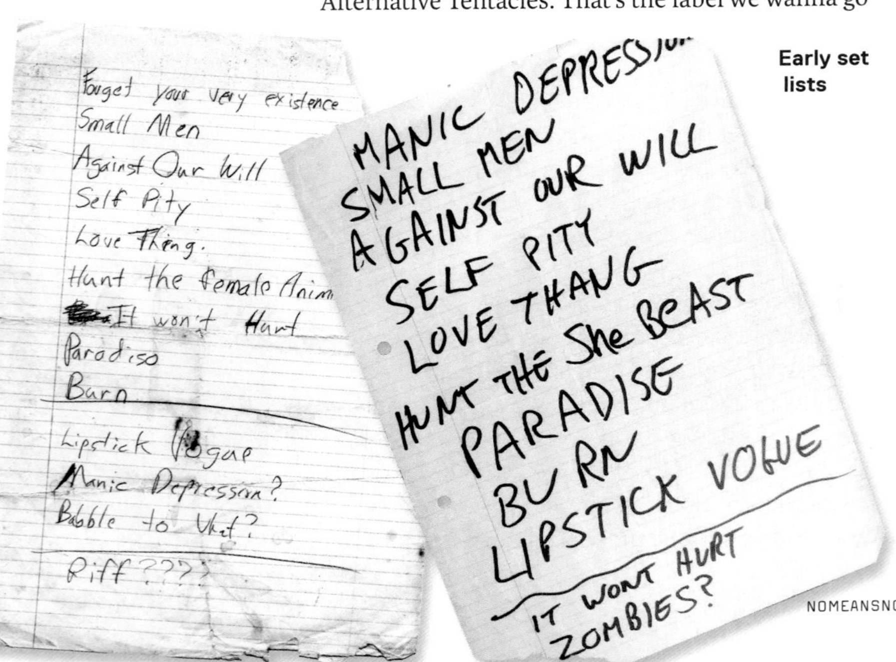


Early set lists

for." I said, "But they have no money!" So I'd suggest something else. "No, we don't wanna do anything like that. No, we don't wanna do that. No, we'll do it ourselves." It's like, holy cow! Right from the get-go, Rob had seen D.O.A. playing at UVic, and that's what he wanted to be. He wanted to do it like D.O.A. did it. Biafra represented something unique, and they didn't mind that it had no commercial appeal. That became our goal, because that was important to the guys.

Most of the bands I was working with didn't have any music out there, so I decided to put forward a compilation cassette, which was called *Undergrowth 84*. That thing had everybody from Skinny Puppy and Slow to Death Sentence and NoMeansNo, who had a little song called "Self Pity." It was a demo version with Rob singing.

***Undergrowth Vancouver 84* cassette, released by Collectors RPM record store**

**Jeff Walker—Collectors RPM record store** We put *Undergrowth 84* out on Undergrowth Records, which was the "label" I was running out of my record store. We did another one the next year, aptly called *Undergrowth 85*.

**Laurie Mercer** When I decided to get into the music business, I had made the commitment that I would always be the guy with the white hat. I'd always pay my bills. I would always do as I said. I would never promise anything that I couldn't get done, and I'd tell the truth. To this day, you won't find a band from that era that did not get paid, even while I was fucking dying. I'd be dealing with not having the rent and two screaming kids at home and my wife hating it.

**Andy Kerr** We opened for the Violent Femmes for two shows: one in Seattle and one in Vancouver at the Commodore. We always thought, "Wow, playing the Commodore, wouldn't that be great?" It was a huge crowd, and they started with the two-piece, and I joined for the last four or five songs. I remember it went over really well. I really was into Violent Femmes. I thought their second record was really good, which was the album they were touring with.

**Opening for Black Flag at the OAP Hall: Rob and Andy**

**Randy Strobl** I was with them when they opened for the Violent

FOE Hall, circa 1983–84

Femmes in Seattle. Of course, the Violent Femmes were a big band then, really popular. We met them briefly during the sound check, and they went on their way. They were at the back of the room when NoMeansNo went onstage, and they had a killer set. They had the crowd of seven hundred to eight hundred people just bouncing. There were several encores. The Violent Femmes guys came to the side of the stage for the last few songs just looking blown away. They also had a great set that night, but not as good as NoMeansNo. The next night they played the Commodore Ballroom in Vancouver, and the Violent Femmes *killed* it. They totally brought their A-game. They hung out with NMN that night and treated them like peers, not like some shitty opening band.

**John Wright** We had such a great show in Seattle. We were like, "Fuck, we just fucking nailed it, man! That was so good!" So the next time we went to Seattle, I thought, "Fuck, we're going to have such a good show! All these people are going to come out." But there were like ten people or something.

That might have been the show where we slept on Chris Cornell's floor. It was one of those very first Seattle shows. Susan Silver was the promoter, and she was Chris Cornell's partner at the time. She might have even done the Violent Femmes show and then had us back.

**Bruce Ployart** Laurie and I did the Violent Femmes at the Commodore, and right in the middle of the concert, he came up to me and said, "Hey, man, I gotta talk to you. There's just not enough money for two people." I knew eventually this was coming, because I hadn't really done very much for a while. Laurie was doing everything. He had kids, a family, and I was only twenty-two at that point. I'm like, "Ahh, that's okay. Carry on, soldier." Laurie took it all over, got an office, and carried on with his connection with Jeff at Collectors RPM. Eventually, I just faded away.

CHAPTER SEVEN

# YOU KILL ME

## "Nobody knows you and nobody wants to."

The trio of Rob, John, and Andy were becoming more tightly knit by mid-1984. They were spending all of their time together writing, rehearsing, and playing shows in Victoria and Vancouver. With their new manager, Laurie Mercer, working on getting them press and college radio airplay, they made plans for a professional recording session and a cross-Canada tour.

Unfortunately, Rob Wright developed nodules on his vocal cords, which made singing very difficult and painful. Despite the benefits of Canada's universal health-care system, the surgery took some time to be scheduled. While they waited for Rob's operation, Andy was tasked with taking over vocal duties for many of the songs, including tracks for their next release, the *You Kill Me* EP.

**Kev Smith** Rob and his partner, Emma Lee, and their friend Deborah, who was my girlfriend at the time, had moved to a house way down at the bottom end of Gordon Head Road. It had a good-sized basement where they built a jam room, which I think was essentially the whole purpose of moving there. Rob told me that when they looked at the place, the landlord said something about the basement having plenty of outlets to plug in all your power tools. Yeah, right, "power tools."

### LETTER FROM ROB WRIGHT TO LAURIE MERCER, 1984

Dear Laurie

Here is your percentage of our grand western tour.

> 10' Henry's = $37.00 (the entire door, they were nice and honest, only totally disorganized)
>
> H.C.'s = $150.00 (H.C. went into the red for a few bucks but was straight and helpful and quite complimentary. Again a distinct lack of promo but basically I think Calgary's scene is just about dead at the moment.)
>
> Spartan's Hall = $200.00 (Over a hundred people all very appreciative for whom we played very well, a real boost after the Calgary gigs.)
>
> ————————
>
> $387.00
>
> ————————

15% $60.00

So if money is the source of all corruption your relations with this band continue to be as pure as the driven snow, hopefully we can blacken it up as time goes by.

I've just got back from the hospital and the doctor said that my vocal chords were basically thrashed but that they may heal fully if I take care of them and allow them a long rest. I told him about the Sept 7th gig and he seemed to think that was not too soon, dependent upon quick recovery. I'll be in to see him again in a week.

I plan to see a voice coach as soon as possible so that I can build my voice back up properly and hopefully learn how to take care of it better. If not, I guess I'll start singing the blues and become a second Tom Waits.

Please send us a couple of Discorders so that we can feed our voracious egos.

Hope you and your sweetie are well.

Thanx

Rob

**Emma Lee** When we lived on Gordon Head Road, the band would practise in the basement. They'd pay a portion of the rent to have the practice space. I remember my kids having to sit three inches from the TV because the band was playing so loudly downstairs. It was stressful for my family. Then the buggers would come upstairs for what I used to call the "post mortem," where they'd talk about how the practice went. Finally, I said, "Listen, I have to put up with the noise, so I don't want to put up with listening to you afterwards!" I'd make them leave, and they would go to Bino's coffee shop and talk about it there, which was fine with me.

**Sylvia Kenny—friend, Fracas** I used to do a radio show with Tom Holliston on CFUV, the campus radio station at the University of Victoria. The show was called *Deviated Septum*. Tom was good friends with Andy Kerr. So Andy and I became friends, and then we became a couple, from about 1985 to '89, something like that.

It was Andy and Rob who turned me on to writers like Kafka, Gertrude Stein, Burroughs, and James Joyce. They referred to those philosophical concepts and social issues and politics in the songs. It was interesting being a young, skinny, sweaty kid on the dance floor. I remember they would often stop the music and say, "Look, you burly guys, you've got to watch out for the other people on the dance floor and don't be so aggressive." They brought their politics to the music as well.

**Rob Wright** Eventually, I lost my voice. Andy took over most of the lead singing, and John did too. I ended up having surgery to get a polyp taken out of a vocal cord. I had abused my vocals completely. I just screamed and yelled and smoked.

I give full credit to Andy for the success of the band when we toured widely, because he was a great performer. People centred on him. He could sing, he could play, and he could make it mean something. He wasn't just coming along for the ride.

**Andy Kerr** Rob had gotten the vocal cord surgery, and then he and I took singing lessons from a woman in Gordon Head. We had done those shows with the Violent Femmes, where I'd sing two songs each night and completely trash my voice. Robbie's voice was literally trashed with the nodules. John couldn't sing the entire set because he was playing the drums. So we took singing lessons. We went once a week for a few months. We just learned the basics of using our abdomen to push air out and not just trying to sing from our throat. We sang things like "I Only Have Eyes for You," and other standards. We learned about how to reach notes and how to relax. We didn't do it for too long, but it did help. It helped save our voices years later.

**Sylvia Kenny** When Rob started singing again, it was kind of tentative, like, "Is this going to be an issue?" We were all nervous on Rob's behalf, thinking what a loss it would be if he couldn't sing anymore. It did change the way that he sang. The earlier albums, the two-piece recordings, his voice is a little bit higher, and then later it became that deeper, guttural sound. Luckily, he didn't have any lasting problems. Andy, at the time, took vocal training, probably because he saw the problems Rob had. He learned to sing more from his diaphragm. You can see it in his posture in some of the old videos, like how he holds his arm against his tummy. That was from that training he took to avoid overstretching his voice, and to get that sound that he wanted.

**Rob Wright** After the surgery, my singing voice definitely changed. Before, I had this sort of boyish, youngish, highish, and not quite very strong voice. Plus, I was not singing properly. I wasn't singing *out*, and it's much harder on your vocal cords if you're not giving them enough pressure to vibrate with.

**Andy Kerr** We recorded *You Kill Me* at Mushroom Studios in Vancouver, which was a big deal. Although I had recorded with Infamous Scientists at Keye Studios, and *Mama* was done at Keye, this was a big studio in the big city. I think it was Laurie who arranged that, and Jeff Walker at Collectors RPM put up some of the money for it.

**Rob Wright** We went into Mushroom Studios, and we had the night shift. We got in at about midnight and had to be out by eight in the morning so we could afford it. We only had a few days, so we went there and did all-nighters and hammered out the songs and mixed them. It was odd, but it was fun. You don't care, because you're up half the night anyway, and you're getting something done, and it's gonna come out as a record. It was all still new and exciting.

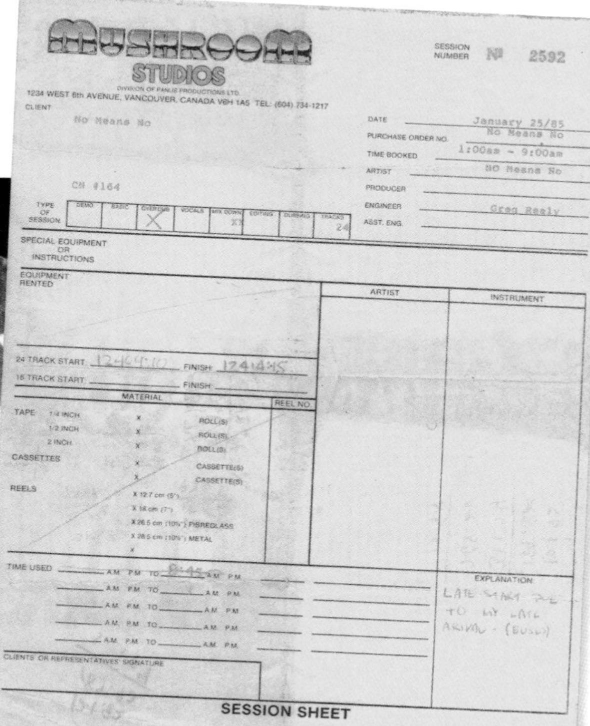

MUSHROOM STUDIOS
DIVISION OF PANLIS PRODUCTIONS LTD.
1234 WEST 6th AVENUE, VANCOUVER, CANADA V6H 1A5 TEL: (604) 734-1217

SESSION NUMBER № 2592

CLIENT No Means No

CN #164

DATE January 25/85
PURCHASE ORDER NO. No Means No
TIME BOOKED 1:00am - 9:00am
ARTIST NO Means No
PRODUCER
ENGINEER Greg Reely
ASST. ENG.

TYPE OF SESSION: DEMO / BASIC / OVERDUB X / VOCALS / MIX DOWN X / EDITING / DUBBING / TRACKS 24

SPECIAL EQUIPMENT OR INSTRUCTIONS

EQUIPMENT RENTED

ARTIST | INSTRUMENT

24 TRACK START FINISH
16 TRACK START FINISH

MATERIAL | REEL NO.

TAPE 1/4 INCH, 1/2 INCH, 2 INCH — ROLL(S)
CASSETTES — CASSETTE(S)
REELS X 12.7 cm (5"), X 18 cm (7"), X 26.5 cm (10½") FIBREGLASS, X 26.5 cm (10½") METAL

TIME USED A.M. P.M. TO A.M. P.M.

EXPLANATION

CLIENTS OR REPRESENTATIVES SIGNATURE

SESSION SHEET

**Mushroom Studios session sheet, January 25, 1985**

**Andy Kerr** I sang "Body Bag" on *You Kill Me*, but Rob originally sang that. Rob also tried to sing "Manic Depression," and it was clear really fast that it wasn't going to work. Then I tried it, but my voice was completely blown from the other songs I had sung. Then John did two vocal takes, the second of which was absolutely amazing and which we ended up using on the record.

**Rob Wright** The "Dead Bob" cover art on *You Kill Me* was my idea, and John's execution. I'd get an idea, but John was the graphic guy. He could really draw. He drew most of those original things, but they were often my ideas. "Back to Nature," that was my idea, his execution. Same with the "Man, Woman, Child" graphic.

**John Wright** *You Kill Me* certainly was Rob's concept. He had this idea of having a name, an image, and a phrase, and they don't necessarily have any obvious connection. It was a concept he was running with, and I ended up doing a few of the drawings. One was Bob, hanging with the YOU KILL ME shirt on, smiling and really happy. "Man, Woman, Child" with the gun, the spider, and the rat, and "FUN," with the guy shooting up. Very dark.

When things are dark, the moments of levity are how you can process it. It's not as though we were out to be this tremendously wise and serious band, but these dark things get under the skin. Once they're under the skin, then you've got to laugh about it. In the end, it's all pretty funny.

MUSHROOM STUDIOS
40 TRACK RECORDING

They say the eyes are the windows of the soul
but I love all the little dark holes
in your body bag
Your little willie, he's oh so pretty
and those titties, and those litties
in the body bag
willie's poised to dive into flesh
something tells me he will leave a mess
in the body bag.
when we kiss, my eyes are closed
my lips are full, i breath through my nose
In the body bag.
See the children play in the mud.
moulding balls of feces and blood.
from the body bag.
All praise for corporal flesh,
the smell of love, the smell of death
from the body bag.
Is it a womb, is it a tomb

1234 WEST 6th AVENUE, VANCOUVER, CANADA V6H 1A5 PHONE (604) 734-1217
DIVISION OF PANUS PRODUCTIONS LTD.

"Body Bag" lyrics

**Laurie Mercer** We pressed *You Kill Me* on Undergrowth, and I think I mailed out 450 copies to every possible place I hoped could make a difference. Every radio station, just anybody I thought would listen. It was such an amazing record, but I didn't understand how to get things on *College Music Journal*, *Rockpool*, or how to get college radio to play something. I became more aware of the financial enormity of what I was trying to do. Dealing with phone bills became a fuckin' nightmare. Postage bills. Every record mailed would be like twenty bucks outta my pocket, and I didn't have twenty bucks. It was just an endless hustle, hustle, hustle.

After that, I let the Undergrowth label go. Jeff Walker had helped me subsidize the *You Kill Me* EP and also helped us put some money into some other local things. I liked Jeff, but there was no room for both of us, financially or managerially.

**Andy Kerr** I was credited as "Somebody" on *You Kill Me*. Maybe it was a little nod to the fact that I thought

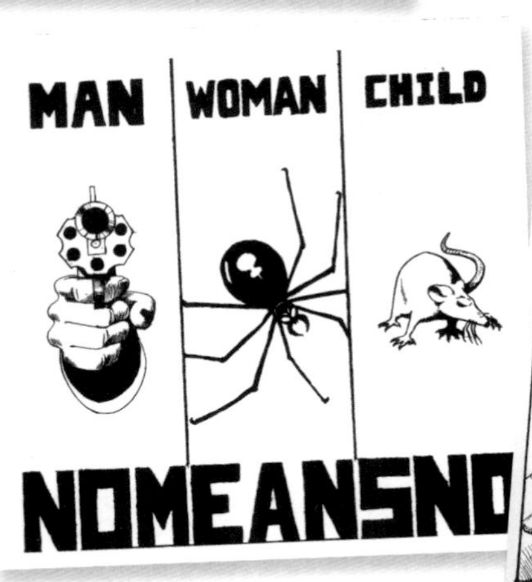


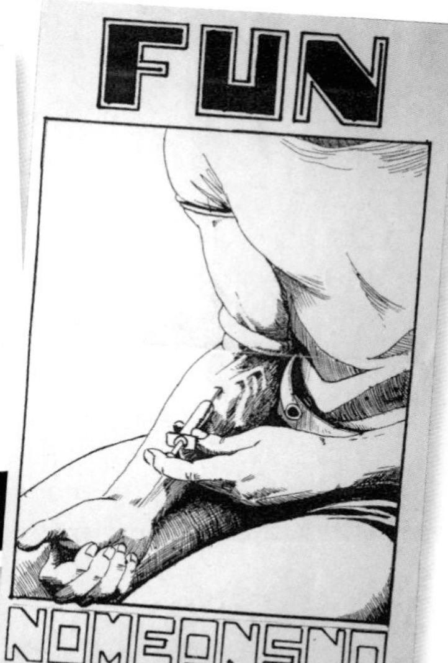

NoMeansNo began life as a Wright brothers project, and I wanted to have my own identity. It kept with the NoMeansNo idea of screwing with traditional promo norms. I thought that by being an anonymous person and changing it every time, people would still figure out who I am eventually. After a show, I wouldn't say, "Hey, you can't know my name," or anything like that. Not at all. If there were interviews, I would be Andy. It was just something to put on the record.

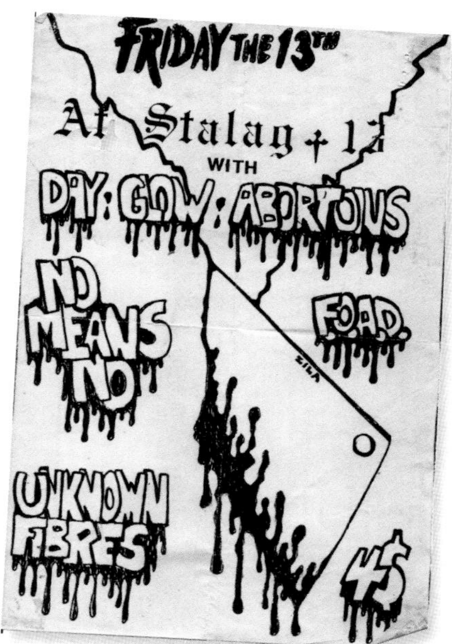


**Craig Northey—Odds** My gateway was the *You Kill Me* EP with "Manic Depression." It was so huge and powerful. It's easy to murder a song like that by going heavier, but NoMeansNo gave it a new elemental power. They captured something in the song that spoke just as loudly as the original, but in its own way.

**Murray "The Cretin" Acton—Dayglo Abortions** The Dayglo Abortions and NoMeansNo played a lot of shows together in Victoria in the early '80s. We'd take turns headlining. We were really the two bands in Victoria that could go over and play Vancouver at that time. Probably the funniest show we played with them was at a squat called Stalag 13. There were a lot of underground, illegal clubs in Vancouver at that time. Some of them were really slick, pretty nice, but Stalag 13 was not one of them. It was sort of bordering on an abandoned building that had been taken over. They had this big basement with a dirt floor, and they built a stage down there, and that's where they'd do gigs.

While we were playing, Simon Snotface, the fuckin' scourge of the Vancouver punk scene, is upstairs, and he lit this guy's fucking room on fire. He's just sitting there laughing, drinking, and the fire department comes. There's a gig happening downstairs, and the firefighters were so unimpressed with everything going on, they just put out the fire and left. Didn't even shut down the show. So we're playing downstairs, and all of a sudden it starts raining through the ceiling. We're like, "What the hell?!" The dirt floor is turning to mud. But the gig still went on. I'm thinking, "That's funny, normally when a building catches on fire, they evacuate it."

**John Kastner—Asexuals, Doughboys** I remember one time in Victoria, Asexuals played with NoMeansNo at this gymnasium. It was an all-ages show. They had this big silver tub full of beer and ice backstage. While we were playing, the Dayglo Abortions showed up. They drank all the beer and then pissed into the bucket. This place was so incredibly hot that at the end of our show I pulled the bucket out and poured it all over the kids, not knowing that the Dayglos had peed in it.

**Rob Nesbitt—Section 46, BUM** The first punk show I ever saw in Victoria was NoMeansNo with Art Bergmann and Poisoned at the University of Victoria in February 1985. I went with these "mod" kids, and I'd never done anything like this. I was freaked out.

They took to the stage, and they started playing. The room blew apart, because all the kids were in motion, slamming into each other. Of course, as time went on and I saw them more and more, I realized that the hardcore aggression thing was really not what they were about, and Rob would often chastise the crowds for getting too rough.

This was Victoria. We had no idea if they were popular anywhere else, but to us, they seemed like people on a completely different level. Like rock stars.

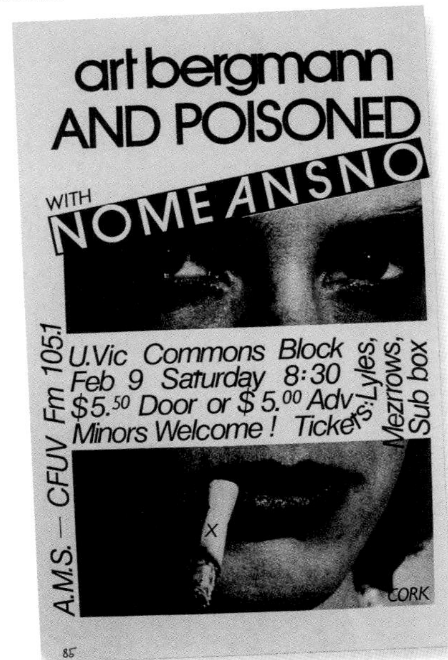

**First Canadian tour: Andy, Laurie Mercer, Ric Arboit, John, Rob, and friend**

**Art Bergmann—musician, Poisoned, Young Canadians** I don't know that much about NoMeansNo's intimate history. I just know that I fucking loved them. They were way before the Red Hot Chili Peppers, doing this hard, hard, fucking white-hot funk that was just brutally good. Just NoMeansNo, nailing down the current and old problems in society. I saw them once at a club in Vancouver, and it was so amazing. It was so intense that I had to leave. They were that good.

**Andy Kerr** NoMeansNo's first long Canadian tour was in 1985. It was us three and Ric Arboit as our sound person. We borrowed the Wright family's station wagon and rented a trailer in which we kept a tent and gear. When I say trailer, I mean a little U-Haul, one you hook on the back and tow.

Laurie managed to cobble together this tour across Canada, and we thought, "Well, we need a sound person to come with us." We asked Ric, and I think we paid him some completely nominal fee, and we got along great.

We would stay in between shows at roadside pullovers and campsites. We took a Coleman stove along to make some food for ourselves. It's one of these things where you go somewhere and the scene is waiting for you, even though they don't have any idea of who you are. You are just *another* punk rock show. The hardcore scene was happening in Canada by that point, so we just fell into that. We were adopted by it, so to speak.

**Ric Arboit** I wasn't going to go, but I think Laurie Mercer and a bunch of other fellows talked me into it. I hate to say this, but I needed to make money, and I wanted twenty-five dollars a night to go on tour, and somehow they found it. I bought my first sleeping bag, I bought a tent, and that's how we toured. I think two of them slept in the back of the station wagon. I remember this amazing cream cheese and salmon spread that John created. We ate that quite a bit on the road, and it was fantastic. I've never tasted it again.

DON'T FALL

HERE ARE THE YOUNG MEN

SATURDAY MAY 25 1985

NO MEANS NO
EUTHANASIA

TICKETS AT CJSR, AURACLE RECORDS AND SOUND CONNECTION

AT GARNEAU HALL
10943 84 AVE
PRESENTED BY
FRIENDS OF CJSR

581-24

**From Ric Arboit's tour diary, 1985, including Montreal shows (right)**

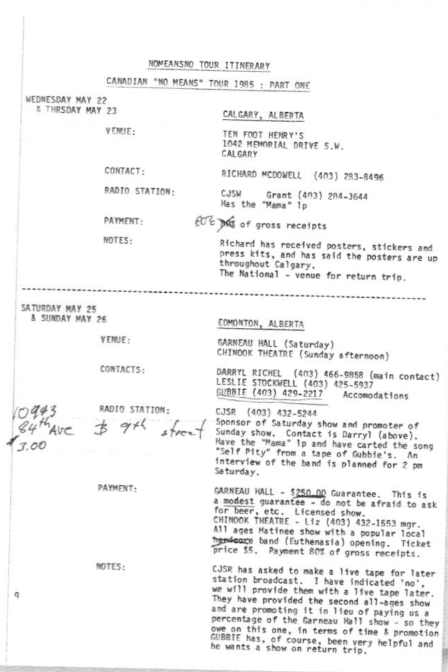

NOMEANSNO TOUR ITINERARY

CANADIAN "NO MEANS" TOUR 1985 : PART ONE

WEDNESDAY MAY 22 & THRSDAY MAY 23 — CALGARY, ALBERTA

VENUE: TEN FOOT HENRY'S, 1042 MEMORIAL DRIVE S.W., CALGARY

CONTACT: RICHARD MCDOWELL (403) 283-8496

RADIO STATION: CJSW Grant (403) 284-3644. Has the "Mama" lp

PAYMENT: 80% of gross receipts

NOTES: Richard has received posters, stickers and press kits, and has said the posters are up throughout Calgary. The National - venue for return trip.

SATURDAY MAY 25 & SUNDAY MAY 26 — EDMONTON, ALBERTA

VENUE: GARNEAU HALL (Saturday), CHINOOK THEATRE (Sunday afternoon)

CONTACTS: DARRYL RICHEL (403) 466-9858 (main contact), LESLIE STOCKWELL (403) 425-5937, GUBBIE (403) 429-2217 Accomodations

RADIO STATION: CJSR (403) 432-5244. Sponsor of Saturday show and promoter of Sunday show. Contact is Darryl (above). Have the "Mama" lp and have carted the song "Self Pity" from a tape of Gubbie's. An interview of the band is planned for 2 pm Saturday.

PAYMENT: GARNEAU HALL - $250.00 Guarantee. This is a modest guarantee - do not be afraid to ask for beer, etc. Licensed show. CHINOOK THEATRE - Liz (403) 432-1553 mgr. All ages Matinee show with a popular local band (Euthenasia) opening. Ticket price $5. Payment 80% of gross receipts.

NOTES: CJSR has asked to make a live tape for later station broadcast. I have indicated 'no', we will provide them with a live tape later. They have provided the second all-ages show and are promoting it in lieu of paying us a percentage of the Garneau Hall show - so they owe on this one, in terms of time & promotion. GUBBIE has, of course, been very helpful and he wants a show on return trip.

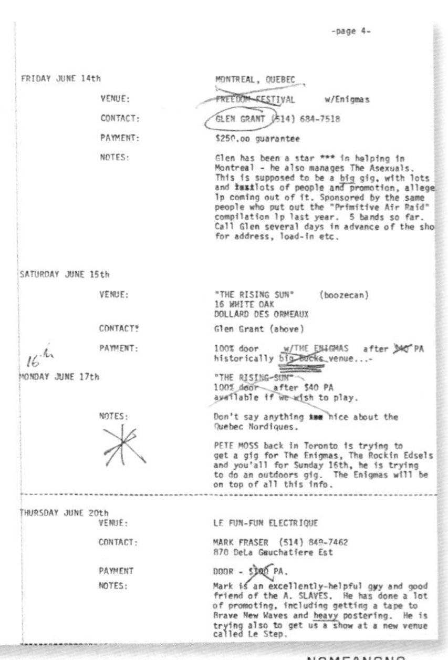

-page 4-

FRIDAY JUNE 14th — MONTREAL, QUEBEC

VENUE: FREEDOM FESTIVAL w/Enigmas

CONTACT: GLEN GRANT (514) 684-7518

PAYMENT: $250.oo guarantee

NOTES: Glen has been a star *** in helping in Montreal - he also manages The Asexuals. This is supposed to be a big gig, with lots and lots of people and promotion, allege lp coming out of it. Sponsored by the same people who put out the "Primitive Air Raid" compilation lp last year. 5 bands so far. Call Glen several days in advance of the sho for address, load-in etc.

SATURDAY JUNE 15th

VENUE: "THE RISING SUN" (boozecan), 16 WHITE OAK, DOLLARD DES ORMEAUX

CONTACT: Glen Grant (above)

PAYMENT: 100% door w/THE ENIGMAS after PA. historically big bucks venue...-

MONDAY JUNE 17th — "THE RISING SUN" 100% door after $40 PA available if we wish to play.

NOTES: Don't say anything nice about the Quebec Nordiques.

PETE MOSS back in Toronto is trying to get a gig for The Enigmas, The Rockin Edsels and you'all for Sunday 16th, he is trying to do an outdoors gig. The Enigmas will be on top of all this info.

THURSDAY JUNE 20th

VENUE: LE FUN-FUN ELECTRIQUE

CONTACT: MARK FRASER (514) 849-7462, 870 DeLa Gauchatiere Est

PAYMENT: DOOR - PA.

NOTES: Mark is an excellently-helpful guy and good friend of the A. SLAVES. He has done a lot of promoting, including getting a tape to Brave New Waves and heavy postering. He is trying also to get us a show at a new venue called Le Step.

**Marty Chatrin—Euthanasia** The first show that we played with them was in the spring of 1985 in Edmonton. Before that, I had this impression after hearing their intense music that these guys were going to be like axe murderers or serial killers.

So up drives this minivan and with the smallest little teeny U-Haul trailer out behind them, and out come these nerdy college-looking guys that were older than us. It was chilly out, and they were all wearing sweaters. I'm just, "Oh my god, look at these guys! They can't be making this music!" What I heard on the cassette of *You Kill Me*, and who they actually were, was just totally opposite in my mind.

**James MacLean—October Crisis** We had a big band house and used to book shows in our hometown of London, Ontario. All the bands that were driving through to Toronto and Montreal, we'd get them a couple shows in London. I got a call that this band NoMeansNo from Victoria was coming through, so I booked them a show at Bullwinkles, and October Crisis opened. We put them up at our band house, fed them barbecue and everything.

One day, we all hopped in our vehicles and drove forty-five minutes from London to Lake Huron, to Grand Bend, a little beach town where my grandparents had this cottage. I can remember the Wright brothers having a conversation with my eighty-year-old granny, because she loved Victoria and had relatives out there. I wouldn't take the Dayglos or Chi Pig to meet my grandmother, but NoMeansNo were just sweethearts.

**John Ondrasek—October Crisis** I remember them asking, "Well, which ocean would this be?" I said, "No, this isn't an ocean. This is a Great Lake." Then an awkward pause ... "Wow, it's beautiful, isn't it?"

**James MacLean** London was a smaller town, kinda like Victoria actually, very friendly, very hospitable. We became friends with the NoMeansNo guys, and they must have appreciated our hospitality, because they thanked us in the liner notes of *You Kill Me*. They came through London many times after that. They just looked like the most normal guys, but then they got up onstage and literally pasted you against the back wall of the venue.

**Eric Popper—My Dog Popper** NoMeansNo came to Montreal in the summer of 1985. They were booked on a Friday night at a place called Station 10, which was a really tiny little bar that was willing to have punk bands play. They didn't have another show booked, but they managed to get two more shows and found a couple parties to play. That's where we became friends, and we'd see each other whenever they came through Montreal. They weren't crazy partiers like many of the punks we were used to. They were happy just to hang out, smoke hash, drink beer, and barbecue.

Rob is so fucking funny, John was always a bit shy, but it was Andy whom I really connected with. We really loved a lot of the same music, but also comedy, like the Firesign Theatre and Monty Python. It was rare in those days to meet somebody into that stuff.

**Lucinda Catchlove—My Dog Popper** One of the really nice things about NoMeansNo is they were really female friendly. They treated all the girls in Popper well, and we appreciated that. When NoMeansNo came to town, especially in the earlier years, we made a big deal out of it. We'd have a big barbecue specifically for them, because we viewed them not just as a band but as friends. We became part of their scene.

Some of their songs are about feminist issues, but you don't really need to be overt to be a feminist. It's really about how you act and how you treat people. It was evident with NoMeansNo that they were just very decent people. I think it's important to highlight that they treated us

with respect, which was not always the case with other bands.

**Andy Kerr** We met a whole bunch of people. That was the most important thing. We were really happy that we did it and came back in one piece. I don't know how much we lost, but we didn't spend that much either. It wasn't a difficult tour. It was lovely, really fun.

**Ric Arboit** After that, the two partners at Nettwerk Records asked me to work for them. In the long run, it all worked out, but I will go on record to say the best time touring I've ever had was with NoMeansNo. It was a blast. Rob could make me laugh. He had a fantastic, brilliant, wise, dry wit. John was the same. We all loved the exact same type of music, and at that age, it is all about the music.

**Andy Kerr** Everyone was making mixtapes around that time. We all made them. Rob made great mixtapes, because he had an excellent record collection. He tended to really like taking extreme left turns. He'd make a tape and put fifteen minutes of just guitar solos on it. Literally just chop them out of songs. Like the beginning of "Cortez the Killer," then into a Hendrix solo, then into a Robert Fripp solo, and then something else. He'd just fuck around with the volume and repeat things.

It's not like it was a competition, but it was a way to show each other what we were into at the time. Robbie would say, "Oh, here's an Aerosmith song." Well, I didn't know fuckin' Aerosmith from a hole in the ground. Or he'd put on "Dr. Feelgood." Both brothers were fans of Blue Öyster Cult. Rob really loved Cream and Jimi Hendrix.

Being on tour, you only have so many tapes, but you have tons of time on the road, and we would play these tapes over and over again. They sort of soaked into absolutely everything that we did, so our albums sometimes sound a little all over the place.

When you are on tour, all you do is listen to the music that you play yourself, or the bands that you're playing with. Once the tour ends, the last thing you want to do is listen to new music. Stuff like the Pixies: a great band, but they just didn't go past our radar. There were all these things happening in the late '80s and early '90s that just went over our heads because we were stuck in the old compilation tapes that we made. We listened to all sorts of stuff, like John McLaughlin, Mahavishnu Orchestra, King Crimson, Killing Joke, Graham Parker, Billie Holiday, Discharge. It was all over the place. On every tour, without fail, we would set aside a special time—usually during a night drive—to listen reverently to the Residents' *Mark of the Mole* in its entirety.

**Daniel Webster—Psyche Industry Records** I put together a compilation record called *It Came from the Pit*. It was bands from all over the country, from the Ruggedy Annes and Stretch Marks to NoMeansNo and SNFU. That's how I first got introduced to NoMeansNo.

We organized a big church basement gig in June 1985 called Communication Riot, and we brought the Enigmas from Vancouver, October Crisis from London, Ontario, and this band that nobody had heard of called NoMeansNo. The Enigmas had a bit of a buzz about them at the time. NoMeansNo ended up doing a bit of a residency in Montreal. For about a week, they played a bunch of different venues. Nobody even cared about the Enigmas after seeing NoMeansNo. We went out to every show that week, and every night it got better. They had the song on *It Came from the Pit* ["No Sex," a different version than on *Mama*], and we told them we wanted to release their next record, which ended up being *Sex Mad* the following year.

**Andy Kerr** So we'd done our first cross-Canada tour, we were very happy with it, and I came back home to my girlfriend, Sylvia, and my day job at the Bapco paint store.

Back in Victoria for the summer of 1985, the guys in NoMeansNo had a moment to breathe and take stock of their situation. The rest of the year would be spent doing gigs locally and in Vancouver. Ric Arboit had been a fine soundman on their Canadian tour, but he had moved on to greener pastures. NMN needed to find somebody more permanent, like a pilot who could navigate the sonic boom of a live NoMeansNo show and all the turbulence that came with it.

## MEET CRAIG BOUGIE

**Craig Bougie—NoMeansNo sound tech** I grew up in Victoria and went to Vic High School. My older brother Paul was there too, along with Tom Holliston.

I was always interested in music, but I could never play it. I had a friend in a cover band, and I would always go to his shows. I got intrigued by the sound guy. He'd come in, and he'd analyze the room with white noise. I thought, "What a neat job!"

John and Craig Bougie

**Paul Bougie—brother of Craig Bougie** Craig at the time was really into music and was getting involved because his good friend Pete Hatch was playing bass in a cover band called Roxxlyde, which were a pretty big deal in Victoria. He was sort of dabbling in being a roadie.

**Craig Bougie** Tom Holliston at the time was a DJ at a local Mexican restaurant called La Hacienda. They started having bands there, and they needed a sound guy. The band Grapes of Wrath were coming through, and their guitar player had me run the board while they played. I did okay at it. I did sound for four or five more shows at La Hacienda, and then NoMeansNo played there. I had never seen them before. In fact, I wasn't really into that scene at all.

**Trevor "Spud" Hagen** I was doing sound now and again for bands at La Hacienda, and either Rob or John came up to me and said, "Craig Bougie's gonna do sound for us. Can you show him how to work a board?" I taught him the basics and kinda watched over him for the night. I showed him how not to overdrive the lines, mark them all out, that kind of basic stuff.

**Craig Bougie** I started doing sound for NoMeansNo more regularly, and then there was a suspicious fire at La Hacienda.

**Tim Chan—Ryvals, Hathead, 64 Funnycars** In October 1985, NoMeansNo and Animal Slaves played a show at La Hacienda, and that same night the club burned down. They lost a bunch of their gear because

## LETTER FROM ROB WRIGHT TO LAURIE MERCER, 1985

Dear Laurie!

Attention! Here is cash for percentages of gigs since we been back. I think this makes us square (I mean I know it does!) Also enclosed is gushing review of DMZ Toronto gig from the NERVE! It was sent by a friend from TO. We done good, eh? Hope you are comfortably sitting behind a large desk in a dark wine coloured naugahyde recliner planning to conquer the concert market of Vancouver and take NOMEANSNO on your coattails up the escalator of success to fame and fortune (the latter at the very least).

I have been staying up all night and sleeping all day, writing songs, reading books and generally enjoying not having to work for a living. I am broke but with two women living here (our friend Debbie has moved in since the kids have returned to their father for a year—in Vancouver actually) who both work in restaurants. I've been eating very well. Last night Debbie whipped up oysters in Cajun sauce on spinach fettuccine (all liberated from her restaurant). Pretty great eh!

How's this for idle chatter—Andy has rented a Marshall and decided that he needs to run his old amp and it simultaneously to get the sound he really wants. He is downstairs right now blowing the walls out of my basement. (Isn't volume wonderful!) With practicing for the Record Release Party (Ha!) I have been inspired to write about four pseudo Ramones and/or hardcore songs. I have also written one extremely long and extremely weird NOMEANSNO song called "Small Parts, Isolated and Destroyed" (I'm not getting older I'm just getting nastier), so be prepared when you hear us again for a band even more schizo than before.

Andy is also on a sort of writing spree, so we will probably have our Third "potential" or shall I say "imaginary" album finished and ready for . . . well, let's not dwell on depressing realities.

John is spending a lot of his time at Club Hacienda (which now has a good sound system) doing sound for whoever needs it. (He starts off by asking for money, then when none of the bands will agree to pay him, he does it for free anyway—what a businessman!)

Give Lenore our love and encouragement (whatever that means), try to keep your mind together, and we'll see you soon (or whenever).

Thanx! Bye!

Rob.

P.S. DEAR LAURIE, IF YOU CAN DECIPHER ROB'S LETTER, YOU WILL BE MORE AWE-INSPIRING IN MY EYES THAN YOU EVER HAVE BEEN BEFORE Love & Kisses —ANDY

## Electrical fault ruled out in fire that destroyed Club Hacienda

Firefighters on Tuesday ruled out an electrical fault as the cause of a fire that destroyed Club Hacienda.

Victoria deputy chief Whitey Severson said the cause of the fire would likely be known today. An arson investigator was at the scene Monday.

The fire broke out on the main floor lounge area shortly after 3 a.m. Sunday, 30 or 40 minutes after the club had closed.

The two floors of the club at 1245 Store St. were extensively damaged.

they left it there after they played. Rumour has it that the owner did the deed himself because he wanted the insurance money. Tom Holliston had moved to Edmonton, so it was Marcus Pollard who was booking it when the club burned down.

**Marcus Pollard** Animal Slaves stayed at my apartment that night, and we got a call at like six or seven in the morning telling us the club had burned down. I lost my record collection in that fire too. I was the DJ there, and all my records were there.

**Ross Hales—Animal Slaves** I remember that night well for a couple reasons. Obviously, because the club burned down and we lost a bunch of stuff. But during the show itself, the crowd was being a little cool when we were playing. People were not as engaged or as enthusiastic as Rachel, our bassist, wanted them to be. So she slipped behind the PA, took all of her clothes off, put her bass back on, came out and played the next song completely fucking naked. At the end of the song, she put her clothes back on and continued playing. That turned the entire gig around. People went fucking mental. It was so fun, and that was so Rachel.

**Sylvia Kenny** I was at that show. I was still not legal drinking age, so I was sitting at home feeling sad. Then I got a call from Andy: "Get down here! Bruno's

Onstage at the OAP Hall, 1984

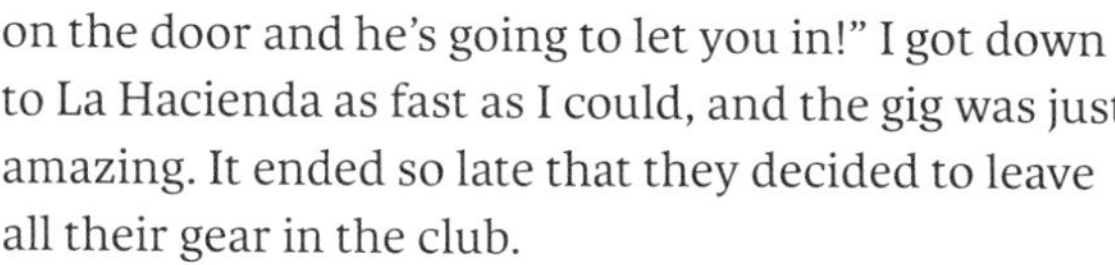

on the door and he's going to let you in!" I got down to La Hacienda as fast as I could, and the gig was just amazing. It ended so late that they decided to leave all their gear in the club.

The next morning, I got this call: "The club burned down." I still remember Andy saying their amps were toast. It was a setback for sure, but they took it all in stride.

**Andy Kerr** I was at Sylvia's house. I got a call in the morning when I'm sitting in her mom's kitchen, and it was John. He said, "Well, I got some good news for you: you'll be able to buy a whole bunch of new equipment." I said, "Oh, why is that?" "Well, the bad news is the club burned down." I was like, "Fuck, well at least I brought my guitar home." I didn't care about the amp, but I wasn't gonna find another guitar like that. Then I turned to Sylvia and I went, "Ahh! My records!" I was DJing at La Hacienda semiregularly then, and about half of my record collection was there. According to Marcus, several months later all these warped, half-burned albums of mine turned up somewhere in a garage sale.

**Eric Lowe** A few weeks later, our band Ryvals played a gig at the OAP Hall to benefit NoMeansNo and Animal Slaves and raise some money for them to get new gear.

**Ford Pier** NoMeansNo venerated the Animal Slaves. They thought they were an incredible band. They were on a Vancouver record label called Mo Da Mu that also did the first 54-40 record. It was more like the recording label arm of an arts collective. Elizabeth Fischer and Animal Slaves were a big part of that, and I think that NoMeansNo's association with them might have led to their selection of Mushroom Studios to do the *You Kill Me* record, because that's where Animal Slaves had recorded.

NoMeansNo were quite aligned with Animal Slaves in a few ways. The prominence of the bass, the different rhythms, the politics, particularly the feminist politics. It was a ready fit. But instead of becoming part of that scene, NoMeansNo wound up finding a way to operate successfully in the hardcore scene and what it grew into in the late '80s and early '90s. It could have gone either way for a while there. If NoMeansNo had happened in Vancouver, that's possibly where they would have been stuck. Pigeonholed with those groups that had a reputation for attracting an *art* audience, a little older, maybe a little bit more sophisticated, certainly more Joy Division or Jane Siberry T-shirts than MDC T-shirts. Instead, they came from Victoria, where they would be perceived under the same umbrella as the NEOs or Dayglo Abortions, Victoria's idea of a punk band. There were more places to play and better communication in the hardcore circuit. They could get out and play for more people.

**Craig Bougie** NoMeansNo were gonna go on tour the following spring, and they wanted somebody to go with them down to the States for three months. I said, "I'd love to." That was my beginning. My baptism by fire.

**John Wright** Craig was totally into sound. He ended up taking a sound-mixing course, because he wanted to learn more about it. He learned along with us. We knew from the get-go that we needed a soundman who was on our side, and Craig was that guy. We had had enough stupid soundmen who didn't give a fucking rat's ass. Soundmen back then were all cover-band, nightclub guys: "What the fuck? You want to set your drums where? Fuuuck, I've got to move this cord over there. Fuck." So much attitude.

Craig learned how to deal with a very loud band with very inadequate equipment early on, and he got great at it. He basically became like a member of the band. He was our soundman and my drinking partner.

**Andy Kerr** Craig was essentially a fourth member of the band. We had all kinds of other fine folks as well, but Craig was always there. He provided absolutely excellent sound at our shows, sometimes in the direst of circumstances. He was also a great friend. I can't imagine my time in NoMeansNo without him, really. He was very relaxed to be around, and he kept us grounded.

**Ingrid Severson—tour merch, Wrong Records** I came into the picture when I met the NoMeansNo guys around 1985. A bunch of us would hang out at Paul Bougie's house, and I started going out with his brother Craig almost immediately. He was doing sound at La Hacienda at the time and was starting to work with NoMeansNo. We ended up being together for a decade. I went on one of the early tours with them and helped sell merch.

**Andy Kerr** Before we recorded *You Kill Me*, I had this shitty Music Man amp. I didn't really like it very much. Then the fire happened at La Hacienda, and I suddenly needed a new amp. I bought an old Fender for like three hundred bucks. Rob and John said, "Why don't you try adding one of our little PA monitors that we use in the basement?"

We just stuck it on top and plugged in, and it gave this really great piercing sound. I never used any pedals except an echo for a couple of songs, like "Self Pity." Beyond that, it was just plugging the amp in and turning it up. Craig just mic'd the amp and the bigger box, and that was my sound. I played through a Schecter Telecaster, which I still have. I had no idea what pickups were in it or anything. I just went, "Okay, this looks like a Telecaster. Joe Strummer plays one of these."

People were always like, "How do you get that sound? What pedals do you use?" I'd say, "I just turn it up and play." I'm not trying to have false modesty here: it is quite literally just dumb luck that I came up with that sound.

Andy onstage at the Pine Street Theatre, Portland, Oregon, 1985

CHAPTER EIGHT

# THE HANSON BROTHERS

## "No dipsy doodle dancin', it's hockey a la Hanson!"

The Hanson Brothers were NoMeansNo's "alter ego" project, a hockey-themed Ramones-style band. John put down his drumsticks and became the front man, Johnny Hanson. Rob became Robbie Hanson, where he could step back from the spotlight, playing his bass incognito behind a goalie mask with "DUMB" emblazoned across the top.

It began as a goof, a way to do something less serious than the often-heavy content they were used to performing. The Hansons later became a touring and recording band of their own. They released albums and earned fans around the world, some of whom didn't initially realize they were watching the same guys from NoMeansNo.

**THE HANSON BROTHERS**

Johnny Hanson, aka John Wright—vocals, 1985–2014
Robbie Hanson, aka Rob Wright—bass, 1985–2014
Andy Hanson, aka Andy Kerr—guitar, 1985–91
Tommy Hanson, aka Tom Holliston—guitar, 1992–2014
Gary Hanson, aka Gary Brainless—drums, 1985–91
Kenny Hanson, aka Ken Jensen—drums, 1992–93
Kenny Hanson, aka Ken Kempster—drums, 1993–97
Ernie Hanson, aka Ernie Hawkins—drums, 2002–6
Mikey Hanson, aka Mike Branum—drums, 2008–13
Ronny Hanson, aka Byron Slack—drums, 2014

**Rob Wright** My voice was shot for over a year. Andy had to take over for a lot of songs, especially live. I never completely lost the ability to vocalize, but it was bad there for quite a while. I had to get them shaved off with a laser. It's just like calluses or boils that you get on your vocal cords, then you can't shut them properly and vibrate them properly. It was basically from abuse. Onstage, there was no control. It eventually healed and then got stronger.

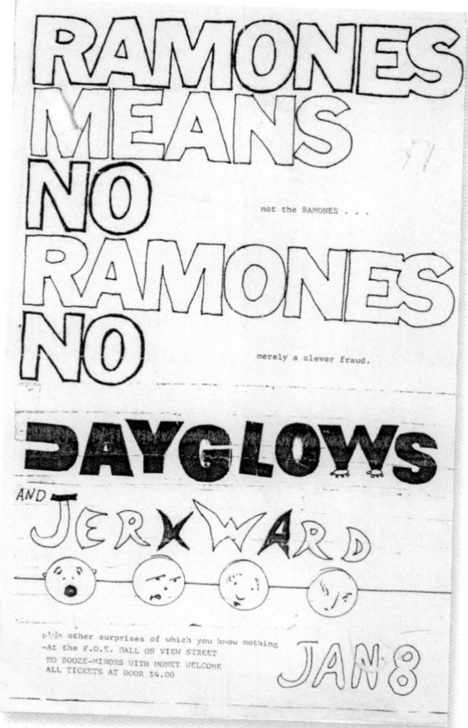


**Andy Kerr** I remember when Rob brought in the Hanson Brothers songs, which included "Dad," and his voice was completely shot at that point. He absolutely had nodules, so that puts it before our next album, *Sex Mad*, for sure.

**John Wright** The Hanson Brothers started as a concept very early, when Andy was in the band. Even back then we thought, "Ah, this is all such heavy music, it would be nice to do something a little lighter," and we all loved the Ramones of course.

We were playing shows around Victoria, and so we thought, "Let's do something fun. Let's do a Ramones show. It'll be something completely *not* NoMeansNo, and we can go up there and pretend to be the punk rock band that we love." We did NoMeansNo Clones the Ramones, with Kev Smith and then Gary Brainless on drums. I think the first one we did was at the FOE Hall, probably '83, '84, and it was great fun.

**Kev Smith** At some point, they decided to do this band called NoMeansRamones, and they asked me to play drums. I practised with them quite a few times before we played a gig at the FOE Hall. We were all big Ramones fans, and I loved the concept, which was to play the first side of each of the first three Ramones albums and then a fourth "side" consisting of all the best songs from the B sides. All four sets delivered in authentic nonstop Ramones style. I was easily the least accomplished musician in the room, especially on drums, but it seemed to work and we pulled it off. Actually, the gig was fantastic, and the crowd flipped. We ran over time, and even though the sound guy shut off the PA, it didn't matter. Since everybody knew all the words, the whole audience did the vocals! They did this again later a few times with Gary Brainless on drums, and I suspect this was the origin of their Hanson Brothers side band.

**John Wright** After doing that, I remember us chatting about, "Let's just write some really straight, Ramones-style songs, just for fun. They won't be part of NoMeansNo or anything, really." Just to see if we can do it. About seven or eight songs just burst out.

We were hanging out at Bino's, talking about this music and what type of band it would be. It'd have to be fictitious brothers; it would have to be Canadian. So it's got to be hockey, and something kinda stupid.

*Slap Shot* was one of my all-time favourite movies, ever. I had seen it in the theatre when it came out in '77. I was literally falling down in my chair laughing so hard. This was the funniest fuckin' movie that I've ever seen in my life! I love that movie; we all love that movie. It's a classic. Of course, it has the classic characters of the Hanson Brothers, the three brothers who start fights and all wear thick-rimmed glasses. We decided this new band of ours has got to be "the Hanson Brothers," and we'll dress up and have this hockey thing to go with it.

**Rob Wright** We did NoMeansNo Clones the Ramones first, and that was the beginning of the Hanson Brothers. We just loved doing that, and so we thought, "Why don't we just write our own little tunes?" John would be up front, and we'd get any rudimentary drummer we could find. He couldn't be too good, because we just required him to keep a beat. He had to be Tommy Ramone.

Tom Holliston John's favourite movie of all time is *Slap Shot*, and it just seemed like this is a natural combination: the Hanson Brothers and the Ramones. For NoMeansNo, hands down, everybody's favourite band for all time, for all of us, is the Ramones. There are only two or three things that have ever really changed my life. One of them was hearing the Ramones song "Suzy Is a Headbanger."

I was living in Edmonton in the mid-'80s. NoMeansNo played a whole show with a band called Euthanasia, but then they came out as the Hanson Brothers. They had hockey jerseys on, and at that time I made a terrible mistake. Somehow I had found a collection of all the NHL teams with their emblems on hockey pucks, and I said, "Hey, why don't you guys give these away at the show?" Which they did. I knew it was a mistake when I saw the crowd throwing hockey pucks at the band while they played.

A couple years later, they did a very successful Hanson Brothers gig at the Town Pump in Vancouver, with Gary Brainless on drums. They did "Clock Strikes Ten" by Cheap Trick as the encore. That was their first packed show. I didn't go, because there were too many people from Victoria going over. I didn't want to be waiting for them to decide what to eat.

When I look at the Hanson Brothers, I think, "Man, John was as good a front man as he was a drummer." It's really too bad that his talents in that direction were never really fully realized.

**Rick Andrews** The *Blobs Vol. 1* seven-inch record that I put out in 1991 was the first appearance of the Hanson Brothers on vinyl. At the time it was just Andy and John. They pretended it was a band, but Rob wasn't involved. It's not actually a Hanson Brothers tune, it's a song that Tom Holliston wrote called "My Girlfriend's a Robot." That seven-inch is also the first appearance on vinyl for Tom's band Show Business Giants.

**Andy Kerr** John, probably more so than Rob, had this notion in his head of doing the Hanson Brothers thing. We all loved the Ramones, and it gave John a chance to be out front and sing, which was neat. We had done the NoMeansNo Clones the Ramones thing with Kevin from the NEOs on drums. He was fantastic, by the way. It was a real epiphany for John, because he'd never been out front with a microphone before. I think he really caught the bug, so to speak, and it was music that he really enjoyed singing.

**Tom Holliston** Andy and I had similar senses of humour, and I think around '86 he said, "We're doing a few shows as the Hanson Brothers. Why don't you write a Hanson Brothers song, Tom?" Andy was very encouraging

about writing and playing. He'd say, "You should play, you'd really enjoy it!" We were good friends at the time. I wrote this song "My Girlfriend's a Robot," which is really good. It's all about misogyny. And the Hanson Brothers recorded it.

**Andy Kerr** "My Girlfriend's a Robot" was a song on the Showbiz Giants' first tape. We had been working on some songs and thought that Tom's song would make a great Hanson Brothers song, although when you first hear it, it doesn't seem like it. There's no drums or big distorted guitar on the original Showbiz version, but it has the total structure of a Ramones song. Rob wasn't there for the recording. John sang it, and I played both guitar and bass on that one.

**John Wright** Nothing really happened until we made some demos, which we did at Profile Studios while we were doing the Biafra album. There were times when we were there but he wasn't, so we'd say, "Oh, let's do demos. We got some time here. Let's just bang them down." Those are the demos which ended up in the hands of Greg Werckman at Alternative Tentacles. He called us saying, "These are fucking great, we've got to put this out." We were, "Ah no, it's just a joke!" But he convinced us.

**Andy Kerr** When I was in the band, we did some Hanson Brothers demos and thought, "Okay, well, what are we gonna do with these? Well, we'll just play them live, and if we feel like putting them out, we will." There was never any sense of taking the Hansons on the road, at least when I was still there. Of course, they did an amazing job, actually. It's incredible that they ended up having this whole other band. I think there was one tour where they went across Canada as NoMeansNo and they came back as Hanson Brothers. I just thought that was marketing brilliance.

**John Wright** I'd been working with Tom Holliston in the Show Business Giants for a while at that point. Tom loved the Hanson Brothers and had written a couple of songs, and I remember Rob, Tom, and I were just like, "Well, we're not doing anything. Why don't we just do this for fun?" So we went into Scotty Henderson's basement studio on Shelbourne Street.

**Tom Holliston** I had a crappy Stratocaster, and we tried to record at Scotty's house, but it wasn't working. I ended up buying an SG.

**John Wright** Tom got his brand-new left-handed SG. It was just out of the store. We were recording the album, and the damn fuckin' thing wouldn't stay in tune. Unbeknownst to us, the truss rod was not correct, and the intonation was off. Tom was just so frustrated; he was having a hell of a time. We'd have to do songs in different parts because he was constantly out of tune. Of course we sorted it out, but that whole album was a real chore getting the guitars done. That was the first Hanson Brothers record, *Gross Misconduct.*

I did all the drumming on all the Hansons' recordings, but of course we needed a drummer for live shows, because I was now the singer, the front man. *Gross Misconduct* came out in 1992, and we did a tour down to California and back with Ken Jensen drumming. So, from inception to actually putting out a record and touring, it was almost ten years.

## RIP KENNY HANSON

### Ken Jensen (1966–95)

Ken Jensen was a beloved fixture in the early Victoria punk scene. A talented drummer and bassist, Ken played in local bands Red Tide, Suburban Menace, Gus, and others. He was also the Hanson Brothers' first touring drummer and eventually joined D.O.A. and moved to Vancouver. Sadly, Ken died in a house fire in East Vancouver on January 29, 1995, at the age of twenty-eight.

**Derek Sheplawy—friend** I grew up in Colwood, just outside Victoria. Ken Jensen lived down the road from me, and we were friends since grade five. We were both into music and then it just really went from there. We met the NoMeansNo and Infamous Scientists guys from going to shows and going to Richard's Records, where Scott Henderson worked. Everybody kind of met through there.

**Craig Bougie** Ken Jensen came with us as a roadie on NoMeansNo's second or third tour of the western States. Ken and I would set up John's drums, and since he was a drummer himself, it was quite handy. Sometimes we didn't get sound checks, so he'd play the drums so I could make sure all the sounds were good.

**Andy Kerr** Ken was a really sweet guy and really nice to have on the road. We hired him as a roadie, but Rob and I just did our own stuff. He would be unplugging my amp onstage and I'd be, "Ken, you don't need to do that. I'll just take down the stuff myself. Take it easy." Ken was like, "Yeah, but this is what I'm here for." He was great with helping John tear down his stuff because he was a drummer as well.

Ken Jensen and John Wright

Ken was in Red Tide, a really great band. Listening back to Red Tide now, I think they were doing far more interesting things than I realized at the time. They were three good-looking guys, as opposed to the NoMeansNo guys. They had more of an appeal on that front. We had Craig, but he would always be behind the soundboard, so that didn't help very much.

**Joe Keithley—D.O.A.** Back in 1982, Chuck Biscuits had quit D.O.A. and we were wondering how to replace him. Soon thereafter I got a letter from this kid named Ken Jensen. He was sixteen years old and he wanted to drum for D.O.A. He went on to write, "My band has played with NoMeansNo and John Wright can vouch for me, and my parents say it's okay to go on tour around the world." I showed this to Dave Gregg and we laughed. Fast-forward to 1992 and D.O.A. was looking for a drummer once again. Who should answer the ad? None other than Ken Jensen! He got the gig, and we both laughed when he reminded me of the letter from ten years earlier. Jensen was a really funny guy with a big heart, and he turned out to be one of the best drummers D.O.A. ever had.

**Rob Wright** Ken Jensen was a big part of everyone's life, but he had the stinkiest feet in the world. We would always complain if he took his shoes off in the van, because he travelled with us as a roadie and sometimes as a drummer for the Hansons.

When he died, his parents were crushed. I think he was an only child, and he was a young man. There was no warning, and there's no reason for it. It was one of these stupid things that happen. He had many, many friends, and they all came to his funeral. I was

The Hanson Brothers with Kenny (Ken Jensen) on drums, 1993

one of the pallbearers. They used to go out to his parents' place and have a big party every year, for many, many years, just so his parents would know that people hadn't forgotten him and to celebrate him.

It's a tribute to Ken, but it's also a tribute to the closeness of the Victoria scene. It was definitely like one big family, close-knit, and they cared about each other. The way everyone stuck with his parents and celebrated his life for years and years is amazing, actually.

**Su Pomeroy—friend** Ken and I were really good buddies. We'd go up to his parents' cabin every year after he passed away, on his birthday, and celebrate with them. They've since sold the cabin, but we were going up there for twenty years. Paul Bougie always went. I don't think he missed one year. Ken was awesome.

**John Wright** Ken was a good friend. He was a great drummer and was in so many cool bands, like Red Tide and D.O.A. I delivered the main eulogy at his funeral, and I was a pallbearer. He was a very close friend of us all, and it was all really sad.

**Joe Keithley** John Wright filled in on drums for D.O.A.'s *The Black Spot* album after Ken passed away. John agreed to do it as a tribute to Ken. John was Ken's idol when he was basically a kid. They had a Victoria connection and all that.

**Ken Kempster—Shovlhed, Show Business Giants, Swell Prod., NoMeansNo, Hanson Brothers** Ken Jensen did a tour with the Hansons, and then I think he was getting back to touring with D.O.A., so they were looking for a new drummer. I actually heard it through Scott Henderson, who was my bandmate in Shovlhed. He said, "I was talking with John and he said that they might be looking for you for the Hansons." Pretty soon after that, Rob called me and said, "Do you want to play in the Hanson Brothers?" I'm like, "Yeah, sure." Secretly, I was freaking out because I was a diehard NoMeansNo fan. I thought they were one of the best bands I'd ever heard.

**John Wright** Somebody, I think it was Greg Werckman with the help of Laurie, eventually got the Ramones to autograph copies of *Gross Misconduct* for us. I heard they were kind of like "meh" at the beginning, because there were lots and lots of Ramones cover bands and imitation bands. They didn't really give a shit until they knew we were on AT. I have no idea if they ever listened to it or cared about it, but I got an autographed copy, so that's as close as I ever got to the Ramones, because I never saw them live.

The next album, *Sudden Death*, was a Virgin release because Laurie was a huge hockey fan too and getting more involved. He got his own independent record label going, Essential Noise Recordings, and had gotten some sort of distribution deal with Virgin. A Showbiz Giants album, a Ford Pier single, a few weird things ended up on this. It was fairly short lived, but he managed to get them to pay for a video. They spent more on that video than we ever made selling records. It was our one and only connection to the major label industry, and we didn't care too much about that. The Hanson Brothers were just for fun anyway, and Laurie really wanted to do it.

**Laurie Mercer** John's motivation with the Hanson Brothers was to have fun, to be the centre of attention, and to make people laugh. While Rob liked it, that's John's baby. I don't think they ever argued about the Hanson Brothers.

**Andre McGillvray—fan from Tofino, British Columbia** One of the earliest Hanson Brothers shows happened one night at the Cruel Elephant in Vancouver. Rob Wright had a cast on his leg, and we were told he would play the show on a stool. I thought

Joey Ramone with the *Gross Misconduct* LP

the show would be a letdown, energywise. The opposite happened. Rob kicked high in the air from sitting on his stool through the whole show, but he never toppled over. The man put out more pure, unhinged punk rock energy while sitting down on a stool with a cast on his leg than I've ever seen.

I turned around to scan the room halfway through the set, and there was a lovely older woman sitting behind me laughing and chatting. I introduced myself and met Rob and John's mom. She was grinning ear to ear every time I looked at her.

**Gina Volpe—Lunachicks** The Lunachicks played a show called Hockey Night at the Commodore in Vancouver in 1993, with the Hanson Brothers, D.O.A., and SNFU. We loved the Hanson Brothers and thought they were hilarious, but I didn't understand the *Slap Shot* reference. They were a great live

The Hanson Brothers, 2012

band. We had never heard of them before that. The whole night was super fun, and all the bands that played were awesome. It must've been quite the party, because I don't remember much!

**John Wright** The Hanson Brothers had become a thing, more so than we really expected. It garnered fans who didn't even know who NoMeansNo were. There were definitely people out there who had no idea it was the same band. For us it was like, "Okay, this is good. We can take a break from NoMeansNo, and we don't have to go get dishwashing jobs again."

It was great fun for me. I loved being the front man, but I get far more joy and satisfaction out of drumming. But as a diversion, as something to go out and just do and have some fun with, it was awesome. I had a great time. I was a caricature, so it became more of a grind in the end. When I'm just playing NoMeansNo, I'm just being myself, and it's not work. The Hanson Brothers became work. I had to be a character. I had to be an actor and a comedian. I wouldn't want to do that full time.

**Ken Kempster** We all wore hockey jerseys onstage, and we didn't always have time to wash them. So we would hang them up at the back of the van. After a couple weeks, it was just like, "Okay, we have to do something. This is serious," because the smell was just *so* bad. Laundry day was a very happy day.

**Laurie Mercer** I invented the term *puck rock*. That's one of the things I'm proud of. I've always been a big hockey fan. Joey Shithead and I are still in Canada's second-oldest hockey pool.

I got the Hanson Brothers to play the 1998 NHL All-Star Game in Vancouver. They played on the ice while all of the mascots from the teams brawled in front of them.

We also launched this whole campaign lobbying to get Tiger Williams in the Hockey Hall of Fame. He had the most penalty minutes in the NHL. I got a polite letter saying that while they appreciated my enthusiasm, it ain't gonna happen. I got to know Tiger a little bit, and the guy's such a miserable fuck. I can't believe that we actually did that. He's an awful human being.

**Ernie Hawkins—Removal, Hanson Brothers** In 2002, I joined the Hanson Brothers as their drummer, after Ken Kempster left. It was the *My Game* tour cycle. Bill Johnston and Rob Clark from Removal would do roadie work, play the referees, drive, and do merch. That was also when Craig Bougie and the guys in Removal became the Shittys. The name stems from a joke about local bands opening for NoMeansNo. We would always ask, "Who's the opening band tonight?" and Craig would always say, "I think it's the Shittys again." We'd do a three-band bill: the Shittys, then Removal, and then NoMeansNo or the Hanson Brothers. We did that for a really long time. I was their drummer when they recorded the *It's a Living* live album in Coaldale, Alberta.

**Tom Holliston** The Shittys were Removal with our soundman, Craig Bougie. Craig struggled mightily. You'd think somebody who had such a good ear, who enjoyed so much good music, could play, but he

**The Hanson Brothers: Johnny, Robbie, Tommy, Kenny (Kempster)**

Robbie Hanson, 2012

could play nothing. He played the bass, and his bass consisted of two E strings. They played the same twenty-minute set every night.

**John Sawyer—Terminal Heads** I get a mention in the liner notes of *It's a Living* as "Stage Manager (Kent)." It's a lighthearted nod to my obsessive fanboy stalking of them around Europe for a decade or so. They'd put me up if they could, or let me sleep in the van, feed me, and take me with them between shows.

Invariably, I'd end up drunk and bang on about me having been in the band Terminal Heads and that we hadn't played for a while. One night they just said they didn't wanna hear what I *used* to do anymore. I should get my arse in gear, get the band back together, and come play with them. That's exactly what happened, and we played three UK shows with the Hanson Brothers in 2008 and then later got to open for NoMeansNo in London in 2012.

**Mike Branum—the Freak Accident, Hanson Brothers** I was playing in a band called the Freak Accident with Ralph Spight, and we got asked by Tom to open for NoMeansNo in the Pacific Northwest. It went great. Then we were asked to open for them on an entire European tour. That also worked really well, and then about a month after we got back, I got an email from Tom just saying, "Would you be interested in being in the Hanson Brothers?" Ernie had left the band at this point. It was supposed to just be one last big European tour, but it kind of snowballed after that. We went over there a couple times and did Canada as well.

In 2014, they did another Canadian tour after me, with Byron Slack on drums. That was the Hansons tour to promote John's new beer. I was living in Bremen, Germany, by then, and Tommy got hold of me and asked me if it was okay for Byron to play. It wouldn't have made sense to fly me out for that; it would have been a loss all the way around. I was like, "Yeah. No problem."

Mikey Hanson

Tommy Hanson, 2014

**Byron Slack—Invasives, Hanson Brothers** My band Invasives had opened for the Hansons in Europe. They didn't even know I played drums until our drummer, Hans, couldn't make a couple shows in Germany. My brother Adam and I did this thing called the Linesmen, with him on bass and me drumming. The Wright brothers were like, "Oh wow, you play drums?" I said, "Yeah, I'll play for the Hanson Brothers sometime if you ever need somebody!"

Later they had some fundraising gigs booked in Canada, and they asked me to do it. The first rehearsals were always just me and Rob in the rehearsal space. We did one full band rehearsal, and then we flew out and did twelve shows in a row in Eastern Canada. It was totally insane.

**Uffe Cederlund—Entombed** We were sort of death metal kids in the late '80s and '90s but also into hardcore and punk. The Hanson Brothers played a festival in Sweden, in the forest somewhere.

I was walking to the backstage area, and I heard some fucking punk rock on a smaller stage. I went there, and it's like, "Who the fuck is this?" Someone told me, "This is the Hanson Brothers." I was like, "But this is NoMeansNo!" I was totally surprised.

**Tim Solyan—Victims Family** When the Hanson Brothers came down to California, it was hilarious. Me and John Wright would be hanging out before the show, and he'd just be sucking down beers with me at the bar. It was like, "Dude, you've got a gig!" He was like, "Dude, all I gotta do is get up there and talk shit and sing, I don't give a fuck! I don't have to play a fuckin' drum lick, dude. This is the best ever! Why was I not a singer to begin with?"

**Sean Cox—Portland, Oregon** The Hanson Brothers were playing at some little fucking bar club in downtown LA. I was just jumping around and dancing. I was up front, and there were only like fifty people in the crowd, and I just couldn't understand that. Everybody's got their arms crossed, being very LA, just going, "Hmm, this is curious." Of course, I'm losing my mind and acting like a goddamn idiot.

Robbie Hanson

It was in the middle of winter, and even winter in LA is kind of cold. Rob was wearing old-timey, grandpa thermal underwear under his jeans. As he was playing, I kept yanking his pants down, since this stage was only about four feet high. I'm so glad Rob didn't kick me in the face.

**Darcy Studebaker—fan from Oklahoma City, Oklahoma** I travelled from Oklahoma City with my Quebecois boyfriend to see the Hanson Brothers play in Dallas. This was circa '95 or '96. We arrived very early. No one was at the bar except John and Rob, watching the Stanley Cup playoffs. We sat down next to them and proceeded to order beer, a little starstruck.

I said, "Hey, Rob and John, who are you all rooting for?" This was when Detroit had the Russian Five, and I was a fan. "Well the Canucks are out this year," Rob said, frustrated, "so I guess the Wings." Overjoyed, we proceeded to talk hockey with them for about an hour. They gave us Hanson Brothers stickers and those cheap plastic Hanson Brothers taped glasses.

**Ray Carlisle—Teenage Bottlerocket** Teenage Bottlerocket opened up for the Hanson Brothers at the Starlight in Fort Collins, Colorado. We pulled up to the alleyway, and there was their van, with Canadian license plates. We noticed on the dashboard there were a bunch of hockey brochures from different towns they had played. I'm like, "Did they grab an Avalanche pamphlet at the hotel last night? These guys are the real deal, that's hilarious!"

**Jello Biafra—Dead Kennedys, Alternative Tentacles** Ultimately, the Hanson Brothers kind of hurt NoMeansNo, I think. After Andy left, the writing kind of split into two forks in the road. Rob crossed more into storytelling territory and longer and longer things, while John got more into the poppier punk stuff, most of which was then earmarked for the Hanson Brothers.

**Grant Lawrence—the Smugglers** Eventually, the Wright brothers had the Hanson Brothers fine-tuned perfectly. They would tour during the playoffs, in April and May. We were on a couple of those tours, and they would even strategize with the bars to make sure that they weren't going on while the game was on. So the game ends, and everybody pours out of the bars or the arena or whatever. They're looking to party and the Hanson Brothers are in town! Whether they want to drown their sorrows or celebrate a victory, there were the Hanson Brothers, and it was a hockey party.

That was surreal for us to see, because we thought, "Well, hockey means, like, stupid jocks, right?" But they kind of showed us that hockey and rock could cross over. I remember a great discussion with John. I said, "I just can't wrap my head around this whole sports and music thing. I love the Hanson Brothers, mostly because I love the Ramones. I was a hockey fan when I was a kid, but I got out of it because I got bullied." I was wary of these hockey goons.

John said, "Well, don't you see that a band is just like a hockey team?" I said, "What are you talking about?" He goes, "The layout is exactly the same." He then explained it, and I'll always remember this analogy. He's like, "You got the centre at centre ice. Usually, the captain is the guy that everybody looks to, to win that face-off. That's the equivalent of your lead singer. Then you got your lead guitarist, the winger. He can do whatever he wants, he gets creative, doodles up and down the side of the ice, just like the lead guitarist can do whatever he wants. Then you got your defenseman, who is your bassist, who's holding down the back end. The defenseman works with the goalie, who is like the drummer. If the defenseman and the goalie aren't in sync, then you're going to have trouble. And if the bassist and the drummer aren't in sync, then you're not even going to have a show."

My mind was erupting: "Oh my god, you're right." Then he said, "And if all five players on the ice aren't in sync and working together, you're going to lose the game. If all members of the band aren't in sync and working together, you're going to have a shitty show." I was just like, "Oh my god, they *are* the same!" That changed my philosophy completely when it came to sports and music, because I thought they were at complete opposite ends of the spectrum.

CHAPTER NINE

# ENTER THE RATS NEST

## "Now the rats are coming to feed. Every night they bring more and more of their friends."

The Rats Nest was an all-ages punk venue in Victoria that local legend Gary Brainless and his partner, Betty Norton, ran in the basement of their Cecelia Road home. Located in an industrial area of town known as Burnside/Gorge, the less-than-legal gig space operated off and on from 1985 until 2013 as a dark, sweaty, and smelly place with a low ceiling and lower standards. It was a parent's and fire inspector's worst nightmare but also a true punk hangout for Victoria's kids and skids.

Dozens of bands played gigs at the Rats Nest over the years, including SNFU, Fratricide, Mission of Christ, Dayglo Abortions, DRI, Problem Children, and NoMeansNo. From 1985 until 1991, NoMeansNo also used the Rats Nest regularly as a practice space. In 2013, the house was sold and torn down. They paved paradise to put up a parking lot, and the Rats Nest was exterminated.

**Gary Brainless—owner of the Rats Nest, Hanson Brothers** Well, the name says it all. Rats the size of cats. It was a great place. Everybody congregated there and got to know each other. The best thing for me was all the people I got to meet. We would cram that basement with people; sometimes when it was full, you'd have to surf on top of everyone to get anywhere.

A friend's sister introduced me to NoMeansNo. It was 1985, and I had been at the Rats Nest for about a month. She said, "I know this band NoMeansNo and they're fucking awesome!" and I said, "Okay, I'll check 'em out."

I lived upstairs in the house for the first year and a half before I met Betty. The Resistance were set to play the first-ever show at the Rats Nest, so I got in touch with NoMeansNo, and we put them on the show too.

After that show, I was told they were also looking for a place to practise. They paid me like fifty bucks a month to use the Rats Nest as a practice space, right up until they moved to Vancouver in the '90s.

**Mike Walker—the Resistance** Brainless had just joined the Resistance as a drummer, and we played the first show there with NoMeansNo and a third band that I can't remember. There were always three bands in those days. It didn't have a name yet, so we christened it the Rats Nest, and I think I drew the little Rats Nest logo with a marker pen because we needed something. It's a crappy-ass drawing that Gary ended up using forever.

It was basically a house where we destroyed the basement, and every gig got more interesting. When we realized that people were punching at the ceiling, we put up some fence lattice. But people would swing on it and rip it down, or they'd put their fuckin' joints or their beer up on the lattice. It was a never-ending battle with the ceiling of the Rats Nest and people just destroying it.

**Gary Brainless**

It's all gone now, so I can say this: under the stairs, there was a little crawl space and a walkway that went off from the gig space. It had a little half door on it, so we made that into a bar. We'd sell beer for a buck apiece to help pay the bands.

**Betty Norton—artist, photographer** I had a little darkroom in the basement, so when NoMeansNo would practise I would go down there and develop pictures. Sometimes I would just sit at the bottom of the stairs and listen. I got to know these guys, and they were like big brothers to me. Somehow I got a fake ID and would go see them at the clubs. Bands would often play an all-ages show at the Rats Nest and then go play at a bar, so we got to see them a couple of different times in the same night. Rob and Andy taught me to play darts.

**Gary Brainless** NoMeansNo played the Rats Nest many, many times. If bands couldn't play, because they couldn't get across the border from the States or whatever, I'd call either the Dayglos or NoMeansNo. More often it was NoMeansNo, because they practised there, so it was easy just to pull their shit out of the closet and away you go!

**Andy Kerr** The Rats Nest was the ideal place for us to go and work on our music. Gary and Betty were so kind to us, such lovely people. We came to practise three nights per week, and each practice lasted three hours or so. We were so noisy, but Gary and Betty never once complained. We played in this tiny basement at the exact same volume we did live. Loud. "It goes to eleven" kind of loud. *Small Parts*, *Wrong*, and *0 + 2 = 1* all got worked out at the Rats Nest. We played gigs there a few times too. Calling it "intimate" would be rather an understatement. If there had ever been a fire, we would have all died, but there wasn't, so we didn't.

**NoMeansNo practicing at the Rats Nest**

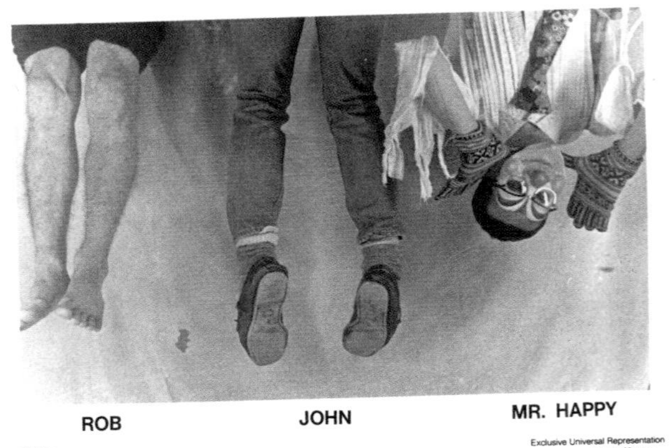

**Mike Walker** I remember Andy refinished his Telecaster at the Rats Nest. He was sitting on the floor in the basement with fucking sandpaper, hand-sanding down his Telecaster. Once he got it down to wood, he restained it a dark navy blue colour. He did that all by hand.

**Betty Norton** I remember a day when we went out and I took all these wild and crazy pictures. One of them ended up being the cover of *The Power of Positive Thinking* EP.

**Andy Kerr** The second name choice after "The Power of Positive Thinking" was "Please Release Me, Let Me Sell."

**Rob Wright** We'd practise at the Rats Nest two or three times a week. It was a good place. Gary Brainless was a very, very good guy for music in Victoria and just in general. He was a solid, helpful, reasonable, funny guy. He certainly put on a lot of good shows that wouldn't have been seen in Victoria otherwise. It was maybe the worst place in the world to see shows, but it was great for local music.

**John Wright** The shows at the Rats Nest were always packed. They built a barrier across the front of the stage because so many people would be crammed in that basement. We'd basically be trapped there. We played a show that was about three hours long once, mainly because we couldn't leave.

Mission of Christ at the Rats Nest

**Mike Walker** It was in an industrial area, so no one gave a shit that we made noise. The James Bay Boys were a bunch of fuckin' douchebag older rocker guys who would sometimes try to wreck gigs. I remember once they pulled up a street sign and smashed it lengthwise through somebody's VW van window out front. Another time they tried to get in and start a fight. There was Bruno, me, Trevor from the Dayglos, and Gary at the door, just fuckin' holding them back so they couldn't get in. We did our own security, though it wasn't like we were tough guys.

The cops came one time, after the gas station around the corner got robbed. A couple of uniforms showed up, along with a real dickhead in plain clothes. They were looking for this robber and said, "We're not here to shut down your gig. We just want to make sure that this guy hasn't come in." Me and the female cop went downstairs, and the gig's in full swing, and it's dark. I turned on the lights so she could look around. The sea of kids' faces looking up at her totally freaked her out. They were literally sardines, shoulder to shoulder, squished down,

Mike Synnuck of Mission of Christ at the Rats Nest

By Michelle Dawson

What can you say about the Rat's Nest?

Andy Kerr, of NoMeansNo, stands against the back wall of the Rat's Nest and smiles like a maniac when Mission of Christ takes the floor and the place explodes into action. "Ah," he says. "Now *this* is a *gig*."

The Problem Children, a band from Toronto who would have nowhere to play in Victoria if it weren't for the Rat's Nest, have a song about their music — how everyone (including "the bastards who run this town") tries to make them change their errant ways. The song applies to the Rat's Nest as well. "Fok yuz all," they say, "we made it anyway."

Mike, who plays guitar for local band The Resistance and helps run the Rat's Nest, talks about how the place is looked down upon by Victoria's alternative music gentry. There must be some reason for the scorn — and I've seen it — awarded the Rat's Nest by other self-described promoters, including CFUV. "We can do it," Mike says. "They can't." Then he says, "It's not a big thing. It's just a place to *play*."

I think it's a whole lot more than that.

The Rat's Nest is Victoria's most important underground alternative music venue, and also its least celebrated. In a city where promoters so exasperatingly concentrate on establishing themselves (or furthering their finances) by presenting only the tried and proven, or the already famous, or bands with their friends in them, the Rat's Nest is the only place to go for people who truly crave adventure in alternative music. Want to see bands who've never played here before, bands who get little (if any) recognition from CFUV, bands who want to play here and no one else has their act together well enough to put them on? ... the Rat's Nest is essential. Not only that — admission is cheap, all ages welcome, and the reckless, happy atmosphere beats the hell out of anything you'll find in Victoria, clubs and hall parties both.

Gary, who plays drums for The Resistance, has been putting on gigs at the Rat's Nest for about a year. He also lives there; the Rat's Nest is his basement. He'd like to say thanks to Mike, mentioned above, and Pia, who runs the door, for helping him with the place from day one. Day one was a spontaneous house party and benefit gig for NoMeansNo, who'd lost equipment in the fire at La Hacienda.

"It was so cold in there when we played," Andy Kerr says, "that John (Wright)'s bass drum pedal broke." He borrowed another one, and it broke too. The playing space was smaller then — people crammed in in overcoats and jumped around and apparently had a good time.

Since then, there have been about fifteen gigs at the Rat's Nest. Bands of various kinds from all over the place have played there:

D.R.I. (Texas),
Beach Mutants (Winnipeg),
Johnson Unit (Eugene, Oregon),
Problem Children (Toronto),
Dehumanizers (Seattle),
Fratricide,
the Spores,
and Active Glands (Vancouver); and local bands: Dayglo Abortions, Mission of Christ, The Resistance, Bedspins, Noise Generation, and NoMeansNo.

It's not cold in the Rat's Nest any more; the place literally steams and sweats with energy. All kinds of people go to watch, sometimes in astonishing numbers (close to 300 for Dayglos, though more modest crowds of a hundred or so are the norm). Two hundred people went to see D.R.I., including metal types and hardcores and trendy haircuts and one hippie (besides me), and part of the admission price was a can of food for the food bank.

"There are always one or two assholes," Gary says about crowds, but at the Rat's Nest they often get surrounded and subdued by others who simply want to enjoy themselves. Gary asks people to "please have a little respect for the place, 'cause people do live there" and such consideration is generally apparent. If you're going to bring beer, bring **cans** (please!), and if you see someone doing damage, do something about it or find someone else who can.

"I do this for fun," Gary says. "If I did it for money, I would have quit a long time ago." Proceeds from the door at the Rat's Nest cover minimal expenses (under $100 for a P.A. that provides surprisingly good sound) and the rest goes to the bands. When there's not enough money for opening bands, they play for beer.

Publicity is via posters handed around a network of interested people who spread the word, often as far as Vancouver (about 30 people from Vancouver showed up at D.R.I., an impressive accomplishment for any promoter). The Rat's Nest is also now used as practice space by two local bands, as well as The Resistance, and the modest rent charged goes entirely into paying heat and power bills.

Mike points out that since both he and Gary are in a band, they understand the problems of other bands looking for a place to play in this city. With reasonable sound facilities — you might want more floor space, a bigger "stage", more headroom, better ventilation, but these are minor complaints — and common sense and simplicity of operation, the Rat's Nest has quietly succeeded in Victoria while other venues and promoters have and are currently failing loudly. Succeeded in that a headlining band doesn't have to be Tupelo Chain Sex or D.O.A. to be paid well. Succeeded in opening doors otherwise slammed on certain bands (and their fans) in this city where who you know too often seems more important than how well you play. Succeeded in keeping tickets cheap, and while not making money, in not losing any either. Succeeded in being happy with that, while others complain and go bust and disappear and carp endlessly about the good old days when things (I'm told) were easier.

Meanwhile, CFUV and the silly self-appointed Victoria alternative upper crust remain aloof from the Rat's Nest and what goes on there. It's their own loss; the Rat's Nest people are doing their work for them and doing it well, and — of necessity — doing it independently. There is an effete snobbery in some quarters at CFUV that says, in effect, "*We* don't go to gigs in somebody's *basement*", a ridiculous attitude that robs the Rat's Nest of the respect and wholesale enthusiastic support it deserves from an alternative radio station. It's up to CFUV to overcome this unwarranted superiority complex (considering CFUV's own difficulties with gigs) and *willingly* — nobody should have to twist arms and pull teeth — offer cooperation and (I think) apologies. This would clearly be to CFUV's benefit (as I've seen with other radio stations that finally acknowledge and help underground promoters), and it would make the Rat's Nest an even better place.

It's pretty damn good right now, though. The Victoria underground is alive and well and living in somebody's *basement*. Never mind the bullshit, get out there and enjoy yourselves.

Coming up at the Rat's Nest on December 20 (Saturday): NoMeansNo with Euthanasia (from Edmonton) and A.M.Q.A. (from Seattle).

*(If you know of any bands wanting to play in Victoria, or if you'd like to volunteer help in any way, call Gary at 383-8835. Any comments, ideas for improvement, etc., can be sent to U. Brainless, 468 Cecelia Street, Victoria B.C., V8T 4T5 ... that's where you'll find the Rat's Nest, in the basement ... all enquiries will be answered.)* ■

sitting on the floor. They couldn't find the gas station robber, so they left.

**Murray "The Cretin" Acton** The Dayglos song "Drugged and Driving" is about the events after a NoMeansNo show at the Rats Nest. People would come in the front door, but there was a back door where everybody could peel out if the cops came. The cops would show up in force, up the front, while everybody was just spuddin' out of the back door. By the time they got down there, there would be no one in the house! "Where did they all go? There was a huge raging party of bands playing here five minutes ago!"

One night at a NoMeansNo show, Bonehead was the last guy to get out. He came running to get in my station wagon. I used to fit ten people in that thing. I'm yelling, "C'mon, Bonehead, run!" There's a cop car in the driveway, and Bonehead stopped and got down on one knee and started tying his shoes in the driveway, blocking the car so we could get away.

**"Rancid" Randy Stubbs—artist** The Rats Nest was a rocking place; it was amazing. I remember getting back from a really stressful Dayglos tour, and the first thing we did was go to the Rats Nest for a show. I had a cold and had taken some Benylin with codeine, and then I bought some beer and had six or seven of those. After a while, I was completely fucked.

It wasn't turning out that well until someone gave me some acid. That sort of cleared my head, and I could start to see things right. I tried to go up and talk to people, because I could now fuckin' focus, but because of the codeine and the beer, my jaw was slacking, and I was going, "Nerdwerbere." I realized this is what it must be like to have cerebral palsy—you can't speak, but your mind is attentive. Some guy was hitting on my girlfriend, and I was like, "Hey! Neerdweergwer." Then he punched me. I ended up somehow going outside, leaning up against the chain-link fence, and bats were flying at me. It was one of the worst nights of my life. I loved the Rats Nest.

**Gary Brainless** The Rats Nest ran from 1985 until 2013, when the house got torn down. We did shows there throughout that whole time, but there were stretches of time when it was just my house, when I had kids there and stuff.

**Andy Kerr** The band's best moments, in my humble opinion, were the three of us practising at the Rats Nest and going for food afterwards at Bino's. All the rest was gravy!

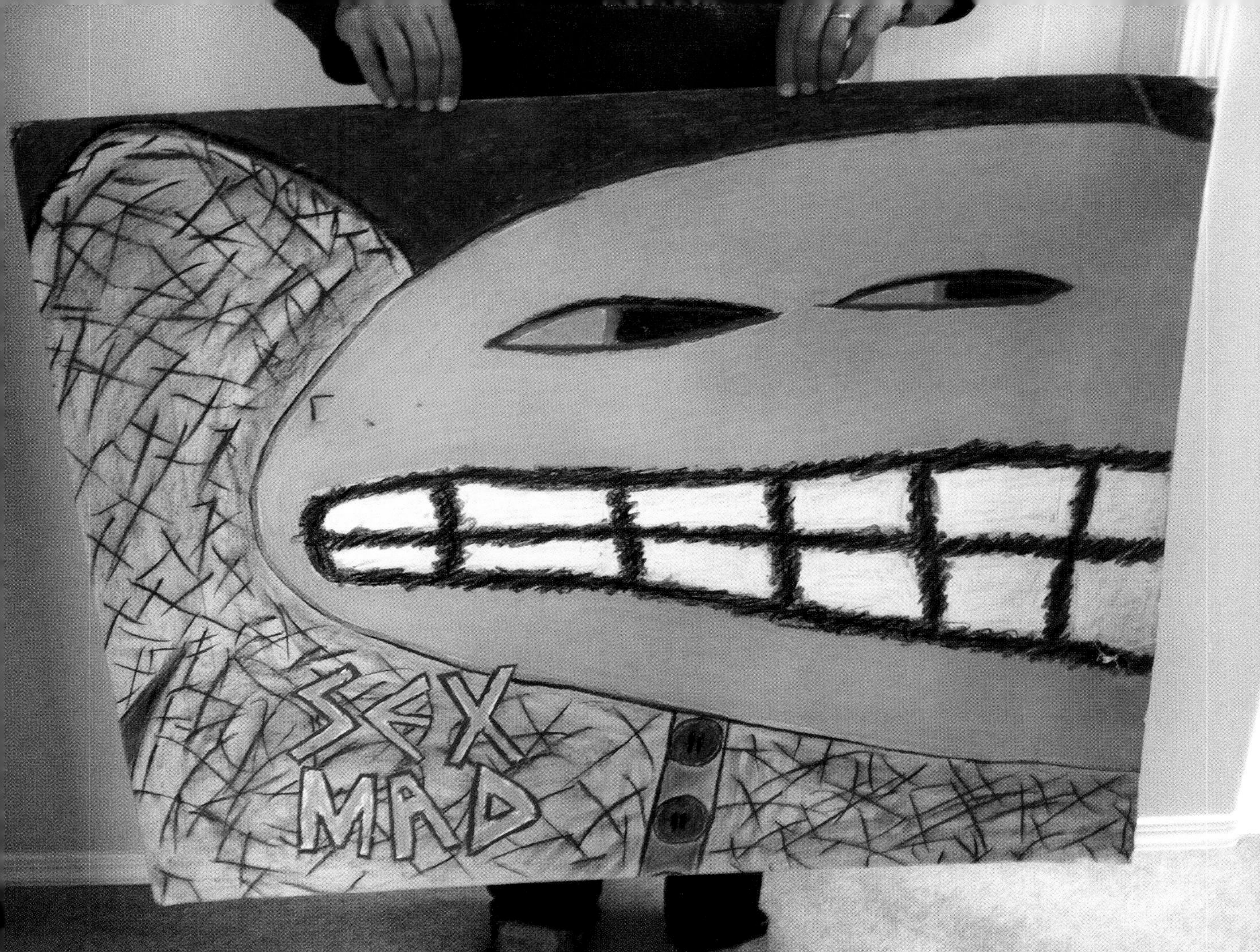


CHAPTER TEN

# SEX MAD

## "I'm seriously considering leaving home."

By early 1986, NoMeansNo had more than a hundred shows under their belt as a three-piece and were gaining notoriety across Canada. Although they had dipped down for a handful of shows in Seattle and other points in Washington and Oregon, they wanted to do a full US tour. They were still promoting the *You Kill Me* EP and were in a highly creative groove. They were writing new songs and honing them live, and many of these would comprise their next album, *Sex Mad*.

The shows in the US not only garnered them new fans, they also introduced the guys to many fellow musicians, some of whom became lifelong friends. The band also caught the attention of Dead Kennedys front man Jello Biafra and his label, Alternative Tentacles.

**Laurie Mercer** I sent them to San Francisco and across the United States, with just the worst itinerary. They were so determined to do it. I sent out hundreds of records to radio stations all across the US with just no feedback. It took Rob a year of washing dishes to pay all my postage back. They went from San Francisco to New York, doing dates wherever they could. When I think back on it, there were periods where they'd have four days off, then turn up and find out the club had burned down three weeks before. I was booking them from phone numbers collected from other musicians and blurbs in *Maximum Rocknroll.* These fan-driven articles were 90 percent nonsense, but I didn't know that at the time. They spent a good five or six weeks on the road in the USA and did maybe fifteen or twenty gigs. It was terrible in hindsight. We were all learning. There was no circuit yet then.

**Chris Crud—stage tech, tour manager** Laurie Mercer and NoMeansNo hired me for their '86 tour of the US. At that time, I had the choice of doing the tour or working at Expo 86 in Vancouver. The whole Expo thing horrified and sickened me. I just didn't want anything to do with it.

Nobody knew NoMeansNo at all on the American side. We were lucky in that we got onto some good shows and hooked up with a fair amount of bands. Some of them I knew already, like the Circle Jerks and Hüsker Dü. We ended up doing shows with Frightwig, Channel 3, Corrosion of Conformity, and lots of different bands. When we came over the border, we had a letter saying we were recording in San Francisco or Seattle, but it wasn't true.

They hired me because I knew people there and I was a US citizen. I wasn't the tour manager per se. They made me the stage tech, the roadie. They dealt with the money stuff. They needed somebody who could work in the States and deal with all this stuff that had to be done. There were a few situations where I would have to step in and deal with it when it got really heavy and crazy. I was an American, so I could deal with the police in a way that didn't get them in trouble, because we were there doing shows illegally.

**Andy Kerr** It was great to have Chris along, as someone who was outside of our circle, to provide some perspective. He didn't drive, but he certainly did everything else.

We'd been called a hardcore band, so we figured that we might as well accept it, for whatever it's worth.

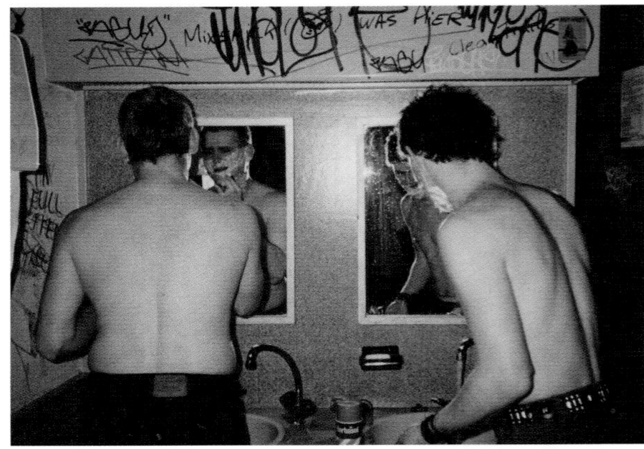

That scene had adopted us, so we thought, "We've *got* to play the States. Let's go!" Laurie did his best to set up a three-month tour. Two months in the United States and one month in Canada. It was insane, really. I don't know quite how we managed to feed ourselves along the way. We were broke most of the time. We really did rely on the Coleman stove and the generosity of strangers. People would put us in their house for two or three days because we'd usually have that long before the next show. We met so many people who we kept in touch with for years.

I think Robbie had sensed, maybe more than John and I, that it was really important to get out there and play. We became more than just three guys playing instruments and some songs. We really bonded, musically, and maybe even personally, on something that intense. And it was very intense.

When it was all done, we thought, "Wow, we made it. We toured!" Canada had seemed like a big deal the year before: three weeks across and back. But two months in the States, that was serious touring. I remember being fifth or seventh on the bill at some fucking hardcore thing in Long Beach and thinking, "What a fucking nightmare," or sleeping in a club in Texas where I woke up with flea bites all over my arm.

**Chris Crud** I pissed off Rob immediately, within the first five minutes of us driving out of Vancouver. I'm sitting in the passenger seat, and either John or Craig was driving the big blue van. Rob reached through from the back and put a cassette in. I was just sitting there with my window open, and all of a sudden Kraftwerk's "Trans Europa Express" came on. I cannot fucking *stand* that song. It was an instant

reaction, and I couldn't stop myself. I just pressed the eject button and chucked the tape out the window. We hadn't even started the tour, and already he was pissed off at me. I was like, "I'm not gonna listen to that song for the next three months."

**Andy Kerr** Rob bought us all pipes before we started the tour, like proper tobacco pipes. He distributed them to us as we crossed the border into Blaine, Washington. One time while driving, Rob rolled down the window and shouted at a lone dog at the side of the road, "*Get a master!*" Then he giggled, as he does.

**Chris Crud** John Wright has an interesting way of ordering food. If you're ever in a restaurant with John and the waiter comes, make sure to get your order in first, because he will take quite a fair amount of time ordering. He wants to know what's in everything. He's a good cook, and so is Rob. Of course, on that first US tour, we rarely ate at restaurants, as there was no money for that. I was the only one out of the group getting paid, so what happened was that every day it would be one person's turn to cook food at the truck stops and rest areas. They were all good cooks, including Craig.

**John Wright** Obviously, I'm the only one with any attention to detail in the whole fucking circus: "So, is that pan fried or seared?" This is the thing with touring. It's all these little things. It's like a *Seinfeld* episode, only it's six weeks long and takes place in a van.

I would stir my coffee in a figure eight, and Craig would bug me about it, constantly. It drove him insane: "Stop stirring your coffee like that!" "It's a figure eight, who cares?"

**Andy Kerr** Ask John how he chooses his drumsticks.

**John Wright** I got teased about this constantly. When you buy drumsticks, you have to look at the grain. The grain needs to run all the way from the top to the bottom in one line, because if the grain crosses at any point, it just snaps there, and it won't even last a show. Every time I went to a music store, I would first roll the sticks, to make sure that they didn't have a wobble in them. If they were straight, then I checked the grain. I got teased a lot about that. I just wanted good drumsticks!

**Laurie Mercer** I think John drove everybody fucking nuts in his own special way. John would circle a block twelve times looking for a parking spot rather than walk an extra ten feet. John would insist, even if they were late for a show, on having a sit-down dinner.

**Craig Bougie** Nobody knew us on that tour, so we would mostly play weeknights, because the weekends were for bands that people actually knew. We had a lot of days off and a lot of scrappy little crowds. Sometimes we'd be playing to less than twenty people. We'd play in backyards, basements, anything we could scrape together. Laurie Mercer was just kind of squirrelling us wherever he could, so it was pretty patchy. Everywhere we went, pretty much everybody was blown away. They were just like, "What is this?!" So that was quite exciting. Soundwise, it was all over the place. I was often barely scratching a PA together.

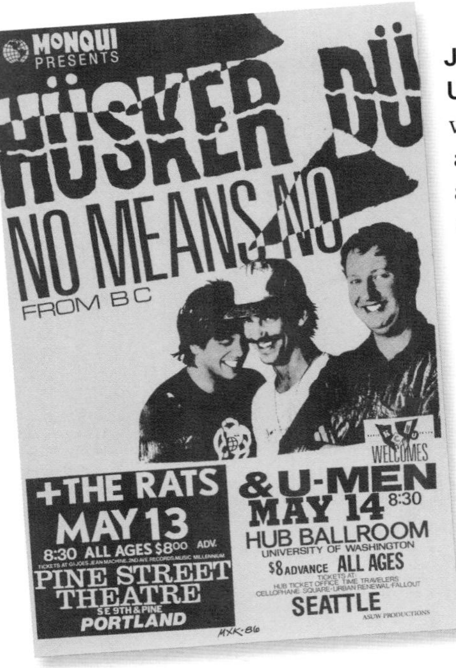


**Jim Tillman—U-Men** We played with NoMeansNo and Hüsker Dü at the University of Washington in Seattle. At that time, there was a bit of cross-pollination between Vancouver and Seattle because of our proximity.

**Chris Crud** At that university show, I was sitting on the side of the stage during Hüsker Dü's set. The kids in the crowd were doing their thing, and the bouncers were beating on them. The kids were just trying to have fun. Some big kid got up onstage, and all the bouncers just jumped on him. They all crashed right through the drum kit, just fucking took it right out and knocked him off the back of the stage.

That was always the problem, especially with the universities. They always got big, pumped-up students who wanted to beat on people. I always had meetings every show with the security, going, "Look. I'll take care of the stage. You don't have to come onstage, and please don't beat on anybody, please." I had to really try and get that across. I'd be spending more time dealing with the security people than the band and the show.

**Andy Kerr** I was a big Hüsker Dü fan, and we probably met them for two seconds. They were quite huge in the alt scene at that point. I don't know what record they were on; I think maybe they were still on SST. I had seen them the first time in Victoria, when they were chucked on the bill, some speed freak band, and they were amazing. I liked them, but I thought that their live sound was just atrocious. It was a mess, and not a great mess. I just thought it was chaotic.

I *loved* the Pine Street Theatre in Portland, because it's this large dance hall. Very high ceiling,

but the whole thing, the *entire* ceiling, was covered in individual lamps, but every one was different. We met the Poison Idea guys at that time, I think.

**Jerry A.—Poison Idea** Ah man, I remember those cats staying at Tom's [Pig Champion] and him telling me about it the next day. I remember being pissed that I missed the show and missed a chance to hang out with those guys. Tom had great taste and used to play them all the time. NoMeansNo were amazing, and those fuzzy misremembered memories are priceless to me.

**Kamala Parks—924 Gilman Street, *Maximum Rocknroll*** I worked at *Maximum Rocknroll*. I was someone who transcribed interviews and did layout. I was the scene reporter for a little while as well, for Northern California. There was a band called Clown Alley who I was a big fan of, and I became sort of their de facto manager. They wanted to do a tour, so I organized for them to go up the West Coast and into Canada to play Vancouver. I think after that Laurie Mercer contacted me: "I'm booking this band, I'm gonna send you their record *You Kill Me*. I'd be interested in seeing if you could organize a show for them." At that point, I was also a guest DJ on *Maximum Rocknroll Radio*, and so I played the song "Stop It" on the air.

I don't think NoMeansNo were on anyone's radar here except for mine. I had started working with this guy Victor Hayden to help with organizing and promoting shows. He helped us find a venue called Own's Pizza. When I heard NoMeansNo, I thought, summer when my parents were abroad. I was house-sitting with an elderly lady who also lived in the house with us. I had convinced her that I had a lot of friends who would often spend the night. So that summer I put up all the bands that I booked. It never occurred to her that it might be odd that a giant truck was parked outside with Canadian tags on it. I do remember waking up one morning and all the NoMeansNo guys were having breakfast with her. She just loved them. All the while I'm just praying that they didn't say that they were a touring band from Western Canada, which they never did.

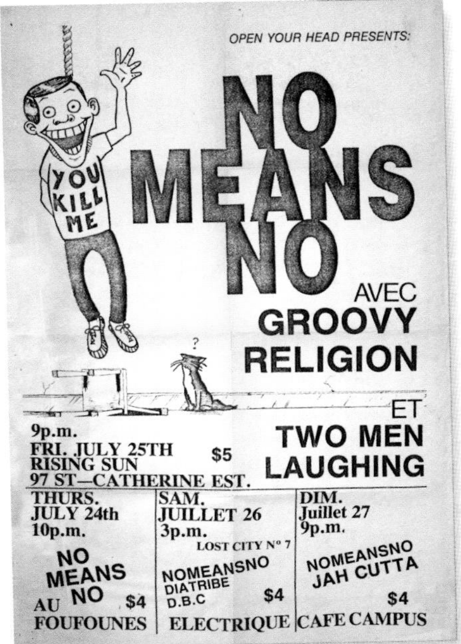

Flyer for Montreal shows, 1986

**Rob Wright** Of course, D.O.A. were an inspiration to us, like they were to many other bands. That first tour across the States, we played in every shithole and got no money. We met up with D.O.A. right at the end, in the Midwest somewhere. Immediately, we were playing to good crowds and making some money. Then the next year we went on tour with them a couple of times, as their backup for the full tour. Amazingly helpful and amazingly good experiences. I love D.O.A.

Through it all, they had brilliant songs, wonderful stage shows. Joe is an original. For all his flaws and drawbacks, he did a lot of stuff. He had a great effect on people from here to Timbuktu. They went everywhere first and blazed all those trails. They worked their fucking asses off.

**Chris Murphy—Sloan** I am from Halifax, and not that many bands came all the way to Halifax in the mid-'80s. I drove to Montreal to see some punk shows, not expecting to see NoMeansNo. I didn't even know who they were at the time. I went to see the Descendents, expecting that to be a big show, and of course, it wasn't. I was just like, "What? How come more people don't know about the Descendents?" But I saw NoMeansNo by chance, in a tiny club with no stage. I just was thrown into fucking outer space by these guys, and I couldn't believe it.

**Anthony Hempell—fan from Vancouver, British Columbia**
When I was sixteen, I first saw NMN at an all-ages show at the Town Pump with less than a dozen people there. I'd known them from listening to *Mama* and *You Kill Me* and a cassette compilation that had "Self Pity" on it. I was excited to see them live. In my mind, I pictured three youngish guys, probably wearing mostly black and being all cool and self-conscious onstage.

The opening band was called Crash Bang Crunch Pop. There was nobody there during their set. I was sitting off to the side with two of my friends. Close to the end of the set, some guy with grey hair who looked like he was in his forties came wandering onto the dance floor. He was dressed in dark grey dress pants and a white dress shirt. It was a Sunday afternoon, and he looked like he had just come from an after-church brunch or something. This guy stands in the middle of the empty dance floor, bobbing his head with a goofy grin on his face. My friends and I looked at each other: "Who the fuck is this guy?" We come up with theories: "He looks like he's the band's manager. Maybe he's one of their dads."

Weird bobbing-head guy is joined by another, even more dorky-looking guy with big funny glasses. They look like they are enjoying the music but also like they would be more at home at an accounting conference.

Flyer for the Independent Music Festival, Vancouver, 1986

Recording *Sex Mad* at Keye Studios

John & Rob Wright, NoMeansNo

The band finishes their set. Later we notice that the dorky-looking guys are setting up equipment onstage. "Those guys are roadies, I guess. Weird." Then they start playing the instruments. "Hey, wait, these dorky guys are NoMeansNo!"

After nearly three months on the road, NoMeansNo returned home to Victoria. While they had barely made any money, they were emboldened by the responses to the shows in the US and the connections they had made. They had been playing and perfecting many new songs, so they decided to record a new album.

**Andy Kerr** We had talked to the folks at Psyche Industry in Montreal about doing a record, and they were interested in releasing it. Laurie kept in touch with them, and eventually some sort of deal was made. The songs for *Sex Mad* were mostly ready to go, even before *You Kill Me* came out. A lot of songs got dragged around for years that only later got recorded.

We recorded *Sex Mad* at Keye Studios in Victoria in late 1986. They already knew us from doing *Mama* and Infamous Scientists. We were completely rehearsed and ready to go. I don't even think we did demos for *Sex Mad*. We had it all mapped out, and we wanted to make use of our time as much as possible. It was very natural. *Sex Mad* was a real mishmash of stuff. We didn't really have any kind of concept for it. I did a lot of the vocals on *Sex Mad*, because Rob was still recovering from his voice issues.

"Dad" was written as a Hanson Brothers song. I remember the lyric sheets that Rob wrote. When Rob was still recovering from his voice, he brought all these Hanson Brothers demos, including "Dad." He could barely sing, so it was just him croaking it along with an electric guitar. Still, it was obvious that it was *completely* different than any of the other joke-band Hanson Brothers stuff. Rob himself said he didn't know where it came from. Both of our sets of parents were lovely. Folks would come up semiregularly and say it was their life story.

**Rob Wright** We couldn't do "Dad" as a Hanson Brothers song. It was too fucking serious. It's not light, it's not funny, it's not stupid. So we did it as

**Recording *Sex Mad***

NoMeansNo. I can't count the number of times people yelled, "Play 'Dad'!" We dropped it from our set eventually, because we overplayed it. Same with "Sex Mad."

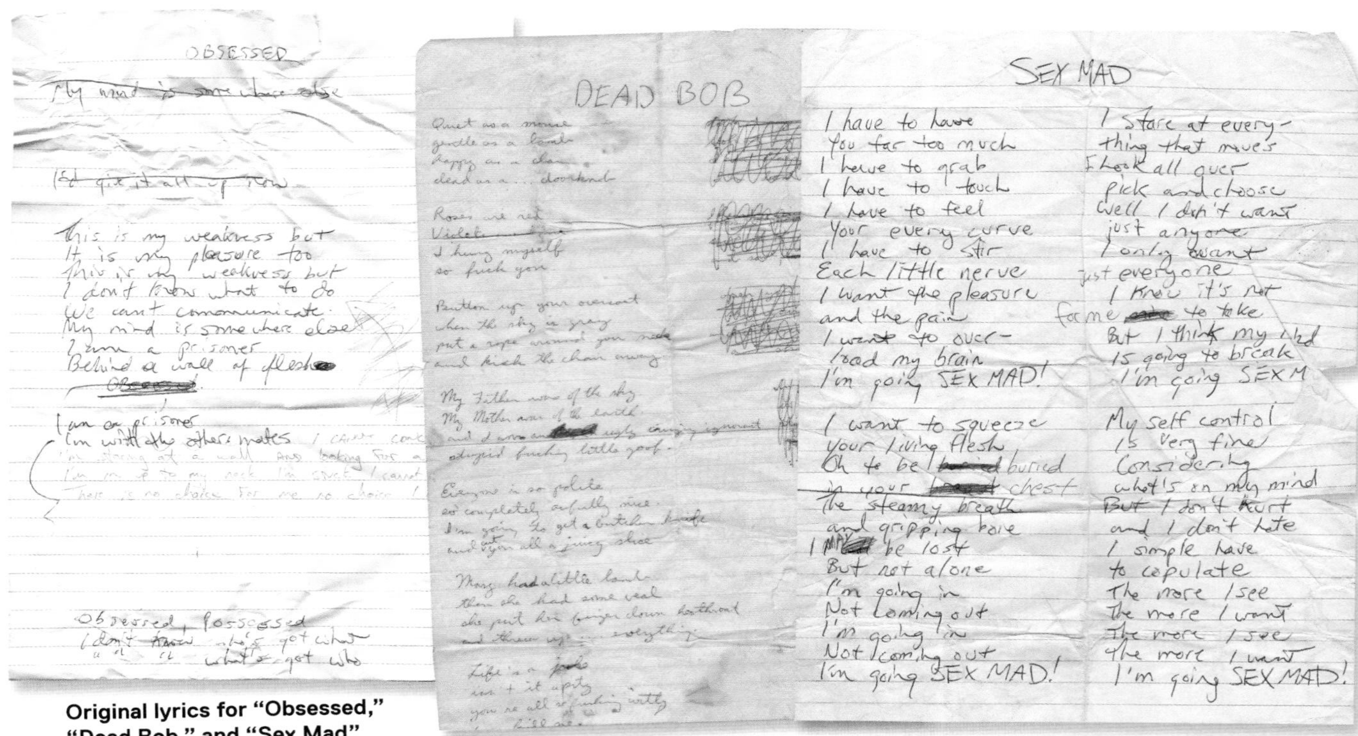

OBSESSED

This is my weakness but
It is my pleasure too
This is my weakness but
I don't know what to do
We can't communicate
My mind is somewhere else
I am a prisoner
Behind a wall of flesh

I am a prisoner
I'm with the others mates

Obsessed, possessed
I don't know who's got what
" " " what's got who

DEAD BOB

Quiet as a mouse
gentle as a lamb
happy as a clam
dead as a... doorknob

Roses are red
I hung myself
so fuck you

Button up your overcoat
when the sky is gray
put a rope around your neck
and kick the chair away

My Father was of the sky
My Mother was of the earth
and I was an ugly cringing ignorant
stupid fucking little goof.

Everyone is so polite
so completely awfully nice
I'm going to get a butcher knife
and cut you all a juicy slice

Mary had a little lamb
then she had some veal
she put her finger down her throat
and threw up everything

SEX MAD

I have to have
You far too much
I have to grab
I have to touch
I have to feel
Your every curve
I have to stir
Each little nerve
I want the pleasure
and the pain
I want to over-
load my brain
I'm going SEX MAD!

I want to squeeze
your living flesh
Oh to be buried
in your chest
The steamy breath
and gripping bore
I'll be lost
But not alone
I'm going in
Not coming out
I'm going in
Not coming out
I'm going SEX MAD!

I stare at every-
thing that moves
I look all over
pick and choose
Well I don't want
just anyone
I only want
just everyone
I know it's not
for me to take
But I think my head
is going to break
I'm going SEX M

My self control
is very fine
Considering
what's on my mind
But I don't hurt
and I don't hate
I simple have
to copulate
The more I see
The more I want
The more I see
The more I want
I'm going SEX MAD!

**Original lyrics for "Obsessed," "Dead Bob," and "Sex Mad"**

**Robert Nichols—Shrug** The first time I heard their music was the *Sex Mad* LP. "Dad" leapt out at me: the harrowing narrative and the power of the guitar and bass chords that reminded me of Dead Kennedys. I also love the funny twist at the end of "Dad," so typical of NoMeansNo. They suddenly spin the whole thing on its head in one quirky comment: "I'm seriously considering leaving home!" I love bands that get hold of your emotions and really tug at them, and NoMeansNo certainly do that.

**Andy Kerr** "Self Pity" is one of my favourite songs, actually. I think it was the first time I was *really* happy with my guitar part, although it absolutely could have been a two-piece song. I sang "Self Pity" on the *Sex Mad* album, but Rob's original version is better. That version ended up on the Undergrowth compilation tape, before Rob's voice got fucked up. He sang very little on *Sex Mad*, actually. He sang "Revenge." We said, "Are you sure about this?" and he was like, "Yeah, I can do it." He wanted to do that one. I wish Rob had sang all those songs, although I did enjoy singing "Dad." I think I did a good job on it.

I always really liked "Hunt the She Beast," despite Rob later disowning it. I like the sentiment of the song too. The song begins with, "Laugh, you asshole, and try to be brave." John does a great drum riff in it, so to me those two things are enough for the song. Where the song goes after that doesn't *really* matter to me.

**Laurie Mercer** "Hunt the She Beast." That song, I fuckin' despise it, loathe it. I hated hearing it. It was just an awful song. But they insisted on it all the way. Something like "Dad" is nuanced. It's not about violence, it's exactly about the opposite. It really weirded the band out when people would get into fights while listening to that song. But "Hunt the She Beast" is just an awful nothing.

**John Wright** I always liked the rhythm, the funkiness of "Hunt the She Beast," but the lyrics kind of missed the mark to some degree. I think it was not really what Robbie wanted to say. The way it ended up was maybe a bit immature or premature or naive. I'm positive it's the lyrics that Laurie and Robbie don't like. Why Andy likes it, I don't know. Maybe he interprets it differently. Obviously, me, I don't really fall down on either side in any real particular way.

There were some lyrics attempted for "Obsessed," and they seemed superfluous. They were quickly abandoned. Plus, it was too hard to sing and play.

# Just a couple of crazy guys

*JOHN MACKIE meets Rob and John Wright, the middle-class mind benders of the Nomeanso band*

"TEMPORARY insanity is okay in certain environments," says Rob Wright, explaining the raison d'etre for Nomeansno, a Victoria band that straddles the line between hardcore punk and other forms — what he dubs "high volume minimalistic post-punk art song jazz-rock fusion."

"A lot of bands have changed and fallen into categories and stuff," says his brother John, 23, who plays drums. "You're a hardcore band or you're a power pop band. In '77, it seemed like everybody just sort of did what they wanted to. A whole new freedom was found, and over time that got whittled down."

"You start playing music instead of expressing yourself," explains bass-playing Rob, the grey hair (literally) of the band at 31.

"Instead of saying: 'What have I got to say? What have I got to feel? What have I got to show?' to a bunch of people and sharing it, you say: [in a goofy, Devo-like voice] 'What style of music do I want to play? What hairdo do I want? What clothes do I wear?'

"They forget that the music is only a tool for self-expression. The music of itself is very little. Even instrumental music, what makes it good will always be the way the artist is expressing himself through it, not the music itself."

John concurs. "Most musicians, if they get back to that basic level of a one-on-one expression with the audience, will turn out really good music. An audience gets off on that, an audience can feel that communication, an audience can understand it. It's not just rattling off some stupid song, this guy actually has a little emotion behind what he's doing. He's actually got some sort of attachment to this song."

"He's putting out something, he's trying to say something 'is me,' " continues Rob. "He's not trying to be somebody. I hate people who go onstage and *are* somebody — there's this wall. There are some people for whom that has worked in an artistic way, but for us, it's like. . ." — he leans forward with a mad look in his eye and puts his arms out to grab the air — "wahhhh."



PETER BATTISTONI

**UNDER COVER: It's Rob (left) and John Wright — and Bob's your uncle**

"We couldn't do it anyways," reflects John.

"If we tried to pose, we'd look ridiculous," agrees Rob.

"The big hair would get in your way. . . you'd trip and fall and rip your tights," says John.

The band, which plays the Savoy through Wednesday with the wonderful No Fun, is rounded out by guitarist Andy Kerr. "Bob" is an imaginary member from the days when the band was just the Wrights and they did a poster called "three guys named Bob." Also of interest is the fact that all three members arenearsighted. "We're known as 12 eyes," says Rob.

The Wrights' father was an officer in the Canadian air force, and they grew up moving from base to base, ending up in Victoria because that's where their dad retired. Rob was born in Halifax, while John was born in Dayton, Ohio.

"It gives you a good perspective on North American life," says Rob. "Total alienation. You have no home.

"We just had sort of a normal suburban upbringing. Shake and bake. I Love Lucy. We figured if Ricky Nelson could be a rock singer coming from that environment, so could we.

"I think our suburban upbringing, like many punk or hardcore bands, tends to give anyone of an artistic bent sort of an hysteria and it comes screaming out in the music," he says. "That's why you find that most hardcore bands are very middle class people. A wild energy comes out of a life that's so stultifying. Whereas working class kids. . ."

"They live it — why do they have to play it?" finishes John.

**An article in the *Vancouver Sun*, July 9, 1985**

**Jello Biafra** "Dead Bob" is a prog rock song, pure and simple. NoMeansNo had that kind of energy and punk fire that takes you for a ride, where you don't pull back and realize, "Oh god, it's a prog rock song!"

**Andy Kerr** I liked the idea of having something that was sort of conceptually irritating. In "Love Thang," you have this middle break, which is an offbeat, of Rob playing a D note, me playing a D note, and John playing a kick drum, and we just go on forever to the point where you think, "Okay, now it's getting really annoying."

**Nardwuar the Human Serviette—interviewer, the Evaporators** In grade twelve, I was the Hillside Secondary School student council president, so I was in charge of organizing the school dances. I was always looking for bands and always asking kids, "Who is the hot band?" One kid I remember said, "You got to check out NoMeansNo. They're amazing." I was totally oblivious, because I liked Cheap Trick and the Beatles. But all these kids put in my mind that NoMeansNo were a cool band.

I opened up the *Vancouver Sun* newspaper one day, and there was an article by John Mackie profiling NoMeansNo. I went down to Collectors RPM and I bought the *Betrayal Fear Anger Hatred* EP. I loved the song "Try Not to Stutter." I really wanted them to play a school dance, but I couldn't get it together.

Later on in the year, I was listening to the CiTR radio show *Party with Me Punker*, and they played the song "Sex Mad," and I couldn't believe it. This is the same band that did "Try Not to Stutter"? I loved both songs but could not believe it was the same band.

**Daniel Webster** We released *Sex Mad* on Psyche Industry. They recorded it out west and handed us the tapes, and we got it mastered, pressed, and made the covers. Andy Kerr did the artwork.

**Andy Kerr** I was just sitting around by myself at home and did this drawing with pencil crayons on a piece of paper. Rob saw it and said, "Oh, that's great! We should use that as the cover." I did a much larger version because it needed to be photographed properly.

I still look at it, and I don't really know what it was meant to be. I like the buttons a lot. I don't know if the person in the drawing is attacking or recoiling. I am really happy with how he's raising his shoulder on the left side of the picture. I'm still happy with it, actually.

**Steve Kravac—My Dog Popper** At the time, I was doing some work for Psyche Industry Records, and NMN had approached them about releasing their next record, *Sex Mad*, in Canada. I'll never forget the day the guys came by the

**Unused *Sex Mad* promo**

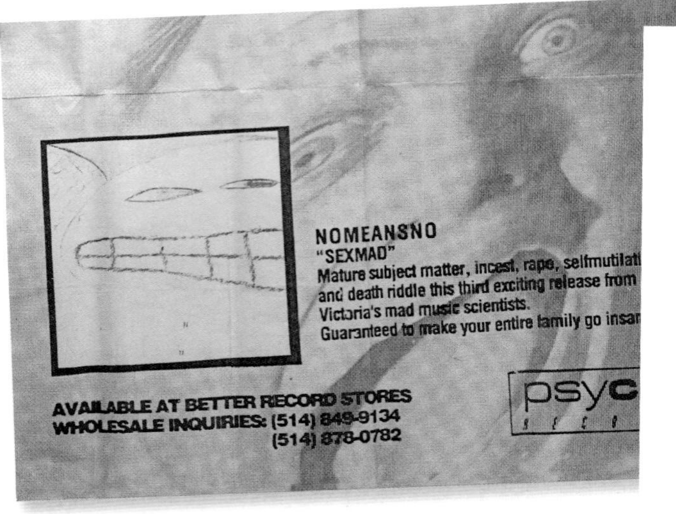

office with a cassette of the record and the artwork. The cover was a perfect expression of what the package contained. *Sex Mad* was a flat-out amazing record. "Dad" was a jaw-dropper.

**John Kastner** Randy and Dan at Psyche Industry were putting their album out, and Montreal seemed like a bit of a hub for them at the time. They'd tour Canada and stay in Montreal for like a week or so. Everybody seemed to know the NoMeansNo guys at that point. They were just part of the family and seemed to be hanging out with everybody.

**Andy Kerr** At some point in my twenties, I announced, "I love Montreal! Maybe I'll move there one day." To which Robbie, ever the nattering nabob of negativity, responded, "No you won't." "What do you mean I won't?!" "You just won't. You'll stay in Victoria." I thought, "Grrr. What the fuck does he know?" Of course, I never did move there. Montreal was always one of our favourite destinations. We got to know a whole lot of lovely folks and played some terrific gigs. Between 1985 and 1991, NoMeansNo came back almost every year, and we always made sure we had at least a couple days off there. Beautiful, bustling, vibrant, cosmopolitan. Old and modern at the same time. If it's possible to have a crush on a city, then I had one on Montreal.

**Rick Andrews** I put out a compilation cassette called *Random Thought: A Victoria Sampler Vol. 1*, which was followed up later by *Vol. 2*. It was intended as kind of an incomplete overview of the local scene. There's a really early NoMeansNo song called "Burn" that wound up later on the *Mr. Right & Mr. Wrong* CD. Then there was the original version of "Love Thang," which is kind of a funny story. They recorded that song for *Sex Mad*, and they decided that the recording they had wasn't quite up to snuff compared to the one on *Random Thought*, so they were gonna leave it off of *Sex Mad* altogether. Jello Biafra freaked out and said, "No, we gotta have 'Love Thang' on this album!" The US version has "Love Thang," and the Canadian version on Psyche Industry has "Hunt the She Beast."

**Andy Kerr** It made the Canadian version different from the American one, which helped both Alternative Tentacles *and* Psyche Industry. Not that we expected people to buy both, but they *might* want to buy the Psyche version because it was a little different.

**John Wright** We made another little change with the AT release. We have the a cappella version of "No Fucking" on there to make it a little bit different.

**Kim Thayil—Soundgarden** My favourite song on that album is "Revenge." I put that on mixtapes back in the '80s that I made for my bandmates or my sister. It was heavy and had that psychedelic component to it. Listen to "Revenge" by yourself looking out the window with your headphones on.

**Mike Watt—Minutemen, fIREHOSE** *Sex Mad* was a trip. It was kind of an opera. One day I'd like to have a talk with them about it. I mean, they shouldn't have to explain it, but it would always open up a can of idea worms in my head. I liked all the stuff, the whole arc, but for some reason that baby made me think, "I want to do something like this. Why can't you talk about fuckin' books in your songs, or paintings?" I like this idea because it's all art, all expression. It's in different forms, but at least when you're taking it from a book or a painting, there's a couple levels of abstraction to keep you from totally fucking plagiarizing. You have to interpret it.

**Chris Crud** Another reason they brought me on was so that I could introduce them to people I knew. We were shopping around for a record company. They needed some way to get their music out to people, especially in the States. I introduced them to Debbie from AT, then Jello Biafra came to their show in San Francisco.

**Jello Biafra** Steve Bailey from the NEOs began lobbying me on behalf of them, and he had the good sense to send me a live tape of the three-piece, not the two-piece. I thought that was really good: "Why can't their records sound like this?" Then they came down and played in San Francisco, a tiny little sparsely attended place called the Vis, which later became the Kennel Club.

Even though I liked that live tape, the real band live was several levels above that. Rob and John were so tight that they played like one person. Me and Ruth

Schwartz from Mordam Records just looked at each other, like, "Okay, who's gonna get this one?" Then off they went on their tour.

A little while later, I got a call from Debbie Gordon, the general manager of Alternative Tentacles. She said, "This new tape came in from NoMeansNo, it's their new album and they want us to put it out." That was *Sex Mad*. Luckily, we had money then. So, like, "Fuck yeah, we're doing this."

**Andy Kerr** Jello came up to us after our San Francisco show in '86 and talked to us. We met him and had a good chat. We were all Dead Kennedys fans, so it was cool to meet him. He said, "Oh god, you are *way* better live than you are on record." He had a way of giving back-handed compliments.

**John Wright** We had already released *Sex Mad* on Psyche at this point. It was Debbie Gordon who said to Jello, "Look, you've got to come see these guys." He came to our San Francisco show, which of course nobody was at. There were maybe twenty people, and most of them were from AT. Jello saw it and went, "Oh, okay, I really like these guys." Debbie was like, "Well, they've already got the record, it's already done, the masters are done. Let's put it out." Jello went, "Okay."

**Daniel Webster** At one point in early 1987, Randy came to me and said, "Well, Alternative Tentacles wants to put out their next record." At that point, we had basically closed Psyche Industry, so it just made more sense for the band. Initially, AT licensed it from us, and we kinda walked away from it. Randy went on to work at a little label called Pipeline that eventually became Cargo Records.

**Andy Kerr** We felt immediately at home with Alternative Tentacles, with the people who worked there, with their attitude, with the scene that we fell into. It was perfect for us, absolutely perfect. We were left to do whatever we wanted to do, without any hassle. If we sold ten records, they'd pay us for ten records. If we sold a thousand records, they'd pay us for a thousand records. At least at that point in time,

**Alternative Tentacles Records**
**P.O. Box 11458**
**San Francisco, CA 94101**

Herein find a little record. It's a 45. Due to modern technology you'll probably be seeing less and less of these things, right? Well, not if NOMEANSNO has anything to say about it. You see, The Three Bobs in aforementioned band find 7" to be the perfect size for serving cheese balls at social engagements. If you do not know what cheese balls are or do not host social functions of any sort, send this record back.

Who are the members of NOMEANSNO? A question often asked and seldom answered. Below find a brief, but true profile on each participant.

ROB WRIGHT. BASSMAN, NOMEANSNO
Particulars: birthdate: March, 1951
birthplace: Plumeflag, Ontario.
physical condition: Labial
ambition: Raise a few chickens, a couple of hogs
thresh hold of pain: So profoundly high, as to be ascertained by a handful of extremely ex-pensive pedigree Dach-shounds.

Rob Wrights' profile compiled by photojournalists W. Buzz Ryan, with the acknowledged asssistance of the Cooley High janitorial staff.

JOHN WRIGHT. DRUMMER, NOMEANSNO
Particulars: birthdate: March, 1941
birthplace: Bunnions Lip, Outer Hebrides, Scotland
clubs, organizations: Cabalists for a better tomorrow.
age began teething: pre-natal.
ambition: discover David Rockefeller Jr.

John Wrights' profile compiled by W. Buzz Ryan, with additional biographical data supplied by the Compton McKenzie historical society, Inverness, Scotland

ANDY KERR. GUITARIST, NOMEANSNO
Particulars:birthdate: October, 1962
birthplace: Smith, Nebraska.
birthmarks: Orange swastika
location: Upper right elbow
see: Duetschmarks.
ambitions: Complete masters degree; Aetiology
main influences on career: Frederick Banting
Carol Wayne

Andy Kerrs' profile compiled by W. Buzz Ryan and Cleve Loowet, Photojournalist

**Alternative Tentacles promo sheet for the "Dad"/"Revenge" single, compiled by W. Buzz Ryan**

Alternative Tentacles was a really good, functioning thing.

That they said, "Yeah, we'll put out your records with a handshake deal," was just unheard of. Biafra would sometimes make suggestions like, "Well, I think that maybe this song would be better off here in the album." We'd say, "No, we want it to go this way," and he'd always be okay with it. Same with the artwork and everything. He's like that with all the bands. "Whatever you guys want, fine. This is the deal, this is how much we take for each record, and this is how much you guys get for each record." We said, "Great, certainly, fine."

**Debbie Gordon—Alternative Tentacles** I was at the AT office when the police raid over the Giger stuff happened. Thank god NoMeansNo had taught us how to play darts. We played darts while the police checked all the stuff in the warehouse.

**Laurie Mercer** Jello is certainly a fascinating character, but he could be problematic for me. He's very dismissive of anybody in the business. When he was first interested, Robbie said, "Oh, I'll call my manager," and Jello would go, "Oh, I hate managers. Tell your manager I fucking hate managers, okay?"

I'd phone Jello with a question, and he'd phone Rob with an answer. He wouldn't take my call; he'd ask whoever was at AT to take my question, and it was so incredibly frustrating. However, in person he was always nice to me.

This is coming off like I don't like Jello, but I don't bear him any ill will. But he'd leave you hanging because you're just a "sleazy manager," someone he perceived as "the man." I was never able to convince him that I'm not a corporate rock manager dude. I'm part of the band. I'm all for one, one for all.

**John Wright** We never signed a deal. There's no contract. It was just simply record by record. He became a big fan, and it was really great. Jello would be like, "Okay, it's great. Put it out." I'm sure there's several albums he didn't particularly like, but by that point he was a fan anyway. Jello didn't interfere with bands, at least not with us. I'm pretty sure that's with everything on AT.

That's exactly what we wanted and what we needed. We didn't want to be someone's employee at a record label. Bands are just contracted workers, and the music is the product. It doesn't work any differently than any other contractor. It's totally annoying, because that's not what art is. It's very, very frustrating.

Once you're on a major label, eventually you just have to do what they want you to do, or else you just don't get any support. It would just be nothing but pressure, like, "Why can't you write something like *this* band?" Whereas, with AT, we did whatever the fuck we wanted and sent it to them.

**Rob Wright** Biafra is a very clever man, a very smart man. I make fun of him a lot, but I admire him completely. He was basically the single most important guy in our career. He did more to help us become a viable band than anybody else, and that was true of lots of people who started on Alternative Tentacles. That was all because he decided to put his money where his mouth was and create an independent record company.

Jello is responsible for our career in a lot of ways. Having *Sex Mad* out on AT gave it credibility and clout, especially in Europe. When we went to Europe, we were getting big crowds from the start, because we were on AT.

**Jello Biafra** There weren't as many labels back then, and I was really uncomfortable having to play God and deciding who to sign. There were always fifty more people I wanted to put out than I could. The main criteria was: you gotta have really good songs, you gotta be really good live, you gotta be intelligent, and *we* gotta have money available. NoMeansNo kinda lucked out, and so did we.

NUCLEAR BLAS
INFAMOUS SCIENTISTS
NOMEANS
PINK STEEL
THE GUEDSTS
THERE'S TWO OF US PRODUCTIONS PRESE
Direct from England:
Angelic Upstarts
TAKE DIRECT ACTION!
Bob's Funnies
This is Bob.
BOB CAN DANCE
Is Bob in jail?
BENEFIT DANCE FOR THE FI
ARRESTED & CHARGED WIT
VARIOUS DIRECT ACTIONS -
JULIE BELMAS
GERRY HANNAH
ANN HANSEN
DOUG STEWART
BRENT TAYLOR
FRIDAY
MARCH 18 8:00 p.m.
UVIC
STUDENT UNION BUILDING
UPPER LOUNGE
FEATURING
NOMEANSNO
ROCKERS
1ST BIRTHDAY
BENEFIT
BASH
NO MEANS NO
PRESSURE POINT
RYVALS
KIDS ACROSS THE HALL
FERNWO
COMM
CENTR
FRIDA
25TH
8 P.M
GET EM AT
TICKETS $5
AUTOMATIC SHOCK
NOMEANSNO
NOMEANSNO
plus
SOLDIERS
OF SPORT
wednesday
JUNE 6th
john
barley's
23w. CORDOVA ST
MR. WRONG PRESENTS:
NO MEANS
WITH
DAYGLOWS
EMILY
RHYTHM MISSION
NOMEANSNO
ANIMAL SLAVES
NOMEANSNO
SAT. DEC. 15 $4
MEATLOCKER
MONQUI PRESENTS
THE HARDEST WORKING BAND IN SHOW BUSINESS
D.O.A.
FROM VANCOUVER B.C.
NO MEANS NO
+69 WAYS
SAT
$5.50 ADVANCE
PINE ST
NOW
INDEPENDENCE
S.N.F.U.
NO MEAN
ON MAY 1st COLLECTORS R.P.M. PRESENTS
WITH VERY SPECIAL GUEST
A.K.O.B.
NO MEANS NO
FRI 28
SAT 1
JESSE BERNSTEIN USUAL
WITH
HOO DUN ITT
UVIC RADIO PRESENTS:
NOMEANSNO
NOMEANSNO
Listen to this...
DEVELOP
YOURSELF.
FRIDAY, AUGUST 26 - 8:3
FERNWOOD
COMMUNITY CENTR
1240 GLADSTONE
$4.00 ADVANCE
$4.50 AT THE DO
TICKETS AVAILABLE AT: RICKARD'S, MEZZROW'S
UVIC RADIO (SUB
MINORS WELCOME!
A RANDOM THOUGHT PRODUCTION
CFUV
Presents:
VANCOUVER'S
ANIMAL SL
And Victoria's
NOMEANS
Saturday
April 5th
Fernwood Community Centre
1240 Gladstone
NO
MEAN
N
from vancouve
+
GUESTS
TUESDAY
JULY
29
$5.00
THE BRIDGE
507 bloor st w
toronto
SPECIAL SURPRISE VISIT
D.O.A.
WITH
NO
MEANS
NO
SATURDAY
JULY 12
1986
7 PM $3
HOUSE
Circle J
WASTED
GA
NO MEA
At THE FARM
SATURDAY,
SHOW 7 PM
ALL AGES WELCOME

nomeansno
NOMEANSNO
FOOD BANK BENEFIT
EXTRAVIGANZA!
NOMEANSNO
RED TIDE
SKINNMANIA!
(THE RESISTANCE)
+ Guests?
SATURDAY, NOVEMBER
7:30 PM
Pro Patria Legion Hall
CITR & CAT PRODUCTIONS
PRESENT
A Hard 'n' Heavy Rock Extravaganza
FEATURING
S. N. F. U.
NOMEANSNO
DEATH SENTENCE
PLUS
THE BILL OF RIGHTS
AND
THE LITTLE RATSKULLS
Friday, November 29, 1985
7:30 PM
UBC Sub Ballroom
ALL AGES WELCOME
TICKETS: VTC/CBO & ALL USUAL OUTLETS
Refreshments Available
Bring I.D.
COLLECTORS RPM
SAVOY in GASTOWN
PRESENTS
SNAKEFINGER
&
NO MEANS NO
..everything can ha
Snakefinger
AND THE VESTAL VIRGINS
+
NO MEANS NO
BEDSPINS
FERNWOOD COMMUNITY CENTRE
NO MEANS NO
YOU
NOMEANSNO
CANADA
GONNA BE
'INTENSE'
SAT. MAY
17
score as you Dare! Costume Party!!
THE SPORES
MARCH 9
SPOILED
NOMEANSNO
FROM CANADA
BACK TO NATURE
NOMEANSNO
VICTORIA SAMPLER
mit der
BEDSPINS
und
NOISE GENERATION
WEDNESDAY, OCT. 22
THE TOWN PUMP
CFUV 105.1 F.M. PRESENTS:
D.O.A.
WITH GUESTS:
NOMEANSNO
AND
MISSION OF CHRIST
SATURDAY, DECEMBER 6 1986
ADVANCE
DOOR
FERNWOOD COMM. CENTRE
1240 gladstone
NOMEANSNO
THE RATS
HOUSE OF COMMONS
BILL OF RIGHTS
HOT OFF AN EXTENSIVE TOUR OF THE U.S.A.
TWO BANDS THAT MAKE UP THE CORE OF CANADA'S WEST COAST MUSIC.
DAY-GLO ABORTIONS
&NOMEANSNO
Dec. 31
8 P.M.
O.A.P.
HALL
1600
Govt.
HAPPY NEW YEAR
RANCID PRODUCTIONS IN COOPERATION WITH

CHAPTER ELEVEN

# THE DAY EVERYTHING BECAME ISOLATED AND DESTROYED

## "First a gentle murmur that calls from the heart, and then a great wind that will blow you apart."

Now that NoMeansNo were on Alternative Tentacles, they began to gain more clout and attention, especially in the often-jaded hardcore scene. After all, if Jello Biafra likes this weird little band from Canada, maybe they're worth checking out. The more they played live, the tighter the band got, so when the time came to expand beyond North America and conquer Europe, NoMeansNo were ready.

**Andy Kerr** We toured across the States and then back across Canada with D.O.A. in late 1987. We met and played with lots of bands on that tour, like the Leaving Trains, Operation Ivy, Marginal Man, and many others.

**Jon Card—D.O.A.** I called their little blue van the "Den for Men," because inside it had this wood paneling, and it just looked like a little den.

**Joe Keithley** When D.O.A would come to town, everyone and their dog would want to get on the bill. We'd have bills where there would be six hardcore bands that sounded exactly the same, and then we'd play. But with NoMeansNo, we had this unique band that didn't sound like anyone else in the world. Plus, we'd add one local band to the bill, which was always a good thing to do.

**Jon Card** John Wright filled in for me on drums for a couple of the shows in Eastern Canada. I had a deviated septum, and my nose started bleeding as we

**Ken Jensen, Rob, Craig, Andy, John, and their "Den for Men" tour van**

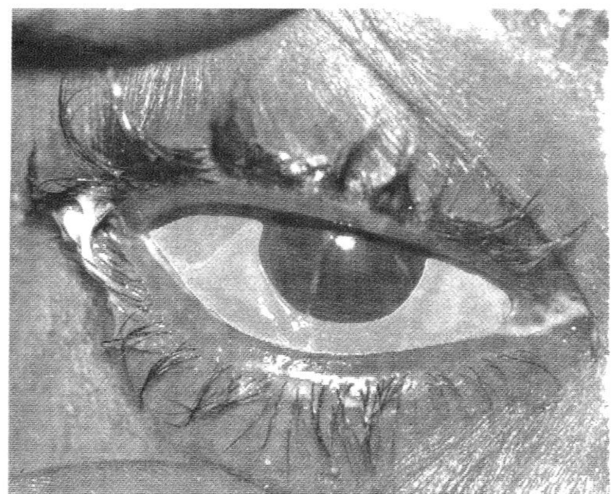


were crossing the border. I was drinking vodka, and I woke up in a pool of blood. They ended up cauterizing it nine fuckin' times because it kept bleeding. I was not allowed to drum the gig because they didn't want me to bleed out on my drum kit.

**Patrick "Hutch" Hutchinson** My mother took Jon to the hospital. She was a nurse, so she took him in to get his nose cauterized. It was a deviated septum, otherwise known as putting too many things up your nose that you shouldn't. We definitely knew that John Wright would have no problem hammering it out.

**Joe Keithley** Jon Card was a little bit of a partier, so these problems were obviously induced by certain things. He got exceptionally high and drunk while we were driving up from Boston to Halifax, and he was out of control. He was bleeding all over the place and just fucked up! We went to the hospital in Nova Scotia, but they kicked him out. They said, "We won't deal with people who act like this." His schnoz swelled up like an orange. They said, "No drumming for about four days."

I asked John Wright to fill in, and he said that he could do it. He knew all the songs, since he had been listening to them the past few nights. We got up there, and the first night went pretty well. John has a different style, so we kind of adjusted to that. In Montreal, we played "To Hell an' Back," and instead of being slower, it was faster and more energetic. I remember turning around and seeing John with a big shit-eating grin on his face. I'm looking at him like, "You fucking idiot, slow down!" In a very friendly way, I spoke to him afterwards, saying, "John, thanks very much for filling in, but there's an awful lot of lyrics in that song."

**Jon Card** Luckily, John knew probably 80 percent of the D.O.A. stuff really well, so he drummed for

**D.O.A. with John (right), New Brunswick, 1987**

me. I got to go and watch D.O.A. play with John on drums, and he did a fine job. I rejoined the tour a few days later.

Me and John, we got along really well. We'd talk shop and have dinner, and then at night sometimes, we'd have these road wars with fireworks. Like, going down the highway in the middle of the night, shooting bottle rockets at each other. We had a great time on that tour. I can't say a bad thing about those guys. I wish I could, but fuck, I can't.

**Joe Keithley** John Wright was one of the only guys I know even from those days who was still using a traditional grip. Everyone at that point was using a "rock grip," where you just grab it like a club. John had grown up learning jazz. His feel was so much different than most guys who got into this high-powered music. I've never seen a guy able to play sixteenth notes that fast with that much rhythm and in time like a machine, while being able to play the high hat or ride cymbal.

We never went down that road of having John join D.O.A., because we knew that NoMeansNo were doing really well. There's no point in breaking up one great band to try to augment another. I guess we could've coordinated it, but we never really thought of that. John is a good friend, and that would've been fun, but it didn't work out that way.

**Jord Samolesky—Propagandhi** I liked the fact that John Wright had an extra tom and that he did all this different stuff to make it sound like he had a second kick drum or a cheater pedal. I could also never really grasp how he gets such a powerful stroke on his snare with that traditional grip, especially the fast punk stuff.

**Ford Pier** The first time I met the NoMeansNo guys was in 1987, when they came and played at the University of Alberta. The show was put on by CJSR, the college radio station where I was working. I was fifteen or sixteen years old, and I interviewed them. Whenever they passed through Edmonton, I would always see them, and we stayed in touch.

I had a band called GOD. We opened for NoMeansNo at the Howlin' Wolf. It is fair to say that all I ever wanted out of playing live rock music was to open for NoMeansNo. I achieved that in 1988, and since then I have plateaued.

**Jon Card** We were in Edmonton, and John said, "Why don't we play around with the crowd a little bit here?" We staged this whole thing where someone threw a beer can and it hit John. He then just dropped and pretended to be out cold. Then Rob said, "We need some help up here. Is there a drummer in the crowd?" So I came running up, hopped behind the drums, and went into the opening drum riff from "Sex Mad." After the song, John came running back out onstage: "He's okay!"

**Dave Genn—54-40, Matthew Good Band** When I saw them for the first time, I couldn't believe how perfect a band they were. They had this weird little punk on guitar, this jazz school dropout on drums, and your crazy science teacher on bass. The thing I noticed immediately that set them apart from the other hardcore bands was that they could *really* fucking play. When you see them live, who do you fucking look at? If you look at one of them, you're missing something from the other two guys. They were just absolutely fascinating live.

**Randy Strobl** There were so many times that people wouldn't know how to react to NoMeansNo. I remember one time this guy from New York City came to Victoria. He was just the coolest guy ever. He had hung out at CBGB's. He'd seen Dead Boys, Minutemen, Ramones. He'd been to England. We took him to see NMN at the FOE Hall. Afterwards, this New York guy was just pacing around going, "What the *fuck* was that? Nobody's gonna believe this! I've never seen anything like that." That's when I really knew that they were good.

**Mark Smith** We had Soundgarden up to Vancouver a few times before they broke big. We basically just paid their gas money to get them up here. They'd sleep on my bedroom floor.

**Kim Thayil** Chris Cornell and I were turned on to NoMeansNo by our first bass player, Hiro Yamamoto. It was a big fuckin' deal for us to be playing with NoMeansNo and D.O.A. When we think of bands

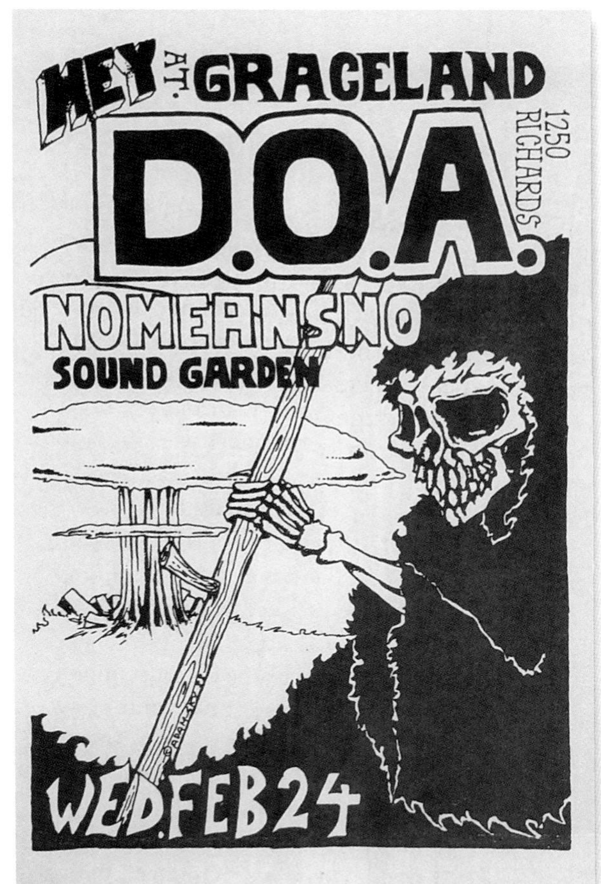


from Vancouver that were somewhat influential, it would be D.O.A., NoMeansNo, and Subhumans (Canada). There were a few others as well. Animal Slaves also had that really cool bass player.

I talked to the NMN guys at Graceland that night. They were drinking Corona beer. In the US, Corona was marketed to yuppies, and we didn't like it. But in Vancouver, the NoMeansNo guys were drinking it, saying, "This stuff's great!" We were like, "Why are you drinking Corona? You've got some of the best beers in the world!" We come up from Seattle and meet this band that destroyed everyone, and they were drinking fucking Corona.

**Joe Keithley** Soundgarden hadn't gotten big yet by that point, and I think they played in the middle of the show, before D.O.A. They played, and everyone looked at them kinda like, "Who are these guys?" You gotta start somewhere, right?

I'm not surprised to hear that Soundgarden and some of those Seattle bands were influenced by NoMeansNo. On those first few tours with D.O.A., it was us and Black Flag primarily touring around North America. You'd go back to a town a second time, and you can tell who had been there first because the opening bands would sound like either us or them. After a while, I'd see bands and I'd think, "Oh, those guys have listened to a lot of NoMeansNo!" That's a good thing. I think they influenced a lot of people.

**Andy Kerr** Soundgarden were very, very good, albeit good at a kind of music that seemed quite retro to our "punky" ears. Back to those '70s riffs, but with a twist. The vocals reminded me far too much of Robert Plant, but I distinctly remember thinking that guitarist Kim Thayil was brilliant. He played with a recognizable heavy sound, but he was obviously trying to do something new with it. I got the chance to speak with him afterwards, and he was a very sweet guy.

**Laurie Mercer** I had brought Soundgarden up to Vancouver a number of times. They were close pals. We formed an alliance between myself, the boys from Monqui in Portland, and Susan Silver in Seattle. Susan was the manager of Soundgarden. We would

"block buy" acts for the three cities, so that we could get a chance against the big concert promoters. That's how we'd gotten those earlier Violent Femmes shows booked.

Promo poster with James Joyce quote

**Matt Cameron—Skin Yard, Soundgarden, Pearl Jam** NoMeansNo played down here in Seattle at the Vogue. I first saw them play probably around '86, right after I joined Soundgarden. It was a small room, so I could really zero in on what the drummer was doing, and I was super impressed. NoMeansNo were a huge influence on us in the '80s. Chris Cornell was really, really into NoMeansNo.

We loved bands that had a really unique signature sound that was completely their own thing. As a young band, Soundgarden really wanted to focus on our strengths and try to forge a sound out of that. We definitely really learned a lot from the bands at the time that were doing that, and NMN was certainly one of them.

**Trey Spruance—Mr. Bungle** I had never heard their music before. We just went to the show. It was in Arcata, California, and it was during the *Small Parts* tour. I don't think any of us had ever seen a rhythm section work that way before. For me, it was the emotional power that came across from the band being so fucking *tight*.

Most of the punk bands we'd see had a lot of fire and energy, but musicianship usually interferes with that direct, emotive power. Here was a band that had all of this incredible musicianship working together to enhance that effect.

I went out and bought the album right after the show. I was trying to use the record to reminisce about how good the band was live. But there's no way you could compare the live experience with the record.

**Chris Crud** In Nevada, the casinos control everything, and they don't like shows happening outside of the casinos. In Reno and Las Vegas, the kids just put on shows in basements or on the Indian reserve. Those are really the only two places that we could play.

We did a house show in Reno, in a basement, tons of people. There was a big party after the show, and we all went. Leaving Reno the next day, we're in the van and John was driving. We're at a stoplight, and as the light changes, this car smacks us and ends up in somebody's yard. There's very little damage to our van, but the whole front of the car is completely ripped out. The police show up, and they're interviewing us, and it turns out the person who hit us is a police officer on a lunch break. So the police thought that they would pin this on these Canadian idiots. They said, "You guys are at fault. We're taking you in. We're impounding the vehicle, jail time, blah, blah, blah." We're like, "What? She ran the red light." A guy who witnessed the whole thing finally came up and said, "Yeah, she ran the red light. I'm a witness. I saw it all happen." They were pissed that they couldn't pin it on us. They said, "Okay. Guess what, boys? You're leaving town and you're not welcome back." We got a police escort out of Reno.

**Jello Biafra** For the first year or two that I knew the Wrights, I thought they were natural blonds. I happened to be in Southern California when they were down there on tour, and we all wound up going swimming at this crowded public swimming pool. Only when I was really close to Rob did I realize, "Oh my god, that's not blond hair at all. That's premature grey, going on white!"

**Craig Bougie** I remember we played a show with fIREHOSE, which was the remnants of Minutemen. Mike Watt came up after the show, and he gave us like an extra five hundred bucks. He said, "Yeah, we were eating your dust tonight, man. You guys were amazing." He said, "D. Boon would have wanted it this way."

**Mike Watt** I have the big trippy poster of *Small Parts Isolated and Destroyed* with the James Joyce quote on it. It's in my practice room, so when I play, I'm staring at this motherfucker, next to John Coltrane for inspiration. There weren't a lot of punk rockers with Jim Joyce connects. In a big way, we felt like kindred spirits.

**Laurie Mercer** On tour in those days, NoMeansNo would spend five shows in a row at sound check playing "Surfin' Bird." They'd master that, then suddenly they'd play some Elvis Costello song. They'd do five or six sound checks until they could fucking blister the song. Then they'd drop it and start working on "Isolation" by Joy Division.

**Angelo Moore—Fishbone** I would hear NoMeansNo a lot on KXLU college radio here in Los Angeles. It would always make me sit up on the edge of my seat. I would go, "Damn, man, that's some badass music. I wanna play music like that!" I would turn it up and go, "Goddamn! Those muthafuckas are *bad*, man!" NMN was a lot of straightforward, focused, and high-energy punk-rock-style type of shit. The attitude stuck out more than most of the bands I was listening to at the time.

**Jay Scott** After the show, we'd pack up, I'd settle the finances, everyone would pile into the van, and I would drive us off into the night. Everyone would be drinking, playing poker or whatever, and gradually they'd all fall asleep. Craig Bougie was almost always the "second shift" driver, after me. He would stay up drinking to keep me company. Eventually, he would just pass out, and he was supposed to be my relief! This would happen over and over again.

I would drive to the next town, and just as we were coming to the outskirts of town, I'd yell at him, "Craig! Craig! I'm too tired, you gotta take over!" He would wake up from a dead-drunk sleep, bolt straight upwards, and go, "Yeah, I'll take it in from here." He couldn't walk, but he was willing to drive.

**Randy Strobl** When NoMeansNo tours, they usually stay at someone's house, but in big or sketchy cities like Berlin, LA, New York, someone always slept in the van. A couple times, break-ins got stopped because someone was in the van.

On that American tour, we went to the New Music Seminar in Manhattan. It's a big deal in the

industry. Laurie was there too, and he had a room at the Marriott in Times Square. We were given badges to go see all these talks and presentations. Jello Biafra was there, Lemmy from Motörhead, Eurythmics, the Police, etc.

What we blatantly saw was how all these underground bands were being bought up by mainstream labels. I remember walking with Rob through the hallways where all these rooms were having different seminars you could attend. There was a sandwich board outside one room that read "Marketing Metal—The Battle Plan." I think that experience really reinforced for them that they were doing the right thing. They felt good about having signed with Jello and Alternative Tentacles because they were able to do their own thing.

**Joe Keithley** We played that New Music Seminar in New York at the Ritz. We played with Danzig and Redd Kross. We ended up getting a record deal out of it. I think it was NoMeansNo, then Redd Kross, then us, and then Danzig closed the show. It was a big show, probably two thousand people.

**Mark Smith** I remember sitting up in the balcony and Iggy Pop and the Ramones were all up there. The Run-DMC guys were there. They're all looking down at the pit, and it was like a tropical storm. They just sat there with their mouths open. The room technically held only two thousand people, but it was so full I couldn't get off the balcony. I'd never seen anything like it.

**Laurie Mercer** I met Hetty and Ingrid from Konkurrent at that New Music Seminar. I met Luc Klaasen from the Ex, who was also working for Konkurrent. Bill Gilliam from the London AT office had given me their contacts. They had seen NoMeansNo play at the Pyramid Club in New York City. There was also a drag floor show on the bill. I ended up missing the show, as the whole thing was a really confusing mess.

With more exhaustive touring under their belt, NoMeansNo once again returned to Victoria in the winter of 1987 to their day jobs and their "normal" lives. They found themselves again with a backlog of new songs that were road-tested and ready to record. They decided to record an EP and a full-length LP at the same time and release them back to back.

**Cecil English—Profile Studios** I'm from Vancouver. The first time that I met NoMeansNo, I had gone over to Victoria to do sound for Art Bergmann, and NMN opened up for him as a duo, just John and Rob. I chatted them up but didn't really see much of them for a while after that. I thought their first couple albums were really good. Then I produced D.O.A's *True (North) Strong and Free*, and those guys were huge D.O.A fans. They actually showed up at my door at Profile Studios one day and said, "We want to make a record with you," which was kind of a common practice. SNFU and the Smalls did the same thing. They just knocked on the door, because the studio was practically going 24–7. We were always there.

They came in and said they wanted to record an EP, to see how it went. I had no idea there was also a full album in progress. At that time, I was more of a "live off the floor" guy than a studio engineer. I think "Brother Rat" was the first song we recorded. We basically slammed everything down, overdubbed a couple of easy things, made a quick mix, and it was done, and everyone was really happy with that first session.

Cecil English at Profile Studios

Profile Studios was a full-on, two-inch-tape analogue studio. The equipment was astronomically expensive, and we were under a huge debt load at the time, so the studio was almost $1,000 a day. I think it was a weeklong recording, for both *The Day Everything* and *Small Parts*. A day and a half of bed tracks and a few days overdubbing and mixing, and that was it. There was no digital manipulation of anything. It was us mixing, with our hands on the mixing board. That's what you hear on the record, in real time.

**Craig Bougie** To produce the record back then, there was no automation, so when it came down to mixing a song, it'd be literally all hands on deck. Like, with one hand you're raising the guitar, the other you're hitting an effects knob. All four of us would be along the board, hitting buttons, trying to get the song right. Lots of takes.

**Scott Henderson** They demoed *The Day Everything* and *Small Parts* on my 388 Tascam Portastudio, which is a portable studio in name only. It's a really big reel-to-reel eight-track/board combination. They would borrow that and take it to the Rats Nest to record. Those sessions yielded some great music. They were still getting off on the songs, because they had just written them.

One of my big complaints about *Small Parts*, and to a lesser extent *The Day Everything*, was that the demos sounded great but then they went and toured them for six weeks and played them to death. So, when they recorded the album, it sounded just a little bit road-weary. Especially songs like "Small Parts," which has the rubato, those pauses. By the end of that tour, the pauses were getting longer and longer.

**Andy Kerr** There are two types of people in the world. There's the people who listen to the CD that contained both the EP and the LP [*The Day Everything Became Isolated and Destroyed*] and hear it in that order. That's really bizarre to me. Then there's the people who bought the original EP and the album, and they see it as two separate things. All the songs were recorded at the same time. We thought, "Okay, we don't want to put out a double album. So these five go here and the rest go over there." They both had the same concept.

**John Wright** That record turned out to be way overproduced in some respects. We had access to the studio and didn't really know what we were doing. It was an odd collection of songs, but really fun to do. I was happy with it in the end.

**Andy Kerr** *Small Parts* was the one where we thought, "Okay, great, now that we're up and running, we want to do something *big*." We had the songs and the basic concept for *Small Parts*, but they all sounded the same when we played them live. When we went in to do the album, we decided we wanted to give every song a different sound. Almost like a mixtape. It didn't really turn out that way, but you can hear the differences in some of them. There are effects on the guitar that I wouldn't normally play live.

**Ralph Spight** I remember being over at Ruth Schwartz's house and having her put on *Small Parts Isolated and Destroyed* before it came out. That title track is Andy at his absolute pinnacle as far as I'm concerned. He basically encapsulated pretty much everything in one song, in terms of the music business and psychology. As a song, it's a philosophical kitchen sink.

**Craig Bougie** I'm the guy in the song "Small Parts" who says, "You know me! You remember me! Can I get in for free?" I was hoping my career in vocals would take off from there, but no.

**John Wright** I had this Mattel Synsonics drum machine that I used on a couple of early demos, like "Dark Ages." It was a stupid toy-company drum machine. It was like, "That's a cool sound, we'll use it here." That's how some of these songs ended up so strange. We were pretty distracted by stuff like that.

**Andy Kerr** I have a memory of Rob being very specific about the way "Teresa" was spelled for "Teresa, Give Me That Knife." He was really like, "No, I don't want it spelled that way. There's no *h*." I remember at the time thinking, "Why?"

"Change" by Killing Joke was on everybody's compilation tape, and when you listen to that song, and then you listen to the main riff of "The Day Everything Became Nothing," you can see big similarities, albeit with slightly different notes. There are several examples of that. They were not meant to be rip-offs; it was just because that's the music we were listening to.

**Jon Card** I played some cowbell and made some pig noises on the song "Beauty and the Beast." I was in the studio when they were recording "Brother Rat." I remember John wasn't sure what to do for the beginning of the song. I showed him this triplet thing, where you do triplets with the hands and then the bass drum is just on the one and the three. He tried that, and he liked it.

Any keen NoMeansNo fan has noticed a character named Slayde who makes the occasional appearance. The *Sex Mad* LP has a "Side Bob" and a "Side Slayde," and *The Day Everything Became Nothing* EP contains a song called "Brother Rat/What Slayde Says." Who is this Slayde fellow anyway? Should we ever listen to what Slayde says?

**Rob Wright** I think Slayde was one of a group of evil twins that I had stored away in my psyche. He's the guy who says, "I don't give a shit. You're an idiot. What you do and whatever issues you have are no business of mine. I couldn't care less." This is not a nice attitude at all. I used to have these feelings, and also more than a bit of cynicism. Slayde was a guy who was ruthless and truly didn't care about anything or anyone around him. He was a villain. Old Slayde was one of my snakes. I had a lot of snakes in my songs. Slayde comes out in many songs, not just "Brother Rat/What Slayde Says." There were a series of songs that have got that sort of cruel but realistic attitude: "This isn't nice, but this is what it is, like it or not."

On the opposite side was the passion for life, which I usually expressed in songs about the feminine side of the world. This is embodied in *Mama* and all sorts of female figures. That was sort of the redemptive. The one that *did* care, the one that was reaching out. The fear, anxiety, and anger were

AND THAT'S SAD

WE SHOULD NOT MAKE A FUSS
WHAT WOULD BECOME OF US?
WE SHOULD NOT
AND THAT'S SAD

WE NEED TO HOLD ON TIGHT
HOLD ON WITH ALL OUR MIGHT
ALL OUR MIGHT
AND THAT'S SAD

I DEMAND WHAT YOU MUST
IN THE NAME OF DECENC
YOU DO THE SAME TO ME
AND THAT'S SAD

WE LIVE JUST KILLING TIME
AND THAT'S THE BIGGEST CRIME
AND THAT'S ALL WE KNOW
AND THAT'S A CRYING SHAME
AND THAT'S SAD

**"And That's Sad" original lyrics**

constantly being expressed in my music. But also love and joy, and suffering, and vulnerability.

Over the course of my songwriting in NoMeansNo, the three touchstones are "Mama's Little Boy," "Mary," and "Faceless May." If you want to know what I was about, those are the ones. It's something to do with the feminine. It's something to do with that link to everything. It's very contradictory: you'll find those songs have both heartfelt and dreadful aspects to them. They're about fear and pain as much as they are about love and trust. They are all intertwined with a sort of semiuniversal feminine figure. Now, *why*? I'm not sure. There's maybe a few personal things I could lay out, but it's really nobody's business. I've written the same song over and over, in a lot of ways.

**John Wright** The people who should be talking about the meanings from song to song are *not* the band. The band has no real objectivity. Once you've recorded and released it, the meaning is what the listener hears. People have asked us in the past,

"What does this song mean?" I'm like, "What's important is what does it mean to you? What do you think? What do you feel when you hear the song? How does it touch you?" Any artist will tell you: the art doesn't belong to you anymore. As soon as you release it, it belongs to the world. It belongs to every individual in their own way.

**Rob Wright** The thing about any inspired artistic act is, it's not you. You are a vehicle. That's where true artistic stuff comes from. It transcends the personal. People who do things that everyone thinks are amazing are not responsible. They're just the ones who managed to spit it out of the ether and put it into material form, whether it's a song, a sculpture, a painting, whatever.

The trouble with artists, of course, is that they all assume it *is* them, thus you get the rock stars, the egomaniacs. Luckily for me, I never thought it was me. I always thought it was something that came to me. A gift, not a production of mine. Is it about me and who I am, who I know, and my personal history? No, not really. It's something else, something that came to me. Where? Who knows where the wild wind blows?

**Sylvia Kenny** I did the background art for the cover of *The Day Everything Became Nothing*. John had some ideas for the cover, and they were looking for some kind of background to put behind John's sketch. I was going to the Camosun College art program at the time. I made those blue textured backgrounds that eventually got used.

**Rob Wright** I used to, and still do sometimes, make these pictures which involve all sorts of weird organic and semi-disgusting shapes and convolutions. I finally thought, "Well, I'll do one for the *Small Parts* cover." I put the swastikas in, and I did that knowing exactly how that would hackle people.

Occasionally, we'd hear something about it, like, "What's with the swastikas, eh?" But again, symbols of evil are there for a purpose. It's because people are evil. This is not political. It's personal. Everything that's political starts out being personal, which is why I never cared much for politics. It's too far removed from reality, which is personal.

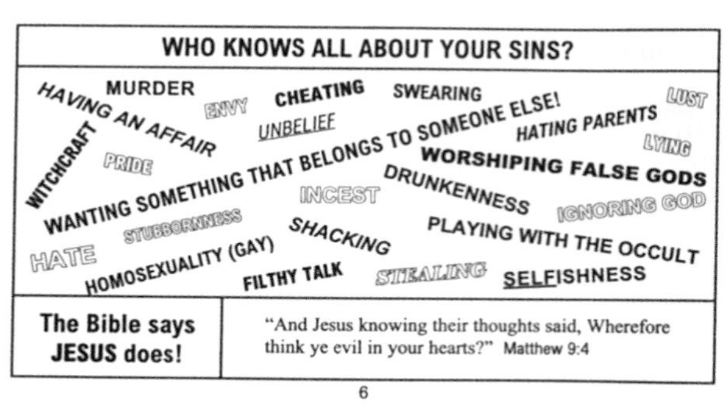

**Original Chick tract (top) and *Small Parts Isolated and Destroyed* insert (bottom)**

**Andy Kerr** I remember distinctly when Rob lived with Emma on Gordon Head. He had drawn that really weird picture on a small sheet of paper. He blew it up using one of those overhead projectors. He took a large sheet of fabric, which became our new backdrop. We originally had a picture of Dead Bob hanging there as our backdrop on our first Canadian tour. The *Small Parts* backdrop took him ages to do.

We would take turns doing album covers. It just happened that way. We'd get together and fine-tune them, but someone would generally take the lead. I remember Rob came up with the idea for *Small Parts*, this weirdo picture with Day-Glo colours. I thought it looked great. To this day, it's one of my favourite album covers that we did.

I think I was the one who found the "Chick tract" that we modified and used as the insert in *Small Parts*. I brought it to Rob and John and said, "Oh, look, we can change this and put, 'Who Knows All About Your Sins—NoMeansNo,'" and we all had a laugh. We were looking at what was actually there, and it's like, "These are our song topics, right here!" It was just perfect for what we wanted to do.

**John Yates—designer** After I moved to the States, I began working for Alternative Tentacles doing design and layout work. NoMeansNo were very much a band that were hands-on. They pretty much always had it planned out, so I was basically doing the grunt work and making their concepts a reality. The *Small Parts* record cover was kind of a nightmare, honestly. This was the late '80s, so full colour was still a luxury, especially for a small punk rock label.

**Nick Evans—promoter** *Small Parts Isolated and Destroyed* and *Day Everything Became Nothing* have this sort of claustrophobic, end-of-the-world aspect to them. It's like the Lars von Trier film *Melancholia*, where this huge planet is about to hit the earth. It really felt like that. They were just screaming at the shadow of the oncoming collision that was going to obliterate the planet. The music that came out was the sound of terror and madness.

**Colin C. Smith** One day in grade eleven, I cut class, took a trolley to downtown Philadelphia, and purchased a used copy of *The Day Everything Became Isolated and Destroyed*. I was already a big fan of Canadian punks SNFU and Propagandhi and knew that I should check out NoMeansNo.

It was not love at first listen. Initially, I was confused and left with many questions. Why did they refuse to write a straightforward punk song? Did this even count as punk rock? What's this about "assured mutual destruction and emotional responsibility"? Who the hell cares what a crow says? But my initial confusion speaks to what makes NoMeansNo so damn good. This is not bubblegum pop, or even pop punk. This music is challenging, and it demands of the listener careful attention and a willingness to meet these strange songs on their own terms.

**Joseph Gray—fan from Poulsbo, Washington** NoMeansNo is a band that when you hear them for the first time, you don't get it. So you listen again, this time to a different album of theirs, and you still don't get it.

But then something will happen in your life, something unexpected that upends your world. That existential moment of clarity is when you finally realize, "Holy shit, NoMeansNo is really fucking good." In that golden second of discovery, NoMeansNo becomes important in a way they never were before.

NoMeansNo is the band I wish I had listened to in high school. I wish I had listened to "Forget Your Life" sooner. I wish I appreciated *Small Parts Isolated and Destroyed* when I was seventeen, instead of when I was twenty-seven. And I wish I would have heard "Lonely" a lot earlier than when I did. They made you reevaluate things in a philosophical way.

The year 1987 had been an incredibly busy one for the band. In addition to recording the new albums, NoMeansNo had done two full tours across the United States and Canada before the year was out. They were gaining new fans and making more lasting connections in the scene. Meanwhile, the AT reissue of *Sex Mad* was being distributed in Europe and perking up some ears. Folks there would soon get to see for themselves what all the fuss was about.

**Hetty Zwart—Konkurrent** I'm one of the founders of De Konkurrent in Amsterdam. Konkurrent is the distributor, and we also had our own label, and that's called Konkurrel, which is an abbreviation of "Konkurrent releases." The concert-booking thing was basically my hobby.

Konkurrent started in 1985. Me and a friend named Richard were the business side, and then Luc and Jos of the Ex were the creative side. Most of us were living in squats, and the first Konkurrel office was in another squat in Amsterdam.

At first, we worked with mainly the Ex, and a bunch of other Dutch bands. But I also loved many of the early hardcore American and Canadian bands, including NoMeansNo. I started asking around, seeing whether we could distribute their records. Then we asked them if they would like to come and tour. All the booking agents in the Netherlands

Konkurrent headquarters, Amsterdam

back then didn't really bother with all these small American bands. I started booking Dutch tours for them. I developed a pretty good network of bookers in different countries, so I would book the Dutch and Belgian dates, and then I hired people in other European countries who booked the shows there.

I was blown away by the *Sex Mad* album. I thought it was so absolutely powerful with this totally dark side about it and this strange sort of humour. I really wanted to see this band. They were on Alternative Tentacles, so I called Bill Gilliam at the UK Alternative Tentacles office. He put me in touch with Laurie Mercer. At the same time, I got in touch with a festival in Holland, and I told them, "I wanna try and get this Canadian band over here. Will you put them on the festival, so they have a good starting point?"

They came over in the spring of 1988 for their first European shows. I went to the Dutch shows, and then I went to England with them. They also went to Germany, Slovenia, and Italy.

**G.W. Sok (Jos)—the Ex, Konkurrent** I was at Konkurrent at the time, and more or less by accident we started to organize some shows for bands from overseas. We distributed Dischord and Alternative Tentacles, and I guess they asked if we could help get their bands some shows in Europe. NoMeansNo were invited to an alternative two-day festival in Amsterdam and Eindhoven, and then they toured Europe from there.

**Ingrid Kerr—Konkurrent** Our friend had warned us already about these three geeky Canadian guys in cowboy boots and leather jackets. Sure enough, we picked them up at the airport, and they're wearing cowboy boots and leather jackets. But they were really fun, really nice, and very friendly. Very different from other bands that we had over as well. We got on really well and started from there. We did five tours together.

I was in charge of the whole tour, but I would hand off different areas to other people. I would section parts off to people who knew the scenes there. There was Dolf in Germany, editor of *Trust*, Arek in Poland, and other people in England. I would say, "We're coming from Barcelona, and we're gonna fly to London. You have this date till that date. Make sure to end up in *this* town."

**Luc Klaasen—the Ex, Konkurrent** Apart from playing in the Ex, I was one of the founders of Konkurrent and involved in the squatter scene in Amsterdam. The whole scene in Holland was quite large, and there were activities and concerts everywhere. The more I got to know the guys in NoMeansNo, the more I appreciated their music. They had a different approach and taste than us, but we shared the same passion. We were more interested in creating super music than becoming popular or rich.

**Randy Strobl** I went on their first European tour with them. I spoke German, which helped. I drove the van and did the merch.

In Berlin in 1988, I remember we went to a club and everyone was so stylized punk: bullet belts, spikes, and multicoloured mohawks. These nerdy Canadians in track pants and shorts arrived for sound check, and these German punks were like, "Who the fuck are you guys?" But then they played "Manic Depression" for the sound check, and everyone quickly changed their attitude.

It got to the point where I would watch that transition happen all the time. In Milton Keynes, NoMeansNo were playing the night after Megadeth played. These metalheads were totally unimpressed with the guys until they heard them play.

NoMeansNo quite quickly became well respected in the European punk scene. They kept their ticket and merch prices low, they would always play free benefit shows, and they would play at squats.

**Kieran Plunkett—Restarts** The squatting culture is incredible, especially in Germany. Just about every town in Germany will have a youth centre, and it's a building that the government subsidizes, and kids go there, and they're always covered in graffiti. They do DJ'ing courses. They run the place themselves: they run a bar, they order the beer, and do all this adult stuff. It's just so amazing.

Poster for Forte Prenestino squat in Rome, 1988

**Hilary Binder—Sabot** The concept of occupied spaces is rather international. I think that the politics behind it are not going to vary that much from country to country. However, the laws regarding squats did vary widely. For example, in northern Europe, there was a lot less repressive state activity to the squatters, and they were able to negotiate contracts and work them into the system. Down in southern Europe, it was a different story. There was not a whole big social movement to support that kind of thing. The government did what they wanted, and people were kicked out. But there, the movement has lasted longer and is more attached to its politics. Whereas in northern Europe, it got more accepted into the status quo.

**Ingrid Kerr** In the '80s, squats were the main focus of the punk scene in the Netherlands. It was the same in Germany, Denmark, Norway, and Italy. People were into the do-it-yourself scene. They had their own record labels, their own bands, their own clubs. Here in Amsterdam we had our own stores where you could rent tools and anything needed to work on your house or your car or your bike. It was a whole network and economy where people helped each other.

I was involved in three squats in Amsterdam where bands would play. We would take care of the food and take care of the sound system. We wouldn't charge a lot of money at the door: just a few bucks to get in. One person would be behind the bar, another person would cook a meal, another would clean up at the end. You were setting yourself apart from the mainstream scene because you wanted to do it all yourself.

We could bring over a small band from Victoria because that culture existed. We were sure that NoMeansNo wouldn't lose money, because we would book them into clubs like the Paradiso and Milky Way [Melkweg], but at the same time we would also do these squats.

**Randy Strobl** We arrived at a huge squat in Amsterdam one time, and after we brought our stuff inside, Andy started doing some dishes. The Dutch punks started falling over laughing: "He broke the record!" They had a running bet going to see how long it took visiting bands to help out and do something. It took about five minutes before Andy went to the sink and cleaned some dishes. They loved that. Many of those people remained friends with the band for years.

**Massimo Pupillo—Zu** I had the great luck of growing up when there was a fervent squat and anarcho-punk scene in Italy in the late '80s. In Rome, there's this huge squat which is still active called Forte Prenestino. NoMeansNo used to come and play, as did many other Alternative Tentacles and Dischord bands. We went to see every single band, even when no one knew anything about them. It was always a big party, and as aspiring musicians, a sort of positive shock to see those bands. Despite the squat's rudimentary PA, we'd be totally blown away. NoMeansNo were already a household favourite.

**Hilary Binder** People say that "Music is a scene only if it represents a movement." This concept of a soundtrack to a social progression. I think that NoMeansNo, and the concerts in those squats at that time, were a movement, especially places that had harder fights against the system. At the time that NoMeansNo were playing in those places, it still was all pretty illegal across the board. I think that there's some energy that happens in those spaces where people really feel like they are truly self-determining. I think that when the spaces are controlled by or provided by the state, or an institution, it has all these other elements that dictate the atmosphere.

**John Wright** The only reason that first European tour succeeded was because people came out to see this band that was on Alternative Tentacles. We owe it all to the reputation of Jello Biafra and AT.

Ruth Schwartz from Mordam Records had a connection to De Konkurrent in Amsterdam, so they were able to book us four shows in Holland. The Dutch government back in the '80s sponsored a music festival every spring that was throughout the whole country. All of these youth centres and art centres would get money, and they had to book a program for

Rob, Leamington Spa, UK, 1988

four days. We got paid well for it, even though we'd never been to Europe and no one knew who the hell we were. The guarantee covered most of our airfare. We ended up being over there for four or five weeks, with shows mostly in Germany, Holland, and the UK. We also went to Ljubljana, Yugoslavia, and met Irena, who we ended up working with for many years.

We didn't totally avoid the industry, we just associated ourselves with a part of the industry that was much more real and palatable from an artistic standpoint. Of course, AT was much more political than we were, in a sense. But it was still a business. We had to sell records. You can't make records if you don't sell them. You can't book shows unless you pay someone to book them. Promoters can't put on shows unless they cover their expenses. It's still a business.

That support is hard to come by. You don't just throw it away because someone dangles some big bucks in front of you. You might lose all your friends over it. It can be that drastic, and you can't get it back. I'd rather work with people who like me and like what I do and are not just concerned with how much money they're going to make off me.

John and Andy, Leamington Spa, UK, 1988

**Rob Wright** We got a good response from audiences in Europe on that first tour. We would get up there and play, but not the standard punk rock they were used to. It was aggressive, angry music, but it wasn't three chords played sixty miles an hour, with people screaming. Hardcore was king when we went there, and I think people appreciated hearing something a lot more musical. It still had the anger, edge, heaviness, and a sense of meaning. It still fit into the milieu completely.

When people asked, "What kind of musician are you?" I always said that I'm a punk rock musician. A lot of people ended up saying, "No, no, no, I don't play punk rock." I remember Hüsker Dü in later interviews: "No, we were never really punk rock." I saw them way back when they opened for Black Flag. They were a great band, but they were the definition of a hardcore band. A lot of people wanted to move on from punk rock and be a little more legit. Me? No. This is punk rock. It's always been punk rock. It's still punk rock.

**Dolf Hermannstädter—*Trust* magazine** I met the NoMeansNo guys in 1988, the first time they came to Europe. I travelled with them on that tour, and a friendship began. I saw them just about every time they toured Germany, about eighteen times. Before I met them, I thought it was pretty awesome for a band to name their album *Sex Mad* but still not be a stupid, childish punk band.

The very first time I met them was at a restaurant on the autobahn. I was barefoot, carrying a radish in my hand. John thought that was hilarious. When I toured with them, I was always so impressed with their technical knowledge when it came to sound, and how they communicated with Craig Bougie, their sound guy. They could recognize feedback in the PA.

In Germany, it was special, because they started pretty small. They came out here as just another punk band from Canada. In the end, though, the German concerts were some of their biggest concerts in Europe, with two thousand or more people.

**"Fat" Mike Burkett—NOFX, Fat Wreck Chords** I consider NoMeansNo to be kind of the other side of the spectrum of Rich Kids on LSD. In '87 and '88, RKL were the most progressive band that played the hardest shit ever. NoMeansNo, on the other side, were more math rock, really doing quirky things. They were very important to punk rock. They made me

**NoMeansNo contract rider, 1988**

CONTRACT RIDER: NO MEANS NO

This rider is an integral part of this contract. If you cannot fulfill any of the conditions herein, you will be put on the band's shitlist. And you will be be jinxed from that day on. Strange things will happen, things will disappear. You will be overcome with sudden feelings of disorientation and panic. You will wake up at night in a cold sweat with nausea gripping your belly. Often. And then, when you least expect it, you will find yourself feeling totally insignificant, completely useless. And you will be right.

PRODUCTION:
1) We must have one hour for a soundcheck, or we will sound noisy. We are a Loud heavy rocking band. **GOOD SOUND = GREAT SHOW!**
2) We need good monitors.
3) Thank you very much.

HOSPITALITY:
1) Chances are good that you are not paying us a lot of cash, so **four hot meals** after soundcheck would be nice, or a cash equivalent (say $100. a head). (two vegetarians).
2) One case of beer, cold.
3) Thanks again.

Well, that's it. Is that too much to ask? Really?

Now you already know the consequences if you don't honor this rider. Now here's the other side - if you do fulfill this rider, guess what? Your life will improve immensely! Really! The sun will shine brighter for you, and you will be confident, self-assured. You will have all the money you ever need. Life will be truly joyful. People will be jealous of your happiness, but who cares? You will **really** be a winner, and that's all that counts!

So. The choice is yours.

Have a nice day.

PROMOTIONAL STUFF & INFO - Alternative Tentacles
c/o GARY STRASBORG 415-861-0688.

think about music differently. They made me want to be a better bass player and also made me want to write better melodies, because they didn't have a lot of good ones. RKL didn't either.

**Barry "Dalive" Ward—Rich Kids on LSD** We played with NoMeansNo somewhere in Germany in '88 or '89. It was rough to play after them. We all stayed at the same place, which was a huge backyard with teepees. Why there were Native American teepees in Germany, I don't know. We had a bonfire and drank and laughed with those guys all night.

**Andy Kerr** Those European tours, from the very beginning, were absolutely crucial. It basically meant that NoMeansNo could exist as a band and get paid. It wasn't a little holiday. It absolutely changed our view on what we could do.

**John Wright** On those first tours of the US and Europe, there was no money for hotels. You were literally just a travelling troubadour. We'd go up onstage and say, "Hey, anyone got a place for us to stay?" And if not, we slept in the van.

It was all part of the adventure. There was no aspiration, like, "Well, we have to graduate to hotels, and we need to be treated differently." The hospitality was the reward. We have friends to this day from sleeping on their floors. You don't meet anybody on a tour bus or in a hotel. The only people you meet there are industry people.

When you stay at someone's house, you get to understand the people that you're playing for,

especially in foreign countries. You get connected to where you are and become more aware of why you are there. Other bands travel all over Europe and don't know what country they're in because no one looks at a map. You might as well not leave home!

**Rob Wright** We did two Peel Sessions, and the first one was really good. The other one was really bad, and that was the end of us with John Peel. They gave us this engineer guy. He had been a drummer with Mott the Hoople. He was just a twit. He was so pompous and arrogant, so we gave him a lot of trouble. I think that got us a bad rap from the BBC.

**John Robb—the Membranes, *Louder than War* magazine** John Peel rarely went to the sessions himself at that time, because he lived a hundred miles away. Sometimes the engineers would not really have an understanding of a band's sound, and bands weren't allowed in to mix themselves. If you have a bass-driven band, you'd just get a straight rock mix,

**Robert Nichols** I hadn't heard NoMeansNo until Ian Armstrong from Meantime Records contacted me. He said he was booking a tour for this fantastic band from Canada and asked if I could book them in Middlesbrough, UK. I was music secretary for Middlesbrough Music Collective. We hosted Monday night gigs upstairs in a pub called the Empire: one pound to get in, one-hundred-person capacity. The gig was amazing; people went nuts. One song ran into another, and then they encored with a load of Ramones songs. Who else would do that? The room was heaving. It was the sort of gig people talked about for years.

where the bass would be put underneath the guitar. If the bass is playing the lead lines, you wouldn't hear them. It would have a big hole in the middle.

**Andy Kerr** I remember not enjoying the Peel Sessions. The producer was your basic rock producer guy. We were just the next time slot he had to sort out. I have heard that other bands had the same experience. Unfortunately, we never met Mr. Peel. The performances aren't bad, but we're a wee bit ragged around the edges. The mix was awful. Both times.

**John Wright** That was exciting to do. It's the kind of thing every band wants to scratch off their bucket list. The first one was funny, because we did "Body Bag" and the only issue was that they said, "Well, you can't actually say 'willy.'" Because in England, it's as bad as saying "cock."

We worked with this great engineer the first time, but the second time around we had this other engineer who was a complete fucking dickhead. He was a typical fucking snobby, stupid engineer who was more important than the job he was doing. He had to show up and record this band from Canada, and he didn't like it. It got a little tense. We were trying to be polite and just do our thing. You have to record it and mix it in one day, all in one go. I just made some comment about the snare or something, and he groaned at me. Then this old engineer showed up and kind of inserted himself in the process, and it got a bit better.

**David DaSilva—fan from Edmonton, Alberta** I was excited to score the last two tickets to a NMN gig at Bonnie Doon Hall in Edmonton. I dragged along my girlfriend, now wife, Kathy, who *really* didn't want to go. We walked up to the hall and stopped outside to talk to the only two guys out there. My bandmate Kelly said, "Hey, Kathy, are you excited to see NoMeansNo?" She exclaimed, "Oh my god, no. I *hate* NoMeansNo. They *suck*!" Then there was an immediate awkward silence. Glances were exchanged between Kelly, me, and the other guy standing there. Kathy said, "Oh shit. Are you in the band?" Andy Kerr said, "Yeah, I am. But that's okay. We do kinda suck."

CHAPTER TWELVE

# SHOW BUSINESS GIANTS

## "I need a demographic."

Victoria was churning out new bands at a frantic pace in the late 1980s. Most would end up in the dust pile of history or as an anecdote in a music blog. Some made records, while others played just a handful of live shows before imploding. The Show Business Giants were a collective of rotating musicians that became known for their unpredictable shows and quirky records. While the lineup of the Showbiz Giants ebbed and flowed, the band was always anchored by Tom Holliston, who was known as eccentric and sometimes recalcitrant. He was also hilarious and had a streak of mischief a mile wide.

### MEET TOM HOLLISTON

**Tom Holliston** We always had music in our house when I was growing up. My older brother, Robert, is a very able and excellent musician. When I was eight or nine, I had an accident, and I lost the top of my thumb. I was right handed, but I learned to write with my left hand, so I was left handed for two years. I was sort of naturally ambidextrous anyway, often doing things backwards.

Young Tom Holliston

I was becoming interested in music and wanting to buy my own records. The first record I bought was "Stop, Stop, Stop" by the Hollies, and Bobby Elliott is still one of my favourite drummers. There was an acoustic guitar in our home that I just monkeyed around with. I gradually got a little bit better. I took a few guitar lessons, but since I was playing left handed, it was very confusing for the woman who was teaching me.

When I was around fifteen or sixteen, I was getting into the blues. I had the Rolling Stones' first couple of albums, Slim Harpo, Robert Johnson, Lightnin' Hopkins. I was attracted to that kind of music. My friend Gavin said, "Oh, I know a guy who likes Robert Johnson and blues stuff too. His name's Atom." Atom Egoyan came over to my house, and he showed me how to play a couple of chords and how to do some licks. He was a really nice guy, and it turned out that my mother and his mother worked together.

**Brian "Jesus Bonehead" Whitehead** Me and Tommy Holliston were in the same homeroom at Central Junior High. He was strange even back then. The great thing about Tom is that he's very introverted until you put a mic in front of him, and then he turns into Elvis Presley.

**Tom Holliston** I didn't finish high school. There was a group of friends, about six or seven of us, who just stopped going. I went to Central and then Vic High, but I left early in the eleventh grade. I had a science teacher named Peter Gammon who was actually taking piano lessons from my brother. On the first day of class, I went up to the blackboard and wrote, "Dear Mr. Gammon, Tom's been kidnapped by aliens." Then I came back three months later and said, "Hi, Mr. Gammon, I was able to escape my alien captors." He said, "I don't think school is for you, Tom."

**Robert Holliston—brother of Tom Holliston** I'm the oldest. Then there is our sister, Margaret, Tom, and then Doug. We were all born and raised in Victoria. There was always music in our household. Our dad had quite an eclectic taste—classical, jazz, etc.—so we were always listening to music. I taught myself guitar and eventually gave it to Tom when he was in his teens. He was always interested in music too, and he was the one who turned me on to the Hollies.

Tom is the most relentlessly inquisitive musical person that I know. His taste is unbelievably wide ranging. He's a walking encyclopedia. He can remember any song that was ever on the hit list. I can mention a song that was on the radio when I was in grade eight, and Tom can remember the band name, even if it was a one-hit wonder. He also listens to Bartók and Shostakovich string quartets and certainly knows his way around jazz.

**Tom Holliston** My first band was called Pat Bay and the Malahats, around 1977–78. My friend Dan came up with the name. There was a guy named Glen Schmidt in the band, who very briefly played with the Dayglos. Glen also tried to sell Amway door to door with a self-made T-shirt that said "I Love Sid Vicious" and had a picture of Charles Manson on the front. There's Glen with a mohawk, like, "Would you like to buy some soap?"

Then there was Gary Field. Gary and I were kindred spirits. We used to buy cases of canned waxed beans. They cost twenty-nine cents each at the corner store. We'd just give them out to people, especially the jocks or the tough guys, because it would confuse them so much they'd leave us alone.

Our drummer, John, suffered a little bit with dyslexia. With Pat Bay and the Malahats, he was in charge of our graffiti. He'd put our name on the side of a wall somewhere, and with him being dyslexic, it meant that the name was always misspelled. We thought that was extremely punk rock.

I had a homemade amp that wasn't grounded, and there was an ant nest inside it. It was like a little Dave Davies–style green amp. It had a fantastic sound, but it was this tiny thing. We were practising in my parents' basement, and I accidentally touched guitars with another guy. I didn't know how serious shocks could be, and I kinda flew across the room. I didn't actually think to check on the ants. I was so discomforted that it never occurred to me. I hope the SPCA doesn't mind.

I couldn't find a lefty guitar anywhere, so I got this weird Kent guitar. I got so frustrated with it that myself and a friend cut it into small bits with a table saw, then put it in a paper bag and left it on somebody's porch. We knocked on the door and ran away.

**Steve Bailey** The first punk show I ever went to was D.O.A. at the Da Vinci Centre, and Tom's band Pat Bay and the Malahats were opening. I thought, "Oh, this is a weird dude." They were very funny, not unlike what the Show Business Giants ended up becoming. Rough and raw, they were playing for a crowd that was ready to explode. They were just holding back the floodgates for fifteen minutes. Then it was the Sikphux, and then D.O.A.

**Tom Holliston** I first heard NoMeansNo when Glen had bought the *Wormies* single. Unfortunately, he put the other side on, and I was like, "This is terrible! I don't want to hear this band, this is awful!"

The first person I think I met was John, although people used to mistake me for Andy, and Andy for me, before we even met. He lived up the road from me, so we also became friends, as we had a lot in common. I used to hang out with Robbie quite a bit because he played darts at the Beaver Pub, which was the greatest drinking establishment that ever existed in Victoria.

**Emma Lee** Tom's a quirky guy. I was housemates with Tom. One time he came into my bedroom in the morning. I'm having my coffee and I'm on my computer. He gets down on one knee and he sings me this song. It's like, "Okay, Tom, who wrote that?" He said, "It's an old Elvis Presley song that nobody ever knew." With Tom you never knew, there could always be a spark of truth in it. I used to call him the "Son of Spike," meaning Spike Milligan.

**Tom Holliston** I've always enjoyed pranks. There is the "ham in the phone" prank. It has to be one of the old rotary dial phones. You unscrew it and just put a tiny piece of meat in the microphone, the speaking side of it. After about a week or so, it'll just start manifesting itself in ways other than the olfactory. Like just a little bit of grease will emerge from the end.

If somebody was pissy, you get a can of tuna and pour the water down the front grille onto their car's motor. It'll burn off, but it will smell really bad for a while.

On a Showbiz tour, Scott Henderson and I found some medication that gets rid of crab lice. When we were staying at somebody's house, we'd always put it at the top of Ford Pier's luggage. People would walk by and say, "Oh Jesus. That guy's sleeping on my floor."

Grant Lawrence was living in West Vancouver, and in his kitchen I put on his calendar: "Thursday, 10 a.m., Grant's proctologist appointment." A week or so later, his father asked him if he was okay.

Or getting croutons and putting them on the top of a ceiling fan at a hotel. The next person staying in the room will turn the fan on, and croutons will go flying around the room. So, that kind of thing. I don't know why.

Biafra and I would talk about pranks, because he's a real ardent prankster too.

**Jello Biafra** I think it's my fault that Tom is a Heino fan. When I found out about Heino, I was weirdly fascinated by how hideous I thought his music was. Those records sound like an ABBA mix. They are a full wall of sound, with everything but the kitchen sink thrown in: children's choirs, saw noises, hula guitars, you name it. If he wants it, it's there, all round that Heino voice. Then I noticed if Heino was put on for laughs at the house, this druggie girlfriend of one of my roommates would leave for the day. The only other music I could put on to get her to leave was Venom. Then it occurred to me, part of punk is about sabotage and pranks and shocking the

Andy and Tom

shit out of people, which should include your own audience.

Everywhere Dead Kennedys played, people got the punk version of something commercial and safe over the PA in between the bands. They got Ramones, Sex Pistols, Generation X. I thought, "Okay, the punk thing to do is to force everyone to listen to at least half an hour of Heino for every one of our shows." We did that from '81 or '82 all the way to the end of the band in '86. It put audiences in the worst edgy mood. It was great.

**Carolyn Mark—musician, Show Business Giants** I recently caught Tom coming out of a laundromat with a fiendish smile on his face. He made this poster with the phone numbers you can pull off: "The Tuneless Whistling Association is going to have a meeting in the campground for fifty-five fun-filled minutes." He's still making prank posters.

**Andy Kerr** At the time, Tom and I were drinking buddies around Victoria. We asked Tom to write some nonsensical press release stuff for us. That was how W. Buzz Ryan was born.

**Tom Holliston** In 1985, I was working at the college radio station in Edmonton, which was great. NoMeansNo were coming through town, and they stayed with me because I knew them from Victoria. I read a terrible promo about them in the newspaper. None of it was true, and I thought, "I can do better." I wrote something up and showed them and they said, "Yeah, why don't you do promo for us?" That's how W. Buzz Ryan came about.

Back in Victoria, in '86 or '87, before they put out the *Small Parts* album, Greg Werckman from Alternative Tentacles got in touch with me and said, "I hear that you do stuff at the university station in Victoria [CFUV]. Why don't you do something to promote the record? Send us like a forty-five-minute tape, and we'll mix it." So I did all these interviews with them. It was great, it was so funny, like, "I read recently that you guys have an interest in Nazi Germany?" "Well, that's true, but I don't think you can necessarily equate the swastika with Nazi Germany." "No. No, you can't." There was all this bullshit stuff. They'd go on tour, and somebody would be like, "One of you is a Nazi, and you have a swastika." AT was like, "Just write this stuff, and give it to Laurie Mercer, and we'll send it to people. Just don't tell us what's in it." It was just the most obvious bullshit.

At one point, several years later, we ended up playing a festival in Estonia, and the poster said something like, "NoMeansNo, recent Grammy award winners for best video by five guys. Produced by Bill Crappelle, who has worked with Night Ranger and Jello Biafra." That information ended up getting on the radio to promote us in Estonia too.

## SHOW BUSINESS GIANTS

Members (at various times):
Tom Holliston
Steve Bailey
Marcus Pollard
Scott Henderson
Calvin Dick
Brock Ellis
Ed Dobek
Gary Field
Andy Kerr
John Wright
Ken Kempster
Chris Buck
Ford Pier
Jennye Rieper
Carolyn Mark
Craig Vishek
Keith Rose
. . . and anyone else who jumped onstage to join in

**Tom Holliston** It all started when I was watching *The Mike Douglas Show* and Shecky Greene was on. He was described as a "show business giant," and I thought, "What a great name for a band!" I learned over time that a band name should never start with an *S* because the "Miscellaneous S" section is the biggest in any record store.

I met Steve Bailey, who was in the NEOs at the time, and I already knew Marcus Pollard because I would see him around Victoria. He was a very charismatic individual and an extremely intelligent man, despite his propensity to dress like a goth.

Somehow, Steve and I decided we'd get together every Thursday and record a song on a little

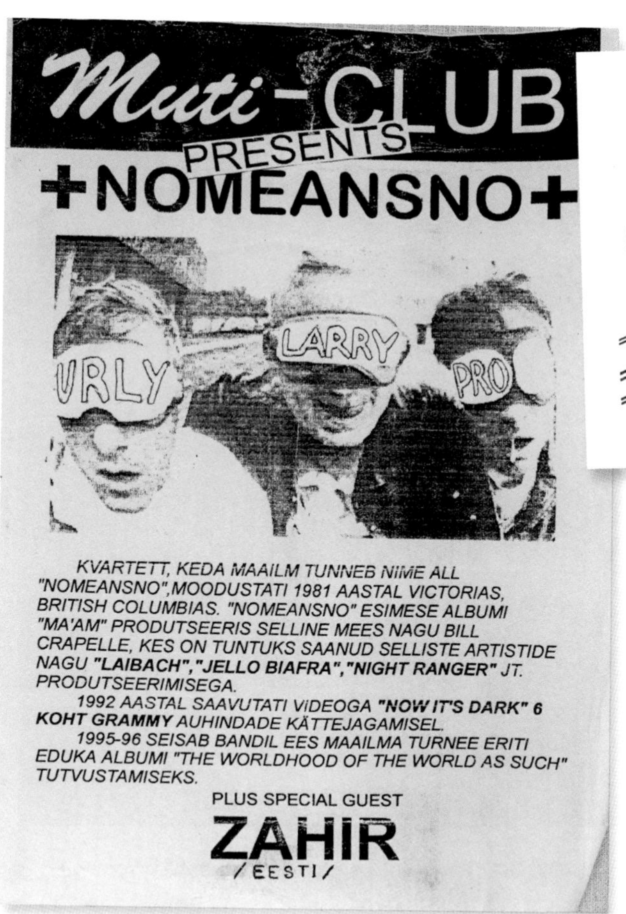

four-track gadget that Steve had. Marcus very quickly seemed the obvious person to play bass. Steve and I wrote all the material at that time, but Marcus just had a great sensibility of how songs should go.

A couple years of this, and Steve said, "Well, Scott Henderson's got a studio. Let's go make a record there!" That was 1989.

Marcus had an accident and broke his wrist rather badly, and Steve didn't really have any great aspirations about trying to take things further. Gradually, the idea was that there would always be different people in the band all the time. Whenever we had a live show, anybody was welcome to be in it, literally. It was never going to be a typical punk rock band.

**Steve Bailey** Tom and I started the Showbiz Giants. I'd seen him in Pat Bay and the Malahats but had never spoken to him, ever. He came up to me and said, "You were in the NEOs. We should play some music." I hadn't played in a while, so I said, "I'm not really playing that kind of music anymore." Tom can be persuasive, so I showed up at his parents' house with a four-track recorder and a guitar. We wrote some songs about local people; "Death of a Dayglo" was one. We started writing songs every time we got together, a lot of which ended up on the first cassette, *Gold Love*. It was around that time that John Wright and Tom became buddies.

Marcus joined, and we became a band. We started doing shows, and different people would show up and add stuff. We both had a quirky sensibility, but he's more talented. I also lived with him for a while, and sometimes I wanted to kill him. I was stunned later when he showed up in NoMeansNo.

**Tim Chan** I got to know Tom at CFUV. We got all these federal grants to employ people to do various art forms. We hired Tom to make radio plays, and he produced them for a year or so. That's how we all met Carolyn Mark, because she got involved with the radio plays too. I think she was still in high school at the time.

Ken Kempster and Carolyn Mark

Show Business Giants onstage: Jennye Rieper, Tom, Scott Henderson, and Andy

Tom started up the Show Business Giants around that time with Steve Bailey. I've known Tom for a long time, but I still don't really know him. Just a total odd duck.

**Marcus Pollard** It probably took five years for the SBG to congeal. The genesis was an impromptu set at La Hacienda. We called ourselves Dressed Up as Firetruck. Costumes, ten-plus musicians, and a version of "Bela Lugosi's Dead" updated with shout-outs to dead people. Another year or two passed before Steve, Tom, and I started jamming on our acoustic Punk Polka concept amongst the shag carpet and cedar paneling of Steve's Gordon Head basement. It seemed like a good idea at the time.

**Tom Holliston** After Marcus broke his wrist, we ended up doing this thing called Dressed Up as Firetruck. We did one other show where we claimed to be a Moody Blues tribute act called Om.

We did a show at the Fernwood Community Centre where Andy Kerr was wearing a strapless evening gown and playing guitar, and I think Steve Bailey was being painted red by Sylvia Kenny. The percussion was people hitting cardboard boxes with Sylvester Stallone hand puppets. We played about twenty minutes, and the Hanson Brothers and the Rockin' Chinamen [Eric Lowe, Tim Chan, et al.] were also on that bill.

Gradually, we did stuff with more people. Jennye played keyboard for a couple of years. Scotty, Ken Kempster, and Chris Buck from Shovlhed played as well. Andy Kerr played for about six months.

**Jennye Rieper—Abbie Hoffman Society, Show Business Giants** Tom worked at a restaurant called Rebar in downtown Victoria, and I was there having a meal. He knew who I was, just from going to gigs. He came to my table and put a cookie down in front of me and said, "There's plenty more where that came from if you play with the Show Business Giants." I was eighteen and thought, "Okay, I'll take that challenge." I showed up to the practice at Scott Henderson's place with tablas that I couldn't play, but that was what I had.

I'd just finished high school, and I'd played music in band, but it was ridiculous to be playing with them. I actually thought at first that maybe they

Show Business Giants promo photo: Ford Pier, Tom, Scott Henderson with Imru, and John

were making fun of me, like it was a hazing type thing. But I diligently stayed on, to learn how to play music. John taught me key shifts and things like that.

I'm very much in the background of the second Showbiz record, *The Benevolent Horn*, but I was much more involved in the next album, *I Thought It Was a Fig*. It was really Tom's baby, apart from NoMeansNo. I think it worked against him sometimes, because people were expecting a much different band to show up, not a quirky inside-joke band. Especially when it's multiple guys from NoMeansNo. Depending on the tour, John was there, and Andy also came along at one point. Even Rob would come along and be the opening act, as Mr. Wrong.

**Ford Pier** I was in bands in Edmonton, and I toured Canada a lot in a group called Jr. Gone Wild. I then moved to Vancouver to be in Roots Roundup. I pretty soon found myself spending all of my time in Victoria, hanging out with Tom, John, Carolyn Mark, and Scotty Henderson. Tom immediately asked me to join the Show Business Giants, so I was making music with Tom and John from '92 on.

**Tom Holliston** The best version of the band was John, Ford, Keith, Scott, and myself, because those guys can all play. We could do anything we wanted. We could stop in midbar and switch tempos, or play something else and then go back to playing the other song, but a half step lower and a little bit faster. Musicians would like us, but people in the audience would be confused.

We'd do all kinds of weird shit. It was just mainly because, "Why shouldn't we?" That was a big thing, like, "Why not have wheelbarrow races while the band plays?" Nobody else seemed to be doing that.

**Rob Wright** I loved the Showbiz Giants. They were brilliant, but Tom had a hard time finding an audience. Unless you're from Victoria at that time, you'd have no idea about the context of a lot of the songs. Tom would sing the "Nanaimo Song," which was some horrible song someone did as a promo for the city back in the day. He would encore with it. It was hilarious, but nobody knew what the hell was going on.

**Ford Pier** Tom and I had a harmony duo act called the Dalai Lamées. We wore lamé jackets and played guitars and we'd sing Show Business Giants stuff but also oddball country songs and other random stuff. We had a couple of props for this. The first was the Stool of Emphasis, which is a stool that goes between us. Neither of us sat on it, but if we had a point to

*The Benevolent Horn* cover photo outtake

make, we would beat our fists on it. We also had this wimple, or turban. These two conical turban things with a line running between them so that we were attached. If it fell off one of our heads, I would start screaming and thrashing about while Tom stood stock-still.

**Scott Henderson** We were playing in Ulm in Germany. We got to this place, and it was like a self-storage thing, way out in the fucking middle of nowhere on the outskirts. We only found it because they had hung an illuminated beer sign out in front. This place was still under construction.

The fellow who was putting the gig on was a dreadlocked man who had a dog. Always a bad sign. We set up and they spirited us into the band room, which had a tropical motif and rattan furniture. It was really strange. There were eight beer fridges against the wall, and they were full of beer. John and I went to find the bathroom, and there were all these little tiny rooms all the way down this hallway. We suddenly realized, "Wait a minute. This is a brothel!"

We gathered four of the rattan chairs, put them in front of the stage, and said to the crowd, "Now, nobody is allowed to sit in these, because members of the Norwegian royal family are coming and we want to reserve these for them. They're huge fans of the Show Business Giants." Of course, in Germany, nobody sat in the chairs because the Germans do what they're told.

Then, in the middle of a song, Tom decided to conduct a fire drill. He announced, "In the Federal Republic of Germany, every new nightclub has to conduct at least one fire drill." So we took everybody outside, and it was freezing cold. We counted the thirty or so people, and we blew the count on purpose a few times. Then Tom yelled, "Now!" and we all ran back in and finished the song. Meanwhile, all these people were standing outside: "What about the fire drill?"

**Nardwuar the Human Serviette** I love the Showbiz Giants. I love them. I love the fact that they did the song from *Star Trek* that Spock sang in the hippie episode. That is a selling point right then and there. I couldn't believe that. That nails it. Case closed. That shows how cool they were. What other band would do that?

CHAPTER THIRTEEN

# WRONG

## "Only so many songs can be sung with two lips, two lungs, and one tongue."

Things could not have turned out better for NoMeansNo on their first European tour, especially in terms of finding a new and dedicated audience. They performed primarily at squats and all-ages venues. They kept their ticket prices low. These three bespectacled Canadian nerds had made quite the impression and were now perceived as the real deal.

They came back home completely inspired by the experience overseas. While they kept their respective day jobs, it was becoming apparent to the band and their friends that NoMeansNo was on the cusp of becoming a full-time gig.

Their reputation as a killer live band with a powerful message was resonating with fans. Professionally, they were known as a convivial and reliable band to work with. Friendships were forged not only with other bands and their fans, but with the booking networks in the US and Europe. People just liked these guys.

Within the next two years, it was tour after album after tour. Just a few months shy of the new decade, NoMeansNo would release an album that would permanently cement their place in punk rock history.

**Sam Dunn** I think that NoMeansNo are truly iconoclastic, in the sense that they sort of turn everything on its head. They are just fucking with you a little bit, and you don't know whether they're serious or not. I think that is the beautiful thing about NoMeansNo.

**John Wright** My family has always been super funny. My sister Shannon is hilarious, and my dad was always very funny. I suppose it's the Irish background a bit. Canadians often make good comedians.

I grew up on all that '70s comedy, Monty Python, Steve Martin, and all those comedians. I watched Johnny Carson all the time, and *Saturday Night Live*. I've always been goofy all my life. Bill Cosby was another one. Of course, he's persona non grata now, but he was a huge influence, comedywise. To this day, my sister still quotes stuff from *To Russell, My Brother, Whom I Slept With*. Rob was a big fan of the Firesign Theatre; he had all the records, and I listened to them too.

**Tom Holliston** Robbie used to take pot when he was a twenty-year-old man and listen to the Firesign Theatre a lot.

**Rob Wright** I loved the Firesign Theatre. "Seekers! I too was fooled by that Venetian gas music." I remember tons of it. I always go, "Holy Mudhead, mackerel!" and of course, "Could be, Seekers, could be." I love that one. I use that one all the time.

**Andy Kerr** Rob, John, and Scott Henderson turned me on to those folks in the Firesign Theatre early on. Firesign fans find it routine to use obscure quotes in their day-to-day conversations with almost anybody. The Firesign canon of comedy records is generally accepted to be *Don't Crush That Dwarf, Hand Me the Pliers*, *We're All Bozos on This Bus*, *The Further Adventures of Nick Danger*, and of course *Everything You Know Is Wrong*.

**Doug Kerr** The whole Kerr family were Python fans. I was big-time into George Carlin, National Lampoon's Lemmings, and Cheech and Chong. Andy and I would laugh a lot at the "Dave's not here" sketch. It was Andy who introduced me to Steve Martin. Andy was always a card. Even when he was young, he would crack up my sister and I at the dinner table with his funny faces.

**John Wright** Often a message gets through if it's accompanied by humour. Humour opens people's minds so that it's easier to deal with stuff that's not so pleasant. People joke at funerals. It's just humans' natural way of coping with stress. The levity of humour keeps your spirits up.

**Alternative Tentacles press release, 1989**

CHECK YOUR PERSONAL RECORD LIBRARY FOR THE ENTIRE NOMEANSNO BACK CATALOG:

| | | |
|---|---|---|
| 1. ESCROW FOR (WHIPPED) CREAM | TUMNUS RECORDS | 1967 |
| 2. UNDER THE MEAT PASTE | SIMBIOSIS RECS. | 1968 |
| 3. ABEDNAGE THE INVINCABLE | COSMIC - ? | 1970 |
| 4. FUCK SHIT CUNT *never issued | | 1970 |
| 5. LIVING ON FRESCA, FOR NOW... | STEREOTYPE | 1972 |
| 6. HOBBY FARM ON THE EDGE OF THE WORLD | STEREOTYPE | 1973 |
| 7. MY MOM TEACHES SCOTTISH DANCING | ARCHIE GRIFFIN RECS. | 1974 |
| 8. I'LL START | DIBBS COUNTY | 1975 |
| 9. NOMEANSNO SALUTE HERSCHEL BERNARDI | CALSTER | 1977 |
| 10. FACTS ABOUT TROY OUNCE | CALSTER | 1979 |
| 11. THE GREAT UNWATCHED. (1973-1978) | KRAATZ | 1980 |
| 12. I SNIFF WATERCRESS FOR KICKS | CALSTER | 1981 |
| 13. MAMA- NOMEANSNO PLAY HIENTJE | CARYBDIS | 1982 |
| 14. BEIGE FROTH | VERDANT | 1982 |
| 15. YOU KILL ME | ZULU | 1984 |
| 16. I COUNT THE SLIP KNOTS | ZOO-LOO | 1985 |
| 17. L.P. ONLY (cassette only) | STANSHALL | 1985 |
| 18. SEX MAP | ALT. TENTACLES | 1986 |
| 19. MEET ME AT THE MORASS | ALT. TENTACLES | 1987 |
| 20. OUR BODIES, OURSELVES (live import only) | PLAIN YOGHURT | 1988 |
| 21. THE DAY EVERYTHING BECAME NOTHING | ALT. TENTACLES | 1988 |
| 22. SMALL PARTS ISOLATED AND DESTROYED | ALT. TENTACLES | 1988 |

ROB WRIGHT SOLO RECORDS:

| | | |
|---|---|---|
| 1. ALL CHILDREN ARE BORN PYGMIES AND WHEN THEY GROW UP THE WORLD MAKES THEM BAD PEOPLE | COSMIC-? | 1969 |
| 2. THINGS WE DO WITH OUR SHOE | DIBBS COUNTY | 1974 |
| 3. WHAT? NO MINTS? | ALLIGATORADE | 1982 |
| 4. ROB WRIGHT PRESENTS THE MUSICAL STILTS OF BOLIVIA | NISHVAULT | 1989 |

It's not so much that we intended to be comedians or intended to be funny. When we played music, we were just being ourselves, and that included joking around. Playing music is fun and playing shows is fun, so humour always played a big part in that. We never really took ourselves seriously. If all you have is really heavy, depressing messages, then it just takes the fun out of it after a while.

**John van Luyn—promoter** NoMeansNo first played the Melkweg club in Amsterdam in 1989. I had seen them the previous year at the Tivoli in Utrecht.

It was sometimes hard to tell how many tickets would sell for a particular gig. It was important to know, of course, so that enough people would be hired for the bar and everything. When we were booking NoMeansNo for the Melkweg, we had a meeting, and I said I thought it was going to sell out. The Melkweg holds about seven hundred people. My director said, "Well, I appreciate that you like the band, but aren't you being a bit too energetic?" I said, "No, no, I think it will be sold out," and he said, "Well, so far, we've not even sold fifty tickets, and the show is in two days."

He wasn't there on the night of the show, but he called me and he asked me how many tickets were sold, and I said, "It's sold out." At first, he thought I was joking. From that moment on, he took my predictions much more seriously.

**John Wright** I'm pretty sure the longest show that we ever performed was on our second European tour, in 1989. It was a squatted show in Amsterdam, and we played for about two hours and then got an encore. We just said, "Fuck it," and just kept playing and playing, for over three hours.

**Ingrid Kerr** We went to Yugoslavia. We drove up, and there were rows of people in front of the venue waiting to get in. We didn't know what we were seeing. It was just insane. Pop music had been forbidden in Yugoslavia up until 1985. We were just a few years after that, so people were hungry. Same in Poland. It was just rows and rows of people. We had to bribe the border officials with booze to let us into Poland that first time.

We went to Northern Ireland as well. I remember sitting in the van, and we had this tank coming toward us: "Okay, this is still not very safe here." I was more scared in Northern Ireland than I was in East Germany.

Travelling with John and Rob was good, because they were Mr. Easy. They never panicked. Not in Germany, not in Ireland, not in Poland.

**Arek Marczyński—promoter** I refused to do military service in communist Poland and decided to go to Holland and ask for political asylum there. I was friends with Jos and Luc from the Ex, who were working at De Konkurrent. I started to do some bookings through them. NoMeansNo came over for their '89 European tour, so I jumped in the van and went with them.

I booked their first-ever show in Poland that year and an illegal one in East Berlin. That was just before the Berlin Wall came down. All of the illegal punk shows took place in church-owned places. Besides NoMeansNo, we also did False Prophets, Soulside, and more. Not many bands came to Eastern European countries at the time. NoMeansNo became a legend, playing here on every tour since, and I ended up working with them for many years.

**Simon Wells—Snuff** The first time I met Arek was in a West Berlin café. The Konk used to have a thing about going to places like Poland and Eastern Europe. They saw it as a cultural mission. No one would earn any money. It was bringing our Western culture to the East.

We were touring in Yugoslavia the week the war broke out. At the old theatre we were playing at, I found this giant wad of banknotes. It was 250,000 zlotys. I thought, "Oh my god, I'm rich!" I showed it to

**Warsaw, May 25, 1990:**
***Live in Warsaw* recording**

John at the Berlin Wall

East Berlin gig, 1989

our Yugoslavian promoter, and she said, "Yeah, you can't even buy a can of Coke with that." That was because of the inflation in the country just before the war.

**Johnny Temple—Soulside, Girls Against Boys** My band Soulside was getting booked to tour Europe through Hetty and Konkurrent, so we were part of that extended punk family. Dolf in Germany helped book some German shows for us and NoMeansNo too.

We were the first American band to play in East Berlin, and I guess NoMeansNo would be the first Canadian band to do that. We travelled in similar circuits as NMN and had a lot of common friends with them. We snuck across the border without instruments, and it was an amazing experience. That East Berlin gig was particularly intense because it was actually illegal to do.

**Ingrid Severson** Besides the many North American tours I did, I only went overseas with NoMeansNo once, on the 1989 European tour. I remember going through Checkpoint Charlie to play in the basement of a church in East Berlin.

**Ingrid Kerr** I had a contact in West Berlin, and in turn he had a contact in East Berlin. Groups of tourists weren't allowed in East Berlin, so we all had to pretend not to know each other. We had to go through the Metro to East Germany not looking at each other. We couldn't bring anything with us. No bags, no guitars, no drums, no nothing. Just a wallet and your smile.

The gig was in a church. The show was in the cellar, so it was literally underground music. We found out later that this was a resistance church, helping young people out. They had all kinds of gigs in their cellar.

There was one little light from the ceiling, and there was this kid's drum kit. John said, "Okay, I guess I gotta play on this." There was one mic. Andy was given a guitar, and there was one amp for the bass. John sitting on the child's drum set was just hilarious!

**Craig Bougie** We went over as tourists, and we borrowed the gear that they had there, which was not up to snuff. But we made it work. That was a crazy show. There weren't a lot of people there, but they just fucking loved it.

Once again, the border cops were interested in me. They always were. The boys looked like they could be dentists, but I looked like somebody who wanted to be a rock star.

**John Wright** It was basically the one place the East German police wouldn't raid. They stayed away from the churches. We had to go over with just our passports and some money. No instruments, nothing.

We get to the church basement and there's the instruments they had for us. This tiny drum set, and no two sticks matched. There was one cymbal—thank god it was a high hat. There was a bass. It had four strings but only three tuning heads. It was really basic gear. Thankfully, one of the Germans who came over knew that there would be nothing, so he smuggled in a distortion pedal to plug the guitar into.

We played our show, and they were all super happy. It was all in the afternoon too. We went over around noon, the show was at three p.m., and we were back by five.

**Rob Wright** It was the greatest thing. The church was helping these people because they were subversive. We played on the most terrible instruments. I had to tune the bass with a screwdriver because it had no pegs, and the strap brought it up to my chest.

They had a little drinking area that we sat down in. I looked up and there's a poster on the wall: "DRI Live at the Rats Nest in Victoria." "What?!" You think you've gone so far, and yet you're just in the same place you always were.

**John Wright** We sat down for some beers and some snacks before the show. They had a bunch of posters on the wall to make it look like a club. We were sitting there, and there's a poster from the Rats Nest! We're in the fucking basement of a church in East fucking Berlin, and there's a poster of our practice space. Turns out Gary Brainless was pen pals with one of the people at the venue.

We picked up a couple of last-minute extra shows around Berlin too. We played Ex, which was a famous punk rock squat in Kreuzberg. There were tons of people, great reaction. There was some demonstration going on, and they asked, "Do you want to come and play at the demonstration?" We ended up playing on the back of a flatbed trailer. We didn't even know what the demonstration was all about! They were like, "Fucking cool, you guys were great, thanks for playing." Getting on good terms with the Berliners!

**Dory Carter** I'm still connected to Andy because he and Ingrid and my mom [Emma Lee] are super close. My mom visits him every year. We went to Paris for four days. We were at this tiny café where the owner didn't speak any English. He went outside to grab this person who could translate. This guy said, "Where are you guys from?" "We're from Victoria." He said, "Are you kidding? My favourite band in the world is from Victoria! They're called NoMeansNo."

My ex said, "We literally just visited Andy Kerr in Amsterdam!" The guy completely freaked out and told everybody outside, "Oh my god, these people know NoMeansNo!"

He told us, "If it wasn't for NoMeansNo, I would have never played music. I saw them in Berlin before the wall came down. They played there in the basement of a church. Nobody was doing what they were doing, and they blew my mind completely. That's why I started to play music."

**Jacob Warneke—fan from Berlin, Germany** It was illegal for them to play in East Berlin. They could only cross on a one-day tourist visa. I was one of the organizers. All we had was shitty East German stuff, but somehow they did it. After the wall came down, the owner of that lousy drum kit died of a drug overdose. He was the first drug victim in the new "free" Germany. We played "Small Parts Isolated and Destroyed" very loudly at his funeral.

**John Wright** There's an interesting end to that story. It comes years later at a festival in Czech Republic. This guy was working with us, and he said, "Hey, I was at that show you did in East Berlin. People were so happy that you came. Someone could go to prison for two years for putting on rock shows back then." He knew that to get the tourist visas, it cost us five Deutschmarks each. He gave us all five euros and said, "I'm giving you this because I am so embarrassed that my country charged you money to come in and play that show. That was just wrong." He handed us the money, and it was so surreal.

This was a music scene that wasn't about popularity. It wasn't about image. It was people doing things and trying to create this scene around them

that was a real alternative to what went on in the industry. It really, really meant something to them. I think what a lot of bands don't quite understand is what an honour it is to come into somebody's life and do something that means so much to them. This is why I have no time for bands that are, "Well, what's on the rider?"

**Andy Kerr** We didn't want to be *that* band. We didn't want to be known as, "Oh, them. They're a great band, but the keyboard player is a jerk," or, "They tore up the hotel room," or, "They stormed offstage." It was the absolute last thing that we wanted to be. We also wanted to be as honest as we could be. It was really important to us, because we saw other bands do the same thing. Bands like the Minutemen. Mike Watt saying, "What band wouldn't want to set up its own equipment? What possible reason would you have not to do that?"

**Mike Watt** Minutemen never got a chance to play with NoMeansNo, but we knew of them. D. Boon

Andy at the back of the tour van, Lyon, France, 1990

was a big fan, but NMN hadn't come down here yet. In some ways, we felt really a kindred spirit to them without even knowing them as dudes.

Our opinion was that you were supposed to bring something original if you want to be part of this thing. Bands didn't need to sound like each other. You're all on the same boat, but you're not clones, rubber-stamped, cookie-cutter versions of each other. NoMeansNo were their own band.

**Rob Wright** For us, it was always strictly about the music, playing it and recording it. We managed somehow to avoid the egos and side issues, the business of music, and the business of being "somebody."

As soon as you get personalities mixed up, it becomes something other than music. It becomes a part of your persona. You see it all the time with famous people. It ends up basically destroying them, and they become a caricature of themselves.

I soon learned that whatever you are in the moment is just what you should put out there. If people are touched by what you do, it's because you're being real. Whether that's nice or not doesn't really matter, because people respond to it.

**Lee Hobson Hollis—Spermbirds, 2Bad, Steakknife** My band 2Bad played a bunch of shows with NoMeansNo in Germany. They stayed at our place in Homburg, and they were the funniest motherfuckers I've ever met. The next day when we got up and had breakfast, they washed all of the dishes. I was just, "What? Why are you washing dishes?" They were *that* friendly. It was the first time I'd ever seen that. Subsequently, I was pissed at every band that stayed at our house and didn't wash the dishes!

**Duncan Redmonds—Snuff** It was common for bands to sleep the night either at the club, the promoter's house, or at someone's flat. NoMeansNo got a reputation quickly that if they stayed at your house, they would leave the house tidier than they found it. They'd hoover up and put everything back and polish the windows. They worked out how to survive around Europe with a van, a cool crew, and cool attitudes.

**Ford Pier** NoMeansNo would usually stay with the promoters and friends they had made over the years, rather than at a hotel. That was one of their major cost-saving strategies. Once you know somebody whom you like, and they have a place where you are welcome, then *that's* where you stay. The more you treat that place and that host with respect, the more likely you are welcome to go back, for the better part of a week maybe, if it's a cluster of shows. You aren't paying for hotels or placing yourself in danger of going home with the wrong people.

I think it's also important to note how NoMeansNo were part of an original group of bands in the mid-'80s who helped establish the European booking network, which persists to this day as the mainstream over there. That didn't exist before those guys and bands like BGK, Negazione, and Fugazi that went and did those tours. Their story weaves its way between so many other important players, and they were witness to so many important developments. They were the first job that a lot of those people had. Somebody who is going to be putting on Santana in Munich today did his first show booking NoMeansNo in Augsburg.

**Laurie Mercer** I had D.O.A. and NoMeansNo on tour simultaneously in Europe in different places. Like a rock star, I'd fly back and forth, just to be with the bands for a bit. I flew from Berlin, where D.O.A. was playing, to Northern Ireland to see NoMeansNo play Belfast.

It was at the Belfast show that I truly realized what NoMeansNo meant to people. They were playing, and they were just fantastic. I'm standing beside the stage, and they start playing "Victory." A boy of maybe eighteen or nineteen years old pushes to the front, and he's horribly disfigured. He's obviously been hurt in a bomb blast. He's got one stump, and half his face is fucked. While they're singing "Victory," this kid wept and screamed at the top of his lungs. This song was obviously of enormous power and value to him. It was one of the most powerful things I have ever seen.

**Nick Evans** When I was about twenty, I moved to Leeds and became a kind of anarcho-squatter. We were all vegan Crass fans, and we ran an advisory service for squatters. I started putting on concerts at a venue in the city centre called the Duchess

of York. The collective was called Flame in Hand Productions.

We put on a lot of Dischord and Alternative Tentacles bands. I think the first tour I booked was NoMeansNo, but I also did a couple of tours for Alice Donut. I ran the whole thing from my bedroom.

Then I met their manager, Laurie Mercer, who came over. I was trying to be professional, but I was really just a punky guy in the bedroom of the squat. They were incredibly gracious to me, all the while very much aware that I was not a professional booking agent.

I would travel with them and be responsible for trying to get press and radio things to happen. I remember sitting for hours with them on those long drives. Rob in particular was a very loving guy. He wouldn't just talk about the band, or T-shirt sales, or getting to the next gig. He would really take an interest in my life.

**Andy Kerr** For *Sex Mad*, our goal was to get the songs recorded in as short amount of time as possible. Whereas later with *Small Parts*, we wanted *every* song to sound different than the song that came before it. Then for *Wrong*, we thought, "Okay, we want the whole album to have a unified sound." Bass on one side, guitar on the other side, not as extreme as the Ramones, but something really straightforward. As few overdubs as possible. A straight punk rock sound. We actually thought consciously about that. Of course, we didn't always know what we were doing. I think the sound of *Wrong* comes down to Cecil and John doing their magic. A lot of it was dumb luck too.

**Craig Bougie** I was hanging around the studio with them, starting with *Sex Mad*, but I feel that the record where I had the most input was *Wrong*. I was convinced that we had to do a Buzzcocks kind of thing. All "hits" from beginning to end. Let's not fuck around. We don't need these moody songs. Let's just dig in and make it a super-rocking record and try to keep the sound consistent throughout. It was John who always wanted to change the sound in every song. Rob just wanted everything loud, basically.

Cecil was great. He gave us the opportunity and gave us good deals, and he liked working with us. We were working late nights again because it was cheaper.

**Cecil English** In the case of *Wrong*, they came in with a completed eight-track recording. It was so good, they could have just released that.

**Andy Kerr** I wrote three of the songs on *Wrong*: "Tired of Waiting," "Stocktaking," and "Two Lips, Two Lungs and One Tongue."

There was a sense that the relationships we were all in were getting strained. We were away so frequently and for so long that it became, "It would be nice if we actually did something together, and it wasn't just all about the band." That's what "Tired of Waiting" is all about. We didn't have any sort of bad feelings toward each other, but you know, it really is this fine line between biding your time and wasting your time. At a certain point, you say, "This isn't worth it. You're a wonderful person, but really, this waiting around is not doing it for me anymore."

Its partner song, "Stocktaking," is about the same subject. They are two halves of the same thing. "Stocktaking" is about literally taking stock of your situation and going, "When does too little become too much?" In other words, too little in a relationship. It overwhelms you and you go, "This isn't worth it anymore."

With "Two Lips," I liked the idea of breaking up what is actually a traditional punk rock song with a sort of utterly minimal solo. I liked messing with stuff like that. It helped that I was also hanging around Tom a lot at that point, but it also goes back to stuff I did with Infamous Scientists.

I think it's quite beautiful on the record. Playing it live, it took on a whole life of its own because I started telling stories, or we'd go into other songs. It just became this sort of gag, a way to kind of yank the audience's chain, as you can hear on *Live and Cuddly*.

**Rob Wright** Andy was always quite timorous in terms of putting his material forward. He was definitely getting more confident by the time we were doing *Wrong*, but I don't think he quite had exactly anything in mind to talk about. Obviously, I did. I was always pretty sure of what I was trying to say.

**Andy Kerr** John was a great arranger of his own songs. He'd play a demo with keyboards and drum machine stuff, and I'd think, "Errr . . . I dunno." Then we'd play it with all our instruments, and it was always like, "Wow!" He'd say, "Yeah, I always hear the guitars in my head." He was great to work out a song with and was open to anything. Except the end of "Stocktaking," which he thought ended too soon.

**John Wright** With *Wrong*, we began to sound like ourselves on record. Those first records have very odd sounds to them. They're all different because we were fishing around for production ideas. A good producer has an objective ear. We were so mixed up in the writing and performing that it was sometimes difficult to have an objective view of what sounds good and what doesn't. It's easy to get caught up in minutiae.

It took us years and years to finally be able to produce ourselves. I think the records got better as they went along. *Sex Mad* has a very odd sound to it. *Small Parts* was a huge production job and over the top, but the saving grace was that the performances were all pretty good.

By the time we got to *Wrong*, we were like, "Okay, we're not going to play around, we just want everything to be as accurately reproduced as possible." That's the approach we took. Not only were they fully formed songs and well seasoned live, but this time we had a very straightforward approach to the recording. Everything kind of came together on that record.

It came out exactly at the right time, because we were gaining an audience. The other albums were odd, but everyone liked the live show. Then *Wrong* came out, and it was like, "Oh, here it is. That's the album! This is the band that I saw live." That's why it remains our most popular and well-known album. It was kind of quintessential in a way.

**Rob Wright** I think *Wrong* was more hardcore than is representative of what we did up until then, and after.

**Andy Kerr** Although we had Cecil there, we never hired a

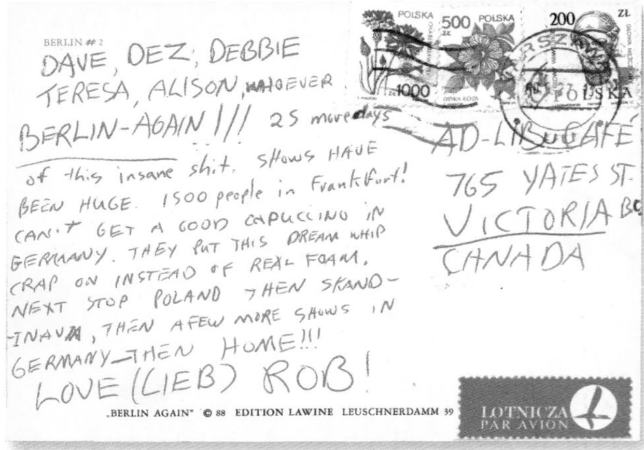

BERLIN #2

DAVE, DEZ, DEBBIE
TERESA, ALISON, WHOEVER
BERLIN-AGAIN!!! 25 more days
of this insane shit. Shows have
been huge. 1500 people in Frankfurt!
Can't get a good capuccino in
Germany. They put this dream whip
crap on instead of real foam.
Next stop Poland then Skand-
inavia, then a few more shows in
Germany—then home!!!
LOVE (LIEB) ROB!

AD-LIB CAFE
765 YATES ST.
VICTORIA BC
CANADA

"BERLIN AGAIN" © 88 EDITION LAWINE LEUSCHNERDAMM 39

LOTNICZA PAR AVION

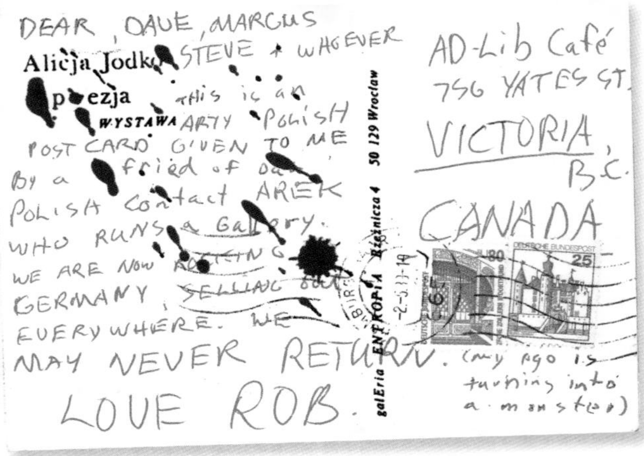

DEAR, DAVE, MARCUS
STEVE + WHOEVER
THIS IS AN
ARTY POLISH
POST CARD GIVEN TO ME
BY A FRIEND OF OUR
POLISH CONTACT AREK
WHO RUNS A GALLERY.
WE ARE NOW ~~ROTTING~~ IN
GERMANY, ~~SELLING OUT~~
EVERYWHERE. WE
MAY NEVER RETURN. (my ego is
turning into
a monster)
LOVE ROB.

Alicja Jodko
poezja
WYSTAWA

galEria ENTROPIA Rzeźnicza 4 50 129 Wrocław

AD-Lib Café
756 YATES ST.
VICTORIA,
B.C.
CANADA

**Rob's postcards to the Ad Lib café**

big, expensive producer. That was partly because we just simply wanted to do it ourselves. Because if we fucked up, then *we* were the ones who fucked up. We didn't want to risk paying some hotshot producer an arm and a leg and then end up with an album that sounds like shit.

**Brian "Jesus Bonehead" Whitehead** The Ad Lib café in Victoria was owned by David Bruce, who did the cover photos for *Wrong* and *0 + 2 = 1*. The Wright brothers worked there at the time. After they went to Europe and got huge, I got their job. The staff were all artists and musicians. David would let us go out on tours, and then we'd still have a job waiting for us when we got back. He was very flexible and cool.

**Rob Wright** I have a feeling the album title was basically an offshoot of the slogan "Be Strong, Be Wrong," which I think was going to be used for a poster or some graphics. *Wrong* ended up being a natural title for that record. I don't even remember who came up with the slogan. I'm assuming it's me, because I assume that everything that happened in the band was my doing, but it might have been Andy. Of course, there's the play on words with *right/Wright* and *Wrong*.

**Tom Holliston** Andy and I were roommates in Victoria when he was assembling the cover for *Wrong*.

**Andy Kerr** For the *Wrong* cover, I thought, "Let's blow up these half-tone pictures of the three of us." I was kind of inspired by the first Public Image Ltd. album. I drew out the word *Wrong* and took John's old, great NOMEANSNO logo, with the letters switching between black and white. We just messed around with that and added colours. I did a really rough version using red and black felt pens. I cut out the heads of the three of us from a blown-up version of it, and then showed it to Rob and John, who said, "That looks cool."

**John Yates** Andy had most of the direction when it came to the *Wrong* cover. For my aesthetic, I like much simpler designs. When I do my own graphic design, I tend to work in one to two colours at the most, so I really liked the stark simplicity of that one. I don't even

DEC. 4/88
- GOT UP LATE. DEBORAH DIDN'T WAKE ME UP TO SAY GOODBYE. SHE'S OFF TO EUROPE FOR A FEW MONTHS.
- BREAKFAST AT SCOTT'S. LOUSY SERVICE NO TIP. THEN ON TO AD LIB FOR N.M.N. PROMO SHOOT W/ DAVID BRUCE (ONE OF THE MORE KIND INDIVIDUALS I HAVE EVER KNOWN). JOHN DRESSED AS A PUNK ROCK GORILLA, I AS A COW AND ROB AS A COP-NAZI-PRIEST-LAWYER. PART 2 IN A SERIES HOPEFULLY. JOHN SUGGESTED FUTURE PHOTO: HIMSELF AND ROB + A HEAP OF LIMBS + BODY PARTS ON THE FLOOR UNDER THE TITLE "ROB, JOHN AND SOME OF ANDY".
- TOM FINISHED TAPE. CALLED N.M.N. UNMITIGATED BASTARDS ON IT. WHAT A SWEETHEART.

**Andy's diary entry about the David Bruce photo shoot, 1988**

think I got photographs; they just sent these photocopies. Andy had hand-drawn the large red *Wrong*.

**Carolyn Mark** I worked at the Armadillo Diner in '88–89 with both Rob and Andy. I also worked at the Ad Lib café with Rob and John. Bonehead from the Dayglos also worked there as a dishwasher and used to steal my tips, although he still denies it. This was before *Wrong* came out.

*Wrong* was a bit polarizing, because a lot of the Victoria punks thought NoMeansNo had sold out because of the good production. They liked the earlier, more obscure stuff better.

I remember later on, the guys came to Ad Lib and were sitting there doing their taxes. I was like, "Oh, okay. They've moved up a layer."

**Sylvia Kenny** I still have a book of poems that Andy gave to me, and it contains some original lyrics for songs that ended up being on *Wrong*.

**Gary Brainless** I never got confirmation, but I'm pretty sure the song "Brainless Wonder" was written about me. Andy said to me, "Remember that time you came into the house screaming, '*Feed me lunch!*' like a robot?" I didn't even know anyone was in the house at that time.

**John Wright** It's not necessarily directly *about* Gary, it's just part and parcel of all the people we were around, him included. The whole way "Brainless Wonder" starts is a rip-off of a Victims Family song. The song is about absolutely fucking nothing, but it's really, really hard to play. I can't even play it anymore.

**Bruno St. Martin** I had gotten myself into a little bit too much shit at one point and ended up getting incarcerated. I spent four or five months at a prison near Victoria called William Head. The NoMeansNo guys were on my "guest list" in jail and would come and see me once a week. We'd just sit and chat for like half an hour. During one visit, they said, "Hey, we

A Bunch Of Things

By Andy Kerr

For
Sylvia Kenny

two lips, two lungs, one tongue

he kept trying
he kept trying
but he couldn't find out
why he couldn't stop crying

only so many songs can be sung
with two lips, two lungs and one tongue

she kept praying
she kept praying
that he would understand
what she was saying

only so many songs can be sung
with two lips, two lungs and one tongue

he kept dreaming
he kept dreaming
of the day they'd realize
what he was feeling

only so many songs can be sung
with two lips, two lungs and one tongue

tired of waiting

tired, tired, tired of waiting
i got tired, tired, tired of waiting
i got tired, tired, tired of waiting
i got tired, tired, tired of waiting

tired of waiting, waiting for news
tired of waiting for things to improve
tired of waiting, waiting for a letter
tired of waiting for things to get better

i got tired, tired, tired of waiting (x4)

tired of waiting, waiting by the phone
tired of waiting here all alone
tired of waiting for something new
i got tired of waiting for you

i got tired, tired, tired of waiting (x4)

tired of waiting, waiting in line
tired of waiting for my clothes to dry
tired of waiting for the show to begin
tired of waiting for my ship to come in
tired of waiting, waiting for the bus
tired of waiting for my shoes to get fixed
tired of waiting, waiting for my cheque
tired of waiting for a change in the weather
tired of waiting for water to boil
tired of waiting for the paint to dry
tired of waiting, waiting for a sign
tired of waiting for my big break
tired of waiting for the dam to break
tired of waiting for the bomb to drop
tired of waiting and waiting and waiting
i got tired of waiting for the end

i got tired of waiting because i found out
that there's only a fine line between
biding one's time and wasting one's time
you know what i mean?

i got tired of waiting, that's all.

Andy on bass

1990 *Melody Maker* photo shoot

wrote a song about you! It's called 'Oh No! Bruno!' We thought it might lift your spirits when you get out."

When I finally heard it, I thought it was hilarious. We used to go to the Beaver Pub and play darts and cribbage, and they sang about that in the song. We'd play for Steinlager beers, the big bottles they had at the Beaver. Over the years, I've had a few people ask me if I'm *the* Bruno from "Oh No! Bruno!" Yep.

**Andy Kerr** "The End of All Things" was the only song in which Rob and I switched instruments when playing it live.

**Mark Critchley—Itch** I am credited as "Mark Critchley—Bells" on "All Lies." You can hear them if you really listen. It kind of fattens out the sound. I did that with my sampler, sort of a tubular bells kinda thing.

**Andy Kerr** It was not at all unusual for NoMeansNo songs to hang around a long, long time before being recorded. "Predators," for example, was around since the mid-'80s, and recorded twice, before being finally put out on the *Worldhood* LP after I'd left the band.

"Be Strong, Be Wrong" references a lyric in the song "I Am Wrong," which I think was written and demoed by Robbie when he lived on Foul Bay Road around 1984. I don't remember why it wasn't recorded for anything before *Wrong*. At a certain point, a song had been baked long enough and needed to be taken out of the oven. You hear about bands booking studio time and then writing in the studio. That was not our modus operandi, at least not while I was in the band.

**Rob Wright** "Rags and Bones" was a song that we definitely overplayed over the years, but we never got

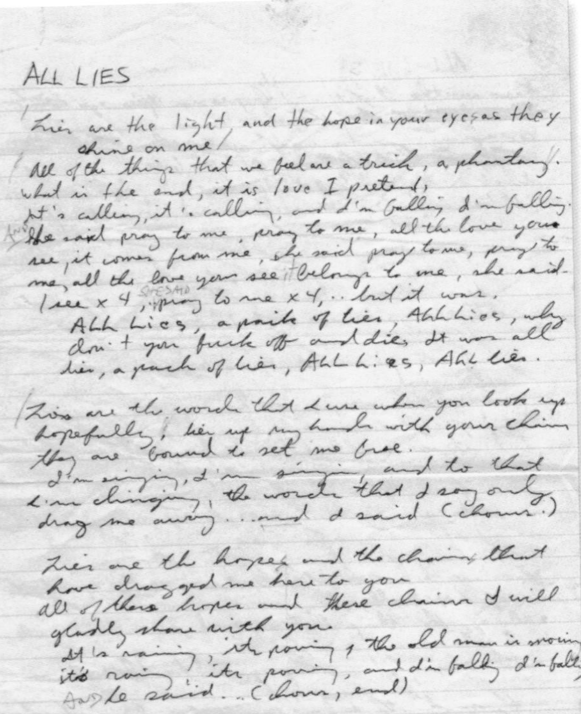

ALL LIES

Lies are the light, and the hope in your eyes as they
shine on me/
All of the things that we feel are a trick, a phantasy.
what in the end, it is love I pretend,
It's calling, it's calling, and I'm falling I'm falling.
And she said pray to me, pray to me, all the love you
see, it comes from me, she said pray to me, pray to
me, all the love you see it belongs to me, she said
I see x 4, she said pray to me x 4, .. but it was,
All Lies, a pack of lies, All Lies, why
don't you fuck off and die, It was all
lies, a pack of lies, All Lies, All lies.

Lies are the words that I use when you look up
hopefully, lies up my hands with your chains
they are bound to set me free.
I'm singing, I'm singing, and to that
I'm clinging, the words that I say only
drag me away... and I said (chorus.)

Lies are the hopes and the chains that
have dragged me here to you
All of these hopes and these chains I will
gladly share with you.
It's raining, it's pouring, the old man is snoring
it's raining, it's pouring, and I'm falling I'm falling,
And he said... (chorus, end)

"All Lies" original lyrics

Leeds, UK, 1989

tired of it. It was probably the most prominent, if you want to put a hierarchy of songs.

**China Miéville—author** I don't know very much about the guys, but it's remarkable to me how many references there are on that album to faith and the sublime and so on. There are lines like, "If I could choose to believe or not to believe / You know I would choose not to / But I can't choose." I have recited that line to myself so many times over the years. It feels like religious music to me. I have no idea if they're religious or not. It doesn't matter one way or the other. That sense of yearning for something bigger.

Lines like, "Christ was married on the cross / My father was married to my mother," and then, "I am married to a cigarette butt, lying in the gutter." To me, this is like the whole tradition of gutter theology, like a kind of radical Christianity. I'm not projecting that onto these guys; this isn't about what they mean it to be about. But to me, that sense of the dirty holiness of the everyday. They express that in a way that blows me away. And that fucking bass line in "Rags and Bones." I mean, Jesus Christ, what are you gonna do? It's untouchable.

**Joe Principe—Rise Against** Luckily, I stumbled upon NoMeansNo while record shopping at Wax Trax in Chicago back in high school. I bought *Wrong* because it was on Alternative Tentacles. I figured, "If Jello likes it, it must be good." "It's Catching Up" hit me in the face like a freight train, and I was hooked.

**Zach Blair—Rise Against, Hagfish, Drakulas** I have played the riff from "It's Catching Up" at sound check for twenty-five years. I don't think I've played any riff more, ever. Every sound check, it doesn't matter where we are, what room we are in. Rise Against toured and opened for the Foo Fighters, and I remember playing these huge halls, and Dave Grohl would shout, "NoMeansNo!" Everybody knows it.

**Mike Morasky—Steel Pole Bathtub** *Wrong* was the rare perfect record. They planted a flag in the landscape of the Nation of NoMeansNo. They carved out this space in a cultural self-identifying universe of people who are probably nothing like them as human beings. It was next door to Fugazi Land. All the squatter punks, along with the more mature smarty-pants fuck-punks, could all identify with them.

**Billy Gould—Faith No More** Hearing *Wrong* for the first time was what really got me into them. When Faith No More opened for Billy Idol on his 1990 tour, we insisted on having "I Am Wrong" playing on the PA before we took the stage.

**Greg Werckman—Alternative Tentacles, Ipecac Recordings** I started working at Alternative Tentacles in November 1989. Before that I had worked in New York City at a talent agency and looked after all the weirdos—Hunter S. Thompson, Timothy Leary, Abbie Hoffman, and Jello Biafra. One of the bands Jello turned me on to was NoMeansNo. The first time I saw them was 1987 at a club called City Gardens in New Jersey.

Two years later, Jello was telling me he needed help with his record label and asked me to move to California to manage AT. I got there right around the time that *Wrong* was released. I became friends with NoMeansNo quite quickly.

My partner now at my record label Ipecac is Mike Patton, from the band Faith No More. I met Mike at a NoMeansNo gig. When I was still at AT, he called up and was like, "Hey, can I get into the NoMeansNo show?" One of the first things Mike said to me was, "If there is one band in the world that I would not want to go on after, it would be NoMeansNo."

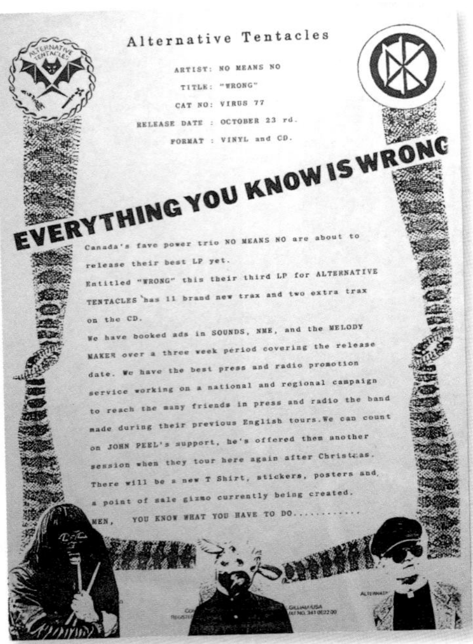

Alternative Tentacles

ARTIST: NO MEANS NO
TITLE: "WRONG"
CAT NO: VIRUS 77
RELEASE DATE : OCTOBER 23 rd.
FORMAT : VINYL and CD.

EVERYTHING YOU KNOW IS WRONG

Canada's fave power trio NO MEANS NO are about to release their best LP yet.
Entitled "WRONG" this their third LP for ALTERNATIVE TENTACLES has 11 brand new trax and two extra trax on the CD.
We have booked ads in SOUNDS, NME, and the MELODY MAKER over a three week period covering the release date. We have the best press and radio promotion service working on a national and regional campaign to reach the many friends in press and radio the band made during their previous English tours.We can count on JOHN PEEL's support, he's offered them another session when they tour here again after Christmas.
There will be a new T Shirt, stickers, posters and, a point of sale gizmo currently being created.
MEN, YOU KNOW WHAT YOU HAVE TO DO...........

**Petr Somol—fan from the Czech Republic** I lived behind the Iron Curtain in Czechoslovakia when *Wrong* came out. Someone smuggled it in from West Germany, and it took my secondary school by storm. There were many local half-illegal underground bands here at that time. We just ignored official rules, which stated that every music group is subject to approval by the censorship bureau. Communism was so weak by then that we dared to ignore them and just play for a bunch of friends in flats and garages. NoMeansNo became the one and only flawless musical drug we got addicted to.

**Nate Mendel—Foo Fighters, Sunny Day Real Estate** I wore that *Wrong* CD out in college. First of all, as a bass player, Rob was huge. If I'd listened a little closer to him early on, I would have saved a lot of time figuring out how to play bass in a rock band, at least in the way I want it to sound. They were so original. No blues, no metal, just NoMeansNo. Of course, there was the jazz influence, but who did that in punk/hardcore? We all loved "heavy" back then, and they simply unearthed a new way to achieve it.

The clever lyrics were great too. I like an earnest hardcore song as much as the next guy, but NMN could get the same lyrical intensity and sentiment in a more original way. It made you laugh, and smile, and feel like you were listening to something truly authentic.

**John Wright** By a long stretch, *Wrong* is our most known and our most popular album. There was good timing involved. We had our first European tour, and it was very successful. Then *Wrong* came out, and that's when people were like, "Okay, so who *is* this band?" I think it was just the right album at the right time. It had a great sound to it, it was super energetic, and it was pretty easy to digest. It was weird enough, but not *too* weird.

**China Miéville** I would be lying if I said that anything hit me as much as *Wrong* did. I'm well aware that among the NoMeansNo cognoscenti, the cool thing to say is that you're into one of the other albums, because *Wrong* is the really popular one. I am too old for that kind of hipster edgelording, and I am just going to admit that for me *Wrong* is an absolutely nonpareil album.

I had a T-shirt with that strange fucking cow's head. I used to wear it all the time. Once in the very

***Wrong*** **promo bumper sticker**

early '90s, I was walking around London. Someone was walking toward me and, upon seeing that T-shirt, just kind of gave me a pleasant nod. It was like I'd made an instant friend, even though no words were exchanged. It was the sense of being part of a subculture, and I know there's something questionable about that. It can also turn into a rather sort of cheesy border-guarding. But when you're a teenager, and you're kind of new to the scene, it feels pretty extraordinary.

To be clear, I realize this is a thoroughly dickish way of thinking about culture. I'm describing the thought processes of a teenager who loved wearing that T-shirt, but it's an exasperated affection. So I wanted that to be someone in a book who was like a young me. One of the characters in my book *The City & the City* sees a punky kid who is wearing a NoMeansNo T-shirt, and the narrator doesn't know what that is. That was basically because that T-shirt became such a talisman for me. It was very much that sense of being an insider and being excited by the music. In the book, it was a depiction of a kind of punky subculture.

This is the perennial border-guarding conundrum of the music hipster. I am so aware when I think about this kind of cultural contempt and the unwelcoming of outsiders. This is ugly stuff.

**Josh Blisters—Cute Lepers, the Spits** I was walking our dog, and this guy was walking by with his kids. He had a hoodie on with the *Wrong* cover on it, so I said, "Hey, man, nice hoodie!" He said, "Holy shit! I don't get very many compliments on this hoodie." I was like, "Best band in the world." He said, "You're goddamn right." So I said, "You know, we're best friends now." He laughed and said, "You're fucking right." I'm sure I'll bump into him again.

**Doni Blair—Toadies, Hagfish** Rob made playing the P-Bass cool. I thought, "Okay, well then, that works for me," and I was trying to get that fucking tone. But his tone is in his fucking hands. It's how he sets everything up, it's how he plays. It's what he gets when his left hand and his right hand touch the bass. No one can ever get that exactly right, but goddamn it, I can fucking try.

**Joe Keller—Night Birds** You can't listen to those songs and ignore the bass. It's always in front. He played a P-Bass, and the tone he gets out of is like Lemmy meets Chris Squire from Yes. That's the best way I could describe it.

**Matt Skiba—Alkaline Trio, Blink-182** *Wrong* to me is like the punk rock *Ziggy Stardust*. Each song is better than the last somehow.

**Rick Mahalek—fan from Campbell River, British Columbia** One of the many times I saw them play was at the Sidetrack Cafe in Edmonton. I bought a CD copy of *Wrong* but didn't have a pen for the guys to sign it. Rob promptly grabbed it, took the sleeve out and bit into it. It's one of my most prized possessions. Maybe I can clone him!

**Bow Campbell—Front End Loader** I was probably sitting on someone's filthy carpet in a share house with a bong in my hand when someone put on *Wrong*. My first impression was, "What the *fuck* is this?" I mean, seriously. How can a band sound so furious, so "punk," and yet be so tight and so precise? How can they be this impossibly heavy when the guitar is not particularly distorted? What's with all the funky time-changing jazzy business? Is that guy with the voice like a prophet of doom actually singing about the personal and the political at the same time? And what the *fucking fuck* is going on with that drum sound?

**Mats Gustafsson—the Thing, Fire!** I used to hang out a lot in a record store called Pet Sounds in Stockholm. It was the best and most important rock store in Sweden. They were always playing good shit on the sound system, and the owner, Stefan, always had good opinions on music. In 1989, he told me to listen to this new record. He told me that I needed to check it out and it even had some "jazz" elements to it. He put it on in my headphones, and my world changed. I could not believe what I heard. Absolute ass kicking and extremely unpredictable. That was *Wrong*. I will never forget the shock. I was sweating and smiling. I bought this life changer of an album right away and have been playing it on repeat ever since.

NoMeansNo began to feel the pressure of promotion. They were now an international touring band with records to sell. They gladly agreed to interviews and were happy to meet their fans, but their promotional materials were often confusing. This proved frustrating for their record label, Alternative Tentacles, as well as band manager Laurie Mercer.

**John Wright** We started goofing up the promo shots. We didn't take much of that stuff particularly seriously, because it has no meaning to begin with. Being goofs was part and parcel of the whole package.

**Rob Wright** Any promo stuff we did was just a joke. One time we did a photo with the three of us that said "Curly, Larry, and Promo." It became fun to do that. Tom Holliston especially loved to do stuff like that. He'd do the W. Buzz Ryan thing, constantly coming up with ways to make it ridiculous. I always appreciated that completely. His real talent is his mind. It's endlessly inventive, and he's so funny.

**Jack Endino—Skin Yard, producer** The single best band promotional picture I've ever seen is the Wright brothers sitting around a card table and playing Scrabble with these two old people. With no explanation. It is just the best.

**Tom Holliston** They did a promo photo playing Scrabble with my parents. They wanted to go out shopping, and Andy and Rob were there. Once again, John was late, and they were just about to leave when he finally showed up. It was a couple hours waiting for John and then about two minutes for Rebecca Kraatz to take the photos.

**Greg Werckman** Promoting the band was a challenge. I have to look at it in two ways. As a human being and a friend, that part might have been funny. But I was trying to sell records, and it was not fun because the music press in general did not have that same sense of humour.

NoMeansNo always had these ridiculous promo photos. I don't know how many times people would say, "This is cute, but we can't use this," or, "Who exactly is this person? Who plays what?" I'd have to explain to them that that's part of who they were. They were not the easiest band to market. Their interviews were all over the place. When people finally did talk to them, they didn't know what was serious or what was sarcastic.

When you're in the music industry, you see bands that are selling out arenas and selling hundreds of thousands of records. Then you go see NoMeansNo play in a sweaty, packed three-hundred-capacity club. You just think, "Okay, the world is wrong here. Let's change this, let's make this right." That was horribly frustrating, and I'm sure Laurie will tell you the same thing.

**Laurie Mercer** The mythology of NoMeansNo has always been a big part of it. That's why all the pictures have the wrong people. It's not just contrarianism; it builds a mystery. It's not about the people; it's about the music. It's also taking the piss. However, opportunities that were created to springboard them were constantly dismissed, turned down, or ignored. It was a constant trail of heartbreak.

Exclusive Universal Representation
Laurie Mercer
S. L. Feldman & Associates

**Promo photo outtakes**

**Zach Blair** I got obsessed. I had to know who they were and how many records they had out. Of course, this was before YouTube and Google, and I couldn't figure anything out about them. Their names weren't on the records at that time. I didn't know Andy Kerr's real name for a long time. I just knew all their voices sounded similar, but you could tell there were different people singing. Everything was misleading about them. You never got a good picture of them.

**Nick Evans** NoMeansNo did weird things with their press: the bags of potatoes or cow's head or Rob dressed as a vicar. They seemed to be against mainstream promotion, yet they always had a lot of interesting ideas to present themselves in a way that was eye-catching. There was sort of an aspect of Zappa there. There was something recalcitrant about them. They were so good that they could say no, and they liked saying no.

**Jello Biafra** One of the promo photos we were told to use was Andy, looking like he's rocking on the guitar, with two sacks of flour. Another one was maybe two or three old men sitting around a table at a little Victoria bar. I'm not sure that we ever had a proper, three-person NoMeansNo promo picture. In that area, I'd be on Laurie Mercer's side. That is not how to get your photo as the lead gig article in the local weekly.

**Tim Solyan** Once *Wrong* came out, NoMeansNo hit this upper level above us. We were so below them when it came to making money. We'd be circumventing the same trail through Europe and see that 1,200 people were showing up to see NMN, and we'd be selling two hundred tickets. We'd play a lot of the same venues and some of those big famous squats. It didn't matter where you went: if NoMeansNo were there before us, there'd be fifty people wearing a NMN shirt that they got the month before.

**Nick Evans** They were playing at the Boston Arms Hotel in London, and it was weird, because Rob was really, really intense about the merchandise. They were constantly trying to get enough T-shirts made. The T-shirt revenue was important, but it wasn't just sales. Rob said, "That's how we spread our name."

**Rob Wright** Merch was the bread and butter of any independent band. The real money was from the bar,

Leeds, UK, 1989

but there's no way we'd ever get a cut of that. The merch sales would often be as much or more than what we'd make for the performance. It was a pain in the ass to transport and organize and costly to get. In the end, though, we had to have them just to make a dime.

We realized at some point that we were basically just a commercial for beer and T-shirts: "What do you do for a living?" "I sell textiles and alcohol." We should have written a song called "Buy the T-Shirts" and played that every night as the final encore.

**Andy Kerr** We always did better on the merch than the records.

**Grant Lawrence** When the Smugglers started touring internationally, I realized the impact of NoMeansNo. One of the most common punk band T-shirts that we saw around the world was NoMeansNo. We saw them in Scotland, Italy, Japan, and Australia. We were just like, "Holy shit, how many thousands upon thousands of fans do these guys have?" We realized the importance of merchandise and having a really good brand that sticks out.

**Mike Hodsall—D.O.A.** One of the cool things about touring in a Canadian band in Europe is that everybody wears their Canadian punk band shirts to a D.O.A. show. It's almost like, "Hey! We know you're Canadian and we wanna support that." You see tons of NoMeansNo shirts, SNFU shirts, and Dayglos shirts. It's really cool because all those people over the years have ended up being friends. We see probably more NMN shirts than anyone else.

**Wilf Plum—Dog Faced Hermans, Two Pin Din** I remember being amazed that NoMeansNo sold so many T-shirts. With the Hermans, if we managed to sell five or ten, then we were pretty happy, but they sold dozens and dozens.

**Milo Aukerman—Descendents** I met my wife at a NoMeansNo show at the Spirit Club in San Diego, California. That was kind of a bond that she and I had. She wasn't as big of a NMN fan as I was, but she went to the show. I was just thinking, "If she likes NoMeansNo, then she's the girl for me!" We started talking, I gave her my number, and it all worked out.

**Brian Lilla—fan from Oakland, California** It was 1989. I was broke, jobless, and living on my sister's

John from the *Wrong* photo shoot

couch in her studio apartment in Portland, Oregon. I had dropped out of college and was financially fucked. All my records sat in milk crates in my parents' garage.

A flyer posted to a telephone pole momentarily pulled me out of my depression when I saw NoMeansNo were scheduled to play the Pine Street Theatre. I had to go. I borrowed money from my sister to attend the show. NoMeansNo had just released *Wrong*. Hundreds of people lined the block to get in. NoMeansNo played a nearly two-hour set. Then the lights came on, and I was soaked in sweat as I walked to the merchandise table with ten dollars burning in my pocket.

Stapled to a board was a *Wrong* T-shirt. The image of a cow's head on a preacher's torso was complemented on the back with the bold lettering BE STRONG BE WRONG. I had to have it.

The next day I proudly wore my new shirt. My sister scoffed at me: "How do you expect to get a job wearing clothes like that? Wear something decent." For weeks, I had been pedaling my bike around Portland applying for jobs and bumming beers. The day after the NoMeansNo show, I walked into Hotlips Pizza and asked if they were hiring.

I filled out the application, and a week later I was hired. One of the pizza cooks had seen me come in and told the manager to hire me. "Why? You don't even know him." "He's wearing a NoMeansNo shirt. Trust me, hire him." That pizza cook, Isaac, along with the other punk cooks, Daniel and Edgar, would become good friends for thirty years. A month of throwing and eating free pizza allowed me to save enough money to get a downtown apartment with Daniel. That NoMeansNo shirt changed my life.

Enschede, Netherlands, 1990

**Niall McGuirk—promoter** Whenever NoMeansNo came to Ireland, they would play two nights, in Belfast and Dublin, and it was always with local Irish bands opening. We had them at a place called McGonagles, and my friend Patrick did the flyer, which was Rob dressed up in a priest outfit. In Ireland at the time, you didn't really make fun of the Catholic Church.

**Paul Timoney—promoter** They already had a very well-established network in Europe by the time I started working with them. When they came to Ireland, they often took a few days off in Dublin. Rob was hugely interested in Irish literature, and Dublin was a city that seemed important to them because of their Irish heritage.

**Michael McKeegan—Therapy?** As with most of the music that made a big impact on me, I first heard NoMeansNo on the John Peel show in 1988. They actually came and played Belfast soon after in 1990, so that was amazing to see. Not that many bands from overseas came to Northern Ireland at that time, so it was a special thing to be able to see NMN in our neck of the woods.

**Tero Viikari—promoter** I booked NoMeansNo's tours in Finland. It started in 1988 when I was helping out at a new venue in Tampere. I had gotten a copy of *Small Parts Isolated and Destroyed*, and I needed to see this band from Canada. I went all the way to London, to the Alternative Tentacles offices there. I walked in and said, "I'm Tero from Finland, and I want to know if they are touring in Europe at the moment." They gave me the address of De Konkurrent, so I contacted them and put a five-show tour together in Finland for the next year.

They came to Finland by ferry from Poland, and I went to Helsinki to meet them. It is a very long ferry ride, many hours, and of course there is not a whole lot to do but drink. I was at the harbour waiting for the guys, and I saw a van pulling out from the ferry. They stopped at customs, and I could see there was some hassle. I saw Craig Bougie was driving the van, and of course they took a breath alcohol test. So, after fifteen or twenty metres of landing on Finnish ground, they got busted for drinking and driving. I

Cedar Hill Rec Center, Victoria, 1989

went in a police car with Craig to the nearest hospital, and they took a blood test and then let us go. Of course, Craig couldn't drive the whole tour in Finland, so John and the other guys drove. It was quite the start for the tour. I heard later that Craig got a letter from the Finnish government asking him to come to court, but it was all written in Finnish. It was several years before they came back to Finland, so the case was old when they came again and there were no issues.

**Craig Bougie** I don't remember much of the ferry ride. I remember the fucking landing though. That's where I got unceremoniously spirited away to the local cop shop. They arrested me on the spot. They took the long route. It was nothing but fucking cobblestones in the back of this tiny little police van. It was horrible, bouncing around, all hungover.

John and I had been up all night gambling and drinking. I drove the van and got busted. John took over, and he was fine.

Tero is an awesome dude. We came off the ferry, and there's Tero, and we'd never met him before. He had this huge pink mohawk, just totally punk-rocked out. The cops and the security guards are all just chatting amiably with him: "Okay, well, we'll sort this out." It was a really odd thing, because everywhere else we'd been, there had been this "punks against the world" kind of thing. In Finland, they all just seemed to get along.

We used to witness a thing we called "Finnish drinking." Basically, 80 percent of the audience never actually got to see the band. They'd just get fucking hammered and lie around like boneless chickens. They would start early in the day, and by the time we came onstage, there'd be like 20 percent of the people who were awake, and the rest were all passed out everywhere.

**Attila Molnar—fan from Budapest, Hungary**
NoMeansNo played in Budapest at the iconic Fekete Lyuk [Club Black Hole]. It was just after the fall of communism. I was seventeen, and it was my first gig. As one from the countryside, it was the first time I went deep into the Budapest underground, with all its mental and visual phenomena. It was the tour of the *Wrong* album, and when I listen to *Wrong*, I can't feel anything else than the mood of this day: sunshine, happiness, juvenility, rightness, wrongness.

**Jay Scott** *Wrong* was immensely popular, and they were selling out big places all over Europe. There was this great moment I remember when some big record executive was telling the Wright brothers, "*Wrong* is such a great album! If we would've handled that album, it would be a million-plus seller, guaranteed, in North America alone!" He was trying to hype it up and impress the guys. I think that might have been Virgin Records. The Wright brothers were just sitting there in their quizzical way and looking at each other. Finally, Rob said, "Well, why would we want to sell a million records? We would have to go support that, and it would be terrible!"

**"Tired of Waiting" video shoot**

CHAPTER FOURTEEN

# THE SKY IS FALLING AND I WANT MY MOMMY

## "There's too many sharks in the gene pool."

Now that the 1980s were in the rearview mirror, NoMeansNo were starting off the new decade busier and more popular than ever before. The intense and positive reaction to the *Wrong* album was unlike anything they had expected. The underground press in Europe and the US were taking notice, and word was spreading. NoMeansNo were now a band performing at peak level.

John Wright was honing his producing and engineering skills during this time as well, working with friends Victims Family, D.O.A., and others. The year 1990 was a busy one, and it would include more touring, an EP release, and a collaboration with their label boss, Jello Biafra.

**Dan Lucey—PufferFish Lampshade** I saw NoMeansNo one time at the Off Ramp in Seattle. A bouncer got so excited by the mosh pit that he coldcocked some teenage kid and laid him out on the floor. I went onto the stage after him, and my friends pulled me off. I complained to the promoter, and she tried to blow it off, saying, "I'm the only person that brings bands like this." I said, "No, no. This is intolerable. This is an all-ages show, and I watched this kid get attacked."

The next night, I'm back at another show in Seattle, and the same bouncer is there. I was all wound up and about to do something stupid when my girlfriend found Andy Kerr. He went over to the promoter and said, "If that guy isn't out of this building *now*, we will not play." As simple as that. She went white, and the guy was gone.

**Jack Endino** I don't think NoMeansNo were influential to the grunge scene at all, because it was a completely different aesthetic. But I do think they were influential to the scene that sprouted up here *after* the grunge scene. That would be the punk rock bands that came about in the middle '90s, a lot of the math rock bands, like Sunny Day Real Estate.

There were a lot of screamcore bands that had tough arrangements and weird mathy stuff. I suspect that when they were younger, they probably thought NoMeansNo were the shit. In the '90s, I just remember noticing a lot more bands that were embracing that kind of proggy, edgy thing, with sort of cynical lyrics and somewhat obtuse, interesting riffs.

**Matt Cameron** Our scene in Seattle was pretty small and pretty tight knit. When a band made an impact with all the musicians and the people who frequented the clubs, the word would spread. I remember a lot of people talking about NoMeansNo, and I would say they definitely were an influence on a lot of those rock bands that eventually became known as "grunge" bands.

**William Goldsmith—Sunny Day Real Estate, Foo Fighters** I've never played with anyone who isn't a huge fan of NoMeansNo, every single person. They've been such a huge inspiration since high school. I was just about to graduate when I first saw them at the OK Hotel in Seattle in '91. They completely changed everything for all of us. We were classic rock kids, but this was a punk rock band that was as technically proficient as Rush.

**Steve "Kicks" Poulin—New Town Animals, the Briefs** I'm a Rush fan, and they're the punk rock Rush for me.

**Rob Higgins—Dearly Beloved** Geddy Lee of Rush is my uncle, so when I was a little kid all I really knew about music was what I was being exposed to. My Uncle Geddy let me hang out with him and his band up until I went to university. I would go to rehearsals and even on tour with them, so I really kind of grew up on prog music. I got exposed to that type of approach and the power trio setup.

When I discovered NoMeansNo, they were the first band that took that level of musicianship and married it to the music that I was attracted to as a teenager. It was the first time a light bulb went on in my head like, "Holy shit, you can fuse prog music and punk music, and it doesn't have to suck!"

**George Smith—Dangermouse** NoMeansNo were probably the most influential band in my peer group in the Tacoma and Pacific Northwest scene. They were obviously super talented, but they didn't wank. They just were incredibly tight and interesting. They had prog and math rock influences, but it was from the perspective of a punk rock band. It wasn't just some musicians showing off what they can do.

**Lori Barbero—Babes in Toyland** I would tell my friends, "I love NoMeansNo." Sometimes guys would be like, "You know, it's math rock for dudes." I'd say, "Well, apparently, I have bigger balls than you."

**Craig Billmeier—fan from San Francisco, California** In the spring of 1991, my friends and I were obsessed with NoMeansNo. They were playing at Gilman Street in Berkeley, so we went early to hang out and talk to them. We were all still in high school. We showed up in the afternoon, and someone working the side door told us that the band were in their van parked down the block.

At that time, this section of Berkeley was an industrial wasteland, and so it was probably dumb and naive of us to have simply popped our heads into the first van we approached. Not surprisingly, we were met by a few homeless old men just lounging in a van with its side door wide open. We awkwardly apologized and turned to keep looking for the band. One of the homeless guys asked who we were looking for. "NoMeansNo." "That's us!" So unassuming, so unpunk, so casual, so *old*. But fuck, did they put on a good show.

**Doug Copley—Clusterfux, Goat Boy** NoMeansNo kicked off their 1991 Canadian tour with the Ex at my house in Victoria. It was a venue

Victoria, 1991

we called the Rubber Room, also known as the Clusterfucks House or the Steele Street House. There were Kewpie doll heads hanging from the ceiling. It was a weird place. Local bands Shutdown and Section 46 opened the show. The NoMeansNo guys were only interested in making sure the Ex got paid well. We sold more than two hundred tickets and made like $2,000 that night, and we paid NMN with a case of Lucky beer.

**Rob Nesbitt** That was an incredible show. We got there early to set up, and they were all there, hanging out in the backyard eating barbecue. I just was like, "These guys are smarter than the people I'm usually standing around."

**Jay Staples—fan from Edmonton, Alberta** After a gig in Edmonton, my roommate informed me that NMN and the Ex were going to sleep at our house that night. I figured I'd keep the celebration going, and I would eat acid and party with these two fantastic bands all night. We got home with all fourteen members of the two bands, I dropped acid, and we ordered Chinese food. Little did I know that the bands just wanted to sleep. As the acid started kicking in, I found sleeping musicians in every room of the house, including my bedroom. I had nowhere to hang out, so I spent the night sitting on my front porch waiting for the acid to stop. Who knew that a touring band would be tired and wouldn't want to party all night?

**Katherina Bornefeld—the Ex** I loved the NoMeansNo guys, and I also had a working relationship with John, because I was able to use his drum kit. We really worked well together, and we liked each other personally. I remember things going smoothly and having fun.

As a drummer, he had a more jazz technique, with a very strong hit with his left hand. He has his very own style, and of course he's well trained. When I looked at him, it was like, "God, I never could do that!" John was also so joyful about playing. When he played, he was *really* having fun.

**Jello Biafra** *The Sky Is Falling and I Want My Mommy* was an unexpected spin-off from the movie *Terminal City Ricochet*. I came up to Vancouver and wound up acting in the movie and trying to come up with some songs for the soundtrack.

The idea was they were going to put a D.O.A. song in, put a NoMeansNo song in, and then maybe have me do one song with each band. It was kind of a ricocheting series of magic accidents, because different parts of what I did each inspired the other. The song "Falling Space Junk" from the movie came from my spoken-word piece "Why I'm Glad the Space Shuttle Blew Up."

With both bands, what started out as being one song quickly mushroomed into an entire album's worth of songs, and everybody was game. Joey Keithley brought in what became "Power Is Boring" when I added the lyrics to it, and it actually got D.O.A. to come out of their shell and let themselves go as musicians a little more. "Full Metal Jackoff" was the result there too.

Then with NoMeansNo, they played me the music that became "Falling Space Junk," and of course it was so good and so fierce. I was really having a tough time getting all the words to fit into it, so it actually split into two songs. "Falling Space Junk Part 1" ended up on the *Terminal City Ricochet* soundtrack, and then "Part 2" opened *The Sky Is Falling and I Want My Mommy.*

Sometimes it came down to improv and jamming. The song "Chew," which I believe was my riff, kind of became more of a band song than a Biafra song, so to speak.

**John Wright** "Sharks in the Gene Pool" was an instrumental song that we had demoed before *Wrong*, and Biafra added lyrics to it.

**Jello Biafra** I wasn't sure what to do with the song "Bruce's Diary." That song is written from the perspective of Bruce Coddle, my character in *Terminal City Ricochet.* I had been trying to figure out, "What kind of a person is this guy, anyway?" I was staying in this hotel in Vancouver, near a hill that went down into Burrard Inlet. There were all these other narrow Pringle-potato-chip-can kind of high rises going down the hill. It was dusk, and all these apartments and condos hadn't closed their curtains yet, but they were all lit up, so I could watch all of them, and watch all of them as Bruce Coddle.

I let my imagination begin to roam, then I sat on the toilet and got a little aroused thinking about everything. In my mind, I populated these apartments with sexy women and whatever else. I began masturbating as Bruce Coddle, and luckily, I turned on my handy Sony recorder and just kind of talked about what was going through my head. There were pages and pages of this that I transcribed later. I realized, "Oh my god, I can turn this into a song that fits back in with the fucking movie."

**Cecil English** The whole thing was kind of my idea originally. I had met Jello Biafra in Vancouver after a Dead Kennedys show, and it was during that whole *Frankenchrist* fiasco, where Jello got busted by the FBI for distributing harmful matter to minors. He was facing big legal bills for defending himself. I suggested recording him for some kind of benefit at Profile Studios for free. He didn't take the offer, but sometime later he called me and said, "I've got an idea. I wanna do a collaboration with D.O.A. and

John at the Commodore Ballroom, Vancouver, 1990

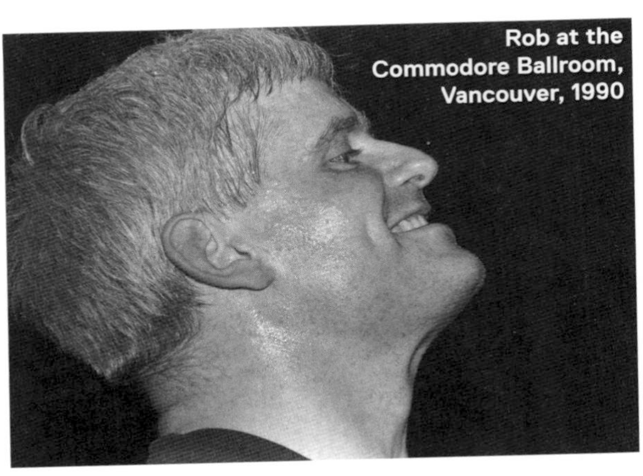
Rob at the Commodore Ballroom, Vancouver, 1990

NoMeansNo, but I've got money. I don't want you to have to do it for free. I'm gonna give you $5,000."

We recorded *Last Scream of the Missing Neighbors* with D.O.A. That went really well, and then the same thing happened with NoMeansNo. We recorded all the bed tracks for their songs, and then Biafra made a few trips back up to Vancouver, where he stayed at my house, and we got all the vocals recorded at Profile. He went back to San Francisco, and I did all the mixing. Of course, this was pre-internet, so I basically had to mail cassettes to him constantly. He'd listen and send back mixing notes, either by letter or by phone conversation.

To this day, the clarity of Jello's mind is still boggling. He can hold a complete album's worth of material in his mind, all the songs and all the parts. He insisted on me keeping every mix that I did, every pass of every mix. I'd be sitting in the studio until six o'clock in the morning, because it was all analogue and I was mixing all by myself, pushing the faders.

I'd put it onto a cassette and send him like fifteen mixes of each song. He'd listen to all those mixes and send me notes about what he liked and what he didn't like, and then I'd do it all over again. This went on for weeks and weeks, then finally he sent me back this huge instruction paper of all the mixes: "Mix 21 of this song, I want you to use that for the first chorus." This was pre–digital editing, so I had to razor-blade everything together as per his instructions. I spent weeks on that, tying everything together. In the end, it was really magical.

NoMeansNo were less the backing band than D.O.A. They were pretty assertive. It was a weird symbiotic relationship. They were kind of at odds the whole time. D.O.A. is more of a meat-and-potatoes band, while NoMeansNo is quirky. When you put quirky people like Biafra and NoMeansNo together, it's never gonna be smooth sailing.

**Jello Biafra** We did some rehearsals at the Rats Nest in Victoria, and I stayed there for a couple days. I had a kind of sporty Subaru, and I commuted back and forth up to BC steadily for six months to get the movie and the albums done. I did drive up from Victoria to Nanaimo once, just to explore the island. I'd gotten a tip about a really good record store called Fascinating Rhythm, which is still there. I got a ton of old 45s and used LPs. I went there a couple times actually. I'm really grateful that substance addiction doesn't run on either side of my family; we don't have the genes. I do have one addiction, and it is music. Especially vinyl.

**Betty Norton** Jello Biafra was in town doing *The Sky Is Falling* album with NoMeansNo. He was here for a

Andy at the Commodore Ballroom, Vancouver, 1990

CHAPTER FIFTEEN

# 0 + 2 = 1

## "The hoot of an owl in the dreams of a mouse."

NoMeansNo could do no wrong. Accolades were pouring into their jar, and they were confident and insanely busy. If they weren't on the road, they were in the studio. Day jobs were now a thing of the past, and precious little got in between the band and their objectives.

Their tour schedule was packed, and their shows were getting the reputation of being events that needed to be experienced. While the gigs were getting better, they were also getting bigger.

Normally, this would be a good problem to have, but the band remained somewhat wary of any success at the cost of integrity, and some opportunities were being passed up intentionally. In particular, Andy Kerr would soon begin feeling unsure if the trajectory they were on was the path he wanted to be treading. But for now, their jar was heavy.

**Tero Viikari** We were driving in Tampere before the show, with John and Rob. We were looking for a music store. We had used some free studio time at the local radio station to record an ad promoting the NMN show. Suddenly, the radio ad came on. It was me and my friend shouting our lungs out in Finnish

about NoMeansNo. The Wrights heard it and said, "What the fuck was that?" I said, "That was your ad that we made!" Afterwards, I sent the ad on a cassette to Canada, and it ended up as the intro on the *Live and Cuddly* album.

**John Wright** *Live and Cuddly* was fun to record. We had two pretty good shows and took the best from each show. We worked with a lot of the original Dutch people we met when we first went over. They were all involved in that.

**Ingrid Kerr** Dutch producer Dolf Planteijdt had just got a bunch of new recording gear and mentioned to me that it might be a nice idea to record some NoMeansNo live shows. Dolf set up all the technical things and recorded them over two nights in Holland. Konkurrel released it in Europe, while in the States it was put out by Alternative Tentacles.

**Dolf Planteijdt—producer** De Konkurrent asked me to record two NoMeansNo gigs in the Netherlands, to release a live album. I rented a stage box splitter, a mixing desk, and a sixteen-track recorder. Together with their soundman, Craig, I placed a few more mics than usual and got it on tape.

They went home, and I mixed everything in Het Koeienverhuurbedrijf. I sent the results by post to Canada and got some suggestions to change a few things, including the order of the tracks. Finally, John said, "It sounds very different from how we would have done it, but I like it."

**Andy Kerr** They set it up, so we really did nothing. The Groningen show was filmed, but I didn't know that until later. I stayed back after the tour and helped Dolf mix it. Dolf is basically the Scott Henderson of Amsterdam. If there was a punk record to be recorded, Dolf would record it in his little studio. He's a real sweet guy and has recorded basically everybody in Amsterdam.

I'm glad that a live album came out while I was in the band. People used to tell us from the time *You Kill Me* came out, "I really like your records, but you guys are way better live."

I'm very, very fussy about live albums. I hate live albums that have tons of reverb and where the band sounds far away. I want any live album to sound like

the Who's *Live at Leeds*, because that's the absolute platinum standard. That and James Brown's *Live at the Apollo*. We wanted a record that had a punch to it. I think it turned out really, really well.

**John Wright** The cover of *Live and Cuddly* was just a family photo from a wedding when I was eight years old. I think it might have been my Aunt Carolyn's wedding. That's me on the left playing the floor tom, and the little kid is my cousin, who was about four or five. The other guy was the drummer in whatever wedding band was there. We were probably like, "Aw, can I bang on the drums?"

**Andy Kerr** The drummer on the back cover of *Live and Cuddly* is Duncan Redmonds, the drummer of Snuff. We were just screwing with our image as per usual. As for the name of the album, we wanted to use the kind of title that was the polar opposite of most live rock LPs. *Live and Cuddly* seemed to fit the bill nicely.

**Duncan Redmonds** Yes, that's me on the back cover. I still get people asking me about this. Snuff were getting a bit of press at the time, in things like the *NME* and *Melody Maker*. Sometimes they mixed up pictures of Snuff and NoMeansNo. They'd put a picture of Rob up, and it would say Andy from Snuff, and then they'd put up a NoMeansNo review, and it would say Andy on guitar and there'd be a picture of Simon. That happened a few times, and I think NMN just did it as a joke. Little did they know that I now have 100 percent of all the profits from that album, for misuse of my image. I have it all, and I'm talking to you from an island near Barbados! But truthfully, it just came from a mix-up, and they just carried on the joke. I'm honoured.

21 April, 1990 New Musical Express—Page

**THE FARM**
LIVERPOOL UNDERGROUND

THE FARM perfectly capture the mood of Liverpool's raging Scally revolution. Clubs have always been important to the average scal about town, but with the House take-over dance mixes have moved to the top of the league, while other more traditional pursuits, like going to the match, have fallen behind in the championship race.

The Underground, an unpretentious shoestring operation playing radical dance sounds, has boosted and responded to this rebellion on the streets, as have The Farm, the original and most infamous of all the Scally outfits.

The atmosphere was one of truly hyped up excitement as over 500 people proved, in the true tradition of Farm gigs, that Liverpool lager frenzy is alive and in staggering good health. The reason for all this feverish anticipation was the launch of The Farm's new label Produce, and new single, a shattering clubwise version of 'Stepping Stone', a long time stage favourite.

The single is typical of their revamped, pumped-up sound; a chugging Go-Go dance beat (in the same mould as Snap's 'Power') overlaid with crashing rock guitar. The Farm haven't gone House, they've just added a Techno surge and some sequenced thump to beef it all up and bring a crucial cross-over dance dimension to their always rhythmic guitar pop base.

Forget anything you've heard from them in the past, on tonight's evidence their ambling rock groove can't fail. They were, as I believe our Mancunian cousins are currently saying, "Top", and soon Dolcis' Timberlands throughout the land will be hitting the dancefloors to the sound of their rugged Scallydelic dance stance.

Without wishing to be in the slightest bit divisive, bugger Manchester. The Farm are nowhere near as ugly as the Inspirals or Mondays, they've got better T-shirts and they don't wear flares. 1990 is going to be Liverpool's year. It could easily be the year of The Farm.

**Kev McManus**

**LES NEGRESSES VERTES**
LONDON TOWN AND COUNTRY

NARROW-MINDED and ignorant of French culture, as I am, Les Negresses Vertes are somewhat of a shock. For a start there's 11 extra-terrestrials on stage, the singer looks like the collective reincarnation of Showaddywaddy and dances like Steve Martin, except he's not kidding.

The sound of a solo accordion absurdly hypnotises you, sweeping us back to '30s–'40s French vaudeville, while the rest of the band trounce on unnoticed. You start wondering if this bizarre circus act would be accepted if they weren't French, and the club wasn't filled to the brim with white-middle-class liberals on a guilt trip (*Who, you?—Ed*).

But you're forced to drop these preconceptions as your realise Les Negresses Vertes are completely off their trolley, and a harmonica heavy, rumbustious ride takes you to heaven. So I close my eyes, and forget how ridiculous they look, and let the blend of African horns, French accordion and flamenco guitar pummel straight-forward arrangements into total weirdness. After a while, the comparison to The Pogues isn't so far off the mark.

Fuelled by alcohol, they get better the longer they stay. Helno, the singer, asks us if we want him to speak in English. When no-one does, he shouts, "F—off, I'll speak English", and then speaks in French. Which is good, because that's exactly how the band are, always twisting and distorting their sound, so just when you think you've got your head round them, they launch into the opposite. It's hard work for the audience, because you're forced to listen, to understand the complexity of it all.

Towards the end, when they're in full flow, I could be spotted down in the front, frolicking like mad, shouting the only French word I know, 'Encore'.

**Simon Dudfield**

**SOHO**
KENTISH TOWN BULL & GATE

AFTER A two million quid contract and little or no returns, Soho are now back in indie-land with a vengeance. How are the *mighty fallen*? Mind your own business. This is probably the best thing that could happen to them, as this new-look group is destined to go places. At least now they can do it at their own pace, and not according to the dictates of some clueless mogul.

The partisan crowd did them favours. There are few venues as cosy and down-to-earth as this one and Soho made the most of a very groovy situation. They've lost the backbone of the group (formerly electronic) and replaced him and his machines with real bass 'n' drums and a turntable scratcher. The guitarist now hogs more of the limelight than ever, but thankfully the twins are still there with upfront voices and moves. The sound is bang up to date: cheesy pop for now people with wrenches thown in.

Soho almost didn't pull this off. The slower tempos engendered by discarding machines were tough to get into at first, but they've gotta move on—can't stand still on one spot pogoing forever. It's to their credit that, at the concert's end, anything faster than the light of day would've seemed out-of-place. Lets talk about the *groove*: percussive injections and rhythm are quite important here and Soho are blessed with some colossal grooves. 'Taxi''s reggae-ish shuffle is decidedly chartbound if recorded properly (ie with a Jamaican producer), and 'Hippychick' is just immensely funky and sugary at the same time.

There is no way boredom could set in. The darting, swooping voices and the mesmeric moves kept you in place. So what if the guitarist occasionally acted the prat? Those clued-in would say he was taking the piss. I think it goes deeper than that. Basically, Soho are back—clear the path. There are very few groups this *sure* and *sussed* currently treading the boards.

**Dele Fadele**

# TO HOLLAND BACK

**SNUFF**
AMSTERDAM DAM SQUARE SQUAT

SNUFF, HENDON's totally abrasive guitar trio, are playing in a squat just off the Dam Square which puts many of London's smaller clubs to shame with its stark-lit but well-engineered set-up.

This gig, part of their current European tour, shows that they're still cutting it, giving off a double burst of urgency and charisma.

Guitarist Simon, sitting around, pre-gig, chatting to some of the punters—including a 20-strong posse from England—is trying to catch up with what's been going on back home.

"We've missed everything," he moans, although with his characteristic, broad grin. "The Poll Tax riots, we haven't a clue what's going on. We only found out *that* happened when we got to Poland . . . Strangeways? What's that all about?"

A month and a half on tour may have damaged their knowledge of current affairs, but apart from that it's done them no harm at all—even though they've had to overcome bouts of illness along the way and the theft of a batch of their T-shirts, stolen from their van in Spain. The thieves also took all the cassettes the band had taken abroad to play in the van between towns, leaving them just one . . . a Pink Floyd LP! Police are searching for a man with good taste.

Other supplies have run out too. When they found out that some of their friends were going over to see them in Spain, they dashed off a fax with the venue details—and a plea at the bottom asking if they could bring with them 12 packets of Hob-Nobs and a box of PG Tips.

Snuff tread the fine line between integrity and bankruptcy. Of the 52 dates on this tour only three will cost more than the equivalent of £3 to get in. But that, if you distil it, is what Snuff are about. They've got a hilarious charisma but they're not taking the piss out of anyone.

"We played in Paris last night," adds Simon rolling a cigarette, "and it was manic. It was a seated venue but they were still stage-diving."

Dam Square is an ideal follow up, a squat party with an enthusing audience. You'd think that their Englishness (the between song banter and the notorious cover versions they do of adverts like the Bran Flakes one) would be a touch perplexing to a foreign crowd, but probably half the audience speak English, and the rest just seem to get a buzz out of the band's resilient thrash-pop power.

*Wot, no windmill guitar? Nice 'n' sneezy does it for Snuff.*

They start off with 'Somehow' from last year's debut 'Snuff Said' LP and then rip through a party-pack of covers including 'Hazy Shade Of Winter' and the Specials' 'Do Nothin'—both lifted from their 'Flibbidydibbidydob' EP.

Snuff actually look a bit mental. Simon, eyes fired up, looks like a fight extra from *Quadrophenia*, drummer Duncan—when he's not singing—grimaces at his kit like a boxer at his opponent.

The gaps between the songs, while they're getting their breath back, are turning into an artform in themselves; a constant flow of one-liners, ads and impressions.

"Someone once timed one of our gaps between songs at the Greyhound," says Andy later "and it was *five minutes*. We don't actually stop, we just 'mill'. We do a lot of 'milling' between songs."

Even so they play for an hour including their own caustic material like 'I See', and the punky 'Not Listening Anymore'. An encore brings a cover of 'Reach Out I'll Be There' and that's it. A lesson in how to send people home happy, and *alive*.

**Steve Lamacq**

PICTURES: MARTYN GOODACRE

# IN THE ARE(N)A!

**HAPPY MONDAYS**
WEMBLEY ARENA

THE MONDAYS at the Arena? A wonderful cosmic joke, but Wembley's seated areas are causing problems galore. Asking this excited, intense crowd to "sit down" is like asking a Loop audience to take a bath: they won't do it and it's cruel to ask. One crazed and tearful teenager offers his dope stash in exchange for my Standing ticket. Like all good tabloid reporters "I politely decline and leave".

Inside, the seated areas have erupted into large scale dive bombing onto the dance floor. One guy leaves his shoes in a security guard's mouth. Another's bell-bottoms fill with air and he literally sails to freedom. Most unfortunates dive straight into the arms of waiting security officials. Unlikely dancing partners in normal circumstances but perfect—hilarious and nonsensical—in tonight's surrealistic setting.

DJs Paul Oakenfold and Gary Clail crank the atmosphere up to an unbearable pitch. I haven't been this excited since The Smiths split up. By the time Happy Mondays appear people are taking drugs to come down. Shaun Ryder shames us all with a few suitably intellectual asides: "(drool) . . . mother—er . . . (belch) c—ts . . . wankers . . ." O, *très charmant*, . . . and not exactly food for thought for all those poor fans defying death as they hang by one arm from balconies to catch Ryder's every word.

However, as a musical force Happy Mondays continue to surprise us all with one of this century's most remarkable growth spurts. Their gigs were once the aural equivalent of having the Tackhead tour bus crash into your groin. Nowadays, early material like "24 Hour Party People", 'Tart, Tart' and 'Mad Cyril' has synthesized into a noisy, totally addictive sprawl. And though the likes of 'Hallelujah' still sound like The Mission sieved through Barney Albrecht's underpants there is a sighing malevolence to tracks like 'Lazyitis' that sounded merely posturing before.

In the middle of all this, Shaun Ryder—Chief Radio 1 Frightener of his day—stands twitchily delinquent, simultaneously aware and unaware of his surroundings. Meanwhile his dad—surely the next leader of the Free World?—cavorts with horrible abandon inside a Viking helmet, waving a cardboard number '1' as his son performs 'Step On' (the next Number One pop-pickers) inbetween simulating sex with backing songstress Rowetta and sending Bez and his maraccas flying off into the wings.

Obviously the salient point of Happy Mondays playing Wembley is not what they do here but the fact that they are here *at all*. The only proof we disco lovers need that the rave will definitely stay on.

**Barbara Ellen**

*Countdown to ecstacy: Bez does his shadow play party-piece*

*Very Happy Mondays fans*

***NME*** **with NoMeansNo mislabelled as Snuff**

**Brian "Who" Else—engineer** I moved to Vancouver around 1990 and started working at Profile Studios with Cecil English. I got hooked up to be the engineer on *0 + 2 = 1*. That was the last record they did with Cecil, but they kept me on for the next five or six years.

The first time I met Rob was at a Music West seminar. He was wearing his full Mr. Wrong priest outfit with the hat and everything, and I actually opened the door for him: "Yeah, go through, Father, it's cool." Then somebody explained it to me after I saw him on the panel, and I went, "Oh, fuck, he's not a priest!"

**Andy Kerr** This was the first time where we went, "Okay, if we're gonna go to Europe again next year, we need another album." At that time, we were putting out an album a year, which is pretty impressive, I think.

We did a lot of talking about it: "Okay, *Wrong* was more straightforward in terms of sound and song structure than the other albums. *Small Parts* had many oddball songs on it." Then it's like, "Okay, where to now?" I think we had the idea that we wanted to have an album which had a little more of a rounder, warmer sound than *Wrong*. Also, I think that we liked the idea of trying to have songs that sort of morphed into the song that came after it. You hear that more on side two.

There was actually more experimentation on the record, with songs like "0 + 2 = 1" and "Ghosts." There are other songs which are far more straightforward, like "Joyful Reunion" or "Blinding Light," which we recorded at the same time. It was heading in two directions at once.

I think that there's sort of an increasing hyperbole in later songs. I think "Mary" is an example of that. "Everyday I Start to Ooze" has that. It's not a lot of subtlety. A lot more blind intensity and rage.

**John Wright** We had always been ahead of ourselves with the music, in the sense that we would play new songs for quite a while on tour, hone them, and then come back and record them. That wasn't so much the case with *0 + 2 = 1*. After *Wrong* and the thing with Jello, we had a few ideas and things we were working on, but we didn't have a slew of songs. *0 + 2 = 1* was the first album that we actually had to take the time and write some music for. It was sketched out, but arrangements were somewhat forced. Some of the songs could have used some editing, which we would normally figure out when we played the songs live. We didn't have that luxury, apart from songs like "The Fall" and "Joyful Reunion." We had played them regularly and didn't change anything. A bunch of those songs just kind of drifted off, and we didn't play a lot of them too much after Andy left, with a few exceptions, like "Now" and "Everyday I Start to Ooze."

**Jack Endino** The apex record for me is *0 + 2 = 1*. I think they completely reached beyond themselves and just made a genius record with that album. Even just trying to get a handle on the lyrics is completely baffling. It's got some of the best lyrical couplets I've ever heard. The whole song "Everyday I Start to Ooze" is so quotable.

John in the studio, early 1990s

**Rob Wright** "Everyday I Start to Ooze" is a rather grisly tale, but it's told tongue in cheek. Most of the lines are there to get a laugh.

**Andy Kerr** "Cats, Sex and Nazis" was a song that was demoed during the *0 + 2 = 1* sessions but didn't make it on the album. Rob wrote the main riff, while John wrote the "zombie" bridge music. The zombie words were the basis of a much earlier NoMeansNo song called "Zombies." We played it a few times in the mid-'80s as an encore song. I don't remember it being an actual song per se but rather a catchy drum riff that repeated over and over with the zombie chant sitting on top of it. "Cats, Sex and Nazis" started with just Rob's two-bar bass part along with his lyrics. One of us at practice saw an opportunity to add the old zombies chant. I think songs like "Cats, Sex and Nazis," had they been given a few more years, may have been turned into better songs.

**Rob Wright** At one point, we were gonna call the album *Cats, Sex and Nazis*. Three things that guarantee success in marketing. It would have been a perfect album cover for us. Some sexy guy with a swastika, holding a nice cute kitty.

**Andy Kerr** I got more into playing a sort of noise guitar than I normally did. A lot of it was watching other bands like Dog Faced Hermans and the Ex and thinking, "Okay, how do I do something different than what I've done up until now?"

Terrie from the Ex had a lot of influence on my guitar parts on the whole *0 + 2* album. From him, and to a certain degree from Fred Frith and Eugene Chadbourne, I cottoned on to the idea of playing the electric guitar less as a musical instrument and more as a physical object.

**Ford Pier** *0 + 2 = 1* had just finished being mixed when I moved to Vancouver and went directly into Profile to start recording with Roots Roundup. Cecil and Brian permitted me to make a cassette copy of the recordings. I was amazed by the consistency of the writing and performance and overjoyed that the pinned dynamics of *Wrong* had been tamed somewhat.

Sometime in October, Craig came over with a copy of the LP to play. I was startled that "This Wound Will Never Heal" was gone, "The Fall" was in, and the sides were switched. The previous version was imprinted on me, so I didn't think this one flowed as well. I got over that pretty quick. If there was one more Andy vocal song for variety's sake, it would be perfect. As it is, I still think it's the band's strongest collection of songs.

**Andy Kerr** David Bruce, who had done the photos for *Wrong*, also did the cover photos for *0 + 2 = 1*. They were not specifically intended for the album. I think they were hanging in Ad Lib café on the wall, and Rob really liked them.

**Laurie Mercer** When *0 + 2 = 1* came out, I received two requests from European pop stars to do remixes of the song "Now." One was the guy from That Petrol Emotion, and I can't remember the other. There was an offer to pay for a remix and put it out as a twelve-inch on a little private label. Rob was like, "Nah." "But Rob, they're gonna pay for it! They just want to promote the band!" "Nah."

**Andy Kerr** Having actually made money was a definite change. It was great, but at the same time it then

became a job. This was the atmosphere around *0 + 2*. Unlike *Wrong* and certainly unlike *Small Parts* or *Sex Mad*, going into *0 + 2* and recording it was just getting down to business. It wasn't a downer to record or anything like that, but it had a little different atmosphere than the other records.

Robbie at this point was living in Vancouver, so he would come over to Victoria for practice. That also made a difference. I had spent a lot of time away from the band in Amsterdam, and then I came back to Victoria and lived there. I think the band was getting together just for the sake of the band.

I don't think we had a real sense of, "Wow, we made this really wonderful record, and we're so proud of it." We just recorded a bunch of songs and went, "Okay. Is that good?"

For me, I find the order is really imbalanced. I remember we were trying to sort out how we could fit the songs we wanted to have on the album. Rob and I were really into "Lost" being on the record. John had written the music to "Lost," but he wasn't so sure. We thought that "I Need You" has got to be on the record. The problem was we had the songs that were tied together, so there was a fifteen-minute-long section on side two that we couldn't break up. "So, what else are we gonna put on that side? Just one long song afterwards or a couple of short songs?" Then we thought, "We'll just put out the other songs as an EP." I don't think any of us were too thrilled by what we ended up choosing. It was just kind of like, "That'll do."

I think it's a good record. I just think it could have been a much better record, and, dare I say, it might have actually been a good double LP. We thought, "No, we can't put out a fucking double LP, that's just completely self-indulgent. No one's gonna buy it."

**Brad Murray—fan from Florida** My experience with Rob goes back to 1991, when they were recording *0 + 2 = 1*. I was sixteen years old, and my friend and I decided to get John's phone number from information. We ended up speaking to their mom, and she said, "John's over at Rob's," and she gave me Rob's phone number. I called and ended up chatting with his wife, who explained to me they were at the studio but I could call back to speak to him later if I wanted.

From there, we went on to have a nice phone relationship where I tried not to be too much of a fanboy. We would chat randomly about various things. I ended up sending him tapes of various bands I'd play in, and he'd send letters. I first met him in person at the Howlin' Wolf show in New Orleans. Saw them only a few more times in Atlanta, Tallahassee, and Chicago. He was always such a kind person. We'd end up sharing life stories. Giovanna, his wife, would also chat me up and ask how I'd been if I hadn't called in some years.

**Rob Wright** There was a guy named Brad from Miami who kept phoning me. I eventually did meet him too, because we did a show somewhere in Florida. He would just phone me up every now and then, and we'd sit there and bullshit for a while. He did this for like fifteen years. It was kind of funny, but he was just a nice guy. I tried to always write back to people who sent me letters. We didn't get a lot of mail, but we did get some. I figured if they're writing to me, I'd write to them.

**Nardwuar the Human Serviette** After I graduated from high school and went to University of BC, I joined CiTR radio. I saw NoMeansNo play at the Commodore Ballroom. Afterwards, I got a hold of them through their manager, Laurie Mercer. I interviewed them for my radio show. I was so proud of NoMeansNo. Here's a band from Victoria on Alternative Tentacles! Every time I did an interview, I would talk about NoMeansNo. I just bragged about NoMeansNo in every interview that I did.

And then in 1989, I put out a compilation record called *Oh God, My Mom's on Channel 10*. I decided to do a follow-up record called *Clam Chowder and Ice versus Big Macs and Bombers*, a Canada versus USA battle of the bands.

The first track on there is NoMeansNo doing "Ya Little Creep." To get them on this compilation, I sent them a VHS copy of some of the interviews I had done over the years. They gave me a song to use on this compilation. I couldn't believe it!

Then they did me even more of a favour: they passed on the tape to Jello Biafra. The next time I talked to him, he was like, "I'll do an interview with you. NoMeansNo gave me a tape of your interviews, I

loved it." Fifteen years later, Jello signed my band the Evaporators to Alternative Tentacles and released my DVD. It was all from NoMeansNo passing on the VHS tape.

**Laurie Mercer** The manager for Jane's Addiction had contacted me and was trying to get me to book them in Vancouver. They were putting together Lollapalooza and asked if NoMeansNo wanted to play. They said they knew that NoMeansNo only wanted to headline, so they talked about putting them on one of the side stages. I briefly mentioned it to Rob, but Rob was adamant at that time that they were only gonna do headlining gigs. Then, when I couldn't put together the Jane's date, they were kind of pissed off at me. I had to walk away after I had made a soft commitment. My relationship kind of went goofy then.

**Ian MacKaye—Minor Threat, Fugazi** I'm surprised to see that Fugazi only ever shared one bill with NoMeansNo, and it was in DC. I feel like they flourished much more in Europe than they did here. In the late '80s and early '90s, bands like NoMeansNo, Victims Family, and Naked Raygun were quite huge over there. These bands weren't in competition, but more like peers. These were bands in Europe that people really talked about.

Part of the deal is when you are orbiting, you don't cross other people's orbits that often. They're out there touring and doing the work at the same time we are. We'd play the same venues, but not at the same time.

We did do one show with them in Washington, DC, in 1991. It was us, NoMeansNo, and the Ex. Wow, what a gig! We had a long-standing tradition of playing in church halls in DC. Not the church itself, or the sanctuary, but the halls. The rationale behind this, especially with Fugazi, was that in DC we never made a penny from the shows. Every show we did was a benefit or a free show. The people organizing the shows, a political action group called Positive Force DC, never took money. The sound people would get paid, and you had to pay for the venue.

The show with NoMeansNo was a benefit for the Washington Free Clinic. There were about 1,400 people there, and NMN and the Ex were great. We had to step up our game following them that night. Occasionally, you play with two bands, and both of those bands are just so unique and so fresh and so original. When you go onstage, you have your work cut out for you. That was one of those nights for sure.

**Frank Turner—musician** NoMeansNo struck me as a completely unique phenomenon in the world of punk rock. They brought so many different influences to the table: jazz, metal, whatever. Their live shows were a marathon that eschewed the traditional brevity of the form, but somehow they were all the more punk for it.

**Eric Chenaux—Phleg Camp** We played with NoMeansNo and the Ex at the Rivoli in Toronto in 1991, and I was completely floored by both bands. I remember being in a van with Rob and him being quite a dry-witted ham. Even though they were both quite a bit older than us, I remember sharply that they were very generous and joyful.

Although Rob had a father-figure vibe, he was not lacking in curiosity. He never made us feel like young kids. In that way, he reminded me of

On tour with the Ex, 1991

Charlemagne Palestine, and I think of Rob sometimes when I reflect upon how to be in public and how to age with music without ever becoming cynical or disillusioned. He had a real grace, albeit a Canadian one, which is reflected in his humility. He took the music seriously, he took being social seriously, but he never seemed to be serious. His intelligence was put in service of his curiosity.

**Grant Lawrence** One of the best pieces of advice the NoMeansNo guys ever gave us was regarding our tour van. Our first few years in the Smugglers, we toured in a horrible rust bucket. A Volkswagen hippie van where the chassis was rusted out. We were so nervous the thing was gonna fall apart on the highway that we would wear helmets in the van.

John Wright was very mechanically savvy. He said, "Listen, your van is the sixth member of the Smugglers. It is literally the extra man. If you don't have a solid van, you are not a solid band." I was like, "Oh my god, okay, but what kind of van should we get?" He said, "I'll tell you what kind of van to get." I swear, it was words that changed our career, because I had no clue.

He said, "You need to get a GMC 350, but basically the same as a Chevy 350." I didn't know what that meant, but I wrote it down. He said the GMC Chevy 350 is the best long-haul engine ever built. He said, "Don't buy a Dodge. They'll break down. You'll be stuck in Thunder Bay for a week as all your gigs spool out in front of you, and you'll be helpless. Don't buy a Ford. They're no good. You want a GMC Chevy 350." So I took that to the bank.

The Smugglers won some talent contest, and we won a bunch of money. The first thing I did was search out a GMC Chevy 350. We bought it, and it had a raised camper. I brought it to John, and he approved it. I had it mechanically inspected, and it was ready to go. That van took the Smugglers around North America like fifteen times and never broke down *once*.

John was also responsible for it not breaking down, because he said, "The secret to keeping rubber on the road is two things," and he gave another two amazing kernels of advice: "First thing, never drive after a gig, because when bands get in accidents, it's after they play a show. They'll get in the van and try to drive to the next city that night. That's when it's deadly, because people fall asleep at the wheel and your van rolls off the road and everybody gets killed." I took that to heart, and then over the years, whenever I heard of a band tragedy, it was always because they had driven after a gig. I always thought back to John Wright.

The other piece of advice from John was, "To keep this thing rolling forever, it's all about the fluids. As long as all the fluids in your vehicle are topped up—gas, oil, steering fluid, windshield wiper, brake

fluid—it'll roll forever." He also said to me, "With engines like that, at every single gas stop, you have to check the fluids." This drove my bandmates crazy, but I'd say, "John Wright said to do it, so we're doing it!" That saved our asses too. The Smugglers became serious touring road dogs. I give all the credit for our touring success to NoMeansNo. They paid their knowledge forward to us, and I'll never forget that, ever.

**Jay Scott** Ken Jensen did some road-managing for NoMeansNo before he joined D.O.A. They came to Dublin, Ireland. It was a sold-out show, and everyone was really enthusiastic. But people started spitting. I hadn't seen that since a Public Image Ltd. show in Vancouver in the early '80s, and it was disgusting. But in Dublin, people started spitting on the band to show their appreciation. NoMeansNo stopped playing and said, "Come on, folks, don't spit on us." They'd start playing again, and someone would start spitting, and they would stop playing. I think that happened like three times, and I think they were actually contemplating leaving.

The crowd eventually stopped, and the show went on, but it was pretty rambunctious. Ken and I were kneeling on the front of the stage, keeping people away from the monitors and pushing people back for the whole show. I am kneeling right in front of Andy, but with my back to him, looking at the crowd. There is this big, tall guy with a blond mohawk who had been one of the main spitters. He's standing right in front of me, looking over at John and Rob. I feel this hand on my shoulder, and Andy sort of leans over me and puts his head above mine and catches this guy's attention. Blond mohawk guy turns to him, and Andy unleashed a mouthful of gob that he must have been saving the whole show. It just covered this guy's face with phlegm. The guy got angry and was trying to get up onstage, but Ken and I both refused to let him up. Andy was still playing, but he was dancing behind us, taunting him.

**Andy Kerr** The T-shirt with STAY HOME—READ A BOOK written on the back was Rob's idea. Henry Rollins had SEARCH & DESTROY tattooed on his back. The polar opposite of that is staying home and reading a book. John did the drawing.

On tour with the Ex, 1991

I'd heard that Henry wasn't happy about that. I don't know if that's apocryphal or if that's actually a thing. I remember at a certain point being interviewed by someone in Toronto. I was going, "Oh yeah. Henry, he's lame. Come and get us," or something like that. Afterwards, I thought, "That probably wasn't the wisest move. I may bump into Henry." You never know, I may *still* bump into Henry. Thankfully, I think he's gotten past that now.

**John Wright** I remember hearing through the grapevine that Rollins thought we were trying to poke fun at him, or it was a criticism of him. It was very short lived and not much of any consequence to him or us. We'd tease Biafra, but he knew us personally, so he grudgingly put up with it.

We picked on Black Flag again with the Hanson Brothers' *My Game* cover, but it's out of respect. That was an amazing album and a classic cover. Our first Hansons album cover was based on the Ramones, our second one on D.O.A., and our third one was Black Flag. I mean, that's just showing respect.

Andy (right) in STAY HOME—READ A BOOK shirt

It was just parodies and jokes, but it was also against the machismo that we eschewed. NoMeansNo railed against the whole toxic masculinity thing a lot of the time. I don't think Rollins was ever a toxic male. It wasn't directed at anyone personally, it was more directed at the *message*. The whole sort of "Search and Destroy," and dehumanizing slogans like "Part Animal, Part Machine." It was just sort of like poking fun, but it's the antithesis.

**Rob Wright** Everyone thinks that I liked to make fun of Henry because he took himself so seriously and had such a hard-edged image. But you know what? He's turned into the nicest guy. I've seen things on the internet with him, and he's grown well. He's gotten very intelligent and reasonable. I'm surprised actually to see how well he's aged and how intelligent and entertaining he is. I wouldn't mind going and seeing him talk. He's a good talker.

In those days, it was just meant to be funny. I loved him in Black Flag. That band was, in a certain way, perfect. But it was also just too much, and they just opened themselves up to be parodied. They took themselves very seriously, but that was encouraged by others as well. I never disliked him. I heard that he would come to shows, but he would never come to see us because he heard we hated him. I don't know why he thought that.

It's just funny to take that kind of grim, hard piece of graphic expression and turn it into something that's a joke. That contrast makes it funny. That's all. It was just about having a laugh. Now, it was a little bit at Henry's expense. I'm sorry, but he kind of set himself up for that. He didn't have much humour about himself in those days. I'd like to let him know, "NoMeansNo loves you, man. Don't be angry." In those days, you were always afraid he would just punch you.

**G.W. Sok** I was working at Konkurrent in Amsterdam and NoMeansNo were coming over for a tour, which meant a *ton* of T-shirts heading our way. At the time, the band managed to survive largely by selling merch. That is to say, T-shirts, records, and even more T-shirts. The band asked us if they could send the T-shirts to our address, where they would pick them up when the tour started. Since our office space was pretty limited, we got permission from the other people in the building to stack those boxes in the hallway. After all, it would only be for one or two days.

The next morning when we arrived at the office, we were told there had been a break-in that night. The visitors had climbed in through a window, didn't find anything fancy there, and went out via the hallway. We ran upstairs, but there was nothing to be

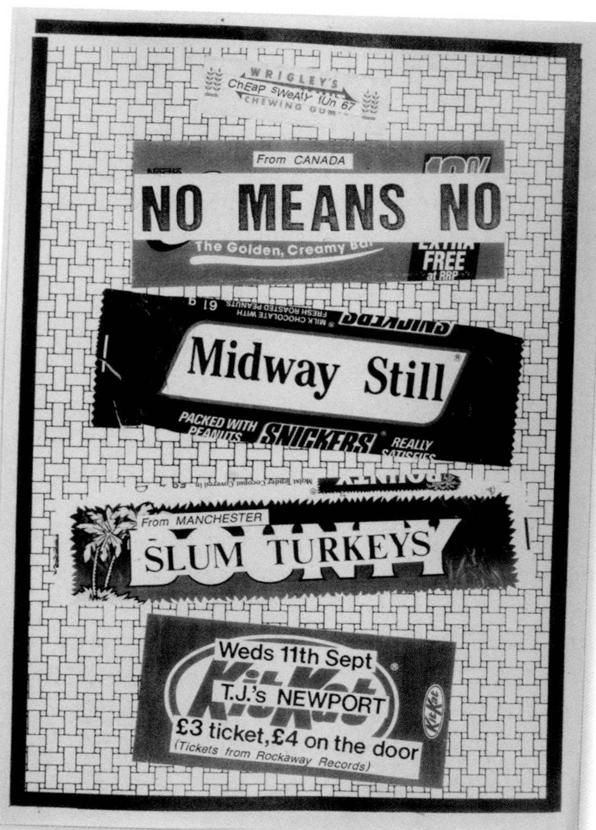

seen. The burglars had taken all the boxes, a total of eight hundred T-shirts that bore the text STAY HOME—READ A BOOK.

I went out into the street and walked around hoping to find people wearing the shirt, but no such luck. Back in the office, however, I glanced out of the window and saw two people with one of them wearing the stolen NoMeansNo shirt. I ran down the stairs, into the street, and followed them. I stopped them short and asked where they got that shirt. They said, "We found it last night in a cardboard box alongside the road, with all the trash." I thought, "Yeah, right."

Later, I realized that maybe they actually did find them. Once the thieves had found out what was in the boxes, they probably had been disappointed and had dumped the stuff on the side of the road. Or maybe these two kids had taken all those shirts home. Eight hundred shirts. That meant that for the next two years and two months, every morning you could start the day with a nice, clean shirt! Nothing wrong with that.

**Greg Werckman** In late 1991, we were putting together the one hundredth release on Alternative Tentacles. I had this idea of asking a bunch of bands to cover songs by Dead Kennedys, and we called it *Virus 100*. Many of the bands picked the big hits to cover. Rob Wright called and said, "We wanna do 'Forward to Death,'" and I was like, "Yeah, okay, that's an interesting one."

I think everyone at the label wanted NoMeansNo to do one of the big anthems and really just blast it, as only they could. Then they sent us their version of "Forward to Death," and it's all a cappella. It was the coolest, most unique thing. That just summed them up to me. They could easily cover any rock song in the world and do the karaoke version, but it was more interesting to them to do something different. Damn, it's just one of the coolest things ever. I remember sitting in the office the day we got it and we played it over and over and over. It was hysterical, classic, and perfect.

**Andy Kerr** NoMeansNo were asked to contribute to the Dead Kennedys tribute album, which we thought was very cool. I brought up the idea about doing our cover a cappella, but with us singing not only the vocals but also the instrumental parts. People do that all the time when describing bits of songs to each other. We just figured we'd do it for an entire song.

We thought of which song would work best and came up with "Forward to Death" from *Fresh Fruit*. Our original idea was for each band member to sing/play their own instrument, but I believe there was some crossover in the end. We listened to the original very closely and tried to replicate the exact parts as best as we could manage. Layer upon layer, it got recorded, one track at a time. I seem to recall John playing the kick drum part on his chest. We were very happy with the end result, but we never played it live.

**D.H. Peligro—Dead Kennedys** NoMeansNo did that version of "Forward to Death," and that just took me back to childhood. Before you even learned how to play your instruments, there was always a song in your heart and you were just able to sing things.

"Let's just put all of our musical talents in the drawer and do vocals and harmonizing and make the melody out of it." Their harmonies and the way they phrased all the musical parts for that song was really excellent.

CHAPTER SIXTEEN

# ANDY LEAVES

## "You're all gonna see a lot less of me."

NoMeansNo seemed on top of the world, but tensions had formed within the band. The constant touring and attention was taking its toll. Andy, in particular, began to question the career arc that was forming. However, the brothers were mostly enjoying the ride, perhaps somewhat oblivious to their bandmate's concerns. By the end of 1991, Andy would be out of NoMeansNo.

"None of Your Fucking Business" was getting tired of the fucking business.

**Andy Kerr** The most common theme is, "Oh, Andy met this woman and was tired of life on the road. Therefore, he left the band, and he moved to Amsterdam." All of which is true, but there was a little more to it than that.

**Emma Lee** Ingrid was their tour manager in Europe. She worked for Konkurrent and was in a punk band herself, as a drummer. She was in Amsterdam, and she and Andy had a back-and-forth relationship for about two years.

There were some tensions in the band then, and Andy basically said, "Fuck this shit. I'm leaving." He wanted to be with Ingrid; he wanted to have a home. He had been on the road for ten years at that point, and he'd had enough. He wanted a place to land

Ingrid Kerr

and have a life. I don't think he has regretted it for a minute. He loves his life in Amsterdam. They have a wonderful son, who I've known since he was young.

**Andy Kerr** After we had done *Wrong* and that tour, it was like, "Well, let's take a little bit of a break here." At that time, I also played bass for the Show Business Giants. John was producing stuff like Victims Family, and Rob had moved to Vancouver. That changed things a lot. I think that I sensed, even before those last tours, that there was a little bit of a dynamic that was changing.

We were having more separate lives than we had before, so we weren't hanging around with each other so much. The thing that I really loved about the band I felt was slipping away. It was now the "industry" of NoMeansNo. There was an urgency reflected in the mixing and some of the songwriting on *0 + 2 = 1*.

Plus, we were getting bigger and bigger audiences every time we went on tour, which was great. We went from playing in front of 200 people, to 500 people, and now to 1,500 people. That meant we didn't have the time to spend with the friends we liked to visit. People we'd normally hang out and spend an extra day with, now we'd see them for like ten minutes after the show.

It wasn't the fame. It was the downside of being popular. Everyone wants to be popular. John just took it as, "Great! More people, terrific." He didn't have any issue with it, nor did Rob. Whereas for me, I was thinking, "I don't want to become one of those bands where everything is the same all the time." I wanted to be in a special band with my special friends and do special things, with us really caring about what we're doing.

That, plus the fact that I had met Ingrid. She was like, "Well, I'll move to Canada." It was never, "Leave the band," or, "I'm gonna leave the band for you." That was never on the table. I was saying, "I don't want to be in the band anymore. I'm tired of this now. I think that I need to do something different, and not to be 'Andy from NoMeansNo.' I just need to be Andy in my life."

I think John and Rob understood that, and there were some arguments. Generally, we didn't fight on the road, but John at a certain point said, "Well, if you're really unhappy, maybe you shouldn't be doing this." Which by NoMeansNo standards was a pretty harsh thing to say. I kind of thought, "Yeah, actually, that probably sums it up really well."

**Cecil English** I was really tight with Andy. He used to come by the studio all the time, and we would hang out and listen to music together, like Neil Young and Roy Orbison, not punk rock stuff. Just smoke joints, drink some beers, sit on the couch in front of the monitors, listen to all this great stuff, and just talk music. I was really good friends with him. After he left, maybe there wasn't as much support for me

On tour with the Ex

in the NoMeansNo camp, because Andy and I were probably closer than I was to John or Rob.

I lived in Amsterdam for a couple of years too, so I knew the magnetism that place has. Andy had met somebody in Amsterdam, so I saw why he wouldn't want to come back to the culture in North America. There was so much support for the mindset that Andy had, and he absolutely loved Amsterdam. He was a natural, he should have been born there. I could see him weighing everything and thinking, "This is my life. As much as I love being in NoMeansNo, and as awesome of a machine as that is, I gotta stop here and carry my life on, from this point and from this location."

Andy is so *not* a rock star; he's like the ultimate nerd. He's the guy who you find dancing alone at the back of the hall while the band is playing and everybody's up front in the mosh pit. You'll find Andy in a dark corner with his eyes closed, dancing his ass off, all by himself. He's 100 percent moved by music, art, and culture. Everything you hear him deliver on NoMeansNo records just totally epitomizes his actual persona and character. Being a rock star would probably have zero appeal to him.

**Jello Biafra** I remember Rob's side of the story to me. He could barely contain the smoke coming out of his ears. He was saying, "I knew he was going through some stuff, but we waited on him for a year. We had all these things we were waiting to go on. Then he comes back and says, 'Well, why don't we be like Wire and break up for a while and then reappear later?'" Apparently, that was what really blew it all up.

**Laurie Mercer** Andy is a really nice guy, and Ingrid's a lovely woman. Andy would always speak up, and he stood for his own truth. He was unhappy touring and felt he would be happier in a new life. He left the biggest thing of his life. It wasn't a small decision for Andy. He had realized the dream. He'd left Victoria, which he didn't ever imagine doing. He phoned me to talk about it too, and it was just very clear that he was choosing happiness at the top. Amsterdam is a really great musical community for someone like Andy. A very experimental community that embraces the outliers.

**Daniel House—Skin Yard** When Andy was in the band, it didn't seem like two brothers. It seemed like three brothers. It was this perfect combination of people, both personally and musically. I was just a fan, but I felt heartbroken for a long time. I can't even imagine being in that band at that peak of creative fitness and then to suddenly have someone leave. It's hard for me to fathom what the experience must have been like.

**Jello Biafra** We were all very close, but stuff like that was kinda kept within the band. Maybe we smelled it coming, because he went off to Amsterdam to be with Ingrid and then he wasn't coming back so quickly. He eventually decided not to come back at all. Some of the frustrations on both ends were aired to me later. Not so much from John, but definitely from Rob, and Andy as well.

He may still be the best guitarist that I've ever worked with, and I've had the privilege of working with many. We're talking Ralph Spight, and Buzz, and Ray, and the rest of them. I knew Andy was good, but that grew when I was actually around him and learning the songs. I loved the way he would just pull stuff out of a hat.

**Craig Bougie** Andy was like, "Well, this is my exit, man. This was a good run. I had fun." Andy had confided in me that he was looking for a soft spot in the canvas just to get out, and so he did.

**John Wright** Ingrid came over and we did a big NoMeansNo tour in North America, which was fun: the six of us crammed into a Chevy van. When that was all done, Andy decided that would be the last of it for him. Rob and Andy were just getting annoyed with each other.

For Andy, I don't think it really had so much to do with Ingrid, per se. I just don't think Andy was ever comfortable with being popular. He was very much into staying obscure. He took that very seriously. He saw it becoming a circus, which is how it often ends up for bands. The funny thing is, he and Robbie were on the same page as far as that was concerned. But he didn't see it that way. As for me, I was like, "Great! Bigger shows. More partying. This is awesome!" We were having fun, and that's how I saw it.

**Ingrid Kerr** We did the whole tour with the Ex across Canada and America. That was really fun, really cool. I went with them and sold T-shirts and merchandise. Of course, I'm very good friends with the Ex as well. That was a really nice tour, and it took a couple of months. We played cribbage a lot in the van.

They were very easy to tour with. Sometimes it's a little *too* easy. But they have to be, because otherwise you drive yourself insane. It almost never went to plan, but it was really fun. The brothers are a force to themselves. You have to let them do their brotherly thing.

On tour with the Ex and Ingrid Kerr (third from left)

**John Wright** We finished up the '91 tours, and that was that. He was going to be moving to Amsterdam and living with Ingrid and eventually marrying and having Dexter, which is all fantastic. He was an amazing musician to play with and such a big part of the band in that respect. I think he made the right decision for himself, and we moved on.

**Ingrid Kerr** Andy's decision to leave NoMeansNo really had nothing to do with me. I don't think it mattered if I was there or not. That was his decision. He wanted something else. He wanted to move to Amsterdam, to move in another direction. Other people would say, "Hey, now we're starting to peak, and we wanna go forward with this." That's exactly what he *didn't* want.

**Andy Kerr** The last show was on December 5, 1991, in Hengelo, Netherlands. Sometimes in the course

Poster for Andy's last show with NoMeansNo, at the Metropool, Hengelo, Netherlands

of a relationship, you just know it's over, and so it was with me and the band I'd been in since 1983 or so. NoMeansNo changed and defined my life in so many ways, almost all for the better. But by the end of 1991, I was unhappy with where we were as a group, and as people. Increasingly, I found myself missing earlier, simpler times, or maybe more what they represented. The last song of the last encore was a cover of "Hey Hey, My My (Into the Black)." Rather than leaving the crowd with the usual "goodnight" or "see ya later," I said "goodbye." And off I went.

**Ford Pier** I think Andy was always the most committed to the conception of the group being a cross between the Residents and the Ramones. They aren't individual personalities, they are a *thing* which descends upon you, and you ask, "Who are they, *really*?" Once that mystery had dissipated a little bit, and people did know what to expect from them, then it didn't appeal to his theatrical sensibilities as much anymore. Fans shouting, "Play 'Dad'!" and all of that.

It's like the D.O.A. thing. Joe Keithley is not fooled. He knows that people want to hear *Bloodied but Unbowed* and *War on 45* material. Every eighteen months, he makes a new record, so there's something new to sell, and then he dutifully goes out with his hirelings. That's a job. It's a machine with some very specific rules. You can do that with a group like D.O.A., which has more of the demotic touch about it. It's almost as though each new visit from D.O.A., or each new album from D.O.A., is a gazette, which reiterates the same things as before. To do that as NoMeansNo would be a disservice to the thing that NoMeansNo is about.

**Andy Kerr** I never regretted my decision. What I regret somewhat is how it all went down. With NoMeansNo, communicating with each other on any kind of deeper emotional level has always been difficult. We loved each other as friends. It never occurred to Rob and John to say to me, "What can we do to convince you to stay?" It was just, "I'm leaving." "Oh, well, that's a drag. Sorry to see you go." I look back on that now and think we were just philistines emotionally.

It's funny, because all the songs we sing about were often about those subjects. We're very passionate and singing and screaming "Real Love," and this, that, and the other thing. Yet, when it actually came to sitting around a table and saying, "Why do you want to leave? How can we make things different?" That conversation never happened. I regret that, and mea culpa, I was part of that. If I could wave a magic wand, at the very least I think we should have communicated and had things laid out more. But I'm not always the best with that. And John certainly isn't. And Rob certainly isn't.

**Steve Bailey** I'm kinda heartbroken about what happened between them. I don't fully understand it, and I never really got the whole picture. It's like when a couple breaks up. You're like, "Why? You're my two favourite people!" I didn't realize at the time that Andy leaving had caused such a personal falling-out between Rob and him. The fact there was negativity between these two people who were great friends with each other and who gave so much to me is very sad.

**Scott Henderson** My wife, my eldest daughter, and I went over for Andy and Ingrid's wedding

Andy and Ingrid

in Amsterdam in '92. Neither Rob nor John came. Actually, very few people from BC made it. I mean, it's a long way. Ingrid Severson I do believe showed up, along with Deborah and Emma Lee, and Andy's mom, dad, and sister.

I suspect the Wright brothers were more inconvenienced than anything. I don't think there was a lot of acrimony in the band. I just think Andy had had enough of touring and wanted to settle down with what has turned out to be the love of his life. They were kind of resentful because, "Hey, wait a minute. We got this great thing going here!" I think if there's any rancour there, that's where it was from.

**Rob Wright** We got quite popular, but it was not a good experience in many ways. I found it to be cumbersome when we got a little too big, which we did in Europe. God, Andy had a great stance onstage. He'd look the part completely. Gaunt and serious looking and a fucking great guitar player. Andy's a family man, staying at home. I've become the same thing now.

**Andy Kerr** It was very hard, because I was here in Amsterdam and they were there. We never had the chance to bump into each other and talk things through. Nothing ever really got resolved. They just sort of carried on their way, and I carried on my way.

Over the years, I would see them when they would come to Amsterdam, and we'd sort of catch up on things. But you're just busy asking each other about your kids. It's difficult being on two continents. Maybe that's better than being the Who and staying together and only talking to each other through your lawyers. At that point, the band is still together, but at what cost?

**Jello Biafra** Andy will probably be very diplomatic, but it was a really gut-wrenching decision for him not to go back to Canada and refire up NoMeansNo. For it to be so hostile after that undoubtedly added to it, although he may have been anticipating that too. Maybe a little part of him wanted to get away from those guys.

With that much touring, there's a lot of pressure to crank out albums faster and faster unless you put the brakes on. I can see how he wanted to get off the road and away from that zoo. It played a major role in me not getting another band of my own going for so long. I didn't realize how sick of the whole grind I was until I was out of it.

**John Wright** One of the lessons we learned from Andy is that you can't be on the road all the time: it's too much and you'll kill yourself. You begin to not have a life. Besides, what are you gonna write about? You have to *live* a life if you want to write about life. It's not like Andy was the only one feeling that, but I think he was the first to realize, "Ah, this is too much." We didn't see it that way at the time. We didn't have a chance to rein it in a little bit. Maybe things would have gone differently.

We did learn that we can't just tour constantly; we need to take time off, or time away. That's when we spoke about touring the Hanson Brothers, because a change is as good as a rest. Even though we were still working and still touring, it had a whole different dynamic to it, so it was refreshing.

Andy, Craig, John, and Rob outside the van

When I finally got a family going in the mid-'90s, it was a difficult balance. I've always found myself trying to satisfy a lot of other people's schedules. It becomes wearisome, but it's what you have to do. Not everyone is going to be satisfied, including yourself. As long as enough things are satisfying, then you're doing a pretty good job.

**Jello Biafra** I just wish Andy had moved *here*, so both him and Ralph Spight could have been in the Guantanamo School of Medicine. That would have been fucking insane. Later, when we put the Hissanol albums out, to me that just laid out on the table what NoMeansNo had lost and what Andy had brought to the threesome.

**Andy Kerr** Had I never met Ingrid and stayed in Victoria, I may have joined another band and stayed single. Maybe I would have joined Biafra's band.

**Kim Thayil** NoMeansNo were huge with bass players and drummers in the Seattle alternative music scene. Those guys were like, "There's this band from Vancouver, they got this amazing bass player, and the drummer's crazy!" That's what I would hear, and I got dragged out to see them. For me, it's like, "What the fuck?! This guitarist is amazing!" I thought it would be one of these rhythm, funky, prog things, but they also had this amazing guitar player. Andy is just a fucking monster on guitar.

**William Goldsmith** I found Andy Kerr on Facebook and I was like, "Gosh, I'm gonna send him a friend request." He accepted and we started having some interactions and getting into some extended conversations. He said, "Oh, my son was talking about you the other day and he likes the pink record, he likes the Fire Theft a lot." I was like, "Dude, are you kidding me? Be sure to tell your son that his dad is the reason those bands existed."

**Andy Kerr** I've had a number of different little projects since leaving NoMeansNo. The main projects that I did were the two Hissanol records with Scott Henderson, my solo cassette, and Two Pin Din. Hissanol and my solo cassette all came out shortly after leaving the band. I just threw up all the music in the course of four or five years.

After I started a family, I made the decision that if I'm going to be a parent, I want to be here. If I was to join a band, then I would want to go all in. That's what I did with NoMeansNo. The band came before virtually everything, and that's how it should be. I've had a couple offers to join other bands, but I thought, "No, I can't do that in all good conscience."

EVENING EDITION
SAVED 866
NAMES OF SURVIVORS
MR. T EXPERIENCE
NOMEANSNO
BLAST
PRIMAL SCREAM
UNIT PRIDE
NO MORE
Let's Speak Freely!!!
A Benefit for Jello Biafra & Independent Rock 'n' Roll
WEDNESDAY, AUGUST 26
D.O.A.
No Means No
Death Sentence · Roots Round-up
Hellcats
GRACELAND
1250 Richards (enter thru alley)
D.O.A
NO MEANS NO
STRANGERS
D. O. A.
NOMEANS
GAME FOR VU
VU LOUNGE
Records and Primordial Production presents
RETURN OF
NO MEANS NO
FROM SAN FRANCISCO
EAT PIGS
AND
DR. NAUGAHYDE
NOMEANS
MY DOG POP
ROCTOPUS
MONDAY FEBRUARY 12
ONLY SHEEP NEED A LEADER
NOMEANSNO
WITH SPECIAL GUESTS
BAD YODELERS
AND
DINOSAUR BONES
SPEEDWAY CAFE
$5.00 AT THE DOOR
505 WEST 500 SOUTH — 532-5733 — ALL AGES WELCOME
ALCOHOL PERMITTED WITH PROPER ID - DOORS OPEN 8:00
BE STRONG BE WRONG
NOMEANSNO
NOMEANSNO
NOMEANSNO
NOMEANSNO
GRAVE CONCERN
SATURDAY
new view Music
in association with KDVS
proudly presents
NO MEANS NO
with special guests
VICTIM'S FAMILY
CARSON AND CKLN 88.1 PRESENT +
no means no
THE RIVOLI + DECEMBER TWENTY-NINE & THIRTY
SUCKER PUNCH AND
FRIDAY W/
Shut My Mouth Present... From Victoria, Canada someplace,
NOMEANSNO
squatting and destroying the U.K.
WALKINGSEEDS
SNUFF
CANNIBAL SUNSET
PLAY Nottingham
MON. 29th MAY
DOORS OPEN 7.30
£2.50/£3.00
STALLS AND FOOD BY VEGGIES
MARCUS GARVEY CENTRE
Lenton Boulevard
SAT
NOMEANS
WITH
$8.00 WITHOUT FLYER
NOMEANSNO
SNUFF
TRELNIKOFF
NO MEANS NO
NOMEANS
LEATHERFACE
PLEASANT VALLEY CHILDREN
Thurs. APRIL 19th
£3 adv. £3·50 door
THE WAREHOUSE LEEDS
8 till late
NO MEANS NO
SISTER DOUBLE HAPPINESS
HELL COWS
DESTROY ALL BLONDS
APRIL 25
4 BANDS 4 BUCKS
VICTIMS FAMILY
THE VICTORIA DEBUT OF SAN FRAN'S
MINDBENDING GODS OF TOTAL
PUNK-PUNK JAZZCORE
NOMEANSNO
RETURNING FROM
& FEATURING THEIR NEW
JOINED BY CHAINSAW-WIELDING
Shovlhed
FRIDAY DEC. 1
CEDAR HILL REC. CENTRE
ALL AGES
FRI JUNE 15th ALL AGES
WITH THE WICKERMEN
AND THE BROWNSOUND
GARNEAU COMMUNITY LEAGUE
MEMBERS & GUESTS ONLY
ADVANCE TIX SOUND CONNECTION
AND CJSR $7 ADVANCE $8 DOOR
PRESENTED BY NIGHT TRAIN AND HSU
NO MEANS
VICTIMS
Eureka National Guard Armory
(across from Sequoia Park)
Doors open at 7:30 p.m.

D.O.A.
MEANSNO
OCT. 24
AGES $6.50 @ DOOR
Ancient teaching
NoMeansNo
BEAT NIGS
PrimuS
VICTIMS FAMILY
Saturday April,23 8pm All Ages
Tix at: The Last Record Store,Backdoor Records
Village Music !
For directions or info call (707) 795-6563
NOMEANSNO
GETEILTE KÖPFE - 2 BAD
EINLASS 19
START 20
ARENA SA. 23.11.91
NOMEANSNO
2BAD
THUD!
XCNTRCX PRESENTS
NOMEANSNO
VICTIMS FAMILY
SHARK BAIT
CAST OF THOUSANDS
$7 ADV. $9 DOOR
FRIDAY FEB. 2ND
AT THE RIVER THEATRE, GUERNEVILLE
TICKETS AVAILABLE AT ALL XCNTRCX OUTLETS
NEW RELEASE SHOW
MEANS NO
FROM CANADA
CKDOG
SATURDAY JUNE 17
VICTORIA'S
NO MEANS NO
ALL AGES
WHO KNOWS ALL ABOUT YOUR SINS?
WHO KNOWS ALL
D.O.A.
ALBUM RELEASE PARTY
with guests
NOMEANSNO
FRIDAY MARCH 9
THE COMMODORE
Cabaret Show 9:30 pm
All Ages Show 6 pm
D.O.A.
MR WRONG
K HOG
EDGE
8:00 SHOW AT 9:30
UBLIK
TH AVENUE SW
PRESENTENT
NOMEANSNO
GRESSIVE H.C FROM CANADA)
+
RKINSON SQUARE
NOMEANSNO !
NOMEANSNO ...
Alternative Tentacles
JEUDI 3 MAI
NO MEANS NO
22 uur f1.7,50
NO MEANS NO
BIG YUCK MOUTH
THE FUMES
OCT. 20 8:30 123ARTS
NO MEANS NO
COFFIN BREAK
SHOVELHEAD
WED. 6/19
DOOR 9:00 • SHOW 10:00
$5
BABYLON A GO GO
FROM NORTH AMERICA
NOMEANSNO
SEX MAD L.P. ON ALTERNATIVE TENTACLES
AND
DAN
SHRUG
MAY 23RD
£2.00
THE EMPIRE
ANSNO
EANSNO
EANSNO
SNO
MEANSNO
MEANSNO
NDAY: JUNE 2
ALL AGES
ID required
doors at 7pm

CHAPTER SEVENTEEN

# MR. HAPPY, MR. WRONG, AND MR. RIGHT

## "You know when I told you that I would never lie? Well, that was the first time."

Andy was gone, and the Wright brothers found themselves back where they had started more than a decade earlier: a two-piece band without a guitarist. The difference now was that NoMeansNo were very popular, especially overseas. The band was firing on all cylinders. However, a major component of that machine was now gone and living in Amsterdam.

While the brothers contemplated what to do next, this in-between period proved to be a productive turning point. Rob and John produced what some fans consider their best album, *Why Do They Call Me Mr. Happy?* It became a favourite of both Wrights as well. During this time, Rob's alter ego, Mr. Wrong, came into its own, and the Hanson Brothers became a tour de force. All was not lost.

**Laurie Mercer** My role as manager was to be the sensible voice. I like to think that when there's a

Recording *Mr. Happy*: Rob, Craig, and John at the mixing board

problem, I always get calmer and more logical and focused. My role is not to react; my role is to handle the shit. For me, that was the process, mainly getting Rob to the idea that there would be a way forward without Andy. They kind of hunkered down in Victoria for a while.

**Rob Wright** I don't think we ever thought about packing it in at that point. We were both totally into it. It was a bump in the road, a serious bump. He was a big part of the band. I don't think that either John or I ever thought, "We can't do this anymore." That's the way the band started, just us recording. It was totally natural for us to keep going.

**John Wright** Rob and I discussed it. "Well, should we keep doing this? We don't have Andy anymore." I'm like, "Yeah, fuck, let's just do it ourselves right now, let's just do an album. We have a bunch of music anyway." It was not so much a setback as, "Okay, once again, we have to just do it ourselves here and see what happens."

**Cecil English** I think there was a vibe in the D.O.A/NoMeansNo camp that I was getting a little too big for my britches. Virtually everyone was coming to me at that time, and I was working seven days a week, twelve to fourteen hours a day. Both D.O.A and NoMeansNo at that point veered away from me and did some records without me. *Mr. Happy* was NoMeansNo definitely deciding they were gonna do something different.

They produced it themselves and got Brian Else to do the engineering. Maybe they were just tired of hearing my opinion about everything! I was young and cocky, and I had a lot of attitude, so maybe they just didn't want my influence. *Mr. Happy* was the first record in quite a few that didn't have my stamp on it.

**Scott Henderson** They recorded *Mr. Happy* at Profile, and they also did some of it at my studio, Dollhouse in Victoria. They also did the entire first Hanson Brothers record there. We had a mutual friend named Dan Ware, who lent Robbie his beautiful Black Beauty Les Paul three-pickup. Almost all of the guitar on that album is this wonderful guitar that Danny lent him.

The writing credits are weird: "written by NoMeansNo," and then there's a bracket "w. A. Kerr" on a couple of the songs. Those were leftovers from the previous record that Andy had participated in.

**Andy Kerr** We were discussing unfinished business. I said that while I had no problem with Rob and John using what they had recorded already, I wanted to have my parts not included on the releases, considering I had already left the group. I didn't want to be hanging around like a ghost, as it were. Rob rerecorded the guitar parts. He mostly copied what I did pretty faithfully, but he put all sorts of his own things in too.

**Brian Else** I was the engineer on *Mr. Happy*. We recorded it at Profile, and I remember Rob playing so loud one time that we got noise complaints from half a block away. There was a little restaurant nearby, and we had apparently knocked some plates off the wall.

**Tom Holliston** Rob got "Cats, Sex and Nazis" from an interview that Spike Milligan did about a book that he'd published. He said he'd asked his longtime manager, Norma, "What's selling?" She said, "Well, pictures of kittens, pictures of tits, and pictures of Hitler." So he thought, "Okay, I'll call my book *Cats, Sex, and Nazis*." Rob and I were both huge *Goon Show* fans, especially Spike Milligan: "When I finally reached the shore, I fell in a heap on the ground. I have no idea who left it there."

**Scott Henderson** "She had to stretch her legs every ten minutes or so, but I didn't, because mine were long enough."

**Brian Else** Robbie got really into sampling on "Cats, Sex and Nazis." We had this old keyboard, and we had an S1000 sampler in the studio as well. Mark Critchley helped with that. We cut that Faith No More sample from "We Care a Lot." Our studio doorbell was in there. We sampled, "Okay, here we go!" from *The Price Is Right*. There is a guy laughing in the background. That was actually Craig Bougie. We sampled LL Cool J. We got permission for them, at least the Faith No More sample.

**John Wright** I know that Faith No More were big fans. I hope they understood that it was all in the name of art. It wasn't meant as an insult, but it suited the song.

**Rob Wright** I would have liked to have seen *Mr. Happy* called *Kill Everyone Now* and have that same picture that's on the T-shirt. There were some things you couldn't do because it seemed like too much. Although I would look at people and say, "What are you talking about? Punk rock? How can it be too much? Isn't it supposed to be too much?"

**John Wright** The name Mr. Happy came from the comedian Robin Williams. He would refer to Mr. Happy being his cock. Not that it has any relationship to how we perceived it or how we used it.

**Rob Wright** *Mr. Happy* is one of my favourite albums. It's a total studio album. I rerecorded Andy's guitar parts, often just copying what he'd done. A lot of those songs became mainstays for the rest of our career: "The River," "Kill Everyone Now," "Cats, Sex and Nazis." It was a very strong release, and I thought it was recorded well too.

**Jello Biafra** At that point, NoMeansNo were a guitar band, and it worked, but Rob had less-than-complimentary things to say about himself as a guitar player. He ain't no Andy Kerr. Nor did he try to be. It may have been the swirling turmoil of that change in their lives that led to some of the depth. *Mr. Happy* has some of the most soulful vocals he'd done up to that point. He was a little more naked than he had been before. Not as much storytelling—more stuff from the heart that he needed to get out.

**Andy Kerr** Rob always said, "I'm not a very good guitar player." I think what he means to say is that when he plays guitar, he tends to rely more on the blues motifs than he does when he plays the bass. His bass sound is so monstrous and wonderful that it has a whole different context. But he is a good guitar player, and he's very precise in how he plays. I was far looser. Rob's a huge Hendrix fan.

**Jello Biafra** I begged them to have somebody remix "I Need You." Someone who had a sense of what it would sound like in a club. I put the UK office to work to see if we could get a commercial hit out of it. If a little bit more had been done to it by somebody who knew how to get stuff on radio, that would've really broken the band.

It's a pop classic. It has these really soulful, sincere vocals, followed by a heavy part, and then back out again. Sometimes people who don't specialize in writing pop hits come up with the best ones. "I Need You" is just staggeringly good for that kind of a song.

**Rob Wright** I always thought the same thing. "I Need You" could've been a hit record, maybe if done by somebody else. The irony is that it's really a religious song; it's not a love song at all. When I say, "I need you," I'm not talking about some gal. Well, it *is* a love song, but not an "oh baby" kind of love song. I don't think I ever wrote an "oh baby" kind of love song. There's enough of them out there.

**Jello Biafra** NoMeansNo were set up in such a way that they could play anything at any time. You rarely see that in a band anymore. You could also say that about Queens of the Stone Age, Led Zeppelin, or the Beatles. They never sat down and pulled out acoustic guitars in the middle of a set. But again, they could play a song like "Small Parts Isolated and Destroyed" or "It's Catching Up" and then turn around and do "I Need You" or the whole *Mama* album. That's very, very rare.

**Tom Holliston** That's me on the cover of *Why Do They Call Me Mr. Happy?* NoMeansNo always took turns doing the cover. Robbie had done *0 + 2*, so it was John's turn. It just took about an hour, but John was late, because he always used to be three or four hours late for everything at that time. He's better now.

At first, he wanted me to stand on a car. I said, "I'm not going to do that, because it's actually private property of an individual we don't know. I don't want somebody running out of the house and looking at what appears to be some complete and utter bum and reprobate standing on their car. I might suffer personal injury." So we didn't.

It would have been late spring or early summer, because I had hay fever. I took one for the team and put on this big plastic nose. My nose was running the whole time, which was unpleasant. I had this hat, and John just sort of dressed me up like the country cousin of Freddy Krueger.

John took a bunch of pictures, and it got used for the album cover and a lot of posters. Nobody knew it was me. I thought that was a real testament to John's creativity. He could take somebody and make them into somebody else.

One thing he was very definite about was having me wear this badge that said MEMBER. I don't really know why. Maybe a joke on how NoMeansNo so very seldom had publicity photos out there? It might have been, "Oh yeah, this is a member of the band." Or maybe it was a reference to Andy not being in the band, I don't know.

**John Wright** Tom had this fucking fake nose on, and his nose kept running because he was having this allergic reaction. He was a reluctant participant, but I appreciated the effort that he made. I kind of had a bee in my bonnet about this picture. I loved the image. The actual cover ended up being a bit bland, I thought. The picture was perfect, but the layout could have been better.

**Jay Scott** I had a challenge to get *Mr. Happy* to number one at college campuses across Canada, which I did. But I think that would have happened without me.

**Byron Slack** In grade nine, a friend gave me a cassette tape with *Why Do They Call Me Mr. Happy?* on side A and the Hanson Brothers' *Gross Misconduct* on side B. I had no idea that they were the same people from the same band. I didn't find that out until we were doing shows with Removal many years later. They were the ones who explained that to me. I was like, "You guys know the Hanson Brothers too? What? They're the same guys?!"

## MR. WRONG—SAVAGE YET TENDER

**Rob Wright** Mr. Wrong really came from the photo shoot of the *Wrong* record. That's where I put it together, and it was just perfect. It's all those power symbols: the clerical, the military, the police, and the businessman in his fine suit. All the pillars of society mushed together made the most evil-looking little character.

The leap then was to do bass and vocal solo gigs. I don't even really remember why that took place. Being Mr. Wrong is much harder than being in NoMeansNo, because you're out there by yourself with the bass and this stupid persona. You better be doing something good, or it's death.

I did do some successful shows, and it did inspire a lot of writing. "State of Grace" was a Mr. Wrong song, and then it was done well by NoMeansNo. I think "Who Fucked Who" was originally a Mr. Wrong song too.

I didn't do a lot of solo things with Mr. Wrong, because I would never, myself, go to a show like that.

Rob as Mr. Wrong

# Mr. Wrong

Mr. Wrong is an invading spirit who, once or twice in every generation, takes over the body of some hapless schmuck in order to promote his putrid, poisonous, yet somehow all too familiar world view. As he himself puts it....."If there is a bit of me in everyone, must there not, therefore, be a bit of everyone in me?" His host this time around is Rob Wright (occasional bassist for the band NoMeansNo) whose heart and mind have become so desiccated by 10 years in the music business that he considers being possessed by demonic forces as something of a holiday. Mr. Wrong's favourite kind of music is white noise.....his other wide-ranging interests include religion, law, military history and the metaphysical ramifications of the numeral 0.

What an asshole.

I would never go to see some guy strumming a guitar and singing some songs. Why would I want to put on a show that I myself would not attend?

**Cecil English** I had a sixteen-track practice space in my basement, and Rob used to come over and do preproduction on the Mr. Wrong stuff. He wrote all that stuff by himself with a drum machine and his bass, right in my basement.

**Rob Wright** I opened for Mike Watt in Vancouver as Mr. Wrong. What a great guy, and great bass player. I loved the Minutemen early on, just brilliant.

**Mike Watt** I got to spend a lot of time with Rob when he opened for us in Vancouver at the Starfish Room. He just came up there and sang as Mr. Wrong. He's a great singer, besides a bass man. I really liked his voice. He reminded me of John Talley-Jones in the Urinals, another favourite singer of mine. That's all he did: he just played bass and sang and it was fucking great, like Woody Guthrie would do, but kinda different. It's so personable; only this man could be doing this.

**Jay Scott** I did one tour with Rob after Andy left, when they went through that hiatus. Rob had put out the Mr. Wrong cassette, and he came out on a solo tour with D.O.A. across Canada. It was amazing. He debuted both "The River" and "State of Grace" on that tour. I won points with Rob when I managed to find a new priest's collar and shirt on a Monday in Regina. It was like trying to find mandolin strings for Spinal Tap!

**Rob Wright** I went on a tour, opening for D.O.A., and I went out with Showbiz Giants. I always remember

Mr. Right (John) and Mr. Wrong (Rob), Victoria, 1993

FROM THE DAWNING OF A NEW ERROR....

WITH SPECIAL GUESTS ROB WRIGHT AS

(THE BASS PLAYER OF NOMEANSNO)

MR.WRONG

AND OUR OWN SKIN BARN

FRIDAY AUGUST 21

TICKETS ARE AVAILABLE AT THE WEST WARD, ATTIC, AND THE RECORD STORE

$8.00 ADV $10.00 DOOR

THE WESTWARD CLUB
120-13TH AVE SW

my T-shirts outselling theirs at the gigs. The KILL EVERYONE NOW shirt was originally a Mr. Wrong shirt, not a NoMeansNo shirt. It got co-opted because it was pretty popular. It would just sell itself. People would buy that shirt because of the image. I still wonder what kind of trouble they'd get in when they wore it around. People would buy it and I'd be looking at them: "Where are you gonna wear that? Is your mom gonna see that?" It's really not cost-effective to be successfully offensive.

At one point, being as repulsively obnoxious as possible was very cool, and you would sell a lot of T-shirts for that. Slowly things changed and no one wanted to stand out anymore. No one wanted to piss anyone off anymore.

**Craig Vishek—Pigment Vehicle, Show Business Giants** I still have my KILL EVERYONE NOW T-shirt. It used to get lots of attention. People would comment, "What do you mean by that?" "Just what it says, lady!"

FRIDAY NOVEMBER 13
MONSTERS OF ROCK
TOUR '92
D.O.A.
MR. WRONG
TANK HOG
WEDGE
DOORS AT 8:00 SHOW AT 9:30
REPUBLIK
219 - 17TH AVENUE SW

**Tom Holliston** I remember once I was walking down a street wearing a KILL EVERYONE NOW shirt, and this woman, who couldn't have been under ninety years old, came up to me and said, "I want one of those."

**Rob Wright** I kicked myself over and over because I could have made so much more out of that. All I had to do was show up. That thing makes such an impression on people, and I never milked it the way I could have. Mr. Wrong could have been a real personality, but I don't have the ambition to do that kind of stuff. Even now if I went on the internet as Mr. Wrong in whatever capacity, I'd garner attention. I enjoyed being Mr. Wrong, but I couldn't take it seriously enough to make a career out of it.

**Scott Henderson** *One Down and Two to Go* is basically a collection of NoMeansNo's early four-track stuff and some stuff they did at Sea of Shit. They brought Brian Else over to help. I came up with the title, and I think I even came up with the album cover concept.

We were sitting around: "What are we going to do with all this stuff?" The idea had already been formulated to mix in the old stuff with the new. Rob was doing a lot of Mr. Wrong at the time, so I said, "Well, John can be Mr. Right. You can just be dressed in white and be like Cupid." At one point, I said, "Yeah, you can call it 'One Down, Two to Go.'" This was right after Andy quit, of course.

**Brian Else** That song "Widget" didn't have lyrics written for it, so it's just John reading the tech specs for the tape machine we were using and throwing some Shakespeare and stuff in at the end.

**John Wright** "Widget" was a highlight on that record for me. I was just reading the manual for the two-inch tape deck at the studio. *Mr. Right & Mr. Wrong* was a hodgepodge. Some songs were around that time between Andy and Tom, and then some blasts from the past.

**Scott Henderson** The fast version of "Real Love" on that album is actually my band Swell Prod. They recorded all the new stuff at my studio, and since Swell Prod. had been doing that version live, it was decided by Rob or John that our version should be on *their* album. Weird, but it kind of worked, and of course it was a great honour to be included.

**Brian Else** *Mr. Right & Mr. Wrong* is pretty weird, because it's all over the place. There's songs on there from like 1979, with Rob singing before he had his throat thing, so they sound like kids. It's funny as hell.

There were unused songs from the *Mr. Happy* sessions and a couple of Mr. Wrong solo songs. There were also a few new ones, like "Remember," "Red on Red," and "Victoria," which of course was a parody of the Kinks song. "All the geeks down at the Forge"—I think that line might have been a shot at me.

**Marlise McKee—friend** I'm from Edmonton, so I knew Tom Holliston when he was living there. I was doing sound for the Show Business Giants for a while. I moved to Victoria in the early '90s and ran into Tom, and that's how I met John. This would have been just after Andy had left NoMeansNo. I started dating John, and that's around when they started doing the Mr. Right and Mr. Wrong stuff. I actually designed and made the white suit that John wore as Mr. Right.

The Wright brothers and Laurie Mercer decided to create their own record label. Wrong Records was launched in 1992, primarily as a place for their friends and peers to release music. It also served as a home for Rob's Mr. Wrong project, reissues of some early two-piece NoMeansNo material, the Hanson Brothers, and more. It was the epitome of a homegrown operation.

**Joe Keithley** John Wright produced two D.O.A. albums, *13 Flavours of Doom* and *Loggerheads*, in 1993 and '94. They were both done at Profile Studios and released on Alternative Tentacles.

Laurie Mercer was also our manager at that time. He got some money from Virgin Records and had his own label, called Essential Noise. He put out the D.O.A./Show Business Giants split, a D.O.A album in '96, and he was working with the band Another White Male. They didn't go too far but seemed promising at the time.

Laurie also had a house on East 22nd and Rupert in Vancouver, so that's kinda where they ran Wrong Records out of for a time, and Rob's wife was running the show there. She took care of all the business and made sure things actually got done.

**Giovanna Di Francesco—Wrong Records** I married Rob Wright in 1990, and soon after that we moved to Vancouver. I started working for Laurie Mercer around '92–93. He needed an assistant, so I helped him with his management of NoMeansNo and a couple of other bands.

We decided to have our own little mail-out record label called Wrong Records. It was really just meant for NoMeansNo merch, T-shirts, some CDs, and things like that. They were still on Alternative Tentacles for their major distribution. We were just trying to do stuff via mail order, sort of like a fan club thing. Later, we put out a few other things jointly with Wrong Records and AT.

**Ingrid Severson** I ran the Wrong Records label for a while too. Part of the time it was with Rob's wife, but a lot of the time it was just me running it out of Laurie's basement.

**Laurie Mercer** Rob's mandate for Wrong Records was to put out records that nobody else was interested in. That's idyllic. It comes down to actually paying for the fucking records by selling them, but you're putting out records that nobody wants to hear.

**John Wright** We did *Mr. Right & Mr. Wrong* so there would be a NoMeansNo release on Wrong Records. Laurie Mercer really wanted Wrong Records to be a proper label and release things. Laurie wanted us to not be on AT anymore, but we were hesitant, and loyal. We didn't want to leave AT. To his chagrin, it wasn't super important to us. Of course, we did leave eventually.

CHAPTER EIGHTEEN

# TOM JOINS NOMEANSNO

## "Addition and subtraction is a cold and sober art."

More than ten years had passed since their humble beginnings in the basement of their parents' home. But in 1992, the Wright brothers found themselves right back where they had started from. NoMeansNo needed a third member who could handle the catalogue they had built but also someone who was dynamic and interesting onstage. Perhaps most importantly, they needed someone who would gel with them onstage and off.

**John Wright** From my perspective, and I think Rob's too, there was no way we could go back to performing just as a two-piece. It's now our reputation, and the vast majority of the songs were not two-piece anymore.

**Rob Wright** After we'd released *Mr. Happy*, it was like, "We gotta go on tour to support the record. Something's missing here." We originally thought anyone could play guitar. Eventually, it was not about the guitar player, it was about the person. If you're in a band with somebody, it's gotta be about the person as much as anything.

We went with Tom Holliston eventually, although I was doubtful, because he wasn't much of a guitar player and this stuff was starting to get complex. Hard-edged-type music was not what he was into. We asked him, and he wanted to do it. He wanted to be onstage and he had the fire to do it. Oh, I fucking tortured that guy for weeks. Oh man. It was just painful, but he never gave up.

**Ralph Spight** I did talk to John about possibly playing in NoMeansNo at one point during that time, but I demurred. I was getting sober, so I kinda knew I wouldn't be able to do that. I just needed a little time. I had also talked to Faith No More at that time, and it was kinda the same thing. I really needed to make a choice so I could survive. Within a couple of years, I got my feet on the ground and was able to go back out and start touring again. I do wonder, though, if my approach would have been right for NoMeansNo.

**Jello Biafra** It's interesting that Ralph has never told me that. That would have been closer to the Andy sound, although Andy's melodies are different to Ralph's for sure. They're each very strong stylists and writers in their own right. I'm not sure how Ralph would have felt if what he brought to the table was minimized like Andy was on *0 + 2 = 1* or like Tom was on the later albums.

Ralph writes songs for Ralph to sing, and that's fine. A lot of great albums have come out of that, with more to come. On the other hand, let's not forget that Andy was a trifecta with lead vocals when he was in the band, so Ralph might just have brought some of his songs and gone from there.

**Tom Holliston** I was the person who tried to talk those guys out of asking me to be in the band. Ralph Spight is a fantastic guitar player. I think probably the main reason why he was considered and then rejected was because Ralph's also a really good songwriter. I doubt he'd want to be in a band without having a greater input into the songwriting process. I'll just include myself with Ron Wood, considering that Rory Gallagher turned the Rolling Stones down before they finally ended up with Ron. I'm in pretty good company there.

I also thought over the years, "Well, you two could still do an album with Ralph." Bands like the Ex have done that for years, with people from different countries. It's an opportunity to move in a whole new direction. That's more my idea with Show Business Giants, which was really inspired by Fred Frith. He's played with everybody, in all sorts of different musical projects.

But Rob wanted the band to be the band, and that was that. He was very much inspired by John Fogerty and Creedence Clearwater Revival in that way: "This is the song. This is how it's going to be played live."

**Ford Pier** I also was approached, but in a very casual way. I think just because they had faith in my abilities as a performer. I was pretty fearless at the time. John and I had played together in Show Business Giants, and Robbie had been along on a short Pacific Northwest tour that we had done, where he was opening as Mr. Wrong.

They were like, "Do you want to try learning some of the new songs with us?" It didn't really go anywhere; it wasn't a formal proposal of marriage, or anything like that. John and Tom and I were all living together at the time. Certainly, it was an exciting idea, but I didn't think that I could do it, and so I didn't pursue it. Then they came back from the Hansons tour and Tom was in and it was off the table.

**Laurie Mercer** The news got out that Andy had left, and there was a little bit of a kerfuffle in the indie music scene that NoMeansNo were looking for someone. I started getting inquiries from a bunch of people. It brought Rob to the point where he was beginning to think about life after Andy.

I got FedExed a large box with KEEP THIS SIDE UP stickers all over it. It was about three feet by three feet. When I opened it, it was a large clay model of a stage. There was Rob, there was John, and there was Bob Wiseman with all his keyboards in the corner. Bob had just left Blue Rodeo. He's a fantastic multi-instrumentalist weirdo. His albums are very inaccessible to people, because they are so idiosyncratic. He makes puns out of time signatures.

I brought Rob into the office and showed it to him. He thought it was pretty funny, but he said, "Nah." He didn't even want to know who Bob Wiseman was. He just said, "Keyboards ... nah." It

Tom Holliston

was also because Robbie didn't know him. They wanted somebody they knew.

**Bob Wiseman—Blue Rodeo, musician** I had seen NoMeansNo two or three times in Toronto, and I thought they were the shit. They were doing something that really was close to my heart immediately, both musically as well as politically. I'd already quit Blue Rodeo when I heard that their guitarist had left.

I was in communication with different radio people, being a musician in Canada who was self-managed. Eva Rucki and her partner, Terry Walters, ran the radio station CKMS in Waterloo, Ontario. They were fans of NoMeansNo as well, and we were talking about how Andy had left. I mentioned something about wishing I could join the band or audition. Eva then made an appeal for me. I think she wrote them herself, and she made a plasticine replica of me, as a keyboard player in the band, and it was hilarious. I thought, "Well, this is a totally fantastic audition, whether they're interested or not!"

Then I heard from Rob. He basically told me that his brother also played keyboards, and that was part of his thing. It didn't jibe with their vision, and that was it. It was just kind of short and sweet. It wasn't until many months later that I heard that Tom had joined NoMeansNo.

**John Wright** It was the old question: "Who do we get for a guitar player?" It was very important for us, because Andy was a good friend. We had become friends first, and that's why we ended up working together. Maybe Rob and Andy didn't end up on super-friendly terms, but that's how it all started. The thought of auditioning guitar players was just tedious.

With the Hanson Brothers and Show Business Giants, we were already working with Tom. It was like, "Tom, do you want to do this, or do you think you can?" He was pretty reluctant, because it was daunting, hugely daunting.

**Tom Holliston** Out of the blue in '92, it was like, "Greg Werckman asked us to do a Hanson Brothers record for Alternative Tentacles, because we're not really sure what we're going to do with NoMeansNo." I didn't even know Andy had quit. He was very quiet, and he hadn't talked about it. John said, "Andy can't do it." I said, "John, I can't play guitar like that. I just strum and make my own songs." He said, "Oh, we'll help you out."

It was really fun, but it was like, "Are you sure you don't want Andy to do this? Why don't you ask Dave Carswell from the Smugglers? He's a way better guitar player." "No, no, we want you to do it with us."

Tommy Hanson, 1993

The Hanson Brothers, 1993

Rob would ask me certain questions, like, "What do you want to do with music? Why do you play music? Do you want to sign a record contract?" I just said, "No, I've never really thought about that. I just want to play shows, that's all I want to do."

We did the Hanson Brothers record, and then there was the *Virus 100* record release party in San Francisco. They said, "Why don't you come down and do this with us? We'll just do some Hansons stuff." Then they said, "Oh, and by the way, learn how to play 'Dad' and 'Oh No! Bruno!'" So I learned them.

We went down there with the late Ken Jensen playing drums. Kramer from Shockabilly was playing, and Alice Donut, who are my absolute favourite band of all time. Biafra did something with them, and a band called the Didjits and Victims Family. We did a thirty-minute set of Hanson Brothers, and then, "Okay, Tom, we're going to do five NoMeansNo songs, and you come up at the end and play 'Dad' and 'Bruno' with us." "What?!" "Come on, you've got to come up and do this."

**Ford Pier** It would have been the AT *Virus 100* release party, where Hanson Brothers played. That was before they had an album out. The Hansons were sort of a mystery to everybody who went to that show. John and Rob did a short two-piece set, and Tommy joined them for a couple of songs. That would have been the first time that he actually played NoMeansNo songs with them in front of an audience.

**Mike Morasky** We [Steel Pole Bathtub] played at that *Virus 100* show at the Kennel Club in San Francisco. Most of the bands that were on that compilation all came together and played. Mojo Nixon was there, Alice Donut, lots of bands. I remember we were kind of sharing gear to a certain degree, and it was a bit of chaos. You could feel that oddball vibe, especially since the NoMeansNo guys came out three different times. There were sort of these weird interludes like Mr. Wrong. Everybody was free to be weirder than they normally would be. People were jumping up and joining in with other bands, Jello was doing songs with us and others, that sort of thing.

**Jello Biafra** I had met Tom Holliston before he was asked to join NMN, because he was close to Steve Bailey. I'd run into him when I'd visit Victoria. He'd often bring me records he thought I should have. Steve would say, "Oh yeah, he's this weird guy that finds the strangest records in thrift stores, and then

**Poster for the Alternative Tentacles *Virus 100* release party**

**Robynn Iwata—cub** Grant Lawrence, our pal and singer for the Smugglers, was handling publicity and PR at Mint Records in the early '90s, and he also booked practically all of cub's shows for the first couple years. The Smugglers had a tour coming up with Seaweed and the Hanson Brothers.

That tour was something special! Firstly, because it was our first cross-Canada/US tour, but playing gigs with the Hanson Brothers was like touring with some superheroes' alter egos. We knew who they *really* were and what they were *really* capable of.

For our last gig together on that tour, in St. John, New Brunswick, we played a very rough-and-tumble cover of "Rockaway Beach" that we figured out earlier that day as a Hanson Brothers tribute. We all got the taped plastic glasses that they were selling as tour merch, and Neko wore her Tacoma Rockets jersey, but alas, I forgot to pack my Canucks one.

**John Wright** Working with Rob and I would be a challenge for anybody. Tom had to face that and if he gets tired of them, he just leaves them at a bus stop."

**Tom Holliston** Then in early '93 it's, "Why don't you do this Hanson Brothers tour with us, and it's going to be just three weeks in the States, and we'll be opening for Alice Donut. You don't have to do a full set. People don't really know who the Hanson Brothers are." It turned out that more people *did* know. They were kind of self-effacing about that. That tour was so fun.

While we were on tour, Laurie Mercer said, "Hey, why don't you guys go out on the road in Canada for five weeks as the Hanson Brothers?" So we did a thirty-one-date tour across Canada with the Smugglers and a band called cub. Neko Case was playing drums with them. It was fun, actually, because for the entire tour, we never washed our stage gear. Those uniforms smelled horrible. There were flies, but it kept the Smugglers out of the dressing room.

**cub dressed as the Hanson Brothers: Robynn Iwata, Neko Case, and Lisa Marr**

deal with it, of course. Tom knew what he wanted to do, and that was go out and play shows, and we were doing that. He felt very, very lucky and happy to have been brought into that situation and be able to have a long musical career, doing what he loves to do.

Even as strong willed and opinionated and as difficult as Rob can be, he also was able to listen. He wanted things to be his own way, but not entirely. If you are completely uncompromising, you're just going to drive everyone around you away. We managed it pretty well, but we also suffered from the same personal dynamics that happen to every band.

**Ford Pier** Tom went off on that first Hansons tour and he had a really good time. Of course, he got along great with everybody. He was a natural fit that way. After that tour, he thought, "Oh wow, this is fun. I could get used to this."

For a year or so, there was little or no NoMeansNo activity. Robbie started doing Mr. Wrong shows, and the Show Business Giants were very active. I was in the band by then. That lineup had John playing drums, so Tom and John were playing together all the time.

There was the recent acquisition of John's boat, which everybody was working on. They were together a lot. To them, it was really more a question of, "Do we have access to somebody with a musical mind, who we can live with?" Those qualities were all taken care of with Tom. It was just a question of Robbie inviting him over every afternoon and torturing him, making him play things a particular way and making a different kind of guitar player out of him.

Because of a lacrosse injury, although he was right handed, Tom started playing left handed, and that led him to figure out his own way of doing things. The songs that he writes are based on very labyrinthine chord structures, as opposed to the rhythmic or riffy foundations that a NoMeansNo song is built on. When you're in NoMeansNo, the whole thing is a rhythm section. He knew that it would take work and didn't know if he was up for it.

**Craig Bougie** Tom Holliston was actually living with me and Ford Pier at the time, when he was sequestered in his room trying to learn all those NoMeansNo songs.

They had tossed a few names around, and Tom came to the forefront and put in the legwork to figure it all out. Tom was not a particularly good guitar player, but he was an interesting songwriter. He was kind of a goofy, folky guy, like a Jonathan Richman kind of dude. He wasn't really geared up for the NoMeansNo style at first. That wasn't really his way, but he managed to figure it out.

**Mark Critchley** We did a show at a club called Station Street in Vancouver. It was the old Cruel Elephant club. It was August 1993. The show was billed as "Itch with Special Guests." The special guests were NoMeansNo playing their first live show in Vancouver with Tom, after their hiatus. They wanted to remain a little incognito. It was a special moment.

**John with his boat, the *Goombah***

**Tom Holliston** They told me, "Well, in September, we've got this offer to go down to New Zealand and Australia with D.O.A., as NoMeansNo. Do you want to try it?" *Mr. Happy* was just coming out at that time. I was like, "No, I can't play this stuff. I can't play fast, I can't play sixteenths!" They said, "Why don't you try it, and we'll see how it goes. We're only opening. You already know a few of the songs. We'll do those, and maybe a couple of harder ones for you to tackle."

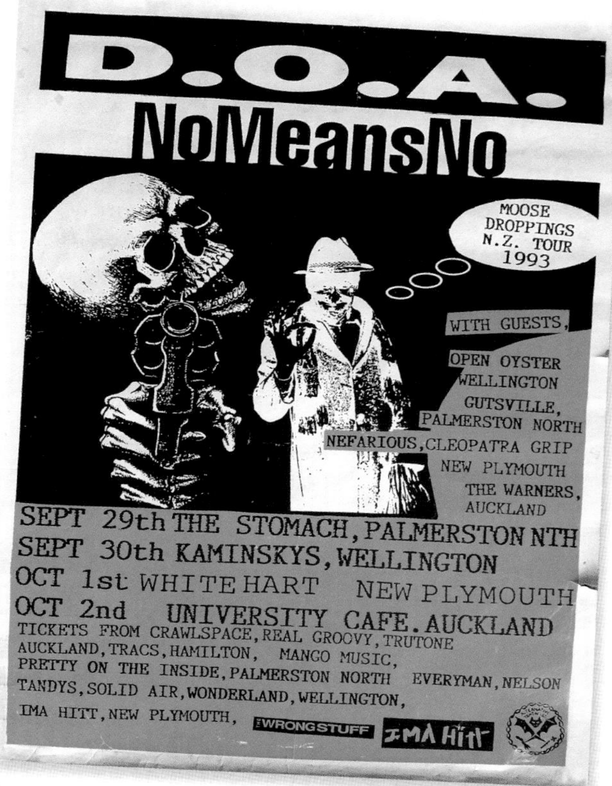

**Poster for NoMeansNo's New Zealand tour, 1993**

I said, "Well, I'd love to go to Australia and New Zealand, but really, I'm not good enough to play with you guys, honestly. I don't sing well enough. I'm too pitchy. I think you should ask Dave Carswell. You know Dave. You've just been on the road with him." They said, "No, no, we'd like to ask you." So, "Okay, I'll do my best."

We did some warm-up shows in BC, and it wasn't working out. The first five shows were like, "Oh shit, I can't play." Robbie was getting a bit impatient, but John was like, "Just go out there and rock out. Go out and do your best. You won't get any better if you're really nervous. You have to relax, and you have to change your technique a little bit." I worked on that. I practised six to seven hours a day for a solid couple of months. Learning another guitar player's technique is really fucking hard.

I eventually became a decent guitar player. A couple of things came naturally to me, like "The River." Rob said I played it better than he did because I was doing something that naturally fit in with John's drumming. Those guys have great ears, and they were always listening to everything. I learned a lot.

**Ken Kempster** They hadn't been to Australia before. They felt like this was a good way to bring Tom into the band because people weren't going to be sitting there looking at him like, "Oh, I've seen Andy Kerr five times and who are you?"

**Tom Holliston** For the first show in Australia, I learned three or four songs. I already knew "Bruno" and "Dad" from the Hanson Brothers tour set. Then we did "Bad" as an encore, so that's three songs. I knew "The River" and "Machine." "Madness and Death" was the hardest song, because there were sixteenths in it. Then it was, "You should sing a song too. How about we do a cover and you sing 'Ride the Flume' or 'Male Model'?"

**Joe Keithley** We went to Australia and New Zealand with them. A local band would play, NoMeansNo would play, then D.O.A. would close the show. By that point, they were pretty established.

That was an odd tour in the sense that we both got completely ripped off by the promoter. We probably did like fifteen shows. We played around Sydney, which is really big. We played seven shows in

**John and Tom in Sydney, Australia, 1993**

# NOMEANSNO

## THE BIO

***NOMEANSNO*** are a band.
Originally from Victoria, B.C.
A city known for crumpets. And flowers. And old people.

***NOM EAN SNO*** were originally two brothers - Rob Wright and John Wright.
Rob plays bass (sort of). And guitar (sort of). And sings.
John plays drums (a lot). And sings (sort of). And keyboards. And some other stuff.

***Nomeansno*** have released a bunch of records and toured a lot.

***NoMeanSno's*** first single embarrasses them. It's called, "Here Come the Wormies".
You've never heard it.
You never will.

**NMN** then made a 7" ep. It didn't have a name. People gave it one.
**noMEANSno** recorded their first album. Called *Mama*.
Pressed a whopping 500 copies.
And toured a little bit. In Victoria.

***nomeansno*** added a guitar player. Who was never credited by name on the albums.
His name is ... uh... never mind.

Of course they made some more records.
Sex Mad. The Day Everything Became Nothing. The Power of Positive Thinking. Small Parts Isolated and Destroyed. 0+2=1. Live and Cuddly. You Kill Me. Wrong. A collaboration with Jello. Other stuff.

Then ***NoMeAnSnO*** toured.
Canada. The United States. And particularly Europe.
And people liked them. Sometimes.

The guitar player now lives in Amsterdam. He left the band.

And ***NoMEANSNo*** continued. (Sort of)
Rob was taken over by an evil spirit called Mr. Wrong.
Mr. Wrong toured. His motto was "Kill Everyone Now".
Nasty bugger.

John produced some bands.
Maybe you have heard of them: D.O.A. . Victim's Family. Show Business Giants.

The Hanson Brothers came out of retirement. It was Rob, John, Ken and Tom.
Puck rock. Hockey and the Ramones in an evil brew.
They wreaked havoc, typically. Played a bunch. Drank a bunch. Fought a lot.
And then were sent back to the minors.

And now they have made a new ***NoMeansNo*** album.
For some reason it is called, "Why do they call me Mr. Happy?"
It is on Wrong Records, but licensed to Alternative Tentacles.
(That means Jello makes a little money, too).

And ***NomeAnsNo*** are going to tour again.
Who's in the band?
You'll see.

Where are ***NO MEANS NO*** going?
Australia and New Zealand get them first, Sept - Oct 1993.
And then? And then? And then?
You'll see.

More misinformation is available from Wrong Records,
P.O. Box 3243 Vancouver B.C. Canada V6B 3Y4.
Their career is completely mismanaged by Laurie Mercer.
Abuse: (604) 684-9338 Fax: (604) 684-9337

**Wrong Records bio of NoMeansNo, 1993**

the Sydney area. I remember the first one being really great, and then we played different suburbs. I remember that by the seventh one, there was nobody there. Everybody had already seen D.O.A. and NoMeansNo.

**Bow Campbell** We [Front End Loader] didn't even really start playing live until '92. We were all in our late teens or early twenties and all on the dole. We were just jamming and playing, punching cones, and generally faffing about. We'd managed to make a bit of a name for ourselves as a decent band, and one that was not afraid to play anywhere, anytime. In fact, that's all we really wanted to do.

Anyway, this dodgy prick of a local promoter suddenly considered himself a big shot and thought he'd bring D.O.A. out here. He contacted us to see if we'd be up for being local support for an Australian national tour. I don't remember any of us being huge D.O.A. fans at the time, mainly due to unfamiliarity, so at first we were a bit "meh." Then he said, "Oh, they're bringing out this other Canadian band, NoMeansNo. You guys ever heard of them?" At which point, we all completely lost our shit and said, "Yes, fuck yes, fuck yes, fuck yes, we're in!" So we did a very long, very arduous national tour of Australia with D.O.A. and NoMeansNo in 1993.

**Joe Keithley** We stayed in this awful rooming house in this old part of Sydney with these huge cockroaches. We made the best of it. Craig Bougie and I were standing outside this hotel, and this beer truck going up the hill had the back gate down. A beer keg rolled off the back of the fucking truck and almost ran over Craig.

**Bow Campbell** There was one night at the Lansdowne in Sydney when their sound engineer, Craig, was nearly killed by a keg of dark beer which fell off the back of a truck while he was having a

smoke outside. They did what any self-respecting band would do: they dragged the keg into the band room, tapped it, and we all drank it. Hilarity ensued, as you'd expect.

**Tom Holliston** I remember we had a day off in Australia and we went to this children's park. It was so strange, because we were on this little children's train looking at all this Australian wildlife. I was scrunched in, giving myself permanent back problems, next to Joe Shithead: "Look at that, Tommy, it's Tasmanian devils there." It's like, "What the fuck am I doing here? This is something I never, never thought about in my entire life."

We're playing at a place north of Sydney called Newcastle, and we're backstage, and it was a boy's club put on by some really wonderful police officers. It was basically, "Let's try to keep kids out of trouble. They can put on these shows and we can help them." It was great. There were a couple of Australian cops backstage, and Shithead had just bought a bottle of Jack Daniels, and he'd bought some ice, but all he could find was a block of ice. "I can't get at the fuckin' ice," and one of the cops said, "Hey, mate, use this," and he gave Joe his gun, and Joe started pounding on the ice with the cop's gun, going, "Yeah, thanks."

We went to play in New Zealand, and I was bugging Joe about being from Burnaby or something. He's a very strong man, and he put me in this headlock, and I thought he was going to kill me. I was smoking at the time, so I put my cigarette out on his forearm, but he was so pumped up that it took him ten or twelve seconds to realize that his skin was burning. He was like, "What did you do that for?!" I was like, "Joe, you were going to kill me!" "All right, fair fight, fair fight!"

**Jello Biafra** Tom Holliston entered the picture, and he wasn't quite as strong a force in the band as Andy was. Maybe in part because they wouldn't let him. The Holliston lineup of NoMeansNo does not play Tom's songs, and it was clear to him that they weren't interested in him bringing in any songs to the band. That was a huge mistake in my opinion.

It still sounded pretty goddamn good, because Rob and John are such great composers, but it will sadden me forever that the decision was made to not let Tom write for NoMeansNo. It would have been neat if Tom's composing had been given the John and Rob treatment, because they're all crack arrangers too. That would have been fascinating; it still would be.

**Rob Wright** Tom Holliston is a brilliant songwriter, but none of his songs suit NoMeansNo. That was always a shame. He's got reams of wonderful material,

**D.O.A. and NoMeansNo in New Zealand, 1993**

but it's this whimsical, funny stuff that wouldn't have fit into the heavy, serious, monolithic NoMeansNo.

**Laurie Mercer** When they added Tom, I was shocked, because Tom was not as competent as an instrumentalist. He was nowhere near what Andy, Rob, and John were producing. They just felt he would learn on the job, which, to his testament, he certainly did. Robbie was so hive-minded that I wondered if he was actually looking for contributions. Tom and Ford Pier delighted in coming up with absurdities, so a little bit of that got into NoMeansNo. He added to the silliness.

**Sylvia Kenny** It's interesting that Tom was the one who took over Andy's role. He wasn't a substitute, because he made his own mark on the band. They were both close friends and had similar personalities. They also had similar intellectual and musical influences, Elvis Costello and a little bit of that Fifties vibe. Tom was the natural person to jump in when Andy moved to Europe and to continue on with NoMeansNo.

**Gijs de Wit—tour manager** To be quite honest, I think Tom was a great substitution, because he brought a persona into the band that was incredible, but he didn't fight the brothers.

**John Wright** Tom was in over his head at first, there's no doubt about it. He knows a zillion chords, but he didn't have the experience with playing solos and crazy rhythms. Andy had such an incredible sense of rhythm, and Tom just wasn't at that level. That's not disparaging Tom at all. That's not where his talent lies, but he practised his ass off. We were friends, so it was all good. We were having fun together despite the stresses. He worked hard, like we all did. Robbie and I had to work hard to play the way we played. We went on for another twenty years with Tom.

CHAPTER NINETEEN

# EVERYTHING LOUDER

## "I'm beating my head up against the wall, and on each single separate brick is a picture of you all."

A time of transition often presents the opportunity for experimentation. John and Rob now had their replacement for Andy. Tom Holliston joined up, and NoMeansNo were doing shows again. An impromptu jam overseas sparked the notion of adding double drums to their live shows. NoMeansNo were back beyond full force and louder and bigger than ever before. Though they had lost some steam after Andy's departure, the engine was revving again.

### MEET KEN KEMPSTER

**Ken Kempster** I first saw NoMeansNo during a daytime show at the OAP in early 1982. I had not started playing the drums yet. My brother brought home a drum kit and that was all she wrote. I met Chris Buck in grade eleven and we immediately clicked. After a few forgetful bands, we ended up playing with Scott Henderson. Scott had been playing in various bands and doing his solo stuff for years but had not been able to find anyone who could play some of his more rhythmically challenging music. Chris and I took up the cause, and in the summer of '88 Shovlhed was born.

A year and a half later, Tom Holliston recruited me for a new version of Show Business Giants. Andy Kerr was on bass. He and John Wright were still in Victoria at this point. John started doing live sound

"Button Boy" Ken Kempster with friend

for Shovlhed and SBG as well as recording Shovlhed's second release, *Stove Boy Serves Daily Special.*

By '91, Shovlhed had broken up, and for a short time all three of us were playing in the Show Business Giants. The next year, Andy Kerr left NoMeansNo. Scott and I formed the short-lived Swell Prod., and the beginnings of a more fully realized Hanson Brothers was in the planning stages. Tom maintained a version of the SBG with John and Scott and eventually moved to Vancouver, as John had done months previous. When I was asked to join the Hanson Brothers and eventually NoMeansNo, it was just a continuation of the musical relationships created several years before.

**John Wright** Tom had been pretty reticent to join in the first place and was very nervous about trying to fill Andy's shoes. We didn't want a nervous wreck playing beside us, so if Tom's going to be in the band, we're going to have to make it work for him.

Rob and Ken in the tour van

We thought about how we could take a little of the tension off of Tom.

We had talked about having two drums for years, even when Andy was in the band. I remember seeing Tankhog play with two drummers in Victoria, and it was just so cool.

We'd gotten to know Ken Kempster really well with the Show Business Giants, and he's such a great drummer. We thought, "Let's give it a try and see what happens. We'll mix it up." He ended up doing about half the set. For the encores on that first tour in the States, I got off the drums and played keyboards.

**Ken Kempster** I had been in the Hanson Brothers for about a year. We had been touring all over Canada and the States, and that was great. Then there were discussions of Tom joining NoMeansNo. I remember we were coming back from the tour and they were talking about the future of NoMeansNo.

They said, "Well, the Hanson Brothers tour is over, and we're gonna get back to NoMeansNo. Tom, how do you feel? Do you want to be in the band?" Tom's like, "Well, yes, I do." Then they asked, "Ken, we've been thinking of maybe adding a second drummer. Are you interested?" I'm like, "Well, yeah, totally."

**Tom Holliston** When we came back from Australia, they said, "Tom, we're going to make it a bit easier for you. We're going to do about twelve dates down the West Coast with Ken Kempster. We're going to have a second drummer, and that'll ease you into it a bit more." I was surprised, like, "Really? You still want to do this? Because I don't think it's working out." "We'll start the show off as a two-piece, and Ken will play

Hanson Brothers promo photo

'Red Devil,' and then you will come on, and we'll do 'Land of the Living' and 'The River,' and this is how we'll do the show. Every time we go on tour, you'll learn another two or three songs." That continued for the next few years, with Kenny playing the drums until *Worldhood*, on which I played guitar on everything.

**Marlise McKee** NoMeansNo had played with the Ex in Europe and they had done "Red Devil" with two drummers. John really thought it was a great thing. He loved the sound. They also realized if they hired another drummer, they could tour across Canada as NoMeansNo and then come back as the Hanson Brothers and play the same venues.

**Rob Wright** Hey, more drums! There were a couple reasons we decided to get a second drummer. I thought if Tom had another new guy, and it was a different context, then the pressure would be off him a little bit. Ken was a really good drummer and a really nice guy. He added a lot, I think. I remember playing "Red Devil." We killed the performance, just bass and two drums. Fucking great to do that—it was fucking awesome. I just loved being surrounded by guys banging away like that. In some cases, it may have been too much, but I love bands with two drummers.

At that point, it was kind of the peak of our popularity too. With two drummers and all the gear, we needed an extra guy with us to help with loading and stuff. We had two vans. It was more of a production.

**Ken Kempster** We did our first NoMeansNo practice. After a couple of minutes, I thought, "Wow, this is really hard. This is really gonna take a lot of practice and a lot of work. I'm not as good a drummer as I thought I was." I suddenly realized how good John and Rob really were. The Hanson Brothers were basically Ramones songs, simple by definition.

I changed the way I played, and I worked with John on that. From that day I realized, "I really need to pay attention and get better at my craft. I can't take any of this for granted." I wanted to do a good job. I didn't want to disappoint anyone. I wanted to play music, and I wanted to tour.

**Jay Scott** Ken Kempster joined in, and holy fuck, it was so powerful. Kenny was a disciple of John's and had so much respect for him. Ken didn't overplay, and they were just so good together. On that first US tour with two drummers, Ken Jensen and I flew down to see them at the Great American Music Hall in San

NoMeansNo as a four-piece: John, Rob, Tom, and Ken

Francisco. They played "Red Devil," which was just so loud, it was insane. They did a cover of the Residents' "Would We Be Alive," with John playing timpani mallets, and it was so syncopated, like a drum machine. I couldn't believe it was live drummers. It was phenomenal.

**Ken Kempster** With their new guitar player and adding me as a second drummer, it seemed like Rob and John decided to try some different things with the live shows. One of those things was getting John on keyboards for some songs. There's a song on *Why Do They Call Me Mr. Happy?* called "Slowly Melting," which is John's song. There's a big keyboard line to it, so they thought, "Well, we can do that song now. And let's bring back 'Forget Your Life,' because it's got a big keyboard drone to it."

We'd mix things up. Sometimes Rob would come out and do just a song on his own, like "Sitting on Top of the World." Then John would come out and the two of them would do "Red on Red" or "Who Fucked Who." Then Tom would come out. Then I would come out, Tom would disappear, and we would do "Red Devil." We did the "build up, break down, build up" kind of thing. Playing around with stuff like that, we also got a little more improvisational. "Wiggly Worm" was a song where we started doing this two-minute strange introduction of just making bizarre noises.

**Steve Bays—Hot Hot Heat** The first time I tried mushrooms was at a NoMeansNo show in 1994 when I was fifteen years old. Pigment Vehicle opened that show. I was in the pit when the mushrooms kicked in. I probably weighed like ninety pounds, and there were all these guys in their twenties and thirties with their shirts off, and I was just getting thrown around like a pinball. It was verging on a bad trip, but for whatever reason that just rewired my brain to associate NoMeansNo with the most decadent psychedelic escapism.

**Matt Morris—Plaid Retina** We opened for Victims Family and NoMeansNo at Gilman Street in Berkeley. I remember they had the two drummers. It took them fucking forever to set up, but it was a great show. At the end of the night, I went to get paid. Rob Wright split the money evenly, three ways. I protested. I was like "Dude, we're not from far away. A hundred bucks would totally do us. You have two vans!" He was just like, "No. We just finished two nights in San Francisco and sold them out." I was like, "Okay. I'll take the money." No fucking headliner ever did that. That was just so cool and generous.

**Adam Pfahler—Jawbreaker** Jawbreaker got to play with NoMeansNo in the spring of 1994 in Albuquerque. We'd been listening to *Small Parts* and *Wrong* on a loop the past handful of years, so we jumped at the chance to support them. At the end of the night, Rob Wright plopped down at the table to count the money. Without a word, he forms two equal piles on the table, effectively cutting the money in half. It was way more than our guarantee. I sat there in stunned silence. I looked at the cash, then back at Rob, like, "Is this right?" After a long beat, he pushed one of the stacks toward me, and with a little sparkle in his eye, he smiled and said, "Bonus night, eh?" which is like the most Canadian thing ever said.

Tucson, Arizona, 1994

**Jay Scott** We went to Petaluma, California, and we were playing with Victims Family at this big theatre downtown. There had been a child abduction in Petaluma a few weeks before we arrived. It became international news, with the story repeating endlessly on CNN. Tragically, a couple days before we got there, they had found her dead. The memorial for her was being held at another place just a block down from our venue. The theatre marquee said, in big letters, "NoMeansNo," and underneath, "Victims Family," so people started coming into our theatre, thinking this was the memorial. We had to keep turning people away all night, sending them down the road. It was so weird.

Canada is a vast country. From Victoria, BC, to Halifax, Nova Scotia, it is a 5,800-kilometre (3,600-mile) drive over mountains, across prairies, and through several weather systems. It's a pain in the ass for any touring rock band who makes the trek, only to realize they now need to get back home. John and Rob thought they had the perfect solution. They'd tour from west to east as NoMeansNo, then turn around and head back west and play all the same towns again, but this time as the Hanson Brothers.

**Ken Kempster** Two bands for the price of one. Touring across Canada as one band and then back again as another worked well in theory but failed in execution. Canada is a huge land mass and has a limited number of venues. The NMN tour now had a second drummer and a second van to carry the extra people and equipment. Driving across Canada in two vans is expensive, but there was enough money touring as NoMeansNo to go into profit.

Going back as the much lesser paid Hanson Brothers was a different story. We had two vans, a full crew, but with smaller venues. Ten days from Halifax to Vancouver meant that the only profit the four of us made was the $1,000 we were paid at Lee's Palace. Unfortunately, that money disappeared after being left unguarded in the dressing room. We retired the one tour/two bands routine.

Later, we would practise for upcoming Hanson Brothers shows while touring as NMN. We would do three Hansons songs during the second encore. Unfortunately, most audiences in Europe were perplexed by this change of musical direction. Many approached us saying things like, "Why are you doing this? Is this supposed to be terrible? Please stop." The mini-Canadian Hanson Brothers tour that followed, however, was a resounding success. The Canadians got us.

**John Wright** Eventually, what wore us down was the logistics. The sound checks took like two fucking

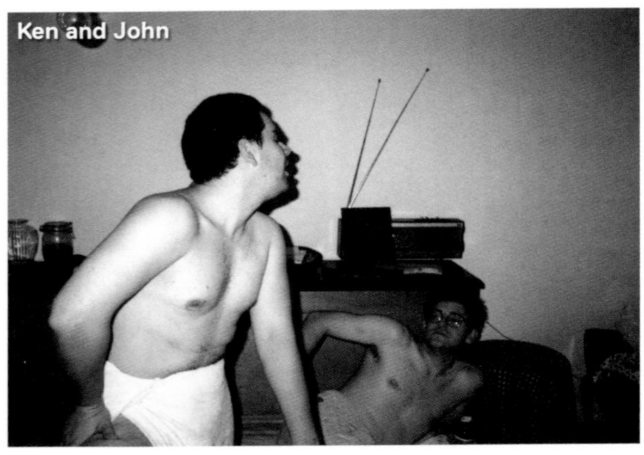
Ken and John

hours. Every stage manager in the world hated us because of the two drum sets, the keyboards, and having to change everything around for this stupid band.

## ROSKILDE FESTIVAL, DENMARK, 1994

"Hello! There's been a mistake. We're not NoMeansNo . . . Hello, Tokyo! We are Cheap Trick! This one, I'm sure you all know . . ." —Rob Wright

**Rob Wright** The Roskilde Festival in Denmark was amazing and hilarious. I had a great time. Apparently, Sepultura needed to switch their spot because they had to make it to another festival the next morning. When we got there, they said, "Sepultura's got to play in your slot. We want you to play on the main stage, after Peter Gabriel."

We went out and I introduced us as Cheap Trick because it was just the whole rock experience, which we'd never done. It was sixty thousand people, and you can feel them. They had two sound towers close

Roskilde Festival, Denmark, 1994

and two towers back. They were on a lag so they wouldn't interfere with each other, because they were so far apart. Craig was back there. He's used to driving a little Cessna. Now he's on a 747. He's got this unbelievable sound system to work with, but he's a hundred feet away. We played pretty well, and everyone liked it. We had a really good show.

**John Wright** Roskilde was a four-day festival, and there were like seven different stages. We were supposed to play a smaller stage, but Sepultura had some scheduling issues. We got moved to the main stage on Friday night, playing last, after Peter Gabriel. That's the fucking primo spot! They asked if we'd mind switching, and Gijs said, "Yeah, fine!" We never played to a bigger crowd before or since.

We set up and sound-checked in the afternoon, and Craig was way the hell over there in a tower. Craig was, "Okay, I've never done this before." The house tech was there and helped him figure it out.

Peter Gabriel played, and frankly he was kind of boring, not a lot of energy. Apparently, Peter had been up late the night before and was hungover. He had Billy Cobb on drums, which I was stoked about. He didn't really do much, though. He just played along to the drum machine.

He played till midnight, and then there was about an hour before we went on, while another band was playing a side stage. We got all set up, and it's still kinda light out, dusky. Word got around that we were gonna be playing, so about three hundred people started gathering. I'm thinking "Boy, this is going to be a pretty lonely little crowd in front of this big giant stage." I didn't know what to expect.

We're all ready to go, and the MC asks, "Who are you guys?'" "We're NoMeansNo from Canada." He announced us, and we walked out. I looked out, and I couldn't see the end of the people. Literally, there were about three hundred people out there who actually knew who we were and sixty thousand who were wondering, "What's going on?" We played for an hour and got big cheers. Everyone was happy, and we rocked out as hard as we could. It was just so surreal. Tom wore his bright blue lamé jacket.

Gijs was there with us, and he was selling our merch. He said there was no business really going on. A woman came up and was looking through our CDs,

John and Ken on the beach in Brighton, UK, 1994

and she said, "You show me seven and I'll buy two." Then she pulled up her skirt and took a shit, right there. She bought two CDs and left.

**Tom Holliston** Peter Gabriel also had a blue lamé jacket on, but *my* blue lamé jacket was better than his. He was hungover, and it was incredibly boring music. Everybody in the crowd was so out of it by that point. There were like forty people at the festival who were there for the music, and everybody else was there to get chlamydia. Rob and I did an interview backstage with a Polish rock magazine, and I said that Rob and King Diamond had collaborated on a project and were putting out an album later that year. Eventually, I got a copy of the magazine and it was all there, word for word. Some people are really good writers, and some people are just there to drink the free beer backstage.

**Rob Wright** That was our one big rock 'n' roll mega experience. Sixty thousand drunken fucking Scandinavians. I really liked it. It was so bizarre that it's just special.

**Tom Holliston** When we were on that '94 tour, my mom was getting very sick from cancer. They said, "We can stop the tour right now if you want to go home." I didn't want to do that, because my older brother had told me, "Tom, when you're playing and performing, a lot of people in the crowd have people who are dying, children who are very sick. They are coming to you because it's your job to lighten their mood. That's the whole thing about 'breaking a leg.' It means you have to go on because other people have broken legs, so you can help them feel better." I think

Rob, Ken, and Tom, Brighton, UK, 1994

that is very true. We were all good at supporting each other that way.

**Robert Holliston** Tom was on tour with NoMeansNo in 1994 when our mother was diagnosed with cancer. It was very serious: she had only a few weeks to live, and he was on tour in Europe. She actually lasted until he got home.

**Paul "Gigs" McGivern—promoter, author, tour merch** I remember the second-to-last date was in Hamburg, and I was doing the merchandise. The amount of money these guys made on merchandise was unbelievable. I had this huge box, and in the bottom of it, I'd screwed in a safe. There were tons of different currencies in there, and at the end of it, we went back to Amsterdam to unload everything. We all just sat in the Konkurrent office and had all these huge piles of money. They all just put it about their person and flew home with it. It was tens of thousands of dollars' worth. For a little punk band in those days, that was an awful lot of money.

John counting money during a tour

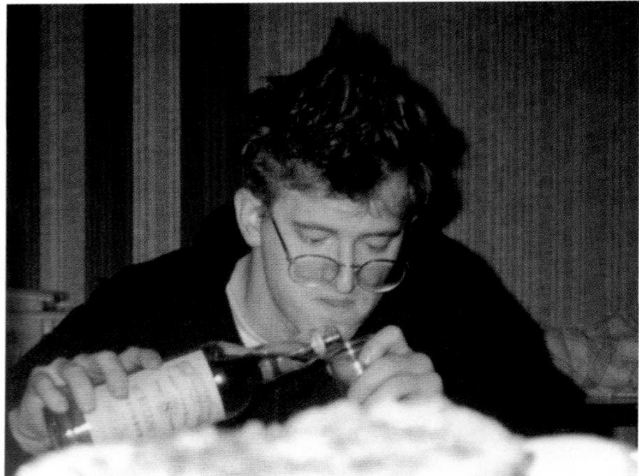

**Marc Belke—SNFU** In the mid-'90s, I remember talking to John Kastner from the Doughboys, and he said, "The biggest bands in Europe right now are Fugazi, Bad Religion, and NoMeansNo." They were regarded as a true headliner, because they would play huge halls. They made a good living and carved out a huge legacy in Europe.

**Rob Wright** We flew into Vancouver from Europe, and I had my bag searched by customs. There was a plastic bag with all sorts of stuff, and they said, "What's this?" and I said, "It's about $60,000 in seventeen different currencies." In those days, they didn't really care.

We used to get about eight hundred people for a gig. Now we were getting double that. After Nirvana and all that faded out of the limelight, our crowds disappeared. The extra people weren't really into it anyways. It was just what was going on at the moment.

You get too popular and it just becomes consuming. You think, "Why? All I do is think about the business. I'm not thinking about the music." It's too much, unless you have a team of people. Managers and minders doing all this shit for you. Then all you have to do is get up there, pick up your instrument that someone else has tuned for you, and play it.

You start worrying about promoters and halls and contracts and money. It becomes showbiz, and showbiz is a business. There's a traditional way of doing it, which was alien to us. We never wanted to learn the shit, but we had to get involved with it. When you're playing two-thousand-seaters, you're not going with the local kid promoting shows.

CHAPTER TWENTY

# THE WORLDHOOD OF THE WORLD

## "It is the art of tearing it apart, and when you know what you know, let it out, let it go."

Wrong Records was humming along nicely in Vancouver, and NoMeansNo were operating at full capacity once again. Ken was still joining the tours as a second drummer. Tom Holliston, having conquered his initial doubts, now felt like a proper member of the band. They decided to return to the studio and work on the next album by writing new material and also tossing in a couple of oldies that had not made the cut in the past. Rob's songwriting was becoming more inward and philosophical, while musically the brothers were on top of their game.

**Matt Skiba** The first time I saw NoMeansNo was at Fireside Bowl in Chicago in 1995. I was working there, helping bands load and doing security. It was completely sold out. It had been a while since NoMeansNo had played in Chicago, so we were expecting a big show, and a possibly violent show.

I remember seeing this guy in the front row, kind of a tweaked-out punker kid, next to this girl, and they were irritating each other. I remember the girl slapping him, right before NoMeansNo were about to play. Just as the band is getting onstage, this tweaker guy turns around and full-on punches this girl in the

John in the studio with his son Aidan, 1996

face like he was hitting a dude. He completely fuckin' just knocked her out. That was a split second before Rob's boot hit this guy's mouth, and it was even in time with the first beat of the song! The dude was just out cold. And that was the *beginning* of the show! I've never been happier to see someone get their teeth kicked out.

**John Wright** We recorded *Worldhood* at Scott Henderson's Sea of Shit studios in Colwood. We had a little more flexibility because we were at our friend's place and not paying a lot of money at a twenty-four-track studio in Vancouver. We did the recordings for the *Would We Be Alive?* EP at the same time.

We recorded at Scotty's, and then we took it over to Greenhouse in Vancouver to mix it. Greenhouse had an SSL with some automation, which made life a lot easier. It was our first chance at automating. We probably spent about a week mixing.

**Scott Henderson** It was overwhelming, because we had two drum kits. We had Rob's bass rig in the green room, which unlike the main room was not soundproofed, and you could hear Rob's bass rig at the liquor store a fucking block away.

They mixed it at Greenhouse with Brian Else. Brian was okay, a really crusty metal/punk kind of guy. He stayed at my place a few times, and this man chain-smoked. My house smelled like cigarette smoke for a year.

**Brian Else** Scott had a dog named Imru. It's this big yellow ... I don't know what the fuck it was. Like part pit bull, part hound. It had the most evil bark in the world. At the very end of *Worldhood*, you can hear a dog barking and then "Ooh, my leg." That's Imru.

**Scott Henderson** It was actually Imru's predecessor, a German shepherd named Roger who had done the awful deeds that earned the studio the name Sea of Shit.

**Tom Holliston** "Ooh, my leg." That was Ken Kempster. There were always catch phrases that came up, just things to help pass the time. There was an entire tour where we started talking way too much like Charlton Heston. One time, we were coming back from dinner in San Francisco. We heard this voice coming out of the alley saying, "You touch my butt, I'm gonna bust your ass." Ken has got a real talent for mimicry. A little bit later we heard somebody, again just out of sight, say, "Ooh, my leg, I think I've hurt my leg!" So Ken just started saying that. That's where it came from. We'd use these weird things to sort of dispel the frustrations of touring. Just having these sort of ridiculous word associations to smooth things over and make life seem more real.

**John Wright** I had done a piano demo of the song "Humans" that had a different chorus than what ended up on *Worldhood*. I didn't like the original chorus, but I remembered a song I had written years earlier for Infamous Scientists that never got used for anything. I really liked *that* chorus and the chord changes, so I just stuck that into "Humans" instead.

**Brian Else** Tommy Holliston had a really hard time singing "Wiggly Worm." When you listen to it, he goes, "Wiggly, waggly, wiggly," and he keeps mixing it up. That outro, where he is fucking it up, that's real. It was a real tongue twister for him.

**Tom Holliston** I couldn't stop laughing, and that was the take that ended up on the record.

**John Wright** We recorded a version of "Predators" for the *Worldhood* album, but we had been playing that song for years. It even predates Andy, back in our two-piece days. It had never found a home. We resurrected that because we really liked it and it was something Tommy could sing.

**Tom Holliston** They always had a backlog. They always had the next album written while the previous one was being recorded.

The only thing I really contributed to on the *Worldhood* album was "Victim's Choice," where I came up with a couple of guitar parts for that song. We also recorded an extra few songs, like "Would We Be Alive?" by the Residents. That was something that Robbie wanted to do. He and I worked out an arrangement for it together. I also came up with the "Sunshine of Your Love" bit at the end of "Rise." I was starting to feel a bit more comfortable bringing in ideas.

**Marlise McKee** John and I got married and had two sons together, Aidan and Liam. Aidan is the baby on the cover of the *Would We Be Alive?* EP, and that little drawing on the back was Robbie's little homage to him. When Aidan was really little, he and Robbie had an excellent relationship. Robbie would take Aidan golfing every week, when he was like two years old. Robbie bought him little tiny golf clubs. They would go out golfing and then to McDonald's.

**Laurie Mercer** Rob would tour with a book by Heidegger for a year. He just kept rereading it, to try to fully understand it. They'd play me a song, and it would be so incredibly profound, and I'd say, "Rob, that is just brilliant! Where did you get it?" "Ah! Heidegger." He had studied something philosophically to the point where he completely understood it

and could transform it into something that's a current understanding of angst. Just brilliant.

**Rob Wright** I am a great believer in the stupidity of the human race and its overweening self-importance. People think they are the centre of the fucking universe. The universe doesn't give a shit about them. The Buddhists are right with their philosophy: the self is a sickness. People who are constantly concerned about themselves are less and less living in reality and more and more wasting their time.

What you have with human beings is a reasoning, language-driven mind in the body of an ape. Humans have been apes for like four million years, but we've only been reasoning, rational people for a few thousand. Who do you think rules? It's the ape. The ape still rules. You can see it in everything that people do. The mind is a great tool, but that's all it is. The human monkey is a very strange and delightful creature, but don't trust him for a second.

You've got to look at yourself as what you are: one monkey amongst many. What's true of them is

**Outtakes from the *Worldhood* photo shoot**

Hey Ken,

Here' a little Christmas bonus I guess you weren't expecting. Konk licensed the Fish Tank EP to Touch + Go in the States and damned if they didn't go and sell a few thousand of them. Who would have thought! Anyway, this represents your 25% after commissions. My advice to you---put it all on Red. HO HO HO!

Love

Rob

true of you. If you want to find hypocrisy and ignorance and cruelty in the world, you don't have to look far. Just look at yourself. That's the only place you can make any changes and the only place you can find any answers. You can't control other people's behaviour.

**Ford Pier** When NoMeansNo were demoing *The Worldhood of the World*, they would practise downstairs in the house in East Vancouver that Tom, Craig, and I lived in. Every morning Craig and I would sit there and play chess while the band practised. I remember at one point looking at the chess board and saying to Craig, "When the fuck did that happen? I'm not in check!" He was like, "Well, I guess you are, fucker." I said, "No way, no way." We went back over our moves and figured out that his piece had just vibrated over onto that square from the sound coming from downstairs.

**Jon Active—Alternative Tentacles UK** I worked for Alternative Tentacles in the UK, taking care of the mail-order catalogue. People would send in order forms with a cheque or a postal order. Sometimes we got letters from people in Russia or Poland saying, "I have no money, but I really love this band. I can trade. I will send you a bottle of vodka. Will you send me this record?" Credit to the boss, Bill Gilliam, because he actually *did* accept that offer on at least a couple of occasions, and we got a bottle of vodka through the post.

**John Wright** We did the *In the Fishtank* EP with the same guy who recorded the *Live and Cuddly* album, Dolf. We knew two Dolfs, German Dolf and Dutch Dolf. This was Dutch Dolf. He had his studio outside of Amsterdam, and we did that *Fishtank* record there, which was super fun.

**Dolf Planteijdt** NMN were invited by De Konkurrent to make a twelve-inch in their *Fishtank* series. That was a very good experience for me. John had a particular way of recording the punch of the drum kit. He placed two SM58s on both sides of the bass drum near the ground on table stands as a kind of stereo underhead. I still use that technique sometimes.

Alternative Tentacles helped arrange a full tour of Canada and the US for three of its bands in the fall of 1995. The lineup was NoMeansNo, Alice Donut, and Japanese band Ultra Bidé. The bands all got along famously and became great friends. After that North American tour,

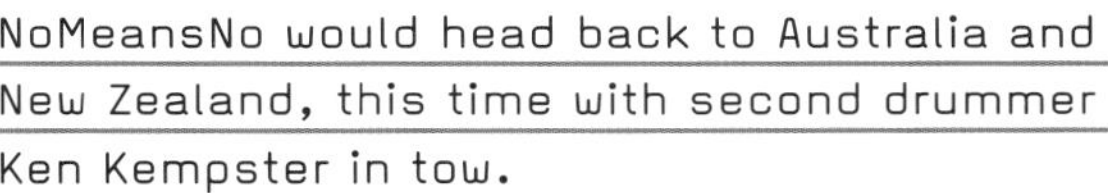

NoMeansNo would head back to Australia and New Zealand, this time with second drummer Ken Kempster in tow.

**Tom Holliston** I like all the people in Alice Donut personally very much, and I loved watching them perform. We did a tour where they opened for us in Canada and we opened for them on the East Coast of the States. They are everything I want in a rock 'n' roll band. I always really enjoyed touring with them.

**Tom Antona—Alice Donut** We had done shows with NoMeansNo before, going back to the mid-'80s. We became friends immediately, and they stayed with us when they'd come through. Alice Donut played in Victoria one time, and we were drunk and fighting and we kind of broke up onstage. John Wright brought me to his parents' house to sleep down in the basement that night, but we were back together to play Vancouver the next day.

**Rob Wright** Tom Antona. Oh boy. He would disappear on tour. It'd be three days to the next show, and he'd just show up at the gig. Where he'd been and what he'd been doing up till then was known only to him. They were crazy, but also a wonderful live band and a joy to play after. I always liked it when the other band was really good, because it just sets people up for a full evening of good music.

**Stephen Moses—Alice Donut** We were driving west through Canada, maybe Alberta or Saskatchewan. This was back when CB radios were a thing. I was driving and the Ultra Bidé guys were in a van behind us. They were like, "Steve, we're bored, tell us some taxi-driving stories," because between tours, I was driving a cab.

I told this story about these hookers getting in the cab, and I'm embellishing it with some extra-colourful curse words. The cops had been listening on their CBs. They pulled us all over and took apart our van, but they eventually let us go. At least they didn't find the weed that was buried in my sleeping bag. After all, we still had a bunch of gigs left.

**Tom Antona** Those years touring with NoMeansNo and Ultra Bidé were really happy days. We all just hit it off so well and became good friends. Not just the three guys in the band, either, but everybody associated with them: Ingrid, Craig, Laurie, and Booza, their Australian roadie.

**Tadayuki Hirano—Ultra Bidé** We were introduced to NoMeansNo's music by the guys in Alice Donut, and we got hooked up with them because we were also on Alternative Tentacles. Our first show with them was at the Commodore Ballroom in Vancouver. They had Ken as a second drummer on that tour. We toured with them all the way across Canada and then down through the USA. We then convinced them to come do some shows in Japan a year or so later. We had nothing but a good-ass time.

**Stephen Moses** NoMeansNo never really blew up on the East Coast of the United States. When we toured together, Alice Donut would headline the shows out east. On the West Coast, NoMeansNo would headline. We all jammed together sometimes onstage, and I remember whipping my trombone out at some point with them, I forget which song. Again, that would be the marijuana.

**Laurie Mercer** There were so many thwarted opportunities. I'd go to Rob with an idea that I knew would work. His only caveat would be, "Well, somebody else has to pay for it." Then when I would line up somebody else to pay for it, suddenly there would be new rules.

In the mid-'90s, I got a distribution deal with Virgin Records Canada. We put out the Hanson Brothers *Sudden Death* LP on that, in 1996. They only put out the Hansons because they wanted to put out something, anything, by NoMeansNo. The guy at Virgin *loved* NoMeansNo. I didn't make any guarantees, but said I would talk to them. He gave me an entire label deal, so NoMeansNo would have all of the rights.

When the Hanson Brothers album came out, I got the actual Hanson brothers from the movie, the actors. I got so many things lined up to help promote it. We released the record, but then Rob said, "We don't want to do anything with the Hanson Brothers right now. I want to go to Europe as NoMeansNo." I said, "But Rob, we've got this record coming out. Virgin's willing to do all this stuff. They love the record. They want to promote it." "Nah, we're NoMeansNo now." It was just such a horrible fuckery.

I had to go back to this guy and say, like, "Thank you for the label deal, but . . ." I wound up putting out a fucking Show Business Giants record on Virgin, like that was ever going to sell. I was just trying to do anything to convince them that this would be a home for NoMeansNo. I'm sorry, no disrespect to Tom, but there's no major label ever going to make a nickel off of a Showbiz Giants record.

**Joe Keithley** We toured all the way down to Texas with NoMeansNo in spring '96. Craig mixed both bands for the entire tour. In San Francisco, Jello came out, and we arranged to get two drum sets onstage and extra amps for the encore of "Full Metal Jackoff," with NoMeansNo and D.O.A playing together. It's a big, long song. Rob and Tom hadn't played it before, so I went over and showed them the chord changes. A week later, Jello caught up to us in Texas and we sang it again in Dallas. This time, I hadn't bothered going over the chords with those guys, and it was horribly fucked up.

**Ford Pier** San Francisco was always a really good show for both NoMeansNo and D.O.A. We'd stay at Biafra's place for a week, doing little day trips to all of the places in the Bay Area. It was great having the one place that you could stay at, do laundry, and have a base of operations that is relatively stable. You'd drive to the Oakland show, or the San Jose show, or the Sonoma County show, and just drive back to Biafra's every night.

There was one show at the Maritime Hall in San Francisco. It was put on by the Family Dog, who were this venerable organization that had put on all of the Jefferson Airplane, Electric Flag hippie shows with their fabulous light complement. We assumed it would be well organized, but it wasn't. Everything about it was terrible.

The NoMeansNo sound check only took place after they put their foot down and said, "No, we are not going to use the drum riser. We always set up with the drummer on stage left." The technical staff grumbled about that.

Then they started running the tests for the oil-drop light show thing while we were playing: "Can you turn that off?" "We're just testing it out to see where you guys are going to be standing." We explained to them that they are not going to be shining that thing on us while we are playing. They were, "But that is the whole point of the show!" NoMeansNo were

**Ford Pier at the merch table at Maritime Hall, San Francisco, 1996**

just like, "Look, who's the light guy? Okay, you get the night off. Just turn them all on and go away."

Then there was some elf who they sent over. Ingrid, who was doing merch for both bands, was approached by someone with a little envelope for her to fill with Family Dog's take from the merchandise. The contract riders for both bands specifically stated we don't do that. Our merchandise money is our merchandise money. This is not negotiable. They had signed this, of course.

Then Joe and John were set upon by some people who were, "This is how we do things here. It is a community thing." "Ah-ha, no it's not." They had decided by now that we were not team players, and there was a definite frostiness between the two bands and the organizers.

Then they decided to start setting up their own merchandise table, and what do they have for sale? Shirts with the poster for the show silk-screened on them, which of course has NoMeansNo and D.O.A. on it. "Sorry, excuse me. This is bootlegged merchandise here." I told them that they can't sell D.O.A. or NoMeansNo shirts here. The entire experience was so unpleasant. John was about one centimetre from saying that NoMeansNo would not be playing.

**Ingrid Severson** I had a big fight with those people because they were freaking out on me. I had to go get reinforcements. They were getting all irate, old-hippie-style. They wanted a cut of the merch, and that never happened.

**John Wright** It was a terrible venue, terrible promoters, just fucking awful. They were so stupid too. They ended up overpaying us because they were morons. I was collecting the money for NoMeansNo, and Joe was getting paid for D.O.A. They were counting the money out, and they counted out a thousand dollars too much. I started, "Ah, but . . ." and literally Joey fucking kicked me. I almost blurted out, "Hey, you're paying us too much!" If they'd been cool people, we would have pointed it out, but they were dicks, so it was like, "Fuck you, you idiot."

**Ford Pier** It wound up being fun at the end of it. There was a big encore of "Full Metal Jackoff" with Biafra singing, and Tom and I were careful to bring our Dalai Lamée wimples. Then we all went into "Ob-La-Di, Ob-La-Da" by the Beatles without telling Biafra. He scuttled away as quickly as his little legs would carry him.

**Jello Biafra** I jumped up with NoMeansNo, and we played "Bad." Then, in a prearranged joke on me, they started playing "Ob-La-Di, Ob-La-Da." I caught wind of what was going on, so I got the hell off the stage, in no small part because I didn't know the words anyway, let alone that it was a *Beatles* song!

**Joe Keithley** I remember we had some time off in the afternoon before that show at the Maritime Hall, so we decided to play a hockey game. Let's just say it was about sixteen to nothing. The Hanson Brothers may have talked a good hockey song, but we schooled them pretty badly then. I just wanna put that on the record.

**Joey Shithead (Joe Keithley) and Tom**

Colin "Booza" Pickup

## RIP BOOZA—ROADIE LEGEND

**Tom Holliston** We had a marvelous Australian guy named Colin Pickup, affectionately known as Booza, who was our roadie for a few years. We had more than one incident where John was playing the drums, and he'd put one foot up on the top of his rack of toms, and Booza would run over and tie his shoes. Of course, John's tongue would still be sticking out of the corner of his mouth, even when his shoe was being tied.

**Scott Henderson** Booza could take a Marshall cabinet, lift it with one hand, and put it on his shoulder, and then take another one, put it on the other shoulder, and walk up two flights of stairs.

**Craig Bougie** He'd throw those amps up on his shoulders like headphones and walk them into a room. When we toured in Australia, he drove us straight through the outback, instead of going around. We ran out of gas, but he was the world's best roadie. I was really sad when I heard years later that he had died, apparently from carbon monoxide poisoning in his house.

**Rob Wright** Oh god, Booza was amazing. He was the youngest of seven brothers from the north of Australia. Complete boyo, working class, rough boy. He was hugely strong and had an edge on him too. He got in with us, and I think what he discovered was that you could be with a group of guys and not have to be a tough guy twenty-four hours a day.

It was nice to have him in the van, because if you got into any trouble, you had a guy there who could solve it. He got to like me a lot, and I don't know quite why. I think because I was straightforward with him. I didn't treat him like menial help right from the beginning.

Over the years, we became good friends, but it was hard being his friend, because he was on speed all the time. That's why he had to smoke so much marijuana: to calm himself down. He was a driven guy with a lot of aggression. I really liked him, and I was really sorry to hear that he passed in such a way.

**Paul "Gigs" McGivern** When he was younger, he raced motorcycles, so he was something of a daredevil, adventure seeker. His nickname was "Booza," but he never drank at all. When they were in Australia, John was driving and Booza said, "You've gotta watch out for the kangaroos on this road!" John asked, "What happens if a kangaroo jumps in the middle of the road?" Booza just went, "Miss it, mate."

**Tom Holliston** Booza was about 160 pounds, wiry strong, but he had a phenomenal sense of balance. He was made for tai chi. He could walk the length of the Commodore Ballroom floor on his hands and then walk back. He had the greatest saying when

Booza onstage

you were talking shit. He'd say, "Wake up to yourself, mate!"

He became our roadie in Australia because at that time you couldn't bring your own crew down, because of union rules. We had Craig Bougie listed as "second guitarist" or something, that's how he made it down.

We played a show in Melbourne, and there was something wrong with one of the amps, and while we were having dinner backstage it was like, "Where's Booza?" He was downstairs fixing the amp, so I put a plate of food and a drink together and brought it to him. He was like, "No one's ever done that for me! I've toured for years and no one has ever paid attention like that. Thank you, guys." I was like, "Really? Well, everybody on tour shares the flat tires along with the great shows. That's how it is."

**Tom Antona** What was amazing about Booza is that he had this very sunny disposition. The NoMeansNo guys loved him. They would have him roadie whenever they could. You don't need to fly somebody from Australia, but they did, because he's just an awesome dude.

**Ryan Rodier—fan from Saskatoon, Saskatchewan** NoMeansNo were coming through Saskatoon on their two-drummer '95 tour with Alice Donut and Ultra Bidé. I heard they needed a floor to sleep on, so I jumped at the chance to volunteer for them to stay at my house. To my surprise, my parents agreed.

After the show, I jumped in one of NMN's two white vans and I guided John to my house. We stopped along the way at 7-Eleven to get some veggies for Rob. We arrived and slunk quietly into my parents' basement. My mom had mattresses and hide-a-beds all set up for them with fresh linens and pillows. When everyone went to sleep, their roadie, Booza, found our hammock outside and slept there instead. Rob and John's sister Shelley worked at the University of Saskatchewan Law School, and they drove to pick her up in the morning and brought her back for breakfast at my house. Booza and Craig whipped up some banana pancakes for everyone. My younger sister got the band to sign her trombone case. Tom Holliston wrote, "Enjoy your slush pump."

Tom, Gijs, John, and Rob

Rob in Prague, 1998

disturbed by the fact that he was sitting there losing money in that slot machine and that somebody was making noise.

**Aaron Chapman** Rob was going through this big Miles Davis period during that time. He'd play Miles all the time in the van, at quite a loud volume. I didn't know a lot of people in punk rock circles who were listening to jazz. Rob recommended a couple albums and got me into it as well.

**Rob Wright** You know who the greatest musician in the world was? Miles Davis. Because he'd say, "I'll set it up, you bring your instrument, and we'll play. Whatever you want to play, play. If it's right, it's right. If not, I'll tell you. Play what happens *now*, right at this moment, with all these other people around you doing the same thing."

We were never at that level. My limitation is that I needed it to be the same. We did often go off the track, but by no means were we an improvisational band. I never jammed with anybody. I wasn't secure with that. I didn't see how it could be focused and to the point, which I liked it to be. Perhaps that's a little anal on my part. I was a bit of a control freak with music, but it worked for us. People often said, "Whoa, you did all this weird stuff." No, we did all the same things that we did last night. Every fucking note is in the same place, the same way.

**Rick Cook—friend** I first met the guys in Dallas, Texas, in 1997 in a club called the Orbit Room. It was a Hanson Brothers show, and I approached Rob after the show to get an autograph, and he said, "Sure, no problem, but what we really need is a place to stay." They ended up staying at my friend Tim's that night.

Two years later, they came through Dallas again as NoMeansNo. My wife, Lisa, and I had a big house by then, so they ended up staying with us from that point forward whenever they'd come to town. Lisa would usually cook a big barbecue for them, and Rob would typically go golfing at the course nearby.

The house was actually my grandmother's house. The boys loved being there, because they would

Tom in Prague, 1998

stay up watching VHS tapes of Jack Benny that my grandmother had. They also enjoyed hanging out and talking to her. She would love having them there.

**Lisa Cook—friend** I love Rob, because he's very deep. I was suffering through some depression, and we talked about that kinda stuff. It was really cool to find out his perspective on things. They are just awesome people, and we loved having them stay with us every time they came through town.

**Rob Wright** We were in Green Bay, Wisconsin, and we were loading back in. For some reason, we put all the money in my computer bag. There was about $10,000 in US cash in it and another ten grand as a bank draft. Someone either stole the computer bag while we were moving stuff into the club or I left it sitting in the parking lot when I got the van. You don't really want large amounts of cash floating around, but that was the way we did business for most of our career. It was all done cash money. We were eventually able to recoup the bank draft, otherwise we would've been out $20,000. That was an eventful time. We were making quite a bit of money, so there was always cash lying around. It had become a business, a fly-by-night, do-it-all-yourself business. It was no frills. If something happened, you were screwed.

**Keith Rose** Those guys never got upset. No one pointed fingers. No one was perturbed in any way. They just kept going on. It's like, "Oh well, that happened." That was their work ethic: just keep going. I think by the end of the tour they still made money.

I had my wallet stolen one time. I had been saving all my per diems. I wasn't drinking on tour, and I had probably four or five hundred dollars saved up. The next day, Rob came up to me and handed me a pile of money and said, "I talked to Giovanna, and I wanna give you this money, and if you can pay it back, great. If you can't, that's no problem." He gave me like five hundred bucks.

**Aaron Chapman** Rob would say, "Rock 'n' roll is one of the last great cash businesses." They would amass a significant amount of money, especially from merch sales and the guarantees. It's important not to underestimate how well NoMeansNo did in merch sales.

Before the shows, the guys would usually go for dinner around the time the doors opened. I couldn't leave, because the moment the doors opened there would be people at that merch table, and I'd be busy selling stuff until the end of the night.

**Ernie Hawkins** They had a bunch of money stolen on tour, which screwed them up financially. That meant they had to tag on a bunch of shows to make up for that money, so they put us on the opening slot. That was the beginning of a chapter in NoMeansNo's life where the seven of us, the two bands and Craig Bougie, were a team for years. We toured together in Europe and Canada multiple times.

**Bill Johnston—Removal** They put out the second Removal album on Wrong Records and had us open up for them on a few shows and then on a big Canadian tour in '99. It was two three-piece bands, and it seemed to work out really favourably for everybody involved. We were gung ho to tour all the time, and they were as well. We didn't mind being on the road for six months of the year.

After John's marriage with Marlise ended around 2000, he moved into the apartment in my house in

Rob on laundry day

Vancouver, and he lived there for about two years. That also facilitated more closeness between us. Then Rob and his wife moved in for a few months after John had moved out. Rob had sold his house and hadn't yet bought a new place.

**Rob Clark—Removal** I had first seen NoMeansNo in my hometown of London, Ontario, at a club called Call the Office in the mid-'80s. Later, when I moved to BC, I lived right around the corner from the house in East Vancouver where NoMeansNo practised. I figured out roughly their schedule, and when they'd jam, I'd sit in the park across from their house. They were so loud I could hear them in the park. I'd drink a coffee, smoke a joint, and listen to NoMeansNo practise.

**Aaron Chapman** Rob was always good with the fans if anybody came up and wanted a photo with him or an album signed. But before shows, he would usually just stay in the van by himself. He liked to have a bit of quiet before he hit the stage. He wasn't always watching the opening bands or making himself available before the show. After so many years of people wanting to talk to him and everything, he was probably a little tired of it.

Rob couldn't understand the really crazy, passionate fans. For example, if someone had a NoMeansNo tattoo, John would sort of get a kick out of it. Tom would usually say something silly, but Rob would say, "God, look at these people! They're going to regret that." There was no concept to him that this was really quite a tribute. He just didn't understand why anybody would want to do that.

**Lesley Bell—fan from London, Ontario** I have a sizable Mr. Wrong tattoo on my arm. They came through London, Ontario, and I knew I'd better seize the chance to get my picture taken with the fellas, since they didn't come our way all that often. I met the super-nice Tom and chatted with the amazing John, who really dug the tattoo. He told me to track Rob down for sure. Finally, after a nudge from a friend, I met Rob. He was pretty surprised and said, "Look at *that*! You're walking around with this mug on your arm forever?!" He graciously agreed to take a picture with me.

NOMEANSNO
nons
is better than no sense at all.
NO MEANS NO
WRONG
RIGHT?
WRONG
NOMEANSNO
KILL EVERYONE NOW
BE STRONG BE WRONG
WRONG
NO MEANS NO
KILL EVERYONE NOW
WRONG
KILL EVERYONE NOW
RACE EVERYONE NOW, A guy.
GO MAN, GO!!

NO MEANS NO
WRONG
HANSON BROTHERS
Yankee Sandwich
NMN
KILL EVERYO
WRONG
CHUCK WOOD
Minor Threat
Cops & donuts
CATS SEX & NAZIS
NO MEANS NO
MAMA
0+2=1
ALTERNATIVE TENTACLES
no means no
NOMEANSNO
15 JUIN 07
CCM J. LENNON

CHAPTER TWENTY-TWO

# ONE

## "Of course I think about it. I think about it all the time."

A superstitious person might look at the events in Poland and the stolen money in Green Bay as an ominous portent. Perhaps it was. Rob was really starting to dislike the grind of constant touring and did not handle the stress well. The century was coming to a close, and the world was a little on edge. Change was in the air. However, NoMeansNo soldiered on, recording a new album and continuing to tour relentlessly.

**John Robb** NoMeansNo are political, but it's human politics. A surreal political commentary. It's not a manifesto, and it's not simplistic. It's kind of sketching out a situation that forces you to think. If you overstate your case, people switch off. It's too much to expect people, just because they're in a band, to get everything correct. As long as they get most things in a human way, then actually that's a quite powerful political statement.

**Rob Wright** I loved the whole thing about punk rock, but it was so laced with complete contradictions and hypocrisy from the punks who were like, "I don't care, I'm going to inject myself with urine," to the ones who said, "We are going to end racism tomorrow with our music."

**Marc L'Esperance** When we started doing *One*, I was really excited by it. I liked getting away from the chainsaw guitar and the super-unrelenting pounding. I liked that there were more dynamics to it, and Rob was sort of doing more storytelling in the songs. To me, it hearkened back to that *Mama* type of sound, where there was more subtlety and more nuance to it. I think the band was pretty happy, because they got me to remaster a bunch of their earlier releases not too long after that.

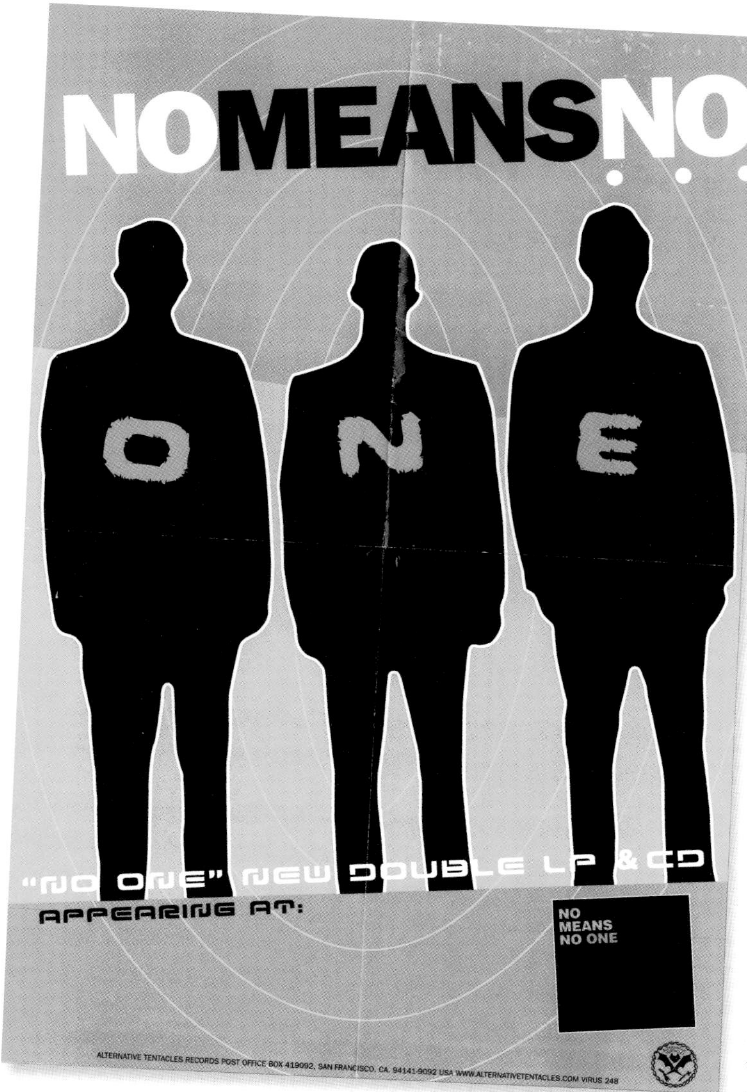


**Rob Wright** John's songs were always sort of against the flow, like "Hello, Goodbye." That's a pop song. It's a beautiful pop song, but it's not the type of song that NoMeansNo cut its teeth on. John would always like to orchestrate. I was always sort of against that. We would argue about the production. It was just two different tastes, two different sensibilities going at the same thing. To me, stripped bare was always the best. Whereas ornamentation and orchestration was what really delighted him. He loved bands like XTC. I liked them too, but that was never what I was looking for. I was looking for John Lee Hooker.

**John Wright** At the time, we weren't selling a lot of records, and that kind of music was not that popular. It's too weird, too original, too not hip. *One* is an album that requires you to actually listen to it, pay attention, and enjoy what it has to offer. It's not a party album. It's also an album I would mix again, but I think it has a really nice feel. As an album, it has that sense of a whole piece.

The version of "Bitches Brew" was a very specific idea that Rob wanted to do. That arrangement is all him, and it worked out awesome. But that one's a commitment: "Okay, I'm going to listen to this *whole* song." Then we put the slowed-down version of "Beat on the Brat," and that was us just being cheeky. It

**Jello Biafra** Andy said after one or two albums without him, "It's obvious nobody says no to Rob anymore. No one edits him." Thus, *Headless Bourgeoisie* and *One* were double albums, with a lot of meandering.

**Tom Holliston** *One* is probably my own personal favourite of the stuff I worked on. I was most comfortable when we were demoing *One*. I got songwriting credit for "A Little Too High" and "Under the Sea." I think Robbie said, "Well, we can just split the songwriting credits three ways." I also really like the song "Our Town," even though it was really hard to play. Rob overdubbed the sixteenths, because I can do sixteenths with my right hand but I can't fret with my left hand. That's just my tale of woe.

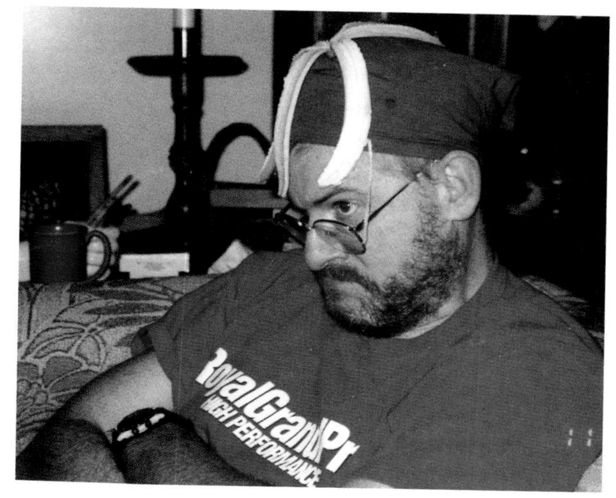

Craig and Rob

had been a long time since we put a cover song on an album. We thought that after covering Miles Davis, then the bookend would be the Ramones. We turned that one on its head too. We played that song live sometimes, just for fun as an encore. It would drive people crazy: "It's too slow!"

**Rob Wright** "Bitches Brew" is one of those songs on the album everyone skips over. I think some of our best stuff is the stuff that's the most unlistenable. Anything over five minutes and you're really asking a lot of any listener.

**Mark Critchley** They brought me in for the *One* sessions to play the piano part on "Bitches Brew." I wasn't sure what they wanted at first. Did they want me to invent something, or did they want me to try and imitate the version from Miles Davis? I played a bunch of things, and they said they were happy with it.

**Marc L'Esperance** The songs on the *Generic Shame* EP were all part of the *One* sessions. There was just too much to fit on a double album. It came out about a year later.

**Jello Biafra** Things were stalling enough with the *One* album. If they had said they were making their next album with Ipecac or with Southern or Konkurrel, I would have understood that. We'd done what we could do. The sales on *One* were not that good, and they weren't happy about it. I also had to tell them, and this probably didn't help, that *One* is not exactly their best album. *Headless Bourgeoisie* justifies itself as a double album; this one does not.

The other thing I had to tell them was, "How much do you really expect to keep going and selling albums down here, when you hardly ever play down here anymore, and you only play the West Coast? In San Francisco, you're not playing at Great American Music Hall or Slim's anymore. Instead you're at a tiny little bar in Berkeley called the Starry Plough, over and over again. When you do that again and again,

people kind of forget about you. Plus, it used to be that bands could boost each other, and you've never really done anything to help us with the newer bands. You never put Dead and Gone on, you never put Thrall on. You never put the newer bands on."

Rob was like, "Yeah, but they're not any good."

"Have you *heard* any of them?"

By then they had Wrong Records going, so the logical thing to do was to take a Wrong Records band with them. It makes perfect sense, except they brought the Royal Grand Prix down as the sole opening act three or four times in a row, and somebody like Dead and Gone or the Fleshies couldn't even get on as the third band. The audiences down here were tired of the Royal Grand Prix. Then they kept coming through with Removal, who never really clicked that much with audiences to begin with. It really, really blew a huge hole in their draw. That, in turn, led to a declining interest in the albums around that time, not just of *One* and *Dance of the Headless Bourgeoisie*.

**Rob Wright** Looking back, I think leaving Alternative Tentacles was a mistake. Our manager, Laurie, had it in his mind, "We can't go anywhere on this." He determined that we were going to get off Alternative Tentacles and get on a more reputable, commercial, rational, businesslike label and make tons of dough and become huge stars. So we got off of AT. They were having a lot of trouble at that time too with their English affiliate. Plus there was the whole trouble at Alternative Tentacles with the Dead Kennedys lawsuits and everything.

**Jello Biafra** It was during an incredibly bad period, of course, because we'd lost this evil trial, with wholescale perjury on the witness stand from ex–Dead Kennedys members and others. Of all the bands of that time—Alice Donut, Victims Family, or even D.O.A.—my closest friends in the whole family were NoMeansNo. They were very, very dear friends. It was another huge body blow for them to leave.

Rob called me up one fine day out of the blue and said, "I have some bad news. We're pulling the entire catalogue from you. We're doing it because we're afraid that East Bay Ray and company are gonna steal our music. As far as I can tell, Mordam and Alternative Tentacles are totally moribund and you seem to get yourself into so much trouble, and I don't want to work with you anymore anyway."

You can imagine how that felt, especially when a super-nasty letter from Laurie Mercer arrived the next day. I could tell he was taking total delight in the whole thing, sticking it to AT and sticking it to me personally. I don't know what I, as a label, ever did to him. That really kind of showed me where Laurie stood. It was just devastating, absolutely devastating.

**Rob Wright** We spent a lot of money buying back our back catalogue, which I think pissed Jello off even more. Laurie Mercer later went on and said, "I can't do this anymore, I've got other things," so we got off our label Wrong Records and found ourselves without a label. It was a mistake. We ended up on Southern Records in England, and they did nothing eventually, except steal our money.

**John Wright** Laurie wanted to get off AT. He had bigger things in mind. Laurie wanted to set up this deal with Southern. Jello and Laurie didn't get along. It's just frustrating when your manager and your record label are not on the same page. AT was the perfect home for us, really. None of us really wanted to leave. In the end, it had more to do with the fact that our material just wasn't available in Europe. Everyone complained about Mordam Records over there. We needed better distribution in Europe, where we were doing the strongest.

America had long since dwindled. We'd play and get good shows in certain cities down the West Coast. There were always pockets of fans, but our audience was not growing in the United States. Europe was where we still did big, good, strong numbers. Our shows and our tours were successful, and people were excited, but Europe was the hardest place to find our records. It was frustrating. We didn't want to leave AT, we just wanted to be better distributed over there. Jello was very loyal. He had worked with Mordam all the time, and he wasn't about to change that.

I certainly made it clear that this had nothing to do with him or the label. It was just trying to improve our pastures elsewhere. It certainly wasn't anything personal. In some respects, I don't think we should ever have left AT. It was kind of pointless. At the time, it seemed like the right thing to do. Ipecac put out the next two records in the States. We liked working with Greg Werckman, and he had moved from AT to Ipecac.

**Jello Biafra** Rob got me to put him on the guest list for a spoken-word show at UBC a while after that. He wanted to at least talk it out, and for Rob I would do that. Instead there was a little note left for me saying, "I couldn't do it, because ... life really fucking sucks, I really don't feel very well." He just left; I never saw him. It took quite a while before I could even bear to go to a NoMeansNo show again. I mean, how would I have any fun when all it feels like is heartbreak?

They never should have pulled their catalogue. I mean, sure, move and do your new album somewhere else: that's fair. But to yank your whole back catalogue and then never reissue most of it? That is another kind of spite.

**Greg Werckman** There wasn't a lot of drama when NoMeansNo decided to leave AT, but Jello was extremely disappointed. NoMeansNo weren't bean counters, but they kept an eye on the business end of things. Maybe they didn't feel like they fit in at a certain point with the other bands on AT. There was no screaming match or claims of being ripped off or anything like that. I do remember Jello was horribly, horribly depressed when that went down.

They had a great relationship, and they still do. There were bumps, and they didn't always see eye to eye. NoMeansNo were never hugely political, and they always found some of Jello's political stuff a little too in-your-face, not subtle enough. The issues that NoMeansNo addressed were social issues more than they were political issues. It all goes to the point that they just never took themselves that seriously. I think they always thought, "We're just musicians. Why

**Backstage with Booza (second from left) and Rob (second from right)**

would anyone want to hear from us about anything but music?"

**Jello Biafra** Only later did Greg put out those two NoMeansNo albums [*All Roads Lead to Ausfahrt* and *The People's Choice*] on his AntAcid label, which was kind of a side thing from Ipecac. I think the AntAcid release came after Laurie was out of the picture. I can't remember.

Eventually, I did go to their shows again, emotionally wrenching as it was. Deep down, these guys were still my very dear friends, and I had to wrestle with that. The next time they came down here, they wound up staying back at my house again. It seemed like Rob was choking back some serious emotions. It really meant the world to him that I'd let him back in my house. The cat had changed, but otherwise it was their Bay Area hotel. As long as they'd come through, and they had some dates, or it was time to master the next album, they would have a place to stay.

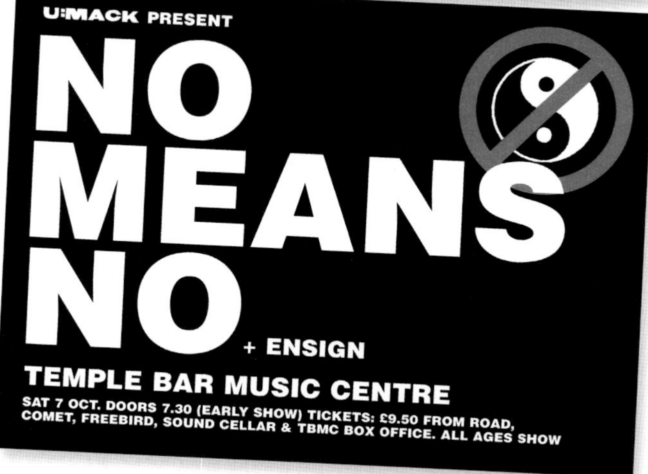


**Tom Holliston** It didn't have much to do with Biafra himself. It seemed for a while that it was becoming very hard to get the band's records in Europe. AT UK was beginning to go under, for different reasons that I never fully got. There were squirrelly things going on. We'd ask them about *Dance of the Headless Bourgeoisie*, and they'd say, "Oh, there aren't that many orders. People aren't buying it." We'd say, "But we played Hamburg last night and sold like 120 copies of it because people couldn't find it in the stores."

I tried to keep an open mind, because I know it can be very hard. We had a well-established manager and overseer with Greg Werckman at AT. When he left, there were a few other people that took his place before somebody finally slotted in permanently. Over time, it was just different. We'd be running low on merch, so we'd get hold of them: "Hey, we're going to be in your part of the woods in California for a few days. Can you please come out and drop off a bunch of CDs and give us an invoice?" It would be like, "Oh yeah, sorry, I fell asleep," or, "We didn't have time." We felt like, "Are we not a priority?"

**Bill Johnston** When we were playing with NoMeansNo in the late '90s, it seemed like it could've gone either way, like they might pack it in. Rob used to say, "Oh well, these are the retirement fund tours."

The joke was they were already too old. I don't want to take any credit for anything to do with them, but we were very gung ho at the time. I think it might've rubbed off a little bit, because touring became really fun and easy for them. I think it kind of reinvigorated them.

**Trey Spruance** In 1999, Ipecac Recordings was just starting up, and there was talk about doing a New Year's show to bring in the new millennium. Greg Werckman knew NoMeansNo through Alternative Tentacles. Of course, Mike Patton was a big fan too. It was the whole Y2K thing, so everybody thought the world was coming to an end, and under those circumstances it was pretty fun.

**Rob Wright** At the end of the 1990s, I basically had a nervous breakdown, and then came the anxiety. I had been the band boss for a long time, and it drove me crazy. It was a necessary role, I thought at the time. But I wasn't suited to it. Being in charge of people wasn't anything I was ever interested in doing. I was interested in playing. When you're in a band, and you're on tour, it's all logistics. It was just constant stress to do all that.

You hear stories of Tommy from the Ramones: he was like a drill sergeant. He kept everyone in line, sometimes violently. Bands often need that, because otherwise artsy-fartsy people just wander around. It may be fun, but nothing gets done. It drove me crazy. Eventually, I just gave it up. I had to. I had to release it.

CHAPTER TWENTY-THREE

# SO LOW

## "I am a crab. I live in a shell. You call this living? I call this hell!"

The new millennium arrived, along with uncertainty and turmoil in the NoMeansNo camp. Going full bore for nearly two decades without consequence is nearly impossible. In this case, Rob's mental wellness became the issue. Being the captain for so long was taking its toll. Some adjustments needed to be made in order to keep the ship afloat.

**Bill Johnston** We were playing in LA with NoMeansNo. There was this big comic book store on Hollywood Boulevard. We were at the counter, and this guy came up with a whole armful of action figures and all this shit. At that time, I was wearing one of those NoMeansNo shirts that had the Henry Rollins tattoo on the back: STAY HOME—READ A BOOK.

This guy looked at me: "Where did you get that shirt?" I said, "One of the guys in the band gave it to me." He's like, "Do you know that's the greatest band ever?" I'm like, "Yeah. Pretty sure. We're on tour with them right now." He said, "What? You're playing in town? Where are you playing?" I said, "Spaceland."

He said, "Okay. I gotta come. What's your band called?" I said, "Removal." He's like, "You got any merch or anything?" So I gave him some stickers. He's like, "Oh, I got some stickers of my band too," and he pulled out a bunch of Green Day stickers. I said, "Dude, there's already a band called Green Day." At that point, I realized that I was talking to Tré Cool.

All three of them came to the show. They came up to the merch table and said, "Yup. I'll take everything. All the Removal stuff. All the NoMeansNo stuff. Gimme one of everything." They dropped hundreds of dollars. We had three or four CDs. NoMeansNo probably had twelve CDs and records and five different T-shirts and hoodies and all sorts of shit. After the show, I was talking to Rob Wright and I mentioned, "Oh, you know, the Green Day guys were all here." He was like, "Yeah, they used to open up for us all the time. Then they got super popular, and did they ever ask us to open up for them? No." I said, "Oh, do you want to?" Rob said, "Well, no. But it'd be nice to be asked."

**Kamala Parks** NoMeansNo played an important role for me, personally, years after I first worked with them in the '80s and '90s. In 2001, I was a teacher at a high school, and I was extremely depressed. So I left teaching, but it had consumed so much of my time that I had actually forgotten how to enjoy myself and have fun.

A couple of months later, NoMeansNo came through town. They played at the Starry Plough in Berkeley, so I went to go see them. I thought, "Oh, this is what I used to do!" I was living in a warehouse at that time, and they came and stayed at my place.

We were hanging out the next day, and they said that they were heading up and playing in Cotati that night. I didn't have a car, and I just said, "You know what, I want to go up there with you," and they were like, "Okay." I just tagged along with them in the van.

We drove to Cotati, and it was wonderful. I didn't really know Tom well at that point, but we just had a little slumber party in the van. Nothing sexual, we were just chattering, and we became immediate friends. I slept in the van, and the next morning I left them and got a ride down to Napa to see my dad.

It was a pivotal moment, a small step out of the depression that I was feeling. Just remembering a life of spontaneity, a life of music, a life of art. It was because of them letting me join them on that trip up to Cotati. They hold a very special place in my heart, both personally and musically, still to this day. If I listen to NoMeansNo, it will lift me out of the doldrums, without a doubt. I will forever be grateful to them. It enhances listening to them, because not only do they make this powerful music but behind that are amazing human beings.

**Rob Wright** When I hit forty-five years old, I came down with anxiety, and it just hit me like a ton of bricks. I got quite sick, and we didn't tour for a whole year between 2001 and 2002. I was not well. I remember on 9/11 being totally pissed off because one of the things I could do comfortably was watch golf on TV, but of course everything got cancelled. This was the extent of my worldview: "What? The golf's cancelled? Why?" I realized that just because I was not well, the world wasn't going to do what I wanted it to do. I learned that the anxiety and depression had nothing

really to do with what's going on, good or bad. It's all just chemical.

I started on the SSRIs, but the drugs are scatter-gun. You're shooting a shotgun to kill a pigeon. All of these other side effects happen, so you don't really want to take them. But if you don't, you end up with your symptoms, and if they're bad enough, they keep you housebound and every waking moment is miserable. Having taken a lot of drugs when I was younger was sort of handy, because when I had a bad experience back then, I'd think, "Well, it's just the drugs, it'll wear off." It was an ongoing battle. It's a vicious thing, and I wouldn't wish it on my worst enemy.

What they say brought it on was an overload of stress to the point where your body cannot produce enough serotonin to keep you in a calm, sane, comfortable state of mind. It's like pushing the panic button, which will never go off. It's like having a phobia, like a fear of flying, but having that all the time for no reason. It can be very severe. You find yourself thinking you have all sorts of symptoms of other things. I'm lucky that it's under control. It gives me a life back.

**John Wright** Rob began in the late '90s, and especially in the early 2000s, to really suffer from anxiety, and it was debilitating. Teeth-grinding fucking *anxiety*. When you have that kind of anxiety, it's like, "Well, where's this fucking coming from?" There's psychological reasons and physical reasons. He had to sort that out. He knew that he needed to get onto the drugs to control it.

He had a tough time dealing with different drugs and trying to find the right one, and he had a lot of therapy. Rob told me that therapy is something that every individual should do, regardless of whether they think they need it or not. No matter how well adjusted you are, you should go talk to someone and discover things about yourself. It's like turning the light on. I mean, it takes courage and discipline to actually open up and talk. Like, *really* talk. He learned from that and had to deal with it for a long time.

I can't say that I've suffered terribly from anxiety or depression myself. I've had some pretty stressful times, but that's stress. I've been pretty lucky. I can sort of detach myself to some degree, to perhaps my old girlfriends' chagrin!

**Rob Wright** There's just nothing quite like it. You figure you're the boss of your own thoughts and consciousness, and then suddenly you realize you're not. You can be overwhelmed from within at any time. It is an onslaught on *you*. The trouble is, you take it personally. You think it's *your* thinking, or *your* life, and *your* history. But it's not; it's something that's attacking you. You've got to separate yourself from your feelings, your emotions, and realize that it's just the chemistry. It's so insidious, because that's exactly where it attacks you, within this state of being that you find yourself in. If you feel terrible, you'll find a million reasons why. None of them have to be true, and none of them usually are. This consciousness is a very, very shady business.

**John Wright** There were times when Rob would be on the floor of the van until showtime, and then he'd come in. He said playing shows was actually the only

time he felt normal. There were a couple tours that were hard for him in that respect.

**Rob Wright** I did tours when I was totally sick. They were torture, but I never really took it to the extreme of thinking the band was done. I was always just waiting to get better, to see what would happen. I never thought that I should consider completely stopping for that reason. It was like, "I've got a broken leg. I can't go on tour now, but when it heals, I'll go back." It was more that kind of reasoning.

**Bill Johnston** I know it was difficult for him and for the other guys, but they got through it and it was okay. Everything wasn't totally perfect and awesome at that time. That was also the only time I ever saw mistakes. I mean, he was on medication, so occasionally you could see lapses in concentration.

They did the Hanson Brothers' *My Game* album, and then a few years later the *Ausfahrt* album. I played on both of those records, and I was in pretty deep then. That was when Rob was getting better. There's several songs that address that whole time. That song "Tranquil" is all about being on medications.

It became a little easier once Rob was getting a handle on his anxiety. At that time, our drummer had the same thing. Ernie and Rob were usually in one van, and the rest of us split up between the other two. So that was the crazy van! I worked as a mental health worker in the Downtown Eastside in Vancouver for years, so I was certainly sensitive to these things. I think it was a good support system for Rob that made it possible.

**Ernie Hawkins** I have been on antidepressants for a long time, and there was a bout there when Rob was having some issues as well. Because of that and our personalities, I got along with Rob more than anybody else. I think the feeling was mutual, but I can't speak for him. He and I toured together in one van, and everyone else was in the other van.

He's a thinker. My anxiety also comes a lot from thinking. He was into meditation and mindfulness before I knew what that was. He also introduced me to a lot of old jazz, like Art Tatum and Coltrane. He introduced me to Éthiopiques, which was a series that compiled music recorded in Ethiopia in the '60s and '70s. Those are just things you don't get exposed to normally, because everyone is listening to the same thing. He's just outside of that. I absolutely cherished that relationship and that access to him.

However, as much as he's a friend, and as much time as I've spent with him and we enjoyed each other's company, he's a loner. The irony there is that his music brings people together and represents community and love. They really tuned in to this later in their career. They had a T-shirt that said WHAT IS THE WORD THAT ALL MEN KNOW BUT FEW DARE TO SPEAK? and then on the back it just says LOVE.

I haven't talked to Rob in years, and I haven't seen him for even longer. Although we had spent so much time together and shared things, he's not going to pick up the phone and call me. He's not even going to send me an email. It's a dichotomy there. I think he appreciates the things when they're there, and that's good enough. Isn't that what we all really want, to appreciate the moments as they happen? That's the Zen moment. If you're thinking about the future, you're being anxious, and if you're thinking about the past, you're depressed. The goal is to appreciate the now, *now*. That's the goal of Buddhists, and I think he read a lot about that, and tried to practise it.

**Tom Holliston** I know that it was very hard on him. Rob is the front man; he's doing the bulk of interviews. He's the face of the band. I've been there. Anxiety makes you feel like, "What the fuck is wrong with me?" You feel dizzy, almost like you have vertigo.

I was just like, "Well, let's make sure that he has as much time to himself as he can. The band will get him a cab after sound check. He can go back to the

hotel and just come back for the show. He won't have to deal with constant people coming into the dressing room or anything like that. We'll look after load-in and load-out. We'll take care of that stuff. We just want him to be well."

The bathrobe phase

It didn't help that around then he also threw his back out a couple times. Putting out your back is no fun, because when you're singing, you feel like puking. Having to deal with inner turmoil is overwhelming. Then a physical injury. It's hard.

**Danko Jones—front man of the band Danko Jones** I once gave Rob Wright my Shoppers Drug Mart backache patches. He used them and gave us a shout-out onstage in Amsterdam. It's a small claim to fame, but I still claim it.

**Bill Johnston** Rob had this "bathrobe phase." There was one tour in Europe where he wore a bathrobe the entire time. I remember we went to Frankfurt to pick up his wife. She was coming to join us for a few shows. I drove him to the airport and, yup, he's got slippers and a bathrobe on. She was like, "Oh my god. What are you doing?" It was funny, and then he started wearing the tie of the bathrobe as a headband. He could appreciate the humour in it, and we all muddled through, and it ended up being okay.

**Rob Wright** The bathrobe phase! I was probably looking for a comfort zone. I remember wandering around a German truck stop at three in the morning in my housecoat and slippers. I didn't care. Basically, from around my late twenties and onward, I just stopped caring. If I could get away with it, fine. If not, well, love it or live with it.

You can get away with all sorts of things if you don't care what people think. I've still got that going, completely. Lots of people think I'm a crazy old man, but I don't care. Everyone is stone crazy. The most crazy people are the ones who act the most normal, because they're on a knife edge. I'm crazy, but I don't try to act normal. What's the point? It's all phoney.

**Paul Timoney** *Ulysses* by James Joyce is a story about a journey across Dublin, Ireland. It begins in this seaside town called Dalkey. In the summer of 2002, I was working with NoMeansNo when they played a really big hall supporting Motörhead. I remember going back to my house with them, and there was a bit of a party going on. When the sun rose at like four a.m., myself and Rob Wright and some other people got a taxi over to Dalkey. Rob

was pointing out across the sea to a landmass called Howth, and he was telling us how this was all described in *Ulysses*. Then he just took off all his clothes and jumped into the sea.

I was just like, "Ah, brilliant!" I remember that day particularly well. Rob was really in his element. We climbed up this hill called Killiney Hill, and I don't think he ever got dressed! We were just walking around this suburban seaside town, and he just had a towel wrapped around him and was picking flowers out of people's gardens and putting them in his hair. It was great fun.

**Rob Wright** Yeah, that was a bit of a bender. In *Ulysses*, there's a bathing area where men took all their clothes off and jumped into the Irish Sea. I met a guy there who said, "I've done this every day for forty years." That's good enough for me, I'll take a dip. I've done this twice actually. It's so cold you almost don't feel it. One time it was October, and it was rainy and overcast and not that warm. I got out and everything felt warm and beautiful.

I recommend reading *Ulysses*, but then again, I don't. A lot of people start it but don't finish it because Joyce is always pushing you. From one

minute to the next, you're like, "What the hell is going on?" I got entranced with that book. I almost bought a first edition of it one time. I wish I had.

**Paul Timoney** Rob always had really high-quality pajamas, slippers, and a dressing gown. We had big punk rock parties at the house in Dublin that I was living in while I was working with those guys. Rob would come home after a gig and then go and change into silk pajamas. He would come back to the party and just sit there, totally content with himself, drinking top-shelf whiskey in his pajamas.

My dad came over to the house one time and Rob answered the door in his classy pajamas. Rob asked my dad what part of the city he was from, and they had this cultural chat, and my dad was just wondering, "What the fuck is going on in that house? Why is there this polite, educated guy who is clearly not from Ireland walking around in his pajamas?"

**Rob Wright** When I was up onstage, screaming at people and acting like an idiot, people loved it. If you show your craziness to people, they appreciate it. Everyone wishes they could tell a perfect stranger their innermost fears and secrets. But they can't. They don't, and they shouldn't. Life would be impossible if everyone was blathering all the time about their thoughts and feelings.

Instead, people put themselves in situations day in and day out in which there is a level of stress and anxiety. It accumulates, and it uses up your resources to stay above it, to still function and feel calm and have peace of mind. If you put yourself through hell long enough, or if your lifestyle does, eventually

it just blows up or breaks down. And then you're screwed.

**Simon Wells** Touring is a mental thing. Originally when the Konk started out, they used to schedule three-month tours. Many bands split up or had mental illness problems. They had to cut it right down to a month. We were the original lot that all used to do these super-long tours. It was crazy. Years of that will have an effect on you. I think a lot of musicians come out of that kind of lifestyle quite broken.

**Matthias Bosenick—fan from Germany** Before the gig in Salzgitter, one of the two Wrights stood at the merch table bare chested, and his belly shone. As we talked to him about everything, what stuck with me was that he always spoke of his brother, beaming and laughing: "My brother, my brother." Everything was tied to his brother. I was deeply impressed by how twenty-three years after the band started, and after forty years of being a sibling, someone spoke with so much love for his brother. The bond between the siblings is stronger than the strongest music.

**Roger Miller—Mission of Burma** I've played in a band with my two brothers, so I know what the sibling thing can do. When you're on the same wavelength, you can do things nobody else can do, because you've grown up together and you've already bonded. It can also cause troubles, because again, you grew up together. The conflicts can be of a different nature than two people who just met and formed a band. It goes back to when you were four and something happened. You're still working off

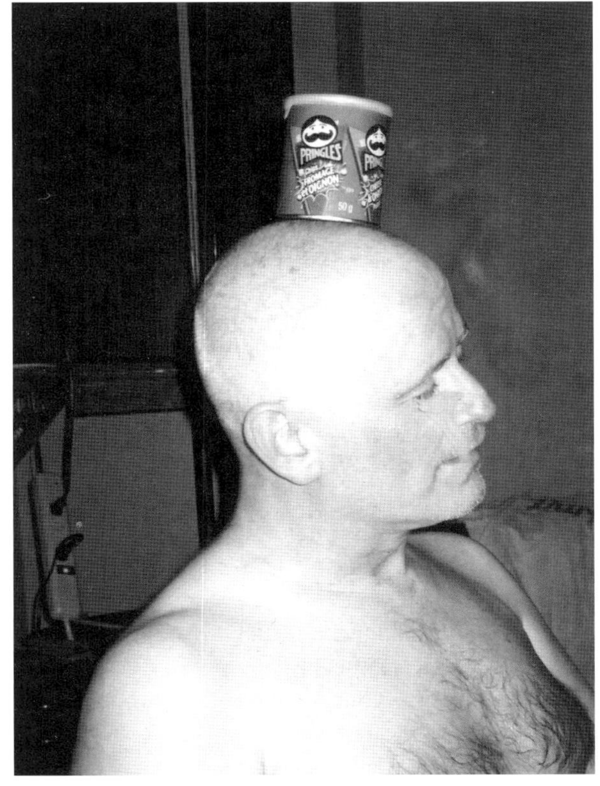

that kind of mentality. It's nuts, but when it kicks, it's amazing. I really felt that with NoMeansNo.

**Bob "Bob 1" Mothersbaugh** I know from experience that having your brother in the band can be the best and the worst of everything. It's weird when you're in the music business and your band is becoming popular. Sometimes it's good to have a brother who you can talk to, and sometimes it's like, "Oh wait, he's being a dick. He's just buying into the rock star thing." You can really sense that when it's a brother. Maybe a little bit of that was negated with us because there were two sets of brothers in Devo.

**Rob Wright** Me and John had our egos, but I think they were subservient to the music because we were brothers and we loved what we were doing. Whenever we got on each other's case or ticked each other off, it was never enough to drive us apart. In the end, it was about doing what we were doing and doing it really well. Usually, arguments were about that. We didn't have a lot of personal arguments. We had serious arguments about music. I was a terrible fuckin' autocrat.

**Jello Biafra** I've never seen two people cut each other down in an argument like John and Rob going at each other in my living room. They were so blunt, but each comment rolled right off the other, and they'd fire back. Only people from the same family could do that and still play together for years to come.

**Dave Lawrence, aka Terry—*FUBAR* writer and actor** The soundtrack for *FUBAR* came out about a year after the movie and featured mostly songs that weren't in the film. It was mostly Canadian bands doing covers of other Canadian artists, with little clips from the movie in between songs. NoMeansNo contributed a cover of Neil Young's "Hey Hey, My My."

**Paul Spence, aka Deaner—*FUBAR* writer and actor** All I can tell you about NoMeansNo is that every time I went to their show I got so rowdy that I got kicked out. Happened probably four or five times between Calgary, Montreal, and Edmonton. When they played as the Hansons in Montreal, I showed up in a Canadiens jersey with taped-up glasses with "Hansons SUCK" written in black ink on the front.

In the middle of the packed-out, insane show,

I was in the pit. Rob saw me, yanked me onstage, and asked the crowd what they thought of this loser. Everybody started pelting the stage with trash, bottles, and cans. It was fucking mayhem. I got tossed back into the crowd and was beaten up in the most friendly and hilarious way possible. I did eventually get thrown out of the club, and as I was getting dragged to the exit, I heard Rob say, "*Hey!* Don't kick that guy out!" But my expiry date had come.

**Rob Wright** I liked the version of "Hey Hey, My My" we did for the *FUBAR* soundtrack. Great song. Great movie, the cinema verité, the mockumentary. The guy who played the main guy was just brilliant: "Turn down the suck, turn up the good!"

**Paul Spence** When we talked to the record label about doing an album, they wanted an album full of Canadian covers. NoMeansNo were definitely my idea. I pitched getting the Hansons to do a song, thinking they'd be into doing something kinda funny. They came back to us and said NoMeansNo wanted to do it. I was so excited, because I came from a punk rock background where all my bands were full of fuckups and wastoids, and none of that was really represented on the soundtrack. I don't know why they chose Neil Young to cover, but it's the best song on the album, and it's not even close.

Despite the struggles that Rob was experiencing trying to get a handle on his mental health, the touring continued. After NoMeansNo's European and Canadian tours in 2002, they decided the following year would be strictly Hanson Brothers shows. Rob was much more comfortable taking side stage and not being the "boss." So Robbie donned his goalie mask and the Hansons spent 2003 on the road, doing a full European and North American tour cycle. NoMeansNo was put on the back burner until early 2004, when it was time to head overseas once again. Early in the tour, a familiar face would join them for one last show in Amsterdam.

**Keith Rose** There was an upcoming Hanson Brothers tour of Europe, and Rob was really having a hard time. John got in touch with me and said, "Look, man, I don't know if Rob will be able to do this tour." I said, "Do you want me to start cancelling the shows?" He said, "No, maybe you better learn the bass parts." I said, "Oh yeah, okay," and I did nothing. The tour went on and Rob was there in the vehicle, and we did the tour.

**Robbie Hanson's goalie masks**

At some point, I think Ernie said to me, "So how many songs did you learn?" and I said, "I didn't learn any." He said, "What do you mean? What if Rob couldn't have done this tour?" I said, "There was no way I was gonna go onstage pretending to be Rob." People would see through it in a second, and I would be the most hated person there.

**Rob Wright** I had my Robbie Hanson goalie mask stolen out of our dressing room after a show in Copenhagen in 2003. A few years later, we were back there. We were playing this amazing squat called Loppen in the anarchic, dope-smoking centre of town. This guy came up and said, "Here's your mask." I said, "Wow! What happened?" Apparently, the guy who stole it had been bragging about it, and a bunch of people got together and said, "Look, you can't do that. Give us the mask," and they gave it back to me. Isn't that great? He also gave me a whole box full of those little tiny bottles of booze you get on planes.

Luckily, I had a backup. That style of mask went out of fashion. They don't make them anymore. It was quite valuable.

**John Wright** Andy joined us for a few songs at the Melkweg in Amsterdam in 2004. I think that was Craig Bougie's last European tour with us too. It was good, because it helped set aside any bad feelings that might have been there, not that there really was. It was crazy, because all of a sudden I had these stereo guitars in my monitors. I was thinking, "Wow, this sounds so fucking huge!" It was really fun to see Andy back up there singing again; he's such a good performer.

**Rob Wright** We did it, and it was, I guess, fine. Again, the sentiment of these things escapes me. It's just like, "So you were a band member at one point, and now we're gonna get all the gang back together again, it'll be like the good ol' days." I wasn't gonna be an asshole about it, but I don't even remember much.

Andy with NoMeansNo in Amsterdam, 2004

Why is he playing onstage? Because he used to? Well, he stopped.

**Andy Kerr** Completely unexpectedly, the brothers approached me and said, "We're playing in Amsterdam and we think it'd be a nice idea if you came up and played some songs with us and Tom." I thought, "What the fuck? Really?" I wasn't sure exactly why I was being asked out of the blue. Then I began thinking, "Well, maybe this is good. Maybe this is something we should have done years ago anyway." We decided on a small handful of songs from my time in the band. I said, "Oh, I also want to do 'Humans,'" because I had actually learned that song, but it wasn't released until after I left.

On the day of the show, I went down to the Melkweg, armed only with my old blue Schecter Telecaster. I walked inside the venue, and there they were, setting up onstage, and Craig was behind the soundboard. Rob had chucked out his back, so he was sitting down. Hi's and hugs were exchanged, and then we got down to business. It was so surreal. Like entering a time machine. Craig was talking to me while he was setting up my guitar sound, and it seemed eerily familiar.

After the sound check, the guys said, "Well, we're gonna go eat dinner." I said, "Oh, okay. Well, I'm gonna go home, and I'll see you an hour or so before the show." "Okay." I remember walking outside, and it was like when Dorothy in *The Wizard of Oz* walks through the door and suddenly it's all colour. It was like walking out of one reality and into another. My old reality versus my current life in Amsterdam. Very bizarre.

A couple of hours later, I went back down to the club for the show and watched the opening bands. It was a great lineup. Then NoMeansNo were up. They played a short set's worth of material and then invited me onstage. They announced, "Oh, we have a special guest here," and so up I went, and it all kicked off. Surprisingly, everything went quite smoothly. It was great hearing and seeing John and Rob doing what they do best, pounding it out at eleven. It was also cool playing together with Tom for the first time in decades. I did "Some Bodies" and a few other songs, and then we did an encore, and I said my goodbyes. I was like, "Well, I'm gonna go home now. See you later." They were like, "Yup, bye. It was nice."

That was that. Off we went again on our usual, separate, disconnected NoMeansNo-ish ways. Looking back, it probably was a healthy thing on some level for all four of us to do, if a bit odd. But it was really a blast, and I'm glad we did it. For a little while, anyways, I could communicate with my old bandmates in a language we all spoke.

NoMeansNo in Amsterdam, 2004: Tom, Andy, Rob, and John

**Tom Holliston** It was a great show. Andy came up, and I think we did five or six songs. It sounded really good. I love the idea of playing with extra people anyway. I know we did "Some Bodies" and "Two Lips," and a couple of others. "Rags and Bones" too. When he came up, I stepped into the back and let him go. That was really, really fun. I'm pretty sure Gijs was mostly responsible for getting that whole thing together.

**Gijs de Wit** When Andy left the band, Rob didn't speak to him for ten to fifteen years. I said, "Rob, you need to speak to Andy." Rob also doesn't talk to me. I think Rob simply doesn't talk to anyone.

**Sissi Schulmeister—Alice Donut** Alice Donut was on that show at the Melkweg, along with the Ex. I think that was one of our last shows we did before we stopped touring that time. I hadn't met Andy a lot, but I didn't get the feeling that there was a lot of animosity. I think sometimes stuff happens. We had a lot of guitar players, and Richard, who used to be in our band, moved to Portland, and when we played a show in San Francisco he would come onstage. It might have been something similar. Andy was hanging out backstage afterwards, and I think everybody had a good time.

**Igor Seke—fan from Serbia** During the wars in the 1990s, the anarcho-punk scene was an essential part of antiwar campaigns in all former Yugoslav countries. Myself, being a part of that scene, got involved and ended up leading a campaign against recruitment and for conscientious objection to military service in Serbia. NoMeansNo were an essential part of the soundtrack of the campaign. All of us involved in the process at that time were huge NMN fans. NMN played in Slovenia a couple of times, but for us in Serbia it was impossible to get there.

In 2004, I was "advised" to leave Serbia for some time, as the military was having a serious pick on me. A peace group active at a university in Barcelona worked out a student visa for me, and I left Serbia in March 2004. I got to Barcelona, and I saw that NoMeansNo were playing just five days after my arrival. I was out of myself with joy. After the concert, I went to buy a NMN T-shirt, but the only T-shirt they were selling was KILL EVERYONE NOW. I am a hardcore pacifist, someone who had dedicated the previous ten years to antiwar campaigning. How the fuck can I wear a T-shirt saying KILL EVERYONE NOW, even if it's just a sarcastic message? But John and Tom were sitting there, signing the merch. I said, "Fuck it," and I bought it. John signed the T-shirt. Of course, I didn't explain all this to him. I just said that in Serbia they have a huge fan base and that it's a pity they hadn't played there yet. I'm a proud owner of a T-shirt of my all-time favourite band, signed by the best drummer in the world, but I never wear it outside of my house.

Stephen Moses of Alice Donut (left) with NoMeansNo

**Milos Svircev—fan from Serbia** I travelled from Serbia to Croatia to see NoMeansNo. I was hoping to buy some merch, but they had trouble at the Hungarian border and arrived without any. I left the gig empty-handed but full-hearted. I was a tad nervous before the trip, since Serbia and Croatia had been separated in a bloody civil war fought during the 1990s. The two countries had remained on not-so-friendly terms ever since.

It turned out I was nervous for no reason whatsoever. The folks in front of the venue figured out my accent in no time, and they were stoked to see a Serb that far from home! The distance is less than four hundred kilometres, but wars and politics bend space and time. We had a friendly chat and shared some beers. I will remember that night and treasure it as long as I'm alive.

**Tolan McNeil** When I was in a band called Gus, we would cross paths with NoMeansNo quite a bit out

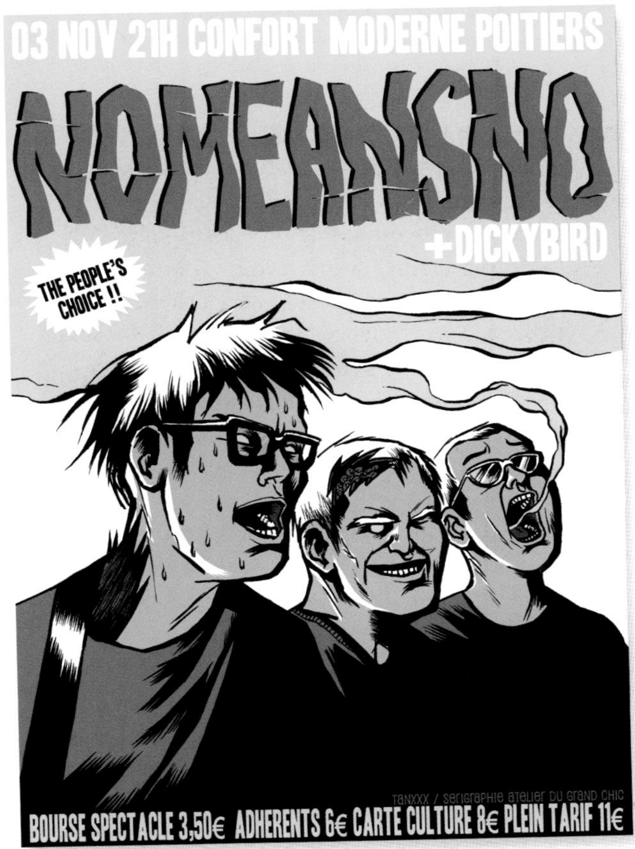

on the road. We were super poor, and they would let us come to the shows and use their hotel rooms for showers, and they would feed us and beer us up: "Come in from the cold, kids!"

Rob had that sunburst 1967 Fender bass. He didn't have a case for it, so it was just sitting on top of the fuckin' amps in the tour van. I was riding shotgun and I was like, "Can I try your bass?" He said, "Oh yeah, go for it." I start playing it in the van and this thing is worn fuckin' out, the frets on it are *flat*. I don't know how anyone could play on it. I said, "Jeez, man, this thing's really kinda beat on, eh?" And he goes, "That thing bought me a fuckin' house!" He is not nostalgic. "It's a *tool*, man! That's not a bass, it's a fuckin' hammer!"

**Rob Wright** At one point, I had the realization that what I was doing was a job. Like a baker bakes bread and a carpenter builds houses, I was writing and playing music. That's what it was: it was a job. It's good, because it's what people need and it's what I have the talent to do.

Everyone needs music, always have. People played and sang music before they were any carpenters or bakers. They say that prostitution is the oldest profession in the world, but I think even before there were prostitutes, people were playing and singing music. Doing it all together too.

**Kyle Bernstein—fan from New York, New York** NoMeansNo played the Knitting Factory in NYC in November 2000. I contacted their road manager in advance and offered to make them dinner, as I was working as a professional chef at the time. I cooked all weekend and arrived at the venue early in the evening with enough food for the bands that were performing that night. I had an amazing time hanging out with them backstage and was honoured to have the privilege of sharing a meal and my talents with the people who'd been sharing theirs with me. We had a few beers, and some jokes and stories were told. I brought homemade chocolate chip cookies but told them nobody could have any until they ate their dinner.

Rob called me a "harsh mistress" and laughed at my ridiculous shoes. John contradicted everything Rob said. Tom came in toward the end of the meal and apologized for not joining us but explained that he doesn't eat before he goes onstage and opted to go for a walk instead.

When NoMeansNo hit the stage, I felt a special connection with them. Then, John publicly thanked me during the break in "Two Lips, Two Lungs and One Tongue." They segued into their rendition of "A Taste of Honey" as something of an ode to my chicken pot pie. What a great group of musicians, and such a fun night.

**Tom Holliston** A lot of people think, "There's probably a lot of sex and drugs and rock 'n' roll on tour." Never. All I wanted to do was play music. It's nice to be liked and appreciated, and it's kind of flattering. I realized that somebody might be attracted to me just because I appear confident while I'm up there playing music.

It was very strange. I was getting to be forty, and this is the first time in my life I've ever been hit on by people. But you gotta load out, and the most important thing is to make sure you're okay to play a good show the next night. I mean, look at all the people from the '60s and '70s who partied all the time. Well, their livers have blown up.

**Keith Rose** We did the tour for the *People's Choice* album. On that album cover, it's the changing room at some venue or squat in Germany, and there's spray-painted on the wall in big letters, "How Fucken Old Are NoMeansNo? Give It Up Granddads!" Then underneath in small letters it says, "That's 'great granddad' to you, fucker! —John Wright." That's their album cover. They could make fun of themselves.

**Devin Townsend—musician, producer** That kind of summarized it. They can take the abuse and just be like, "Oh, fuck it, that's what we are." If you're not pretending to be anything other than what you are, then you never have to remember anything. You never *have* to pretend. If someone wants to call you out for being exactly what you are, your only response is, "Yeah. That's true!"

**Tom Holliston** I had taken that photo backstage somewhere in Austria or Germany in 1994. I

Rob with a different "Give It Up Granddads" graffiti

remember there were other dates on that tour that had similar things written backstage. I'm pretty sure it was SNFU, or a certain member of that band, who was doing that, because they were on tour at the same time.

Let's just say if it had been anybody, it would have been Chi Pig. He was a very eloquent person and a really funny guy. It was obviously the same person, because it was the same handwriting with slight variations, which inferred somebody who was fairly creative. That would be Chi in a nutshell.

**Keith Rose** The tour promo that went out was just their three bald spots, a photo from above of the back of their heads. It was fantastic. Again, there's a lot of mystery involved. Who are these old men?

I remember having these little punks come up to me at the merch table, maybe like thirteen-year-old kids. They'd be in their little zipper suits with their mohawks, looking all punky. They'd look at the stage and go, "How old are those guys?" I'd always say, "Oh, Rob, he's at least eighty now." They'd go, "Oh my god, he's older than my grandfather!" Then they'd see them play, and there was like this wave of revelation over these kids: "Wow, maybe I don't need this uniform to be punk." It was really cool, because you could see these kids having an enlightenment. Here's this old geezer on the drums, and he's wearing goofy Bermuda shorts with little beer stains all over them, and he doesn't seem to care what people think.

Any concerns about the band's stamina were dispelled in 2004. That year, NoMeansNo did three European runs and a Western Canadian tour. While Rob, John, and Tom were back in fine travelling form, not everyone in the circle was completely happy. Their soundman, Craig, was looking for something a bit more settled. Once again, the brothers would find themselves needing to adapt and overcome.

Mark Critchley at the merch table in Dublin

**Craig Bougie** I had a run with NoMeansNo that lasted almost twenty years. John likes to say it was nineteen years and six and a half months. I said, "I should get a gold Maglite for doing my twenty years," and he was like, "Well, you didn't actually do twenty years." "Fuck you, John."

I had made the decision to leave. I was dating a girl at the time, and she had a kid. I just felt like it was time to become a little more stable. Between the previous two tours, I'd started working in film, and the money was basically the same but I didn't have to travel. Besides, we were kind of hitting all the same spots, and it was feeling quite routine. Robbie was kind of losing his nut a little. He'd always be wearing his bathrobe with a samurai bandanna on his head. He was doing weird stuff like collecting little toy Ferraris. He was taking some medication at the time and seemed more aggressive sometimes. I just kind of felt like, "Well, if there's a time to go, it's now." It just felt right. I regret it in some ways, but it was the right decision for me.

Mark Critchley started doing sound; he was gonna take over from me. He came on tour with us as a roadie at first, and I was training him. He was quite a musician, but he hadn't really done live sound. The last show I mixed was in San Francisco. That's when I just kind of handed over the reins to him. Biafra was onstage doing a song or two with NoMeansNo, and he gave a huge shout-out to Mark but didn't even mention me. He was like, "NoMeansNo's new soundman, Mark Critchley!" He was a big fan of Mark's because Mark was just insane, musically. It was sort of an unceremonious departure.

I ended up smoking some of the Petaluma pot that Victims Family brought. I really got quite stoned and then back at Biafra's house, we were sitting around, and I was kind of going like, "Man, I'm just done," and I dropped my bottle of beer on the ground. Biafra was like, "Ahhh!" and he came running around with a cloth and wiped up after me. I'm like, "Oh, sorry, dude. I'm just gonna hit the hay." That was my last show.

**Mark Critchley** In San Francisco, Jello introduced them and came out and sang a song with them. At the end, he gave thanks and said, "I want everybody to turn around and say thanks to Mark Critchley doing

Craig at the soundboard

the sound. It was excellent." Everybody clapped. It was kind of embarrassing.

We stayed that night at Jello's house, and Craig was a little upset, saying to Jello, "Well, how come you never publicly thanked me?" Jello said, "Because you never turned the guitars up loud enough for me to hear. When Mark did it, I could hear the guitar."

**Keith Rose** Craig was incredible. He was a lot of the glue that held the machine together. When Craig departed, it definitely left some boots to be filled. Craig really watched out for Rob leaving his glasses behind and John leaving his earplugs around. He really kept things going. Craig could pull anything together. It could be the shittiest PA and sound like crap, but he'd figure out how to make it sound good.

**Bill Johnston** You can't underestimate the importance of Craig Bougie to the NoMeansNo story. He made them sound the way they sounded. He really was responsible for that. They're great and talented, and John's a great soundman in his own right, but you can't do it all from the stage. Without Craig, they wouldn't have sounded as good.

**Ernie Hawkins** Craig became the catchall. He was the guy who would explain that Rob was "not around right now," because everyone wants to get at Rob. John has no qualms about talking about himself for many hours at a time. He rather enjoys it, but Rob is not that way. Craig was a bit of a bouncer. He'd get them onstage at a certain time, and he'd make sure that the numbers worked out at the end of the night. On top of all that, he was just an absolute sweetheart.

His levity had a way of lightening up the tensions that invariably arise when you have grown men in the van for long periods of time. Craig functioned at the level that they toured at.

**Rob Wright** Craig was very important. He was a good soundman, and he learned how to deal with us. He went through hell too, because we were a very difficult band to mix. He was part of the band.

**Craig Bougie** I loved it. I loved it, man. When I quit, I didn't wanna quit, but it was just time. NoMeansNo were a big, massive part of my life.

CHAPTER TWENTY-FOUR

# ALL ROADS LEAD TO AUSFAHRT

## "Heaven's not in heaven. Heaven's in the dust beneath my shoes."

Things were getting back on track in many ways by the middle of the decade. The tours continued to be successful, and Rob was beginning to enjoy life in NoMeansNo again. Not having Craig Bougie in the van was a change, but not insurmountable. They would hire a series of different sound techs over the next decade, never quite finding the perfect replacement for Craig. Rob, John, and Tom were writing quite a bit, so they decided to get back in the studio. The recording of their next album, *All Roads Lead to Ausfahrt*, took place in January 2006.

**Blair Calibaba—engineer, sound tech** We recorded most of *All Roads Lead to Ausfahrt* at the

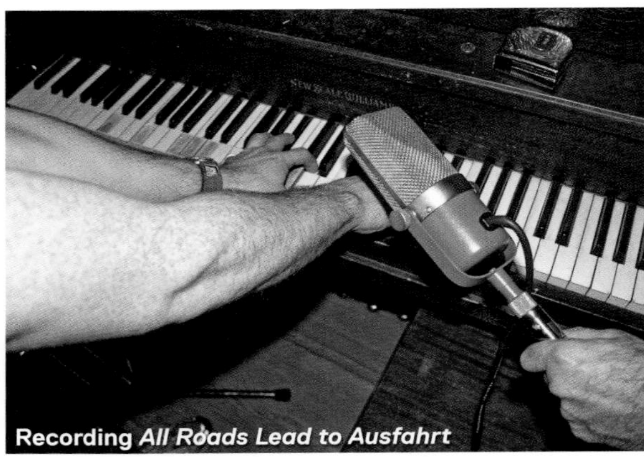
Recording *All Roads Lead to Ausfahrt*

Hive studios in Burnaby. We basically did the bed tracks there, and we did a few overdubs and vocals at Lemon Loaf. We mixed at Hipposonic.

Those were pretty fun recording sessions. We were still getting to know each other a bit, as we hadn't travelled a ton together. We had done a couple tours. They were kinda goofy and playful but pretty serious when it came to getting the music right. They were into capturing performances, not overdoing it, not overthinking it. There's some farts and warts on there that normally I would've ironed out a bit, but they were insistent, and I was on board. It's *their* music, it's *their* record. As a recording engineer, I'm just there to document it.

They had it all sorted out from rehearsals. They're not a layering type of band. They're pretty raw, and they had their parts pretty much sorted. John really had the most visions for the songs. He was very hands-on in the mixing process. You can't really call him the leader, because they all had their own strengths and creative input in huge ways. I'd say it was equal. But on the recording side, he took the lead a little bit. They definitely arrived ready to make a record.

**John Wright** With *Ausfahrt*, I had quite a bunch of song ideas. We really worked on the music and demoed a lot of it. Then Rob sat down and wrote the words to everything. The words kind of spit out after the basic music was done. We decided, "Let's just do a snappy album."

That was recorded on some weird digital format that is long since gone now, which is probably why the masters or the multitrack is no longer available. I wouldn't remix that one. It's a little spongy, but it rocks. It does what it needs to do.

**Rob Wright** Most of that *Ausfahrt* album was bits and pieces which everyone brought in and stuck together. Someone would throw in an idea, we'd work at it, and I'd add some lyrics. In the early years, I would just bring a song: "Here it is, learn it." That

Blair Calibaba, engineer on *All Roads Lead to Ausfahrt*

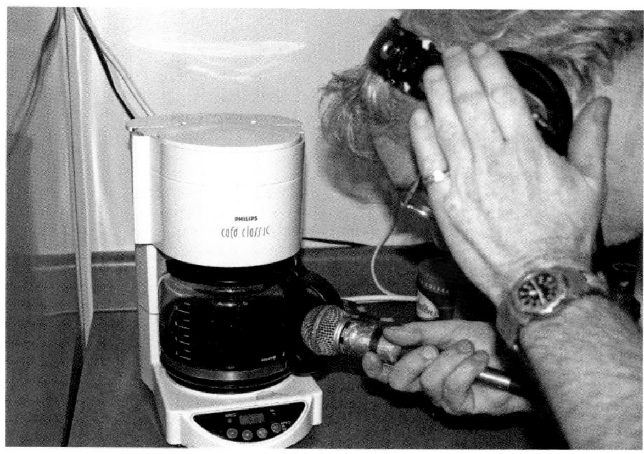


was my attitude, but I got tempered over the years. It's better if you let everybody get into the act. It took me a while to learn that.

On some of the last recordings, I got into drum machines, and I programmed the drums how I wanted John to play. I should have just let him play what he wanted. It wasn't bad, but it wasn't as good as someone who drums like he breathes, which John does. He knew better than I did.

**Tom Holliston** *Ausfahrt* was much, much more collaborative. Basically, Rob said, "Let's just come up with music. I want to write differently this time. We'll bring in our stuff, and I'll go home and write lyrics to it." I think he was listening to a lot of electronic music at that time and becoming interested in a different approach to songwriting.

**Robyn Carrigan—musician** I knew Blair Calibaba because I was a backing vocalist for hire in town, but usually more of a folkier, country nature. I'm a singer-songwriter myself, and a multi-instrumentalist. When I was younger in Nova Scotia, I was definitely very much into punk rock, so I had that side to me, but I wasn't famous for that at all.

Tom Holliston had seen me perform many times, and I knew Carolyn Mark from the Show Business Giants. I have a big voice, and I think Tom liked it, and he would often compliment me on my singing. I think it was Tom who asked me to do some vocals for the next NoMeansNo album. Tom paid me for that gig with a ticket to see a Chopin recital, which I went to see *with* Tom! I ended up singing on a couple of Tom's solo albums too.

I really enjoyed doing it. Their music is so amazing, and it's so beautifully composed and arranged, and it was just a treat. I sang on three songs: "So Low," "Slugs Are Burning," and "Mondo Nihilissimo 2000." I felt honoured to get to sing on that album.

**John Wright** Robyn's got a great voice; she was super. Just easygoing and doing her best to deliver. It was something totally different than she'd ever done before. She did a great job.

**Rob Wright** I love the song "Slugs Are Burning." Don't ask me what it's about, or why we would write about slugs. But it was kind of fun, and it worked. Songs are not necessarily about anything specific. They're entities in their own right. To me, music was always an emotional language, which means it never had to make any sense. It was, by nature, irrational, and I like that about it. I'm a very reasonable person in many ways, but I think my heart is in the mysterious and the uncanny. That's where I am really in my element.

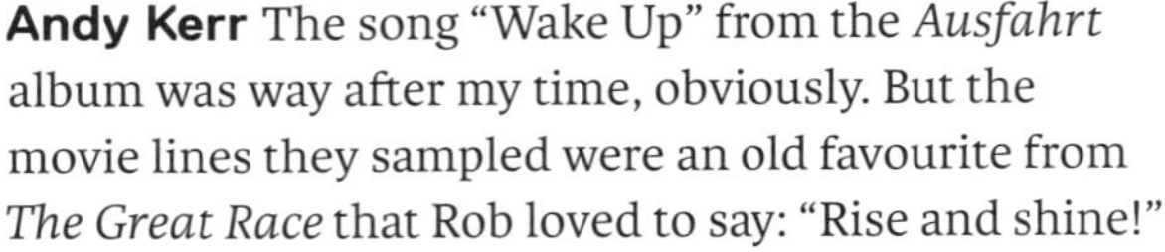

**Andy Kerr** The song "Wake Up" from the *Ausfahrt* album was way after my time, obviously. But the movie lines they sampled were an old favourite from *The Great Race* that Rob loved to say: "Rise and shine!"

**John Wright** In the verses for "The Hawk Killed the Punk," one of us is playing in 3/4 time, one is playing in 4/4, and one is playing in 5/4, but damn if I can remember who did what.

**Tom Holliston** The music for "The Hawk Killed the Punk" was like, "Okay, I'm going to play 4/4. John, you play 5/4, and Rob, you play 3/4," and then John had a middle part, and then I wrote the other middle bridge, and then Rob put the lyrics on that.

"I'm Dreaming but I Can't Wake Up" was definitely written before John and I heard it, though. Rob had a very definite idea about that one.

**John Wright** "Mondo Nihilissimo 2000" is a bizarre song and was added very last minute. We'd written the whole album, but then this song showed up that Rob had written. It was very simple but really fun to do. The drumming was odd.

**Mark Critchley** NoMeansNo had some stickers and stuff with the yin and yang symbol in a circle with

a line through it. I asked Rob what it meant, and he said, "Everything is nothing." He said, "Okay, you've got the black and you've got the white, and they are dovetailed. It's the dichotomy of spirit and matter. I'm interested in the line between the two."

**Rob Wright** The original title for *Ausfahrt* was *Nihilism for Dummies.* I found out we couldn't use that or they would come down on us like a ton of bricks. That would have been funny, but we didn't want to get sued.

**Greg Werckman** I was in a weird position. I had my own record label by then, and they approached me to do *All Roads Lead to Ausfahrt*. It was a strange moment for me, because Jello was the one who gave me my start in the music industry. I felt, "Oh god, shouldn't this be on Alternative Tentacles?" I called Jello and had a talk about it. He totally understood, and said, "Yeah, of course you should do it. They're one of the best bands ever. Why wouldn't you do it?"

**Ralph Spight** During the *Ausfahrt* tour, I was standing next to Larry Boothroyd at Slim's in San Francisco watching them play, and I'm like, "How do these fucking guys keep getting better?" I felt like I understood Rob on that *Ausfahrt* record a lot more. Lyrically, it's not flawless, and it does shift beyond the pale at times, but I also admire Rob's ability to say something where you're like, "Really, dude? Did you have to say that?"

I feel like on that record, it's Rob turning more Zen than nihilist. Even in the song "Mondo Nihilissimo 2000," he's sort of this passive observer. I really think it goes back to Rob having a singular vision. I think he's an enormous intellect; he's a really smart guy. He's funny as shit, and I really relate to him. He kinda reminds me of my older brothers too, the same sort of generational smart-ass kinda thing. I feel a strong kinship with that record. I really feel that's Rob staring death in the face.

**Rob Wright** I think we just have to realize life's limitations. That would be the first big step, which Buddhists really actually did. If you read the Diamond Sutra, the Buddha says, "In the end, it is unknowable, unutterable, and unthinkable." Which means that there's an end to what you can know. An end which knowledge as we process it, through reason and language, does not reach and never will.

It's an absurd universe. "Nothing means anything" comes from that, because you can't conceive it. You can't go to the end without fighting with your logic, without finding contradiction and paradox. Does that mean that the world is meaningless? No, it means that we're all stupid. There's a level where we will always be stupid and ignorant.

The one thing I loved about punk rock was people went, "Yeah, I'm a dummy. I'm a jerk, I'm a creep. I don't know anything." Right! The first step toward wisdom, my friend, is to know that you know nothing. The human brain and logic all developed simply to be a food-gathering tool for a bunch of apes. It's ridiculous to think that's going to be something which can encompass the meaning of existence.

Besides their propensity for avoiding publicity, the Wright brothers also did not exactly have their fingers on the pulse of the new internet age. After several incarnations of fan-driven websites, they would finally get their own official online presence.

**John Chedsey—nomeanswhatever.com, tour merch** The first time I saw NoMeansNo was at a skate park in Mesa, Arizona, in 1994, with the two drummers. After that, I got just absolutely obsessed, and I would go to every show I could. It got to the point where they'd be like, "Why is this guy showing up everywhere we play?"

I'd go up to Canada to see shows too. In early 2005, they were getting ready to do a US tour. They needed a merch person, so Tom emailed me, "Hey, you interested?" I got to do that tour, and everything snowballed from there. At some point, I suggested to the guys that I could build a website for them.

Nomeanswhatever.com started in 2006. They were resistant to just having a traditional website, but they were starting to realize the value of it. People started going there to get the tour dates and stuff. Tom would provide information to me, and we'd see an uptick in discussion when a new tour was announced.

Tom was like, "You do what you want with this." I had a lot of fun coming up with all of the bullshit. I just ran with that idea, and I was getting as ridiculous as possible. We started making the imposter promo photos and fake news releases. The only time I ever put any actual, really true, totally factual updates was on April Fool's Day. I don't know if anyone ever picked up on that or not.

**Rob Wright** Ah, good old John Chedsey. He knows us pretty well. Great guy to travel with. One of these down-home, basic Americans that are a good crew. He's one of these guys who hung on and hung on until it was, "Okay, come along then. You're

Outtakes from the *Ausfahrt* photo shoot

everywhere we're going anyway. You might as well be with us." Most of the time I try to avoid those guys like the plague, but John was one of those people who have something valuable in their personalities and in their willingness to help. Those are the people you should deal with.

**Tom Holliston** There's a great promo shot where we all had those cones that are given to dogs to stop them from scratching themselves. That was Sue Angle's doing: she managed to get a hold of those. Whenever we did a photo shoot, it was not just in front of some indistinct building. It was more like, "Hey, can we go and stand in your backyard and have our picture taken? Then we'll have a beer."

**Sue Angle—friend** I gave them the dog cones because I worked at a vet clinic, which they still haven't paid me for.

**Blair Calibaba** I started as their touring soundman in 2005. I had big shoes to fill, because Craig was a beast. Everywhere I went on those first couple of tours, it was like, "Where's Craig?" It wasn't people slighting me, but everyone loved Craig.

I had never worked with musicians whose technological musicality was so acute. John could help with frequencies he wanted pulled in or out of his monitors, same with Rob. Later on, they trained Tom really well with that too. Moreover, they just knew what the heck they wanted.

However, they're not the most accommodating musicians when it comes to live sound. They wanted what they wanted, and if you weren't able to supply that, they would not be pleased. Rob was the loudest bass player I've ever heard in my life. He didn't care whether it was a hundred-person basement or a ten-thousand-seat arena; his bass was the same volume every night. One of the "charming" things about him is he would aim the bass cabinet directly *at* me every night, and it was not done accidentally. It was quite irritating.

I always found it difficult to make sure the vocals could be heard. I had a shirt I made that said on the front, "Yes, I know the vocals are too low," and then on the back it said, "And I can hear the feedback too." I got tired of people saying, "Hey, you gotta turn up the vocals!" "Yeah, sure, okay, go tell the bass player to turn down." End of conversation.

Rob missed Craig for sure. They were creative souls together when it came to the live shows. Craig knew how to deal with them. I just didn't ever find a way to do it. Craig had twenty years of it. They had a language and everything, and I was just a studio guy who was trying to make the feedback go away every night. I was still kinda green with live stuff, so working with one of the loudest bands in the world was a bit of a task. You learned something every night, technologically and interpersonally as well.

The Hanson Brothers was the only time I ever felt like I was becoming part of the band. I got to put on a hockey helmet or a ref jersey and get up onstage with them and goof around.

**Tom Holliston** We did a show for part of the Vancouver International Jazz Festival. We brought in other musicians, like Luca, the baritone sax player from Zu, and David Macanulty and Mark Critchley on percussion and keyboards. I would have loved to have had different people come in more often; it just enriches you if it works. If the band is essentially a touring band, people will come to the shows

NoMeansNo with Luca from Zu (left), 2006

because they'll wonder, "What's it going to be like this time?"

Duke Ellington would record the same song over and over again, but with different soloists and slightly different arrangements, and it's always sort of, "Fuck. This is a really unique version." There's nothing to stop anybody from doing this. It's almost like self-censorship.

**Sean Cox—guitar tech for Foo Fighters and Tenacious D** The Foo Fighters were playing an arena show. The show ended and Dan Hadley, who is our lighting director, ran up onstage. He said, "NoMeansNo is playing one mile away. I've lined up a ride. Let's go." I'm like, "I've got to tear down my guitar rig. I've got to load the truck! Maybe I'll be ready in an hour and a half." Dan was like, "Come on, come on, come on." I turned around to my backline tech. I was like, "Dude, this is important. I gotta go." We ran out of the arena and jumped into this woman's car. She was somebody who worked at the venue who Dan had coerced into driving us to this place. We got to the club, ran up two flights of stairs, and got within like ten feet of the stage just as they were breaking into "The River." Seven and a half minutes ago, I was standing on this huge stage at an arena, and now I'm in this club. It is one of the top five most magical moments of my entire life.

**Ernie Hawkins** NoMeansNo flirted with the big time, but they were smart enough to recognize that as soon as you expand, you'll wind up spending the money that you make anyway. So they just kept it tight. If you got past the level that NoMeansNo were at, you'd

John and Tom in Europe, 2005

Rob in Europe, 2006

hire a production manager and you'd hire roadies. You'd just immediately screw yourself, because that stuff costs money. It's personnel, it's another ass that smells in the van, and it's another guy who gets drunk and doesn't make the hotel checkout time.

**Laurie Mercer** It was around 2006 when I finally called it quits with NoMeansNo, around the *Ausfahrt* time. It was clear that their course was going to run out and that there was no need for me. There was nothing I could do to build on their career. I said, "Look, I'm stepping back. You're going on this tour, don't pay me a commission." Rob then shook hands and said, "Good luck, God bless you, and I love you. It was a great trip."

It was such a huge part of my life, and while I don't want to be a drama queen, there was a considerable amount of self-sacrifice, and there was a lot of shit that happened that hurt. It was for a good cause, and to not even end up with a friend out of it is heartbreaking. The last time I saw Rob was at a funeral. At that point, Rob had been incommunicado for about nine months, and I tried chatting him up. I said, "Hey, I see you got a new phone number." He smiled at me and said, "Yes," then turned and walked away. I was like, "What just happened?"

I still believe NoMeansNo were one of the greatest bands of their time, so it's unfortunate that Rob's idiosyncrasies torpedoed everybody who wanted to make that more public knowledge. I don't know why he was like that. The easy answer would be that it's the punk ethos. The answer's probably in his lyrics if we are ever smart enough to decipher them. The art of the maelstrom: he just wanted to be the chasm of nothingness. His drive for self-negation overpowered everybody around him who wanted to help, and that included the record labels.

**Tom Holliston** Anybody who has managed a band is coming from a different angle. They want the band to be successful, because it takes up a lot of their time. I think without Laurie and probably Debbie Gordon at AT, it would never have got off the ground. Rob and John needed to just be playing music, and they needed other people to be doing the other stuff for them. I think for Laurie it was incredibly challenging. There's so much bullshit and horror and incompetence that you have to deal with, trying to get something to be successful in the music business. It's like, "Is this really worth it?"

I was booking the band for a while after that, and there was one occasion where I had it set up perfectly. We were gonna tour after Canadian Thanksgiving

Laurie Mercer

and just before American Thanksgiving. I had it all figured out. The dates for Canada were all when schools were out. Then a week before we were to go on tour, John said, "Oh, I forgot. I have to move." We had to reschedule everything to just a few days before Christmas, and then there was the complaining: "Oh, it's really cold. It's snowing." I said, "Yeah, well, then you do it!" and they'd say, "I don't know how to do it." "Okay then, let me do it!" I think that Laurie came up against stuff like that all the time. That still rankles me: "Oh, I forgot. I have to move."

**Jello Biafra** Laurie Mercer can be a very old-school rock manager at times. I tried to get along with him, but it's not as though he wasn't an arrogant motherfucker. Not everyone likes me, possibly including Laurie Mercer. He presented himself to me like he was a big-time manager, and he had it on the way up. The biggest thing he ever had would turn out to be NoMeansNo. There are times when he acted like a sharp-elbowed manager because he had to, both with NoMeansNo and with us. However, I think overall he did them more good than harm.

**John Wright** Laurie just had bigger plans for us, and I think it was a little disappointing for him, because we didn't really play ball. By the time the late '90s were rolling around, we're like, "We're not going to be a pop band, we're not going to be Nirvana, even if we went to a major label. We're not going to sell heaps of records. It's not going to happen. It would be the end of us."

I think Laurie just wanted to see us make money. Bless him, because that was technically his job. We really made his job difficult, because we didn't play the whole promo game. He tried to spin that the best he could. It's just two different ideas of how the band should be marketed and promoted.

**Gijs de Wit** Laurie leaving was a very specific turning point. That's where Rob, in a way, lost control over his own situation. John and Rob would always argue about everything, but that kind of stopped then as well. It became more of John's band. John made the decisions. I could just go to John and discuss it with him. I think that is also when Tom got a bigger piece of the pie, because with the two brothers not arguing, he could actually bring his reasoning into the debate.

I think Laurie may take it a little bit too personal, and I think it's also because Rob was one of his best friends. It's just that things went astray. Nobody's to blame, and it's unfortunate for both Laurie and Rob.

**Andy Kerr** Laurie got us off the island, essentially. We owe a lot to Laurie in terms of him setting up shows for us and being there when we paid him next to nothing. I feel we owe a great deal to all the people who put on shows, like the Konkurrent, the people in Britain, people like Dolf in Germany, AT in the States, and others, but particularly Laurie, because we wouldn't have been able to do it ourselves. It would not have been possible.

I liked working with Laurie. I liked him as a person. He could be really funny and really sweet. The only thing was that as soon as he started talking about labels, big labels, we just basically had to say, "No." That was my only issue with him. He'd say, "Yeah, but you guys are good! What's the difference between small labels screwing you or a big label screwing you?" Well, a big label can screw you way more.

**Craig Bougie** I know that Laurie was always pressing for a record contract, and Rob was always very much against that. I don't know why Laurie left. I think it was out of frustration because he wasn't making any headway.

He tried for years to break NoMeansNo, and the band was always resistant. I remember we got this big six-page contract from a major label. I believe it was Warner Brothers. Laurie was reading through it like, "Oh, this is pretty good." He gave it to Rob, and Rob wrote "NO" on the first page, "MEANS" on the middle page, and "NO" on the last page. And that was that. Managers are used to dealing with bands that want to get big, and the challenge is to get them out there. Whereas with NoMeansNo, it was sitting there, waiting for them, and NoMeansNo didn't want it.

In the earlier days, we got asked to play Glastonbury and all these big festivals. Laurie's like, "Oh, this is gonna be awesome! Finally some recognition, and a paycheque!" The band was always like,

“No, we’re not playing festivals.” It was pretty frustrating for him.

NoMeansNo definitely had this negativity toward the whole machine of popularity. I thought that some of that was counterproductive. It was frustrating to me too, but it must have been incredibly frustrating for Laurie.

**Laurie Mercer** They spent most of their energy trying to obfuscate and hide. For a lot of situations, I was the sole flag-bearer. There was a certain zealotry that was necessary, because the music business and punk rock and all that stuff is a hard river to swim upstream.

I should have thrown the towel in a lot earlier, but I enjoyed the community; I loved the band and the songs. When I got into the music industry, I had decided that I wanted to find a band that excited me and had something unique to say. NoMeansNo certainly did.

NoMeansNo
WITH
VICTIM'S FA
AN ALL AGES SHOW
VICTORIA'S OWN (EVEN IF THEY DID MOVE TO VA
NO MEANS NO
CMG PRODUCTIONS
REPUBLIK
APRIL 5TH
WRONG RECORDS RECORDING ARTIST
NO MEANS NO
PRIMRODS
25 CENT PEEPSHO
RABBIT HAS BRA
DOORS 7:00
SHOW
NOMEANSNO
THE IMAGINEERS
NAKED AND THE DEAD
WED APR 6
POLISH HALL
THRASHERPRESENTS
NOMEANSNO
WRONG
BERBATI'S PAN
DIRTCLODFIGHT MAY6 THERUBYDOE
SUCKER PUNCH PRO
ALTERNATIVE TENTAC
ALL AGES
ITH VERY
PLUTO'S REVENG
ND FROM NEW YORK C
VEHICL
SAT APRIL 2 1994
S AT 7:30
LYLE'S PLACE - UVSS
esday. April 17th
7P.M. ALL AGES
NO MEANS NO.
NILE THEATRE
EMPIRE COFFEEHOUSE
19TH AND G ST
A.
$8.00 advance
NOMEANSNO
D.O.A.
TOTAL CHAOS
X MEMBERS
FRIED WOOD
$10
SATURDAY, APRIL 20th
The Barn
NOM
NO TOMORROW
4 AD
di 4 jun
Boterhalle
vvk : 350 Bfr / 60FF kassa
org. & info: vzw 4 AD
endlich
SNUFF +
DACKELBLUT
+ RIEBE's DACKELBLUTIQE
NO MEANS NO
+ ITCH
4.9.'96
D.O.A. + Gäst
NO MEANS NO
FRIDAY
NOV 19th
TIX $10
DOERS
PAPER LANTERNS
CIRCUIT TRANSFER
NO MEANS NO
THURSDAY 21 SEPTEMBER
guests to be announced
$13 ADVANCE
19+ MUST SHOW I.D.
TICKETS AVAILABLE AT: ORANGE MONKEY MUSIC
ENCORE, BEAT GOES ON & MAPLEMUSIC.COM
FOR MORE INFO GO TO WWW.JANEBOND.CA
G ST. N. WLOO
INFINITE PRODUCTIONS presents
FRIDAY JANUARY
NOMEAN
Royal Gra
and
YOU KILL ME
nomean
mi. 25.09.96: reitschule bern
NSNO
MEANS
OMEA
SNO
NTIMN FRIZURN (LJ)
SREDA, 16. JUNIJ 2004
DIA PARK (VPK), Kranjčeva 20
57° livello
spazi di comunicazione conquistati autogestiti
D.O.A.
+ Braindamage
mercoledi 12 settembre
No Means No
+ ITCH
lunedì 16 settembre
bologna

did, like, this whole little exchange of: "Okay, well, if that's the way you feel." "Oh yeah, that's the way I feel." "Okay, all right, good night." "Okay, good night." He walked out, and then I was just like, "Did I just witness NoMeansNo break up?" Rob turned to me and said, "Can you play guitar?"

**John Chedsey** Tom would sometimes get cranky, like, "Argh! I've had it with you guys. I'm out of the band!" and John would be like, "Oh gosh, well, we have a tour in a week. Do you know where we can find another guitar player?" Ten minutes later, Tom would be back: "Sorry, I was just a little mad."

**Mike Branum** After shows, there was often a party at the club or the place we were staying. About a quarter of the guys would stay and party till late. Usually it was Keith Rose, Will Schatz, John, and sometimes me. Rob would go to bed early, but he would sit there on his laptop, sometimes until five o'clock in the morning. You'd never see him sleeping. He would just be up all night on the laptop, listening to drum and bass and all that stuff.

**Will Schatz** Rob was really getting into electronic music. It was bizarre. A lot of the music that he was listening to in that genre was very interesting experimental stuff: it wasn't boring dance-club techno by any means. He got pretty obsessed with it, and that is what he would spend most of his time doing, other

Mikey Hanson (Mike Branum) and Rob

than reading. I would share a room with him a lot of the time, and he would just have his headphones on and stomp to a beat until about six in the morning. I can sleep through anything, so it didn't bother me. That was sort of his routine.

**Mike Branum** He really, really had a frickin' thing for it. He was a fanatic about it. When we were on tour, he would listen to it on his headphones so loud in the van that Tom would be like, "Rob, can you turn your headphones down? We can hear it all the way up in the front." Oh my god, it was so freaking loud.

**Rob Wright** I had done some electronic music very early on, just experimenting. I borrowed Scott Henderson's incredibly ancient synth. One of my regrets is that I did not get into electronic music early and go at it with a lot of verve. I still think of doing that, but it's a little late to have another career. The learning curve is big, and it's all-consuming. I'd get obsessed with it. I'd be sitting here for hours, diddling around. I don't know if that's a good idea. I don't know if I want to plunge into that. I'm basically exclusively listening to techno.

**Will Schatz** A few times, Rob decided that he wanted to play electronic tracks as walk-in music for NoMeansNo shows. I would hook him up to do that, and it confused the punk rockers. It's funny, because on that tour, it was just me, Keith, and John who had cell phones. Tom and Rob were always very unplugged.

**Paul Timoney** Rob asked me if I knew a producer called Shackleton. He is this Berlin-based musician who made really good dubstep music. I found his contact info, and Shackleton ended up remixing NoMeansNo.

**Sam Shackleton—producer, musician** I almost see NoMeansNo as a gateway band. For a kid like myself, I think hearing NoMeansNo playing unconventional music within a conventional format helped me start exploring nonmainstream music generally.

I have a friend who is a promoter in Heidelberg, Germany, and one day he rang me up and asked me if I had ever heard of NoMeansNo. He met them when they played at his local venue. Rob Wright had been telling him how much he was into Shackleton! My friend passed the phone to Rob at that point, and he explained his remix idea. I could hardly refuse. Rob seemed to think that the other guys in the band regarded it as one of his eccentricities, but they seemed happy enough to indulge it. I wanted to remix "Metronome" at first, but someone else had taken that! So I chose "Dark Ages." It has a lyrical theme that sits well with my music.

**Rich Oddie—Orphx** We performed at Mutek for the first time in 2010. I remember seeing a tall, older guy dressed like a priest in the audience. After the show, he approached us and introduced himself as Rob from NoMeansNo. He talked about their remix project and invited us to contribute. We were both familiar with NoMeansNo and liked their music, so we were naturally excited about doing this. I ended up working on this remix myself. I chose "Metronome" because I liked the sparse arrangement and the lyrics, which could be taken as a commentary on the rigidity and predictability of dance music. The "tyranny of the beat." I was trying to accent this idea in the remix. I also loved the unhinged quality of the vocal.

**Scott Monteith—Deadbeat** I first saw NoMeansNo in Kitchener-Waterloo, Ontario, when I was fifteen years old. In all the times I've seen them play, "The River" was always the tune that I pined for. For me, it is the perfect amalgam of heaviosity and drama. An epic that pulls at the heartstrings and calls the body into the most relentless fucking pogo you've ever done, elbows up, in the middle of the mosh pit, devil be damned!

Venlo, Netherlands, 2011

I was utterly gobsmacked when Robert essentially cold-called me over email to request a remix. Initially, I didn't even believe it was him. He said the whole catalogue was open to choose from, but there was absolutely no question what track I wanted to do. I've had the chance to remix some of my greatest musical heroes over the years: Lee "Scratch" Perry, the Orb, U-Roy, and many others. But as a small-town Canadian boy, remixing "The River" by NoMeansNo was hands down my proudest achievement as a musician.

**Rob Wright** The best songs are those that mix both hope and despair together. "The River" is one of those, where it's apocalyptic but there's all sorts of moments of striving for the good things. "I Need You" is another one. "Forget Your Life" is about defeat and victory. So is "Victory," but the tone of it is all dark, so it's a little unbalanced. The mixture between hope and despair was often too much to the dark side.

$10.70 ADVANCE
NO MEANS NO
ALICE DONUT
ULTRA BIDE
THE LACKEYS
TUESDAY
SEPTEMBER 19, 19
DOORS AT 7:00 PM
BANDS AT 7:30 PM
THE POLISH HALL
& Bishop en culer
Datum: Do. 23.07.2009, Gebäude 9, Köln - Einlass: 20:00 | Beginn: 21:00 | Eintrittskarte: VVK 15,00 EUR
NO MEANS NO
Ritterstrasse 52 * 50668 Köln *Tel/Fax: 0221-131343
email: underdogrecords@aol.com*www.underdogrecordstore.de
GRUPO
NOMEANSNO
NOMBRE
FECHA 19/9/96
BACKSTAGE
Garatge Club
BLACK CAT
1831 14TH ST., N.W.
DOORS OPEN AT 9:30PM
NO MEANS NO
GA2 GA1 1 ADULT
GEN ADMISSION 15.50
WWW.LEESPALACE.COM
NO MEANS NO
LEGAL AGE 19+/NO SMOKING
LEES PALACE
529 BLOOR STREET
SAT APR 18 2009 DOORS 9PM
PAKKO
Helsinki 27.6.1994
NO MEANS NO
NOMEANSNO
& Frank Accident
VVK-Karten nur bei: Rave Up, Why Not und direkt im Flex
Flex präsentiert
NoMeansNo
BEGINN: 19:00 UHR!!!
September 96 REMISE
2, Engertstraße Ecke Walcherstraße
direkt über die Vorgartenstr. erreichbar).
BACKSTAGE
No Means No
DATE: 01194
WHO KNOWS ALL ABOUT
SATURDAY 6TH OCTOBER 2012
NOMEANSNO
INFINITE PRODS. PRESENTS
NOMEANSNO
21 AND OVER
GRACELAND
FRI 23 FEB 2001 8:00 PM
PRICE:10.00
NO MEANS NO
& GETEILTE KÖPFE
30.11.1994
NOMEANS NO
DI. 29 mai 01
21.00 H
Aktionshalle Rote Fabrik
NoMeansNo
18.06. OULU, Cafe Rooba
19.06. TAMPERE
20.06. JOENSUU
nomeansno
Belfast Gig
NOMEANS
THRASH
£3adv
KING TUT'S WAH WAH HUT
NO MEANS NO
MEANS NO
BANE • MULE
mc gonagles
sunday, 15th sept.
be strong be wrong
NOMEANSNO
PETLAMB
TENSION
First band on stage 7.30
Admission: £4.00
718
NOMEANSNO
& Manhole
+ Schtum
Friday 26th November 2010
NOMEANSNO
Tickets £6
Nomeansno onstage 9.30pm
free entry to Freakscene Club
069
Schlachthof
TRUST
25 Jahre Trust-Fest
NoMeansNo
Leatherface
Sex Jams
Fr 03.06.11
20 Uhr
Stehplatzkonzert
VVK: 15,-€
AK: 18,-€
Kesselhalle
Kulturzentrum Schlachthof
www.schlachthof-bremen.de
High Noon Saloon
NOMEANSNO
THE INTERNATIONAL
WORT 89.9 FM
$12.00 Advance
(Plus Service Charge)
Door $14.00
General Admission
NO REFUNDS OR EXCHANGES
NO MEANS NO
ALICE DONUT
Ultra Bide
NO MEANS NO
HANSON BROTHERS
NOCHE HOCKEY PUNK
NOMEANSNO
DOA
ITCH
SEPTIEMBRE
GARATGE CLUB
Victoria Punk Rock
Nomeansno
The Frosted Tips
& Tolan McNeil
Friday
December 2, 2005
SIDETRACK
18+ ID Required
NO MEANS NO
AFRAID TO SPEAK IN PUBLIC
SABADO 22 DE OCTUBRE A LAS 22'30 H
Venta anticipada: 1500 Ptas. Venta en taquilla: 1800 Ptas.
PUNTOS DE VENTA:
Garatje Club.
WHO KNOWS ALL ABOUT
Antena Krzyku i Komuna Otwock
prezentują
NOMEANSNO
HARDTIME
RAIN
27.06.1996, godz. 19.00
klub Stodoła, ul. Batorego 10
BE STRONG, BE WRONG
GENERAL ADMISSION

NOMEANSNO
Admit One - General Admission
NOMEANSNO
Potty Umbre
Rio Bent
NO MEANS NO
a. 94eko Urriak 23 igandea
a: 1.200. Taquilla: 1.500
October 20
NO MEANS NO
With Ford Pier Band
FRIDAY, JUNE 19, 2009
SUGAR NIGHTCLUB, 858 YATES STREET
$18adv / DRS 9:00PM
GAST
N+SNUFF
NOMEANSNO.
+REMOVAL
MAY 10th 1985
FRIDAY
GORILLA GARDENS
D.O.A.
ROCK THEATRE
8:00
$ 6.00 Advance
$ 7.00 At Door
No Means No
& Removal
ASSH
MR. IN-BETWEEN
IN HER EYES
SOLO
ANGE
FALL
MANS
VICTIM
FAITH
HEAVEN
DARK AGES
DREAMING
HAWK
JUNGLE
GRAVEYARD
BILTMORE CABARET
NOMEANSNO
BILTMORE CABARET
27 MAY11 8:00PM DOORS@8:00PM
So. 06.05.01 20.30 Uhr
Bremen
NOMEANSNO
+ LES PETITS FIERS
DIMANCHE
10 NOVEMBRE 1991
19 HEURES 30
ESPACE ORNANO
Heute in der Aktionshalle
NOMEANSN
& ITCH
TIM'S FAMILY
NOMEANSNO
SHOVLHED
DOORS 7:30PM
FRI DECEMBER 1/89
ALL AGES
A BENEFIT FOR AMNESTY
featuring
Canadian hardcore giants
NO MEANS NO
also
TRENCHTOWN
NOT OUR WORLD
KILLERKRUST
SLOTH
THE NEW INN
7PM SUN. 22ND APRIL £3
ALL PROCEEDS TO AMNESTY
NoMeansNo : "...A good record of power and variation, showing sensitivity for melody as well as trying to blow your brains out..." The Catalogue
NOMEANSNO
NoMeansNO
7.11.98 godz 19.00. klub ESKULAP, pozna
a BEZ GRANIC
meansno (can)
28 VI
godz: 18.00
KUPON KONTROLNY
No MEANS No
+ UNSANE AND MULE
at LEEDS UNIVERSITY UNION
RILEY SMITH HALL
Saturday 11th June 1994
Doors 7:30 p.m.
Tickets £6.00 Adv./£7.00 On The Door
NOMEANSNO
from Vancouver, Canada
BIGGER THAN GOD
THE PROBES
start 9pm
NOMEANSNO
Victoria CANADA
Alternative Tentacles Recording Artist
NoMeansNo
Removal
THE STARRY PLOUGH
3101 Shattuck Avenue
in Berkeley
510-841-2082
Friday
March 16th 2001
Doors at 8:00 pm
Admission $12
NoMeansNo
With Guests
Royal Grand Prix
Removal
THURSDAY
FEBRUARY 12, 1998
D.O.A.
+
NO
MEANS
NO
+
FRONT END
LOADER
WED 8
SEPT
NO MEANS NO
29.06.96.
KRAKÓW
CENA - 17ZŁ
FALL
MR. IN. BE
FAITH
NO SEX
DARK AGES
IN HER EYES
HAPPY
TOWER
HEAVEN
A LITTLE 2
RAGS
CAN'T STOP
'IL I DIE
SLUGS
+ BIG DKK
HAWK
SMALL PARTS
+ BITCHES
NOW.
MONDO.
WELL DONE
NoMeansNo
Date: 21/09/2007
Time: 19:00
West Riding
Albion St. Huddersfield
£6 Adv
General Admission
NoMeansNo
With Guests
Royal Grand Prix
Closed Caption Radio
FRIDAY
FEBRUARY 13, 1998
Admission $10.00
NOMEANSNO
NOMEANSNO
Plus Guests
NOSTURI
NOMEANSNO (CAN)
+ support
Pe 17.6.2011 ovet klo 21:00
NOMEANSNO
THU 6. 6. 2013

CHAPTER TWENTY-SIX

# THE END OF ALL THINGS

## "The end of the road looks like freedom to me."

Nothing is forever. By late 2012, NoMeansNo appeared to be winding down for several reasons, including advancing age and Rob's desire to be at home for his new role as a dad. The final active years for the band saw some Canadian dates, one last European tour, and a finishing flourish as NoMeansNo Clones the Ramones. In retrospect, it was a beautiful and perfect way to wrap it all up.

**Jennye Rieper** The Abbie Hoffman Society opened for NoMeansNo for their last-ever shows on

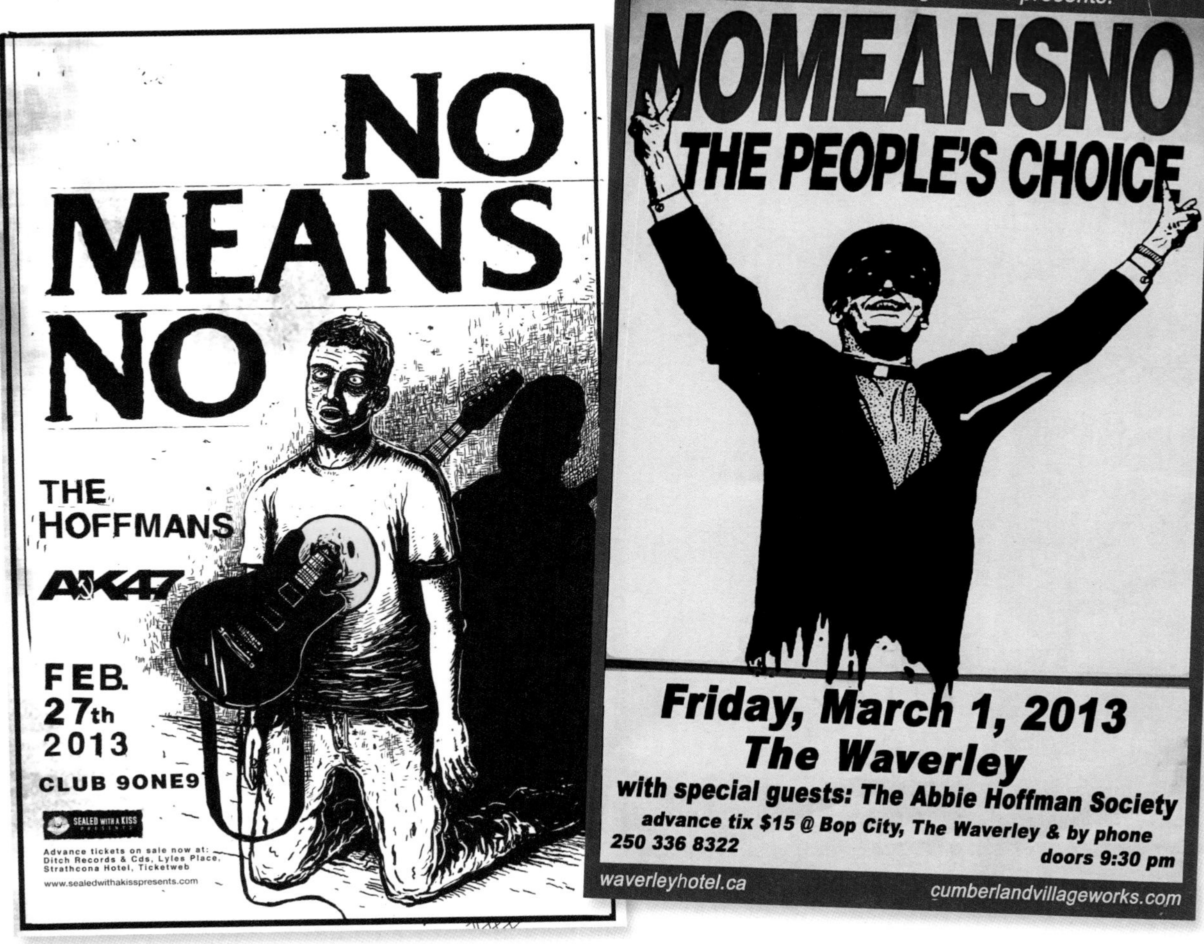


Vancouver Island in 2013. We didn't know they were the last shows at the time. They had been talking about their retirement for years in conversation, but not in any serious way. I'm pretty sure we got asked because I've known them since I was in my teens. I mean, the Hoffmans aren't bad, but we're certainly not good enough to really open for them. It was more like a gift.

**John Wright** On our first European tour in 1988, we played mostly at squats. Later, most of them ended up legalizing. It didn't go unnoticed by me that our very last show in Europe as NoMeansNo was in Frankfurt, Germany, at the AU, which is one of the oldest squatted houses in Europe that is still not legal.

Every year the AU had a festival in their backyard. They had this very sizable piece of property, and they'd get 1,500 to 2,000 people out. They had been asking us for years and years to play their festival, and we never could or did. Dolf was always saying, "They never offer enough money. We can play somewhere else and make more." Finally, Dolf agreed and we thought, "Well, it's time," so we ended up playing the AU Fest on June 8, 2013. That was our final show ever in Europe. Kind of apt that we would end on that note.

**Kieran Plunkett** The AU is one of the oldest and longest-running squats in Germany. It's one of those flagship squats, and they're super well organized. We've played the AU Fest a few times. They have it outdoors, so they have big beer gardens and punk merchandising markets. It's just a really great festival. The Restarts were on the bill for AU Fest in 2013, and I remember there was a bit of a buzz about NoMeansNo coming. It was something kind of special, although no one knew at the time it would be their last European show.

**Rob Wright** The AU lasted longer than most. In Germany, they'd have everything fixed up, and it would be beautiful, with a wonderful PA. There was also a squat in Torino, Italy, which we played on

that last tour. Totally different between Italian and German squats. In Italy, there'd be a squat that had been there for twenty years, and it still didn't have a toilet with a lid. If you could find the toilet.

**Will Schatz** It was kind of perfect, honestly. The final show that NoMeansNo played in Europe was that Frankfurt show, and that was the longest set I've ever seen them play. People weren't really letting them stop. They did a whole whackload of Ramones at the end. Normally, they'd do their two-song encore and that's it. Once in a while you'd get one more out of them. This was a definite three-encore night.

**Tom Holliston** That was the last official NoMeansNo show. It was pouring rain all day, and like the Who at Woodstock, when we came on, the skies cleared, and we ended up playing our full set. Then we played forty-five minutes of Ramones songs, because we knew we weren't going to be touring again for a while. We were just shouting out the songs to each other: "Okay! 'Let's Dance'! 'Cretin Hop'!"

**Keith Rose** I think the way they ended was the right way. With NoMeansNo, you were either there for it or you missed it. They didn't wanna be just these old guys, carting it out again.

As the tour manager negotiating the pay every night, I could see it. The problem was that we weren't making numbers. We were making guarantees, but we weren't going into percentages. That means someone's losing money, and that's not good business. Every night we were about sixty people shy, and that's not a lot, but it was consistent. I said to them, "You guys gotta make another record or do something that gets the press. Otherwise, no one's coming." NoMeansNo were touring so much in Europe, people had the idea, "Well, I won't see them this time, but I'll go see them next time."

**Rob Wright** I'm a believer that things happen when they happen. The longer you hold on to them, the less real they are. I read a lot about Buddhism, and it's exactly that. In certain monasteries, they get together with coloured sand and make these huge mandalas. In the end, they sweep them up and just get rid of them.

I don't hang on to things that are done. If you do, you're wasting your time. The things you could be doing right now in the world are relevant. Those things in the past are not. Trying to grasp something that's already gone? It doesn't exist anymore. What's the point?

**Poster for NoMeansNo's last European show, at AU Fest, 2013**

However, I talk the talk, but I can't claim to walk the walk completely. Those Buddhist ideas are a difficult thing to do. It's an awakening. The most difficult thing is to wake up from the dream and see things just as they are in front of you. I have time to contemplate such things now, whereas on tour I did not.

**Ford Pier** Tom always had his little strategies for insulating himself from the rigamarole of touring life. He would just be out in the van with his bag of popcorn and a beer, reading a book. Then he'd do a little bit of a stretch when it was time for him to play. He was engaging with that life as little as possible. They all did, in varying ways.

**Tom Holliston** As time went on, I needed my own space. I started to ask myself, "Why am I so anxious all the time?" The late Neil Peart was like this too. As soon as the concert was done, Neil got on his motorbike and was gone. There was nothing wrong with Neil; he just wanted to go. You just talk to so many people during the day.

After the show is done, I've got to go, and I think Robbie was the same way. I just want to be in my own space for ninety minutes, read my book, have a glass of Scotch, and go to sleep. I can't talk to anybody anymore. I don't have anything left in the tank.

**Gijs de Wit** NoMeansNo took the piss out of everything. They really didn't care about all the glamour. Look at the shorts John was always wearing. Rob would walk off the stage, have a shower, get into his pajamas, and sit in the van, because it made it easier later when he got to the hotel. He can just go to bed instead of having to put on different clothes twice.

Every single night, John would sit down with people, either fans, promoters, or whoever, and have another drink after the show. He would always be open to having a talk. There was no sense of, "We are better than you." That's maybe why they have such a hardcore fan base—because people could see they weren't fake.

**Tom Holliston** At one point, Fred Armisen wanted us to do something with his TV show. I like *Portlandia*, but I didn't want to do that. I just want to play music. I don't want to be on a TV show. Rob was also like, "Yeah, I'm not an actor." Thank you very much, but no. I just want to go and play music.

When Fred Armisen came to Vancouver, he was hoping that we would make an appearance at his show. I could go there, but I'd have to find a place to park. I'd have to talk to people and get a laminate, which I hate. Then I'd have to go backstage and stand there. They might want to put makeup on me. It's not my element. I wouldn't know what to do. I'm not an actor. But I like the *Portlandia* show a lot. It made me laugh.

**Mike Branum** Something that was really bugging Rob on the last few tours was being away from his kids. He had barely seen them much before leaving on tour, and it was crushing him. You want to just be with your kids, but you're over in Europe with these four sweaty guys and every one of them is going, "Oh, it's not so bad, Rob. Don't worry about it." I have a young kid now, so I get it.

**Tim Solyan** When Rob had that baby, I remember John telling me, "Oh dude, I think Robbie's done." I was like, "What? Come on, man. No way. He's got a kid, I've got kids, you've got kids." He was like, "I don't know, dude. He's going the other way with it."

When NoMeansNo ended, I didn't really take it as a moment of sadness. I cannot believe the amount that they gave to the music-listening community. How hard they fuckin' drove that machine. They never gave it up until the moment they gave it up.

**John Wright** I wasn't terribly surprised. Rob was just burned out. It's like, "Okay, we rent the same vans, we stay in the same places, play the same venues, see the same crowds." It just got to be all too much of the

same for him. He was already losing interest in rock 'n' roll music. All he cared about was dubstep and electronica; that's what he listened to, and that's what he wanted to write. Well, how? We're not that kind of band.

After 2013, we took a break. We did one more Hansons tour to promote the PunkRauch beer I did with Isaac at Le Trou du Diable. I can't really remember when exactly he said that he was finished. Also, his hip was going, which was something he didn't really mention at the time. After the fact, he said, "If I can't move my own gear anymore, I don't want to go on tour." His hip was fucked up. His knee was fucked up. He was turning sixty and feeling older, and he had young kids. He just had enough, and he hasn't picked up his bass since.

**Sissi Schulmeister** If you tour a bunch, it's really hard to have a relationship, because you are constantly on the road. It's hard to have a family, because you miss out on seeing the kids grow up. Alice Donut stopped playing basically when we had kids too. We had a big breakup in '96, but then we started up again later. You never know, in five years maybe they'll miss it and start up again. That's what we did.

**Rob Wright** I was always a fish out of water. With the upbringing we had, I had no hometown. I've had a series of places I stayed at and left. It's one of the reasons I can do something like leave the band. When something's over, it's over. I learned that when I was young. I went from one thing to another, and that was it. When I came back from one tour and Sammy didn't recognize me, my priorities completely changed.

**Melanie Kaye—publicist** I got a call from Break Out West telling me NoMeansNo was going to be inducted into the Western Canadian Music Hall of Fame. It seemed like the band was getting ready to retire, so it felt like a great way to end it. I was unsure if the band would agree to show up, never mind perform. It was a magical night but bittersweet, because I knew this was the end of the road for the band. Everyone had a great time. Rob was even coaxed out to take part in some photos after the show, thanks to a bottle of Oban that I insisted the runner get at the last minute.

**Western Canadian Music Awards, Victoria, 2015: Tom, Rob, and John**

**Rob Wright** The actual last live performance of NoMeansNo was at that awards show in Victoria. Ordinarily, I wouldn't have touched that with a ten-foot pole. It was just a hilarious idea, so I could not resist. John said, "You're probably not going to want to do this, but I've got this offer." I was like, "What? Hall of Fame?" I didn't realize that it was an awards show, like the Oscars, but at a lower level. Grant Lawrence came to moderate it, and I must say, I enjoyed every minute of it. I thought it was so funny. I was having such a good time; I couldn't believe it. I thought being inducted into the Hall of Fame is like the answer to the question "What do we do with the body?" That was the perfect ending. The only reason you get in the Hall of Fame is because you're finished. You should see the award they gave us. I don't know who's got it. It's some sort of little triangle made out of plastic.

We had Tom on acoustic guitar, John on keyboards, and me without my bass, just singing. I think that was my idea. Something I never wanted to do was NoMeansNo unplugged. Being plugged in and loud was the whole point of the fucking thing. Why would we do it unplugged?

They were not going to let us play what we wanted, and we'd have to get together and rehearse like crazy. That would be a nightmare. We would have to sound-check and argue with people, and they're not going to let us be loud. This way it was simple, and I didn't have to play. I could just sing. I didn't have to get my chops back.

I hadn't played for a long time at that point. I'm the kind of person who would have to relearn all these songs nearly every time. If you asked me to play one of my songs, I could not do it. Andy could play every song he ever learned or heard. Tom's pretty good with that too. No, give me a month off and I have to relearn everything. I am not a born musician. Never was.

Rob in full costume at the 2015 Western Canadian Music Awards

Tom on acoustic guitar at the Western Canadian Music Awards

John playing keyboards at the Western Canadian Music Awards

**Joe Keithley** Rob is a unique guy, I will say that. He's great, but he's cut from a different cloth. John is way more down to earth. The eccentricity of Rob is part of what made NoMeansNo. They were always funny too, and that's the key to punk rock. You wanna be intense, but if it's too serious, it gets pretty hard to take after a while. The humour thing is really essential. It's part of what made punk rock fun.

I think that's one of the things that made them unique. They didn't conform to the music business. D.O.A. didn't either, but they were hardcore nonconformist. If somebody offered D.O.A. a good opportunity, we'd think about it. Those guys were really particular. That's a pretty admirable trait on their part. It's really hard to find that quality in people, because most people bend with the wind. I guess another word might be stubbornness.

**Byron Slack** I was asked by the Portland Hotel Society if I could get NMN to play the staff party. I asked them, "Would you guys like to play Clone the Ramones for this staff party?" Rob's one stipulation for doing it was, "If we're going to play the staff Christmas party, then we also have to do the

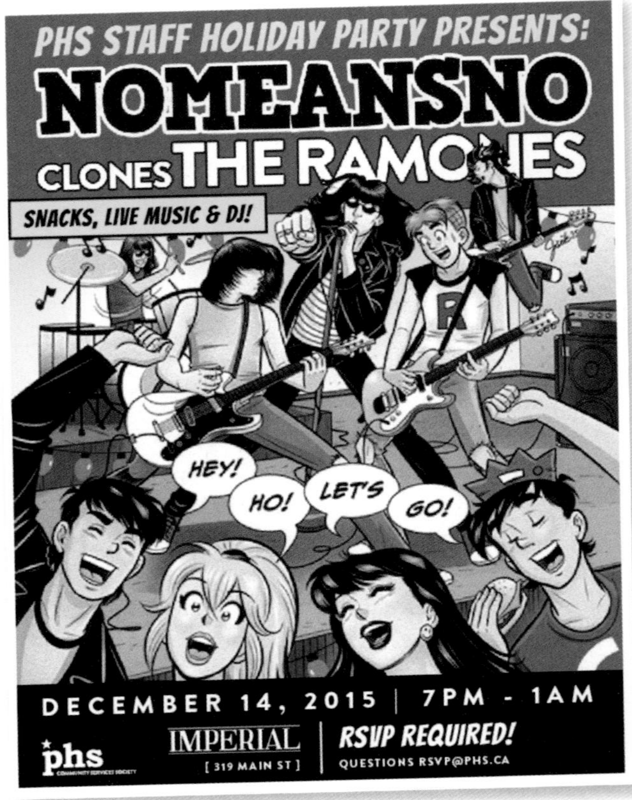

Ramones on a New Year's Eve show. We can do that at midnight, and it will be just like the *It's Alive* record."

When we did that, it didn't feel like the last show. It was just another cool show. A year before, Rob would say things like, "Well, I guess I'm going to do this till the day I die. Poor John could have had a better life, but I dragged him into this one." It flip-flopped between being committed to it and not wanting to do it anymore. But he gave it his all at that last show.

**Rob Wright** Our last show was at the old Biltmore, here in Vancouver. I did it because I was volunteering at a church and they needed a new roof. I said, "Guys, do you want to do this thing as a benefit?" We made about $6,000. It was a big success, and completely so much fun to do. I had a stupid Dee Dee bobbed-hair wig on, which kept flipping down over my eyes. John was brilliant too. It was a gang of fun.

**Byron Slack** It was insane. I came in the front door with the wigs and the leather jackets in my arms, and I just hit a wall of people. John was phoning me, and he's like, "Dude, it's almost midnight, where are you?"

NoMeansNo Clones the Ramones backstage

I'm like, "I can't get in!" John's like, "Get back here, because it's gonna strike twelve." I was pushing my way through; it was near impossible. I'd say the place was oversold. I think their capacity was like eighty, but there were like five hundred people there that night.

There were only two working toilets. People were just peeing in the garbage can, because there was nowhere to go. Everybody was so happy to be doing this thing. It was bananas, but it all worked out. All three of them were like, "Thank you so much for that, because we've made a good chunk of cash." It really felt like it was more than just, "See you next time, we'll talk to you soon." They all got into their cars. Rob drove me home, and that was that.

I think the other two were hopeful that things were gonna continue. I think Rob might have thought, "That's a great way to end it," as an afterthought, but that was definitely not something that was vocalized at the time.

**Adam Slack** As far as them packing it in, it made sense. During the last tour, I could just feel it. Rob was tapped out. Calling it quits is a hard thing to do. I think Rob entertained it for the last couple of years.

**Ford Pier** I don't know whether anybody was really enjoying themselves that much at the end. I knew that they were finding it hard to write. I didn't really like their last record, although there were some good things about the last couple of EPs.

There comes a point in your life when you've been doing a thing really well for so long that *not* doing it would not only be hard, it would be an existential threat. To intentionally dismantle that is an attack on your identity. There is a lay belief that any sort of artistic pursuit is a calling, so why would you stop? Maybe you just don't have any ideas anymore. Maybe you don't like that sort of stuff anymore.

The resentment that I saw the last couple of times out was something new. I didn't really believe that they all liked all of the music they were playing, but it was their job, and they had to do it. I think that they should have stopped a while before they did. They were always worth seeing live, but the energy that animated it had waned.

**Joe Keithley** Usually when bands pack it in, they do a farewell tour, or like D.O.A., they come back to do another farewell tour. You think it would be an obvious thing. To me, personally, I will keep playing music live in front of people until either I can't do it anymore or nobody shows up.

People would've been really excited about a farewell tour. They could've done their favourite spots. To me, that would be a satisfying and a sad thing. When you've been playing music all your life, it's pretty hard to turn off the tap. John's still involved with music. I don't talk to Rob much. I bet he's sitting around playing his bass when he's not being a dad. Or maybe he's like, "I've done that for forty years, enough."

**Rob Wright** One of the reasons I was happy to end it was that we did everything we wanted to do. We made our own music our way. We kept control of it. We made a living. We had a career. We went all the way around the fucking world. At the end, we

weren't doing it as well, because the environment had changed, and we lost relevance.

NoMeansNo is a great band. I also think that the old recordings of Sidney Bechet in New Orleans from the '20s are great. However, it's no longer relevant to this culture and the people who are now listening to music. Neither is NoMeansNo. Neither is hardcore, or punk, or even, goddamn it, any kind of guitar-based rock. It's things that refuse to die. They walk around like zombies, but there's no reason for them to exist.

**Byron Slack** In the entertainment industry, there's a lot of mistrust, but those guys are really honourable people. That was at the core of every decision they made. They'd call you out if you were being a jackass. They didn't want something to get wrecked by an outside source or have somebody take advantage of the hard work they had done. I think that's why they never signed to a major label. They would always rather have been a big fish in a small pond than just another fish in the sea.

**Rob Wright** Being in punk rock got me out of the shell that I was in. I became another person as I started doing it, and I did things I'd never done before. I'm a very solitary guy most of the time, but being on tour is like people central twenty-four hours a day. There was a purpose then, there was a goal, there was something to do that was important. That something was the movement that was going on. It certainly wasn't just a musical genre or just a fashion thing.

Everyone just wanted that energy, that out-of-control feeling with crowds going crazy and the pogoing. Then suddenly it became regimented. It constantly got spoiled. It calcified over time, and basically it's gone now completely. Things are born, they live, and they die. We calcified along with the scene.

**Keith Rose** I think they ended right. It's better than the running joke of the endless farewell tours. Their whole thing is about myth and legend and mystery, so why would you ever announce a final show? It just ended.

**Scott Henderson** There was no farewell tour. Most rock bands would go out with a big bang and a

NoMeansNo
Sep 24, 2016 ·
Greetings everybody,John here from NMN and with a heavy heart I must announce the retirement of No Means No.A hiatus became a long hiatus and a lingering hiatus has become a permanent one. Thirty-five years and countless miles, a couple thousand shows and many more beers, a bunch of tunes and sweaty hoards of great fans, I can't say thanks enough to everyone.I will continue to post here on our page about the Robots and future projects if and when they happen. Hoping to have the debut Compressorhead album out by next march so you have not heard the last of things yet.So cheers everyone! Raise a glass....xo

7.1K 1.7K comments 2.6K shares

Like Comment Share

flourish, but NoMeansNo were not your average rock band. They never thought about it like that. They just went until they couldn't: "That's it, we're done." From where I sat, it was like, "Okay, well, job well done. That was a hell of a career."

I know a lot of fans wish they'd get back together and do a final tour. I think that is actually one of the reasons they *wouldn't* do it. If they're gonna get back together, they'll fucking tell us. They don't need us to prompt them. They never needed us to prompt them to do anything.

**Rob Wright** I wasn't that angry of a guy anymore. Fear, anger, and betrayal had been trademarks of my personality. I eventually got tired of being that guy. The things that are valuable about those songs are still valuable, but the environment didn't have to be so dark and desperate, bitter and angry.

**Jello Biafra** They definitely ended with a whimper more than a bang, although "whimper" might be the wrong word. They did it with dignity; they did it with class: "NoMeansNo is done and this is all we're going to say about it." There wasn't some dumb internet or social media war going on after that, in no small part because they are all adults and chose to stay adult and stay friendly with each other. There was no public sniping back and forth on Andy after he was out. There were no drama queens in NoMeansNo. They are adults. It is also very much to their credit that you don't get all this bitterness of, "We could've been a contender! Waah!" You don't get that from them. All four of them are grounded and comfortable in their own skin.

**Rob Wright** When I stopped playing, at first it was kind of weird, and then it was such a relief. I don't ever have to ask, "When does the backup band go on?" No more rehearsals. No more tour schedule. No more buying T-shirts. What I felt was relief. Freedom, finally.

Everything I do now is mainly just killing time in between putting the garbage out, washing the dishes, or driving the kids somewhere. I'm living in suburban splendour with two lovely kids, and I'm doing what the hell I want to do.

There's a Chinese sage who once said, "Don't go to the mountaintops searching for enlightenment. It's right there in what you do every day." Most of the rest of it is just a dream. I find myself now trying more and more to be in the real world and out of the dream. That means not worrying about things like careers.

To me, having kids is like a whole new career. In a lot of ways, I think it's a more important job than what I was doing. Not that I think that music isn't important, but bringing up kids is one of the main things in life. You work, you procreate, you teach, you die. In that order. I'm at the teaching stage now, but that dying part is creeping up on me, man.

**Keith Rose** I was going on tour to Germany. I needed a case to put my bass in, and I knew Rob had a good flight case. I phoned Rob and asked if I could borrow his case. Rob said, "Keep it. I don't need it. I'm not going anywhere."

**Tom Holliston** When John suggested that we announce we were retiring, I said, "No, I'm going to quit, because I am not retiring from music." That's why I announced I was quitting NoMeansNo just shortly before the retirement announcement. I told John I respected where he was coming from, but I didn't want the perception that I was retiring musically. The band as a concept, as an idea, was retiring, not me. John said, "Yes, that's fine. I totally understand."

Somebody asked my older brother once, "What are you going to do when you retire?" He was like, "Do I have to retire?" That's the way I think. I'm not retiring. I may just have to take a break because I'm getting older and I can't go on tour all the time. I do solo shows because I'm a musician and I want to. It's my agenda. It's my acoustic guitar and myself. I can decide when I want to go, because I'm driving the car.

**Andy Kerr** We all really loved the music that we played. There's nothing we did that I'm embarrassed about, really. I just think of specific things, like, "Oh fuck, we shouldn't have put that synthesizer solo right there." Really sort of small, petty things. I've talked about this with my kid too. He said, "You guys made *Wrong* and that's a really good record!" I said, "Yeah, I'm really glad I was part of a band that put out a good record."

**Rob Wright** We made lots of friends. A lot of people just made a lot of enemies.

**Tom Holliston** One of the best things about being in that band was how I made new friends, literally, all over the world. I'm not the most socially interactive person, but I really enjoy catching up with people I've grown to know. Maybe having a beer or a meal before the show and just hanging out. I've kept in touch with a lot of people I met from being in NoMeansNo.

**Gijs de Wit** I think the truth is highly overrated. What is the truth about NoMeansNo? There is no fucking truth.

They've done political shows. They've done benefits. But were they political? I have no idea. They were a piss-take in a way. They were on Alternative Tentacles, which means punk music. But were they punk?

Sometimes it's the people who you work with that define what you really are. I've never seen Tom, John, Rob, or Andy as punks, ever, but they were completely DIY. They were doing things in the way they wanted to do them. With John and Rob being brothers and quite often completely opposite in terms of opinions or musical direction, it became very NoMeansNo. They're unique.

Apart from *Wrong* maybe, there's always moments in their records that are very, very uncomfortable. They cannot be put in any category. I don't know if they were even a band.

**Laurie Mercer** Few bands affected people the way NoMeansNo did. I would have people come up to me and pick a lyric out of some song that had been under the radar to me. They would talk my ear off about how it emotionally meant so much to them. That's their genius.

**Trey Spruance** I knew lots of people who were very deeply affected by their music on an emotional level. They were screaming and yelling about the pain and abuse that a lot of the kids in the crowd were going through. When you're out in the middle of nowhere, and nobody is acknowledging any of that stuff, it has a huge impact when a band addresses it in a powerful musical performance.

**Colin Macrae—Pigment Vehicle** NoMeansNo had an incredibly profound ability to shine light on the dark side of the human psyche. They were politically and intellectually savvy. They had this incredibly original musical style. It had a groove, and it was bombastic.

**Greg Werckman** It's so criminal that the world doesn't know and worship NoMeansNo, but for me and my personal experience, it was the people. Andy, Rob, and John were just the nicest people you'd ever want to meet. They realized they were talented musicians, but any time praise or adulation came their way, they were very humble about taking it. Maybe that's the Canadian way. They quickly became some of my best friends.

Each one of them is such an individual too. There were shows where I would want to stand as close to the drum kit as possible and just be like, "Oh my god, how many arms does John have?" He was a machine. Then there were shows where I would just watch Rob and the way he played bass and sang. I do think his songwriting is horribly underrated. Then Andy's funny faces, his odd off-key playing and everything. Later Tommy too. It was all perfection.

**John Wright** We had a core audience, and we could always count on our fans. Around the mid-'90s, there weren't any new young fans coming out. Since we've been retired, sixteen-year-olds are discovering NoMeansNo. "Where were you twenty years ago? Oh, you weren't even born yet."

**Daniel House** NoMeansNo are one of those bands that only sound like NoMeansNo. They're so singular. There was a whole level of intensity, cold sweat, and urgency about their stuff that was just completely undeniable.

It's like that stupid question, "Stones or the Beatles?" Well, both, obviously. The Beatles are the band you wanna take to meet your parents, and the Stones are the band you wanna take to bed. NoMeansNo are the band you want to take to meet your parents, but you just wanna make sure your parents never see them live, because then they'll have a completely different opinion.

**China Miéville** There was something about one's relationship to culture and to subculture when you had to really work at it. NoMeansNo were the first band where I felt that way, partly because the music was so fucking weird. I have this very strong dilemma about wanting to shout about it but also wanting only people who pass an exam to actually be allowed to listen. I have enough insight to recognize this as not my finest hour when I feel this way.

**Ford Pier** The story of NoMeansNo is the story of a group of men whose business was coming up with these startling exegeses on communication, and what it means to communicate, and how you can communicate, and how hopeless it is to try and truly communicate anything. Communication and the study of communication was really what the whole project was all about, but none of these guys were any good at communicating.

**Rob Wright** To me, music is an emotional language. Emotions don't make any sense, and they don't have to. They have to be expressed, and music is the way people express their emotions together. Music is bonding. That's why every culture has had it. Cultures with music are closer together, and they work better together. In primitive cultures, everyone sang. There was no audience. Everyone was doing it. Dancing, singing, rhythm. It's an essential part of the working human community. When I figured that out, then I knew I had a reason to do it.

**Craig Bougie** We never did get a fucking tour bus. That's always been a big disappointment for me.

NO MEANS NO
PLUS
FRIDAY
NO MEANS NO
FIRST EVER HUDDERSFIELD SHOW!!!!
£6 ADV LIMITED TICKETS
NOME
THE FREAK ACCIDENT
Saturday
Wahoo is good eatin'!
NO MEANS
PACK
FRI OCT 9
Advance Tickets At All Safeway
WWW.MIKETHRASHERPRESENTS.COM
U:MACK PRESENT
NO MEANS NO
KIDD BLUNT
NOMEANSNO
KAI KLN
TRICLOPS
MIKE WATT
@ HAPLOWS
OCT 17
2009
BRIAN McKENNA'S 40th BIRTH-DAY!!!
SHOWS
NOMEANSNO
FRIDAY 26TH
BRUDENELL
WITH SUPPORT
STOWARZYSZENIE
MIEJSKI DOM KULTURY W ZGORZELCU
zapraszają na koncert:
NoM
Dr Fleischn
17.09.201
MDK Zgorzelec
start 19:30
NOMEANSNO
THE PAC
NOMEANSNO
CLONES THE RAMONES
ROB JOHN TOM BYRON
A FUNDRAISER FOR THE SAINT BARNABAS COMMUNITY SERVICE
NOMEANSNO
BUTLINS MINEHEAD
NOMEANSNO
+YANKEE SANDWICK
PAC
FANZIN
GRAPH
21H
THE SHAKEDO PRESENTS
NOMEAN
WITH FORD PIER
WE
$10
DOOR

NO MEANS NO
HEKLA BRISTOL
AY 1ST OCT
ADV
DI 27 APR
20:00
CS. BRUNO
(TRENTO)
NO MEANS NO
+ INVASIVES
GOOD BAU MONDO CANE
100
CAN
INVASIVES CAN
'07
DACHSTOCK REITSCHULE
WWW.DACHSTOCK.CH
VVK: ROCKAWAY BEACH, SPEICHERGASSE 35,
INVASIV
SKG
12 07 09 VERA
NO MEANS NO
NOMEANSNO
SATURDAY 9/11 @ DANTE'S
CAM AND LEVER MECHANISM CONTROLS MOVEMENTS OF HEAD, EARS, EYES, TAIL, JAWS, AND SOUND BELLOWS
SILENT ELECTRIC MOTOR OPERATES ALL INTERNAL MECHANISM
TANK HOLDS MILK
GLASS MILKING MACHINE SHOWS MILK COMING FROM COW
ELECTRIC-DRIVEN CENTRIFUGAL PUMP CIRCULATES MILK BACK TO COW FROM MILKING MACHINE
WINE?
RED
NO MEANS NO
EH UP!
NO MEANS NO
THURSDAY 23 MAY WHELANS
NO MEANS NO
TOURNEE FRANCAISE 2012
17/11 . EVREUX . L'ABORDAGE
18/11 . PARIS . LE POINT EPHEMERE
20/11 . TOULOUSE . LE BIKINI
21/11 . BORDEAUX . BT59
22/11 . NANTES . LA BARAKASON
23/11 . LYON . L'EPICERIE MODERNE
NONONO
MEANS MEANS
MEANS MEANS
NONONO
superfifer proudly presents
legendary canadian punk rock
friday 26
LIVE AT THE BRUDENELL SOCIAL CLUB, LEEDS
support from PACK AD
doors 7:30pm
ANTIPOP PROUDLY PRESENTS!
NoMeansNo
Plus The Dead Class
NO MEANS NO
INVASIVES
SEVEN SIOU
2.DEZ
ARENA
THE ART AND SCIENCE OF
NOMEANSNO
WRIGHT
WRONG

# BACKWORD

## from the desk of W. Buzz Ryan

Yeah. I been drinking. Trying to work a tooth loose. There it goes. So. Okay.

I never really knew these guys. I don't know if I met them, either. The No Means No? A power trio?

In about 1990, I was working as a publicist guy for a Death metal group calling themselves Ironic Odor. Cryptic Seed? ... They kept on having arguments and changing their name. Then, the lead singer and lyricist, Scrotus, killed and ate himself.

Maybe a week later the rest of the band also killed and ate themselves. I had all this good promo written but no place to take it to. No band extent! Bane of the A&R dude for sure. Look what happened to Alice Donut. Same thing!

I fell on hard times and was working at my Auntie Leni's kitten disposal.

As chance would have it, I met up with Jello Biafra at a San Francisco eatery called "Garndiments." What a shit hole! Everything on the menu was either a garnish or a condiment and it just sucked. Jello and I went elsewhere. To a reading. Yeah. It was a book signing. Merrill Womach's book.

Back to Jello! I met him at Choate. Yeah, I know. We both went to Choate. Anyway! Now he had a record label. Something to do with Cephalopods? I been awake a long time now. Sorry. Shit. Okay!

this ...

He, Biafra, he told me that some band on his label needed a publicist. I said sure I could do that, although I had no idea about his bands? I had a lot of that shit written already and told him about Scrotus and his band, who had also killed and eaten each other. Could I just use that crap? I had to get a move on because of a certain traffic citation ... SO!!!! I needed cash. Also, my partner had a bad foot.

Biafra told me that would be fine: change a few names, a few dates? Who'd know?

The release was a live album, and it was for some foreign label where they have cheese wheels in that country. So, I did. The band (I guess NoMeansNo?) saw that and liked it. Some A&R guy told me what to change, a financial formality took place, and all was good.

Took maybe five minutes. I never met the guys nor did I ever hear The NoMeansNo on the radio.

They made it into some kind of Canadian Hall of Fame thing?

---

*Editors' Note:* Mr. Ryan's foreword to this book arrived inside a smudged bank deposit envelope in the form of an audio cassette tape that appeared to be well seasoned. There was no return address on the envelope.

The sound quality of the tape was less than ideal and, at times, proved quite difficult to transcribe. However, in the interests of authenticity and despite the rambling nature of the narrative, we decided to go ahead and use it. Several audio filters proved helpful, and we were able to piece together something we hope is at least moderately acceptable to the reader.

We later found out that Mr. Ryan had been living in a small rental flat above a clerical outfitters in Dothan, Alabama. He has since moved along, and despite our best and extensive efforts, his current whereabouts have not been ascertained.

APPENDIX

# THE GEAR

## "I'm a good machine."

Nothing about NoMeansNo's gear setup made any sense, and it was unlike anything I'd seen for a punk band. But the moment they started playing, they sounded *exactly* like NoMeansNo.

For most bands, the lead singer stands front and centre as the focal point of the band. It's telling, and totally appropriate, that for NoMeansNo, that position was given to Rob's bass rig. Crucial to Rob's sound was the use of a 4x12 guitar cab. This accentuated the punchy midrange his tone was famous for. Sitting on its end to the side of the cab was a solid-state Acoustic brand head. This would later be replaced by another solid-state head, this time a Marshall 3530 Jubilee series. These amps produced loud, clean tones without the breakup associated with tube amps at high volume.

Plugged into these would be one of Rob's 1970s Fender Precision basses, one natural and one classic sunburst. These were very much what we would describe as "players" and not lovingly kept in their cases to remain dent and scratch free. These were tools and wore their battle scars proudly with paint and wood gouged out of their top due to Rob's exuberant playing style. Stickers and duct tape adorned the bodies to hold parts in place or keep his strap secure. The metal bridges got rustier and rustier thanks in no small part to the sweat coming off Rob. By the late '90s, both of these basses were finally retired and replaced with a new Fender Precision bass in candy apple red finish. It saw service at both NoMeansNo and Hanson Brothers gigs. In their final European tours, it was quite a shock to see Rob play rented basses that weren't the stock, standard Fender Precisions he had used exclusively to that point.

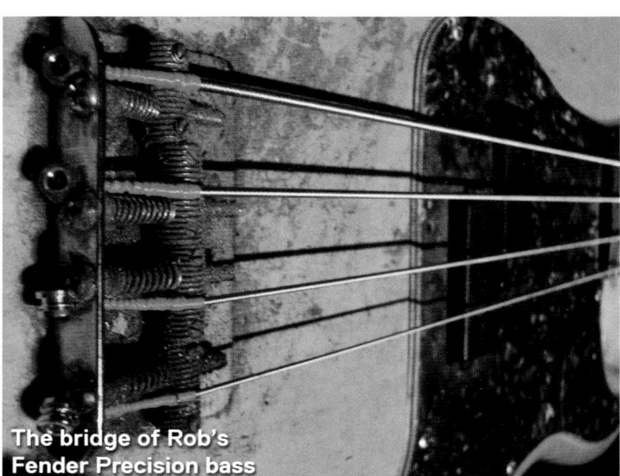
The bridge of Rob's Fender Precision bass

Andy Kerr's guitar rig was to Rob's right as they stood onstage. Most notable were his speaker cabinets, a pair of small 1x12s. The horn speaker in one of the cabinets gave away that it was originally a full-range speaker cab designed for use with a PA unit. Andy used Fender amp heads that were beloved by guitarists for their crystalline, clean tones that, with some coaxing, could be pushed into light breakup: first a 1960s Fender Band-Master and later a 1970s "silverface" Fender Bassman.

Both Andy and Rob took equipment traditionally associated with bright, clean tones and pushed them *hard*. Rob hit his strings ferociously and sent the signal into a solid-state amp turned up way too loud. The subsequent sound was then pushed through a speaker cab that accentuated midrange growl. That gave him the tone so important and memorable for NoMeansNo's sound.

Andy also took amps known for their clean headroom and pushed them way past the point of decency to make them wail and scream. Crucially, the sonic ranges of the two rigs, while far from traditional,

Andy's speaker cabinets (on chair), Fender amp head (on floor), and Schecter guitar

John's drum kit

worked perfectly in unison with each other. Rob pushed into the frequencies usually inhabited by the guitarist, leaving Andy's treble-heavy, angular, and wiry sound to fill the sonic space left unoccupied by the rhythm section.

Andy's guitar was a Telecaster-style guitar but seemed to have two sealed-unit humbuckers and didn't seem to be a Fender, despite having the classic headstock silhouette of an original. Thanks to communication with Andy himself, I learned that it was indeed a Schecter but one that dated back to their origins as an aftermarket parts company. This was before Schecter began constructing and selling fully built guitars under their own name. The guitar Andy owned was the definition of a "parts-caster," being put together from Schecter parts and ultimately finding its way into a local music store fully built for Andy to discover.

I saw the band with Tom many more times than I did with Andy. I was lucky enough to get to hang out with the band and crew for a few days while they were in town. This gave me a chance to see the band's equipment from up close and confirm my long-held belief that it was in as bad condition as I had observed from the pit. There were torn amp and speaker coverings, rusted-out metal parts on the guitars and basses, and missing control knobs on amp heads, effects, and guitars. The thick layer of grime on John's drums would be more commonly found on a studio or practice-place loaner kit rather than on the professional tools of one of punk rock's most lauded technicians.

John's gear tale starts with a piece of equipment gifted by his father, a '60s Ludwig kit that was later broken up and sold for something more modern. For early NoMeansNo work, John went hybrid with the Ludwig kick and rack tom, adding two Pearl toms and a Remo concert snare.

This kit lasted until 1989, when it was upgraded for a Tama Royalstar kit with Ayotte snare. It was used on all North American tours and recordings, and it even made the trip to Europe for the tour with second drummer Ken Kempster. John also brought along his trusty Korg M1 synth for use on a few songs. He mostly used it at home for writing.

Cymbals were primarily Sabian with a Paiste 2002 China. John's signature piece of gear, seen on his kit no matter where in the world they played, was that trusty twelve-inch Ludwig tom, dating back to the kit gifted to him by his father in 1974.

Tom had an interesting setup, running two rigs side by side. One was close to Andy's, with a Fender Bassman head running into a matching Fender 4x12 cab. Alongside it was a Marshall JCM900 SL-X head going into a Marshall 4x12 cab.

Tom's Marshall and Fender rigs

This gave Tom's sound a bit more oomph and crunch when both rigs were mixed together. For guitars, Tom chopped and changed quite regularly. He was most often seen with a black Gibson Les Paul Standard, a cherry red Gibson SG Standard, and a slightly rarer "TV Yellow" double-cutaway Gordon Smith GS-2.

All of these showed significant signs of use, with body gouges from heavy pick usage. They were missing plenty of original accoutrements like knobs and OEM pickups. Sections of the finish had been worn away.

One piece of equipment shared by both Andy and Tom was a standalone echo unit for use on songs like "I Need You" and "Self Pity." Andy used a Roland DC-30 to create the wildly self-oscillating sound that stands out in "Self Pity," whereas Tom used a Boss DM-100 Delay Machine for the same function. Naturally, it was missing several knobs. Effects weren't that big a part of the NoMeansNo sound.

The band weren't gearheads, and the condition of their equipment showed little signs of care or TLC. They bore plenty of scars from being used in a punk band famed for their energetic live shows. Their eclectic mix of amps, cabs, and guitars produced an unprecedented wall of noise and gave them a sound that very few could ever come close to. Their equipment, like the band themselves, defied convention and proved that wrong could very much be right.

**Andy Sandall**
Former President, Morris Museum of Musical Instruments and Automata

# THANKS AND ACKNOWLEDGMENTS

## "Are any of my friends here? I can't see. What about you? Could you be a friend to me?"

It's been said before, and it's cliché, but I'll repeat it. It takes a village. A book like this is only as good as the enthusiastic participation of many. There were many, many people who contributed to what this book eventually became.

First and foremost, I want to thank the four members of NoMeansNo: Rob Wright, John Wright, Andy Kerr, and Tom Holliston. I was blown away when all of you said yes to this, and the fact that I now consider you my friends is like an insane dream.

That brings me to this next guy. Scott Henderson was someone who I confided in with my idea about this book early on. He contacted the band members on my behalf and told them if they were ever gonna allow something like this to happen, then *I* was their guy. It set everything in motion for me. Thanks from the bottom of my beating heart, Scott!

I am eternally indebted and thankful to Paul Prescott, who went from a casual chatter on Facebook to a transcriptionist and then to my #1 amigo. He helped edit this book down to its penultimate form. We spent hundreds of hours together on this, and he did so much work for me with it all. He also became therapist, sounding board, and friend. Paul, you were invaluable and really fun to get to know. Keep the monkeys warm: I'm coming to visit!

A big thanks to Melanie Kaye for being in my corner all these years, and for being the first person to connect me with the band.

I'd like to thank the entire team at PM Press for their incredibly hard work and dedication to this project, especially Ramsey, Steven, Brian, Dan, Wade, David, and Mr. John Yates. I knew from day one that I was in excellent hands.

A massive thanks to everyone who took the time to participate in interviews—the list is in the back of this book. Several went above and beyond for me early on as well. Thanks to Larry Boothroyd, Bill Johnston, Shelley Wright, Ford Pier, William Goldsmith (thanks for that call), Colin Macrae, Matt Skiba, Tom Antona, and Ken Kempster.

My humble thanks to Fred Armisen for writing the foreword and to the inimitable W. Buzz Ryan for dictating the backword.

There was a small army of NoMeansNo fans and friends who took on the task of helping transcribe interviews (and there were a lot!). Big thanks to Paul Prescott, Simon Coopey, Dave Watson, James Mangin, Esther Wurley, Donna Morgan, Ian Roberts, Ian Albertson, Ricky Jak Long, Dorian Kahle, Andre McGillvray, Julie Moore, Sylvia Kenny, Sue Castle, Jeff Hopkins, Alex Araujo, bobEE Sweet, David Briere, Angille Hz, Eden DaSilva, Jacqulin McNicol, Hugo Higgins, Rick Cook, Lisa Cook, Vanessa Violini, Jean Skilling, Kevin Gaudet, Ty Stranglehold, Cary Jackson, Michelle Strangey, Shawn Cox, Christine Albrecht, Angille Heintzman, David Briere, Melissa Erletz, Louise Carlow, João Morais Ribeiro, Matt Morris, Tyler Hrabok, Rian Kelly, Paulina Ortlieb, Yvonne Perrett, Matthew Butler, Pol Plastino, Tom Kelly, Jared Amos, and anyone I may have foolishly missed. It was tedious work but so vital—many thanks!

Thank you to the dozens of photographers and poster artists who allowed me to reproduce their art in here. And thanks to the collectors who gave me access to their archives. There are far too many to name, but especially John, Andy, Tom, Ricky Long, Holger Summer, Kev Smith, Adam Slack, Blair Calibaba, John Chedsey, Brad Bengston, Tyler

Hodgins, Piotr Skotnicki, Ičo Fugazi, Paweł Homiński, Hugo Higgins, Paulina Ortlieb, Pawel Zawislak, Rob Frith, Kareem Kaddah, Gary Brainless, Herve Lethielleux, Bob Mitchell, Fred Garrone, Wojtek Kozielski, and Jose Gurdulu.

Huge thanks to Sophia Swengel, Sam Shoichet, Ty Stranglehold, John Carlow, and Ian Albertson, for your extra help with collages, the Victoria map, gig info, photography, and discography info, respectively.

Thanks to Andy Sandall for the excellent essay about NoMeansNo's gear. It saved me some embarrassment, as I don't know a bass cab from a taxi cab.

Special thanks to Daniel Bastian for early layout help when I truly didn't know what the fuck I was doing. Oops!

Thanks to Paulina Ortlieb for her help and her fantastic documentary *Somewhere to Go: Punk Victoria*.

Thanks to Aaron Chapman, the first real author who gave me advice on this new world I was setting foot in. He was not the last. Thanks to Martin Popoff (chop files!), Derek Emerson, Brian Cogan, George Hurchalla, James Burns, Jason Flower, Ricky Long, John Robb, and David Ensminger.

Thank you to the Zone @ 91-3 in Victoria for employing me (I definitely didn't use company time for this!), and special shout-out to my radio cohost, Dylan Willows, for hearing me rattle on about this project for three-plus years.

Hats off to my fellow NoMeansNo fans and friends here in Victoria for their warm hearts and cold beer. Cheers to Rian Kelly, Scott Duncan, Scott Dunlop, and many others. Thanks to Jordon, Matthew, and Michelle for their endless passion about NMN and for their excellent podcast *NoMeansNo Thing*. You're a great complement to this book—unpacking the meanings of it all with hilarity and insight.

Gratitude to Louise Major for enduring both the book project and me, neither of which could have been easy. Finally, thank you to my son, Martin. You are an inspiration to me. I need you to know that dreams really can and do come true. Luck = hard work + passion + opportunity. Plus a little bit of luck. This book is dedicated to you. Love you, buddy.

# RECOMMENDED READING

## "Stay Home—Read a Book."

Below is a list of titles that helped with the research for this book, and some that I just think are pretty cool and worth checking out.


Azerred, Michael. *Our Band Could Be Your Life: Scenes from the American Indie Underground, 1981–1991*. Boston: Little, Brown, 2002.

Barclay, Michael, Ian A.D. Jack, and Jason Schneider. *Have Not Been the Same: The CanRock Renaissance, 1985–1995*. Toronto: ECW Press, 2011.

Black, Mark. *NoMeansNo: Going Nowhere*. Halifax, NS: Invisible Publishing, 2012.

Boulware, Jack, and Silke Tudor. *Gimme Something Better: The Profound, Progressive, and Occasionally Pointless History of Bay Area Punk, from Dead Kennedys to Green Day*. New York: Penguin, 2009.

Burns, James. *Let's Go to Hell: Scattered Memories of the Butthole Surfers*. N.p.: Cheap Drugs, 2015.

Chapman, Aaron. *Live at the Commodore: The Story of Vancouver's Historic Commodore Ballroom*. Vancouver: Arsenal Pulp Press, 2014.

Cogan, Brian. *The Encyclopedia of Punk*. New York: Sterling, 2010.

Flower, Jason, and Ricky Long. *All Your Ears Can Hear: Underground Music in Victoria, BC, 1978–1984*. Victoria, BC: AYECH International, 2007.

Fontana, Kaitlin. *Fresh at Twenty: The Oral History of Mint Records, 1991–2011*. Toronto: ECW Press, 2011.

Humphrey, Clark. *Loser: The Real Seattle Music Story*. Seattle: MiscMedia, 1999.

Hurchalla, George. *Going Underground: American Punk 1979–1989*. 2nd ed. Oakland: PM Press, 2016.

Keithley, Joey. *I, Shithead: A Life in Punk*. Vancouver: Arsenal Pulp Press, 2003.

Lawrence, Grant. *Dirty Windshields: The Best and the Worst of the Smugglers Tour Diaries*. Madeira Park, BC: Douglas & McIntyre, 2017.

McGuirk, Niall, and Michael Murphy. *Great Gig Memories: From Punks and Friends*. Dublin: Hope Publications, 2020.

Reynolds, Simon. *Rip It Up and Start Again: Post Punk 1978–1984*. New York: Penguin, 2006.

Robb, John. *Punk Rock: An Oral History*. 2nd ed. Oakland: PM Press, 2012.

Sutherland, Sam. *Perfect Youth: The Birth of Canadian Punk*. Toronto: ECW Press, 2013.

szim, Eric Isaacson, and Erin Yanke. *Dead Moon: Off the Grid*. Mainz, Germany: Ventil Verlag, 2022.

Walsby, Brian. *Self Empunishment*. Claremont, CA: Pelekinesis, 2020.

Walter, Chris. *Argh Fuck Kill: The Story of the Dayglo Abortions*. Vancouver: Gofuckyerself Press, 2010.

# CAST OF CHARACTERS

## "I can't stop talking."

All interviews were conducted by the author, Jason Lamb. Dated interviews were conducted on the phone or in person. Thank you to everyone for taking part, and apologies for any I may have missed.

**Jerry A.** Poison Idea (interviewed via social media)
**Jon Active** Alternative Tentacles UK (interviewed May 16, 2020)
**Murray "The Cretin" Acton** Dayglo Abortions (interviewed May 11, 2020)
**Rick Andrews** *Random Thought* magazine (interviewed September 11, 2020)
**Sue Angle** friend (interviewed August 12, 2021)
**Tom Antona** Alice Donut (interviewed March 29, 2020)
**Ric Arboit** Nettwerk Records (interviewed May 19, 2020)
**Fred Armisen** Trenchmouth, comedian, actor (interviewed April 14, 2021, and June 2, 2022)
**Owen Atkins** Seaweed (interviewed November 12, 2020)
**Milo Aukerman** Descendents (interviewed May 25, 2020)
**Steve Bailey** NEOs, Show Business Giants (interviewed August 8, 2020)
**Steve Bays** Hot Hot Heat (interviewed August 5, 2020)
**Marc Belke** SNFU (interviewed April 5, 2020)
**Lesley Bell** fan from London, Ontario (interviewed via email)
**Art Bergmann** musician, Poisoned, Young Canadians (interviewed May 18, 2020)
**Kyle Bernstein** fan from New York, New York (interviewed via email)
**Jello Biafra** Dead Kennedys, Alternative Tentacles (interviewed November 30, 2020)
**Craig Billmeier** fan from San Francisco, California (interviewed via email)
**Hilary Binder** Sabot (interviewed September 21, 2020)
**Becky Black** the Pack AD (interviewed April 3, 2020)
**Zach Blair** Rise Against, Hagfish, Drakulas (interviewed July 6, 2020)
**Mark Blaseckie** friend (interviewed April 25, 2020)
**Josh Blisters** Cute Lepers, the Spits (interviewed March 14, 2021)
**Jurgen Boel** fan from Belgium (interviewed via email)
**Larry Boothroyd** Victims Family (interviewed March 29 and May 24, 2020)
**Katherina Bornefeld** the Ex (interviewed October 25, 2020)
**Matthias Bosenick** fan from Germany (interviewed via email)
**Craig Bougie** NoMeansNo sound tech (interviewed April 20 and August 8, 2020, and March 7, 2021)
**Patti Bougie** Wrong Records (interviewed June 27, 2020)
**Paul Bougie** brother of Craig Bougie (interviewed September 26, 2020)
**Gary Brainless** owner of the Rats Nest, Hanson Brothers (interviewed July 26, 2020)
**Mike Branum** the Freak Accident, Hanson Brothers (interviewed June 29, 2020)
**Doug Burgess** friend (interviewed April 24, 2020)
**"Fat" Mike Burkett** NOFX, Fat Wreck Chords (interviewed March 30, 2022)
**Blair Calibaba** engineer, sound tech (interviewed September 26, 2020)
**Matt Cameron** Skin Yard, Soundgarden, Pearl Jam (interviewed May 22, 2020)
**Bow Campbell** Front End Loader (interviewed via email)
**Pete Campbell** Pink Steel (interviewed May 2, 2020)
**Brendan Canty** Rites of Spring, Fugazi (interviewed May 19, 2020)
**Jon Card** D.O.A. (interviewed July 9, 2020)
**Ray Carlisle** Teenage Bottlerocket (interviewed October 23, 2020)
**Robyn Carrigan** musician (interviewed June 14, 2021)
**Dory Carter** daughter of Emma Lee and Ray Carter (interviewed January 2, 2021)
**Jade Carter** son of Emma Lee and Ray Carter (interviewed October 12, 2020)
**Jeff Carter** Pink Steel (interviewed May 2, 2020)
**Michael Carter** friend (interviewed June 14, 2020)
**Ray Carter** Mass Appeal (interviewed June 13, 2020)
**Lucinda Catchlove** My Dog Popper (interviewed September 23, 2020)
**Uffe Cederlund** Entombed (interviewed December 19, 2020)
**Tim Chan** Ryvals, Hathead, 64 Funnycars (interviewed April 5, 2020)
**Aaron Chapman** Real McKenzies, author, photographer, tour merch (interviewed April 4, 2021)
**Marty Chatrin** Euthanasia (interviewed June 28, 2020)
**John Chedsey** nomeanswhatever.com, tour merch (interviewed May 6, 2020)
**Eric Chenaux** Phleg Camp (interviewed via email)
**Rob Clark** Removal (interviewed August 14, 2020)

**Lisa Cook** friend (interviewed July 18, 2020)
**Rick Cook** friend (interviewed July 18, 2020)
**Sean Cox** guitar tech for Foo Fighters and Tenacious D (interviewed September 24, 2020)
**Mark Critchley** Itch (interviewed May 2, 2020, and May 1, 2021)
**Tim Crow** Suburban Menace, Red Tide (interviewed April 18, 2020)
**Chris Crud** stage tech, tour manager (interviewed June 20 and September 27, 2020, and April 21, 2021)
**David DaSilva** fan from Edmonton, Alberta (interviewed via email)
**Gijs de Wit** tour manager (interviewed April 25 and June 24, 2020)
**Giovanna Di Francesco** Wrong Records (interviewed June 30, 2020)
**Chuck Dukowski** Black Flag, SWA (interviewed March 30, 2020)
**Sam Dunn** founder of Banger Films (interviewed April 2, 2020)
**Dave Edwardson** Neurosis (interviewed November 2, 2020)
**Brian "Who" Else** engineer (interviewed June 20, 2020)
**Craig Else** Twisted Minds (interviewed July 25, 2020)
**Jack Endino** Skin Yard, producer (interviewed May 29, 2020)
**Cecil English** Profile Studios (interviewed June 19, 2020)
**Thedor Erkamps** friend (interviewed August 10, 2020)
**Nick Evans** promoter (interviewed July 11, 2020)
**Sean Forbes** Rough Trade (interviewed May 10, 2020)
**Paul Forgues** sound tech, engineer (interviewed July 11, 2020)
**Dave Genn** 54-40, Matthew Good Band (interviewed October 17, 2020)
**William Goldsmith** Sunny Day Real Estate, Foo Fighters (interviewed April 24, 2021)
**Tommy Goober** Toy Dolls, Goober Patrol (interviewed September 14, 2021)
**Debbie Gordon** Alternative Tentacles (interviewed May 13, 2020)
**Billy Gould** Faith No More (interviewed March 29, 2020)
**Greg Graham** House of Commons (interviewed July 15, 2020)
**Joseph Gray** fan from Poulsbo, Washington (interviewed via email)
**Mats Gustafsson** the Thing, Fire! (interviewed via email)
**Trevor "Spud" Hagen** Dayglo Abortions (interviewed May 5, 2020)
**Ross Hales** Animal Slaves (interviewed August 8, 2020)
**Ernie Hawkins** Removal, Hanson Brothers (interviewed August 22, 2020)
**Anthony Hempell** fan from Vancouver, British Columbia (interviewed via email)
**Scott Henderson** Shovlhed, Show Business Giants, Swell Prod., Hissanol, producer, engineer (interviewed June 27, 2020, and October 12, 2021)
**Dolf Hermannstädter** *Trust* magazine (interviewed April 25, 2020)
**Rob Higgins** Dearly Beloved (interviewed April 1, 2020)
**Tadayuki Hirano** Ultra Bidé (interviewed via email)
**Mike Hodsall** D.O.A. (interviewed June 28, 2020)
**Lee Hobson Hollis** Spermbirds, 2Bad, Steakknife (interviewed December 23, 2020)
**Robert Holliston** brother of Tom Holliston (interviewed May 18, 2020)
**Tom Holliston** Show Business Giants, Hanson Brothers, NoMeansNo (interviewed July 21 and September 19, 2020, and June 19, August 22, and December 2, 2021)
**Daniel House** Skin Yard (interviewed June 15, 2020)
**Patrick "Hutch" Hutchinson** D.O.A. sound tech (interviewed August 8, 2020)
**Robynn Iwata** cub (interviewed via email)
**Murray Jackson** Infamous Scientists (interviewed via email)
**Karl Johanson** friend (interviewed June 20, 2020)
**Bill Johnston** Removal (interviewed April 13, 2020)
**Danko Jones** front man of the band Danko Jones (interviewed via email)
**Mario Kasapi** NEOs (interviewed May 16, 2020)
**John Kastner** Asexuals, Doughboys (interviewed October 7, 2020)
**Melanie Kaye** publicist (interviewed May 14 and August 24, 2020, and March 1, 2021)
**Joe Keithley** D.O.A. (interviewed October 15, 2020)
**Joe Keller** Night Birds (interviewed March 30, 2020)
**Ken Kempster** Shovlhed, Show Business Giants, Swell Prod., NoMeansNo, Hanson Brothers (interviewed April 5, 2020)

**Sylvia Kenny** friend, Fracas (interviewed July 11, 2020)
**Andy Kerr** Infamous Scientists, NoMeansNo, Hanson Brothers (interviewed April 22, July 1, and October 4, 2020, and April 11, May 16, August 8, and October 24, 2021)
**Doug Kerr** brother of Andy Kerr (interviewed via email)
**Ingrid Kerr** Konkurrent (interviewed May 17, 2020)
**Luc Klaasen** the Ex, Konkurrent (interviewed via email)
**Steve Kravac** My Dog Popper (interviewed via email)
**Domas Kunčinas** fan from Lithuania (interviewed via email)
**Michel "Away" Langevin** Voivod (interviewed October 24, 2020)
**Dave Lawrence** *FUBAR* writer and actor (interviewed April 12, 2021)
**Grant Lawrence** the Smugglers (interviewed October 24, 2020)
**Emma Lee** friend (interviewed May 14, 2020)
**Kev Lee** Infamous Scientists (interviewed July 12, 2020)
**Marc L'Esperance** producer, engineer (interviewed June 25, 2020)
**Brian Lilla** fan from Oakland, California (interviewed via email)
**Nancy Lipsett (formerly Castle)** Castle (interviewed June 10, 2020)
**Eric Lowe** Ryvals, Automatic Shock (interviewed September 12, 2020)
**Dan Lucey** PufferFish Lampshade (interviewed August 16, 2021)
**David Macanulty** Roots Roundup, Royal Grand Prix (interviewed December 16, 2020)
**Ian MacKaye** Minor Threat, Fugazi (interviewed April 24, 2020)
**Artur Mackowiak** Potty Umbrella, Something Like Elvis (interviewed via email)
**James MacLean** October Crisis (interviewed October 3, 2020)
**Colin Macrae** Pigment Vehicle (interviewed April 18 and October 14, 2020)
**Rick Mahalek** fan from Campbell River, British Columbia (interviewed via email)
**Matthew Mallon** *Random Thought* magazine (interviewed September 26, 2020)
**Arek Marczyński** promoter (interviewed via social media)
**Carolyn Mark** musician, Show Business Giants (interviewed April 4, 2020)
**Steve McBean** Jerk Ward, Black Mountain (interviewed April 6, 2020)
**Andre McGillvray** fan from Tofino, British Columbia (interviewed via email)
**Paul "Gigs" McGivern** promoter, author, tour merch (interviewed August 15, 2020)
**Niall McGuirk** promoter (interviewed July 25, 2020)
**Marlise McKee** friend (interviewed May 24, 2020)
**Michael McKeegan** Therapy? (interviewed via email)
**Brian McKenna** promoter (interviewed May 16, 2020)
**Jacqueline McLaughlin** musician, artist (interviewed April 18, 2020)

**Tolan McNeil** Mission of Christ, Gus (interviewed August 22, 2020)
**Nate Mendel** Foo Fighters, Sunny Day Real Estate (interviewed via email)
**Laurie Mercer** NoMeansNo manager (interviewed August 2, 2020, and February 28, 2021)
**Brad Merritt** 54-40 (interviewed October 17, 2020)
**Tim Miedecke** fan from Melbourne, Australia (interviewed via email)
**China Miéville** author (interviewed November 14, 2020)
**Maya Miller** the Pack AD (interviewed April 5, 2020)
**Roger Miller** Mission of Burma (interviewed December 16, 2020)
**Tara Miller** artist (interviewed April 21, 2020)
**Andrew Molloy** Bed Spins, BUM (interviewed August 12, 2020)
**Attila Molnar** fan from Budapest, Hungary (interviewed via email)
**Scott Monteith** Deadbeat (interviewed via email)
**Angelo Moore** Fishbone (interviewed November 9, 2020)
**Mike Morasky** Steel Pole Bathtub (interviewed May 16, 2021)
**Matt Morris** Plaid Retina (interviewed July 29, 2020)
**Stephen Moses** Alice Donut (interviewed May 3, 2020)
**Bob "Bob 1" Mothersbaugh** Devo (interviewed March 31, 2021)
**Chris Murphy** Sloan (interviewed June 20, 2020)
**Brad Murray** fan from Florida (interviewed via email)
**Nardwuar the Human Serviette** interviewer, the Evaporators (interviewed April 29, 2020)
**Rob Nesbitt** Section 46, BUM (interviewed December 12, 2020)
**Blaine Newberg** fan from Minneapolis, Minnesota (interviewed via email)
**Robert Nichols** Shrug (interviewed via email)
**Stefan "Scream" Niemann** friend, photographer (interviewed November 25, 2020)
**Craig Northey** Odds (interviewed via email)
**Betty Norton** artist, photographer (interviewed May 9, 2020)
**Rich Oddie** Orphx (interviewed via email)
**John Ondrasek** October Crisis (interviewed October 3, 2020)

**Kamala Parks** 924 Gilman Street, *Maximum Rocknroll* (interviewed March 14, 2021)
**Casey Pechet** engineer (interviewed June 6, 2021)
**D.H. Peligro** Dead Kennedys (interviewed August 2, 2020)
**Mauro Pezzente** Godspeed You! Black Emperor (interviewed December 28, 2020)
**Adam Pfahler** Jawbreaker (interviewed via email)
**Ford Pier** Roots Roundup, D.O.A., Show Business Giants (interviewed April 15 and September 10, 2020)
**Dolf Planteijdt** producer (interviewed via email)
**Bruce Ployart** promoter (interviewed October 4, 2020)
**Wilf Plum** Dog Faced Hermans, Two Pin Din (interviewed via email)
**Kieran Plunkett** Restarts (interviewed January 2, 2021)
**Marcus Pollard** Show Business Giants, promoter (interviewed October 14, 2020)
**Su Pomeroy** friend (interviewed August 30, 2021)
**Eric Popper** My Dog Popper (interviewed June 27, 2020)
**Joe Principe** Rise Against (interviewed via social media)
**Johnny Puke** promoter (interviewed October 22, 2021)
**Massimo Pupillo** Zu (interviewed via email)
**Chris Rankin** Sabot (interviewed September 21, 2020)
**Duncan Redmonds** Snuff (interviewed August 31, 2020)
**Jennye Rieper** Abbie Hoffman Society, Show Business Giants (interviewed August 22, 2021)
**Deborah Ritchie (née Mitchell)** friend (interviewed May 23, 2020)
**John Robb** the Membranes, *Louder than War* magazine (interviewed October 30, 2020)
**Ryan Rodier** fan from Saskatoon, Saskatchewan (interviewed via social media)
**Keith Rose** Roots Roundup, Royal Grand Prix, Show Business Giants, tour manager (interviewed April 19, 2020)
**Jord Samolesky** Propagandhi (interviewed April 2, 2020)
**Bill Sample** teacher (interviewed December 6, 2020)
**Steve Sandve** friend, promoter (interviewed April 16, 2020)
**John Sawyer** Terminal Heads (interviewed via email)
**Will Schatz** sound tech (interviewed May 2, 2020)
**Sissi Schulmeister** Alice Donut (interviewed September 21, 2020)
**Jay Scott** Cattle Prod Productions, Wrong Records (interviewed June 26, 2020)
**Igor Seke** fan from Serbia (interviewed via email)
**Ingrid Severson** tour merch, Wrong Records (interviewed April 18, 2020)
**Sam Shackleton** producer, musician (interviewed via email)
**Derek Sheplawy** friend (interviewed June 29, 2020)
**Matt Skiba** Alkaline Trio, Blink-182 (interviewed September 17, 2020)
**Adam Slack** Invasives (interviewed April 17, 2021)
**Byron Slack** Invasives, Hanson Brothers (interviewed April 5, 2020, and April 17, 2021)
**Colin C. Smith** Penn State Department of Philosophy (interviewed via email)
**George Smith** Dangermouse (interviewed September 26, 2021)
**Kev Smith** NEOs, Mission of Christ (interviewed via email)
**Mark Smith** Cattle Prod Productions (interviewed June 27, 2020)
**Winston Smith** artist (interviewed via email)
**G.W. Sok** the Ex, Konkurrent (interviewed via email)
**Tim Solyan** Victims Family (interviewed March 28 and September 27, 2020)
**Petr Somol** fan from the Czech Republic (interviewed via email)
**Paul Spence** *FUBAR* writer and actor (interviewed via email)
**Ralph Spight** Victims Family (interviewed May 24, 2020)
**Trey Spruance** Mr. Bungle (interviewed August 9, 2020)
**Jay Staples** fan from Edmonton, Alberta (interviewed via email)
**Bruno St. Martin** friend (interviewed May 16, 2020)
**Randy Strobl** friend (interviewed May 1, 2020)
**"Rancid" Randy Stubbs** artist (interviewed October 26, 2020)
**Darcy Studebaker** fan from Oklahoma City, Oklahoma (interviewed via email)
**Milos Svircev** fan from Serbia (interviewed via email)
**Johnny Temple** Soulside, Girls Against Boys (interviewed November 28, 2020)
**Kim Thayil** Soundgarden (interviewed May 15, 2020)
**Jim Tillman** U-Men (interviewed September 11, 2020)
**Paul Timoney** promoter (interviewed May 9, 2020)
**Devin Townsend** musician, producer (interviewed April 9, 2021)
**Isaac Tremblay** Le Trou du Diable Brewery (interviewed June 9, 2020)
**Frank Turner** musician (interviewed via email)
**Jeremy Turner** friend (interviewed May 30, 2020)
**Ben Valle** Viagra Boys, Isotope Soap (interviewed December 13, 2020)
**John van Luyn** promoter (interviewed April 23, 2021)
**Frank van Schaik** fan from the Netherlands (interviewed via email)
**Tero Viikari** promoter (interviewed September 26, 2020)
**Craig Vishek** Pigment Vehicle, Show Business Giants (interviewed March 15, 2021)
**Gina Volpe** Lunachicks (interviewed via email)
**Jeff Walker** Collectors RPM record store (interviewed August 3, 2020)
**Mike Walker** the Resistance (interviewed September 28, 2020)
**Barry "Dalive" Ward** Rich Kids on LSD (interviewed via social media)
**Jacob Warneke** fan from Berlin, Germany (interviewed via email)
**Mike Watt** Minutemen, fIREHOSE (interviewed May 8, 2020)
**Daniel Webster** Psyche Industry Records (interviewed April 4, 2020)
**Simon Wells** Snuff (interviewed May 30, 2020)
**Greg Werckman** Alternative Tentacles, Ipecac Recordings (interviewed May 9, 2020)
**Brian "Jesus Bonehead" Whitehead** Dayglo Abortions (interviewed October 26, 2020)

**Bob Wiseman** Blue Rodeo, musician (interviewed March 7, 2021)
**John Wright** NoMeansNo, Hanson Brothers (interviewed July 21, September 7, and October 10, 2020, and June 19, August 28, and December 2, 2021)
**Rob Wright** NoMeansNo, Hanson Brothers (interviewed July 22, September 14, and December 7, 2020, and March 12, June 20, September 11, and September 27, 2021)
**Shelley Wright** sister of Rob and John Wright (interviewed April 17, 2020)
**John Yates** designer (interviewed April 13, 2020)
**Hetty Zwart** Konkurrent (interviewed October 3, 2020)

## ADDITIONAL INTERVIEWS

**Toren Atkinson** (interviewed September 9, 2021)
**Daniel Bastian** (interviewed November 16, 2020)
**Jacopo Battaglia** (interviewed via email)
**Aaron Beam** (interviewed via email)
**Brent Belke** (interviewed April 4, 2020)
**Ferdy Belland** (interviewed August 17, 2020)
**Brad Bengston** (interviewed May 5, 2020)
**Mark Black** (interviewed May 14, 2020)
**Jason Bonneau** (interviewed June 28, 2020)
**Abe Brennan** (interviewed April 18, 2020)
**Andy Cairns** (interviewed via email)
**Bertrand Castagnet** (interviewed via email)
**David Clark** (interviewed October 5, 2020)
**Claude Coleman** (interviewed via email)
**Alan Cross** (interviewed April 24, 2020)
**Bob Cutler** (interviewed via social media)
**Alan Dickey** (interviewed September 30, 2020)
**Dave Dictor** (interviewed via social media)
**Doug Donut** (interviewed via social media)
**Paddy Duddy** (interviewed May 10, 2020)
**Dave Fortune** (interviewed August 10, 2020)
**Tom Gaffey** (interviewed via email)
**Fred Garrone** (interviewed via email)
**Gerry Hannah** (interviewed via social media)
**Tim Hoey** (interviewed November 28, 2020)
**Steve Ignorant** (interviewed December 12, 2020)
**Chris Jackson** (interviewed March 25, 2021)
**Michael Jung** (interviewed May 3, 2020)
**Brendan Kelly** (interviewed October 23, 2020)
**Steve Kicks** (interviewed March 14, 2021)
**Kim Kinakin** (interviewed via email)
**Todd Kowalski** (interviewed March 29, 2020)
**Joe Lally** (interviewed via email)
**Peter Litwin** (interviewed June 28, 2020)
**Ricky Long** (interviewed April 19, 2020)
**Andy MacVannan** (interviewed April 1, 2021)
**Lisa Marr** (interviewed via email)
**Jimmy May** (interviewed via email)
**Grant McDonagh** (interviewed June 20, 2020)
**Rachel Montpetit** (interviewed via email)
**Keith Morris** (interviewed via social media)
**Hakim Rashad Muhammad** (interviewed via social media)
**Bif Naked** (interviewed August 22, 2020)
**Brian Nothing** (interviewed May 30, 2020)
**Fred Nus** (interviewed via email)
**Paulina Ortlieb** (interviewed August 8, 2020)
**Andy Pearson** (interviewed via email)
**Justin Pearson** (interviewed via email)
**Tom Pitts** (interviewed October 10, 2020)
**Martin Popoff** (interviewed December 16, 2020)
**Josh Ray** (interviewed September 20, 2020)
**Josh Robins** (interviewed April 25, 2020)
**Andy Sandall** (interviewed September 20, 2020)
**Larry Schemel** (interviewed May 22, 2021)
**Mia Simmans** (interviewed October 13, 2020)
**Chris Slorach** (interviewed July 16, 2020)
**Aaron Stauffer** (interviewed November 5, 2020, and via email)
**Michelle Strangey** (interviewed May 16, 2020)
**TANX** (interviewed via email)
**Carmela Thompson** (interviewed October 10, 2020)
**Mike Throneberry** (interviewed via email)
**Dale Tomlinson** (interviewed May 23, 2020)
**Pete Tower** (interviewed via email)
**12 Midnite** (interviewed via email)
**Cactus Vella** (interviewed via email)
**Rey Washam** (interviewed October 25, 2020)
**Rob Wrong** (interviewed May 22, 2021)
**Chet Zar** (interviewed July 25, 2020)
**Pawel Zawislak** (interviewed via email)

# IMAGE CREDITS

We have done our best to identify photographers and folks who supplied posters, but we didn't always have (or remember) complete information and may have missed a few. If you are a photographer, poster artist, or contributor who was not credited, please contact PM Press and we will add your name in future printings. Thanks again to everyone for their contributions.

Page vii: courtesy of David Deggeller
Page 1: photographer unknown, courtesy of John Wright
Page 2: (left) Betty Wright, courtesy of Shelley Wright; (right) Emma Lee
Page 3: photographer unknown, courtesy of Thedor Erkamps
Page 4: art by John Wright, courtesy of Karl Johansen
Page 5: (left) photographer unknown, courtesy of Julie Moore; (right) photographer unknown
Page 6: (bottom left) photographer unknown, courtesy of John Wright; (top right) Jason Lamb
Page 7: (top left) photographer unknown, courtesy of Patty Castle; (bottom right) courtesy of Patty Castle
Page 8: (top left) courtesy of Glenn Parfit
Page 12: Emma Lee
Page 14: Bill Blair
Page 15: art by Sam Shoichet
Page 16: (top left & right) Russ Beinder; (bottom right) Steve Sandve
Page 17: Rana Long
Page 18: (top left & right) Russ Beinder
Page 19: (top left, top right, & center right) Julie Moore; (bottom left) Gregor Schmidt
Page 20: (top left) Jason Lamb
Page 21: (top left) Marcus Pollard; (bottom left) Steve Sandve
Page 22: photographer unknown, courtesy of Steve Sandve
Page 23: (left, top right, & bottom right) photographers unknown, courtesy of Andy Kerr
Page 25: (left & right) Steve Bailey
Page 26: (top left) Steve Bailey; (top right) Jason Lamb
Page 27: (top left) photographer unknown, courtesy of Paulina Ortlieb; (center left) courtesy of Murray Jackson; (bottom right) courtesy of Andy Kerr
Page 28: (top) art by Andy Kerr; (bottom) Andy Kerr
Page 29: (top left & bottom right) Steve Sandve; (top right) Emma Lee
Page 30: courtesy of Ricky Long
Page 31: Emma Lee
Page 32: Steve Bailey
Page 33: (left & right) Emma Lee
Page 34: art by John Wright
Page 35: (center & right) courtesy of Andy Kerr
Page 36: (top right) photographer unknown, courtesy of Scott Bennett; (bottom left) art by John Wright; (bottom center) photographer unknown, courtesy of John Wright
Page 37: (left & right) Emma Lee
Page 38: (left) Emma Lee; (right) photographer unknown, courtesy of John Wright
Page 39: (top) courtesy of Andy Kerr; (bottom) courtesy of Ricky Long
Page 40: Gregor Schmidt, courtesy of Tara Miller
Page 41: (top left, top right, & center right) Steve Bailey; (bottom left) Steve Sandve
Page 43: (top left & right) Russ Beinder; (bottom left & right) courtesy of Ricky Long
Page 44: (left) courtesy of Ric Arboit; (right) Steve Sandve
Page 46: Emma Lee
Page 47: (left & right) Stefan Niemann
Page 48: (left) Stefan Niemann; (top right) Emma Lee; (center right) photograph by Emma Lee, courtesy of John Wright
Page 49: Stefan Niemann
Page 50: (left & right) courtesy of Andy Kerr
Page 51: (bottom left) Steve Bailey; (top right) Jason Lamb
Page 52: (top left & right) Andrew Tolson; (bottom left) photographer unknown, courtesy of John Wright
Page 53: Alison Leslie
Page 54: (letter) courtesy of Laurie Mercer
Page 55: (top) art by Jesse Rivard; (bottom left) Ingrid Severson; (bottom right) courtesy of Andy Kerr
Page 56: (top) courtesy of Laurie Mercer; (center) courtesy of Ross Herman; (bottom center & bottom right) art by John Wright, courtesy of John Wright
Page 57: (top) courtesy of Murray Acton; (bottom) courtesy of Kem Kempster

Page 58: (top left) Emma Lee; (bottom right) Ric Arboit
Page 59: courtesy of Ross Herman
Page 60: (left) Joel Robinson; (right) Bev Davies
Page 61: photographer unknown, courtesy of John Wright
Page 62: (letter) courtesy of Laurie Mercer
Page 63: Derek Sheplawy
Page 64: (top right) Andy Kerr
Page 65: Tracy Marander
Page 66: Mischa Veenema
Page 67: courtesy of Ricky Long
Page 68: (top left) photographer unknown, courtesy of John Wright; (bottom) courtesy of Tim Chan
Page 69: courtesy of Richard Hanes
Page 70: photographer unknown, courtesy of John Wright
Page 71: Kai Korinth
Page 72: (left) Eddie Malluk/AtlasIcons.com; (top right & center right) courtesy of Jason Lamb
Page 73: (top left) Mischa Veenema; (bottom right) photographer unknown, courtesy of Laurie Mercer
Page 74: (top left) Mischa Veenema; (bottom left) art by Adam Swinbourne; (bottom center) courtesy of Jason Lamb; (bottom right) art by Niall McCormack
Page 75: (left) Christian Kock; (right) John Carlow
Page 76: (top left) Marc Gaertner; (bottom left) art by Esther Nina
Page 77: (left) Blair Calibaba; (right) Tony Crosgrey
Page 78: courtesy of Brittney Salmond
Page 79: (top) Lisa Mitchell; (bottom) Betty Norton
Page 80: (top left) photograph by Betty Norton; (top & bottom right) Dan Walters
Page 81: (top left & bottom left) courtesy of Gary Brainless; (right) courtesy of Rick Andrews
Page 83: photographer unknown, art by Andy Kerr, courtesy of Andy Kerr
Page 84: Andy Kerr
Page 85: (left) Cory O'Brien; (right) photographer unknown, courtesy of John Wright
Page 86: (right) photographer unknown, courtesy of Andy Kerr
Page 87: (bottom) photographer unknown, courtesy of John Wright
Page 88: photographer unknown, courtesy of Andy Kerr
Page 90: (left) Jay Brown/jfotoman.com
Page 91: courtesy of Jimmy May
Page 92: (top left & right) Johnny Puke; (center) courtesy of Johnny Puke
Page 93: (top) courtesy of Chris Murphy
Page 94: Rory Mahony
Page 95: (top) Bob Garlick
Page 96: (left) courtesy of Blair Calibaba; (center & right) courtesy of Andy Kerr
Page 97: (top) John Mackie; (bottom) art by Andy Kerr
Page 99: (left & right) photographers unknown, courtesy of John Wright
Pages 102–3: collage by briandesign
Page 104: photographers unknown, courtesy of John Wright
Page 105: (top left) photographer unknown; (top right) courtesy of Kareem Kaddah; (bottom right) photographer unknown, courtesy of John Wright
Page 109: Patrick Hart
Page 110: Shane Kurenoff, courtesy of Andy Kerr
Page 111: photographer unknown, courtesy of Cecil English
Page 112: Patrick Hart
Page 113: courtesy of Andy Kerr
Page 115: courtesy of Andy Kerr
Page 116: photographer unknown, courtesy of Andy Kerr
Page 117: (top) courtesy of Carmelo Seminara; (bottom left) courtesy of Paweł Homiński
Page 118: Andrew Giles
Page 119: (top) Andrew Giles; (bottom) courtesy of Jimmy May
Page 120: (left) photographer unknown, courtesy of John Wright; (right) Murray Bowles
Page 122: Rebecca Kraatz, courtesy of Tom Holliston
Page 123: photographer unknown, courtesy of Tom Holliston
Page 124: (bottom) Ken Kempster
Page 125: (left) John Wright; (right) courtesy of Andy Kerr
Page 127: (top right) courtesy of Marcus Pollard; (bottom right) Rachel Montpetit
Page 128: Kai Korinth
Page 129: (top) Rachel Montpetit; (bottom) courtesy of Ken Kempster
Page 130: Rebecca Kraatz
Page 131: David Bruce
Page 132: (top) photographer unknown, courtesy of John Wright; (bottom) courtesy of Hugo Higgins
Page 133: photographer unknown, courtesy of John Wright
Page 134: (left) photographer unknown, courtesy of John Wright; (right) photographer unknown, courtesy of Andy Kerr
Page 135: photographer unknown, courtesy of Andy Kerr
Page 136: (top) photographer unknown, courtesy of Andy Kerr; (bottom) Hugo Higgins
Page 137: Gorazd Repse
Page 139: (top) courtesy of Kareem Kaddah
Page 140: (top left & top right) courtesy of David Bruce; (bottom) courtesy of Andy Kerr
Page 141: (top) photograph by David Bruce; (bottom) courtesy of Sylvia Kenny
Page 142: (top left) Patrick Hart; (top right) Katherina Bornefeld; (center right) Piers Allardyce; (bottom) courtesy of Andy Kerr
Page 143: (top left) Andrew Bannerman-Bayles/abayles@mac.com; (top & bottom right) Rob Ben
Page 144: (top) courtesy of John Tugby; (bottom) courtesy of Bill Johnston
Page 146: (top) photographer unknown, courtesy of John Wright; (bottom) photograph by Rebecca Kraatz
Page 147: (top right) photographer unknown, courtesy of Andy Kerr; (bottom right) Ingrid Severson
Page 148: (top left & right) Andrew Bannerman-Bayles/abayles@mac.com; (bottom) David Bruce

Page 149: Herman Nijhof
Page 150: (top) photographer unknown; (bottom) Rebecca Kraatz
Page 151: photographer unknown, courtesy of John Wright
Page 154: (left) Andrew Tolson
Page 155: courtesy of Jason Lamb
Page 156: Kai Korinth
Page 158: (top left) photographer unknown, courtesy of Mark Twistworthy; (top right & bottom left) Kai Korinth
Page 159: (bottom) art by Winston Smith
Page 161: David Bruce
Page 162: (left & right) photographers unknown, courtesy of John Wright
Page 163: (left) photographer unknown, courtesy of John Wright
Page 165: (top) Marlise McKee; (bottom) courtesy of Andy Kerr
Page 167: courtesy of Ian MacKaye
Page 168: (top & bottom) Katherina Bornefeld
Page 169: Katherina Bornefeld
Page 170: (top) Mark Twistworthy
Page 173: Rob Ben
Page 174: (top & bottom) Katherina Bornefeld
Page 175: photographer unknown, courtesy of Andy Kerr
Page 176: (left) Katherina Bornefeld; (right) courtesy of Andy Kerr
Page 177: (left & right) photographer unknown, courtesy of Andy Kerr
Page 178: (top) Emma Lee; (bottom) Katherina Bornefeld
Pages 180–81: collage by briandesign
Page 182: John Wright
Page 183: photographer unknown, courtesy of Sue Angle
Page 187: (left) Ken Kempster; (bottom right) Rachel Montpetit
Page 188: (bottom) courtesy of Ross Herman
Page 189: (bottom) photographer unknown, courtesy of John Wright
Page 191: photographer unknown, courtesy of John Wright
Page 193: (top) photographer unknown, courtesy of John Wright; (bottom) Kai Korinth
Page 194: (top left) Kai Korinth; (bottom right) courtesy of Kareem Kaddah
Page 195: (right) courtesy of Ross Herman
Page 196: (top) photographer unknown, courtesy of Robynn Iwata; (bottom) Marlise McKee
Page 197: (bottom) photographer unknown, courtesy of Tom Holliston
Page 199: (top left, bottom left, & bottom right) photographers unknown, courtesy of John Wright
Page 201: Ray Auffrey
Page 202: (top left) Russ Beinder; (bottom left) photographer unknown, courtesy of Ken Kempster; (bottom right) photographer unknown, courtesy of Laurie Mercer
Page 204: (top) photographer unknown, courtesy of Ken Kempster; (bottom) Ken Kempster
Page 205: (bottom) Ken Kempster
Page 206: (top) Tom Holliston; (bottom) photographer unknown, courtesy of Ken Kempster
Page 207: (left) photographer unknown, courtesy of John Wright; (right) photographer unknown, courtesy of Ken Kempster
Page 208: (left & right) photographers unknown, courtesy of Ken Kempster
Page 209: courtesy of Ken Kempster
Page 210: (top) Marlise McKee; (bottom) Ken Kempster
Page 211: Marlise McKee
Page 212: (top, outtakes) Rachel Montpetit; (center right) courtesy of Ken Kempster
Page 213: (top left) Aaron Chapman; (top & bottom right) Corey Hamilton
Page 214: courtesy of Ross Herman
Page 215: art by Jimbo Phillips
Page 216: (top & bottom) Ingrid Severson
Page 217: (top left) Ken Kempster; (bottom right) Ingrid Severson
Page 219: Aaron Chapman
Page 220: Eric Stone
Page 221: (top left) Corey Hamilton; (bottom center & right) courtesy of Mark Critchley
Page 222: (bottom left) Ken Kempster; (top right) Keith Rose
Page 223: (left) Ian Roberts
Page 224: (top left) photographer unknown, courtesy of Ken Kempster; (top right) Ken Kempster; (bottom left) Ken Kempster; (bottom right) photographer unknown, courtesy of Tom Holliston
Page 225: (left & right) photographers unknown, courtesy of Ken Kempster
Page 226: photographs by Aaron Chapman
Page 227: Ken Kempster
Page 229: (top right) photographer unknown, courtesy of John Wright; (bottom left) art by Todd Baricklow
Page 230: (top left) Ronny Kvalvaer; (center) courtesy of Hilary Binder
Page 231: courtesy of Gijs de Wit
Page 232: photographer unknown, courtesy of Tom Holliston
Page 233: (top left) Ernie Hawkins; (top & bottom right) Ičo Fugazi
Page 234: Ken Kempster
Page 235: Ken Kempster
Pages 236–37: collages by Sophia Swengel
Page 239: (top left) courtesy of Paweł Homiński; (bottom) Bill Johnston
Page 240: (top left) Bill Johnston; (bottom right) courtesy of Paweł Homiński
Page 242: (top left) photographer unknown, courtesy of Tom Holliston; (bottom right) photographer unknown, courtesy of John Wright
Page 243: (top left) photographer unknown, courtesy of Tom Holliston; (top right) courtesy of Paweł Homiński; (center right) art by Niall McCormack
Page 244: art by John Seabury
Page 245: photographer unknown, courtesy of John Wright
Page 246: Bill Johnston
Page 247: (top) John Chedsey; (bottom) Keith Rose

Page 248: Mike Branum
Page 249: (top) John Chedsey; (bottom) Bill Johnston
Page 250: (left) Darcy Studebaker; (right) Corey Hamilton
Page 251: (top left) photographer unknown, courtesy of John Wright; (top & bottom right) Bill Johnston
Page 254: Jason Lamb
Page 255: (top & bottom) Jasper de Jong
Page 256: Tom Antona
Page 257: (top) art by TANX
Page 258: Tom Holliston
Page 259: (left) Carmelo Seminara; (right) photographer unknown, courtesy of Mark Critchley
Page 260: (left) Mark Critchley; (right) art by Malleus
Page 261: Blair Calibaba
Page 262: John Chedsey
Page 263: John Chedsey
Page 264: John Chedsey
Page 265: (top left) courtesy of John Chedsey
Page 266: (left & right) John Chedsey
Page 267: (left) John Chedsey; (right, outtakes) John Chedsey
Page 268: John Chedsey
Page 269: (top left & center left) Blair Calibaba; (bottom right) Paul Clarke
Page 271: John Chedsey
Pages 272–73: collage by briandesign
Page 274: DK
Page 275: (top right) courtesy of Adam Slack; (bottom center) art by TANX
Page 276: Blair Calibaba
Page 277: (top right) Arny Zona; (bottom left) Adam Slack; (bottom right) courtesy of Adam Slack
Page 279: (top) art by Zoltron; (bottom) art by Paul Imagine, courtesy of Brian McKenna
Page 280: (left & right) Adam Slack
Page 281: (bottom) courtesy of Isaac Tremblay
Page 282: Marc Gaertner
Page 283: (left) Byron Slack; (right) John Chedsey
Page 284: art by Laurent Meunier
Page 285: (top) Marc Gaertner; (bottom) art by Niall McCormack
Page 286: (top) Blair Calibaba; (bottom) Adam Slack
Page 287: (top right) art by TANX; (bottom left) art by Graham Pilling; (bottom center) art by Alec James Joyce
Page 288: Mike Branum
Page 289: (top left) Christian Kock; (bottom left) Marc Gaertner; (top right) Laurent Meunier
Pages 290–91: collages by Sophia Swengel
Page 292: Mike Branum
Page 293: (right) courtesy of Laura Balducci
Page 294: (top) courtesy of Francis Antonisse; (bottom) courtesy of AU Fest
Page 295: (top left) Jillian King, courtesy of Paulina Ortlieb; (bottom left) Paul Baines; (bottom right) Mike Branum
Page 296: (top) Cameron Chacon; (bottom) courtesy of Isaac Tremblay
Page 297: Webmeister Bud
Page 298: (top left) John Carlow; (center & bottom left) Webmeister Bud; (bottom right) courtesy of Byron Slack
Page 299: (left) photographer unknown; (right) Carrie Jo Swiggum
Page 300: Mike Branum
Page 302: Marc Gaertner
Page 303: Webmeister Bud
Pages 304–5: collage by briandesign
Page 307: Adam Slack
Page 308: (left) photographer unknown; (right) John Chedsey
Page 309: Andy Sandall
Page 314: Ken Kempster
Page 315: Ken Kempster

# ABOUT THE CONTRIBUTORS

**Jason Lamb** was born and raised in Victoria, British Columbia. After pursuing a career in stand-up comedy in Vancouver for fourteen years, he went back to school for broadcast journalism and moved back to his hometown of Victoria in 2008. Since then, Jason has been one half of the morning show at the Zone @ 91-3. He also produces and hosts *The Punk Show*, a weekly uncensored and commercial-free showcase of punk rock new and old, local and otherwise. It was on this show where he first interviewed members of his favourite band, NoMeansNo. That connection helped convince the band to allow Jason access to their incredible story. When not on the radio or doing stand-up, Jason enjoys full-contact snooker and writing flattering biographies of himself.

**Paul Prescott** is a retired engineer from Maine who currently lives in Belize. He has been a NoMeansNo fan since the mid-'80s.

**Fred Armisen** is one of the great comedians of his generation. A cast member on *Saturday Night Live*, Fred went on to create the comedy series *Portlandia* with Carrie Brownstein (Sleater-Kinney). He has appeared in dozens of movies and television shows over the past two decades. Before his career in comedy and acting, Fred was the drummer of Chicago band Trenchmouth. His band opened for NoMeansNo in Texas in the mid-1990s. Fred is a very big fan of NMN.

**W. Buzz Ryan** is a fictional character who is actually the writing of NoMeansNo guitarist Tom Holliston. W. Buzz provided satirical and strange essays that served as liner notes on many NMN albums, as well as press releases and radio spots. He is a beloved and misunderstood member of the NoMeansNo universe.

# ABOUT PM PRESS

PM Press is an independent, radical publisher of books and media to educate, entertain, and inspire. Founded in 2007 by a small group of people with decades of publishing, media, and organizing experience, PM Press amplifies the voices of radical authors, artists, and activists. Our aim is to deliver bold political ideas and vital stories to people from all walks of life and arm the dreamers to demand the impossible. We have sold millions of copies of our books, most often one at a time, face to face. We're old enough to know what we're doing and young enough to know what's at stake. Join us to create a better world.

**PM Press**
**PO Box 23912**
**Oakland, CA 94623**
**www.pmpress.org**

**PM Press in Europe**
**europe@pmpress.org**
**www.pmpress.org.uk**

# FRIENDS OF PM PRESS

These are indisputably momentous times—the financial system is melting down globally and the Empire is stumbling. Now more than ever there is a vital need for radical ideas.

In the many years since its founding—and on a mere shoestring—PM Press has risen to the formidable challenge of publishing and distributing knowledge and entertainment for the struggles ahead. With hundreds of releases to date, we have published an impressive and stimulating array of literature, art, music, politics, and culture. Using every available medium, we've succeeded in connecting those hungry for ideas and information to those putting them into practice.

*Friends of PM* allows you to directly help impact, amplify, and revitalize the discourse and actions of radical writers, filmmakers, and artists. It provides us with a stable foundation from which we can build upon our early successes and provides a much-needed subsidy for the materials that can't necessarily pay their own way. You can help make that happen—and receive every new title automatically delivered to your door once a month—by joining as a Friend of PM Press. And, we'll throw in a free T-shirt when you sign up.

Here are your options:

- **$30 a month** Get all books and pamphlets plus a 50% discount on all webstore purchases
- **$40 a month** Get all PM Press releases (including CDs and DVDs) plus a 50% discount on all webstore purchases
- **$100 a month** Superstar—Everything plus PM merchandise, free downloads, and a 50% discount on all webstore purchases

For those who can't afford $30 or more a month, we have **Sustainer Rates** at $15, $10, and $5. Sustainers get a free PM Press T-shirt and a 50% discount on all purchases from our website.

Your Visa or Mastercard will be billed once a month, until you tell us to stop. Or until our efforts succeed in bringing the revolution around. Or the financial meltdown of Capital makes plastic redundant. Whichever comes first.

## *Queercore: How to Punk a Revolution: An Oral History*

Edited by Liam Warfield, Walter Crasshole, and Yony Leyser with an Introduction by Anna Joy Springer and Lynn Breedlove

**ISBN: 978-1-62963-796-9**
**$18.00 208 pages**

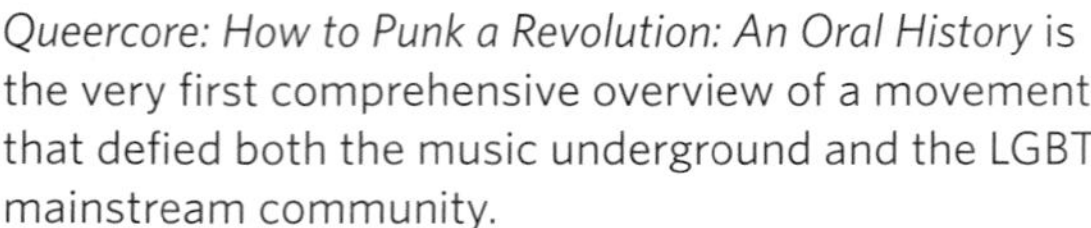

*Queercore: How to Punk a Revolution: An Oral History* is the very first comprehensive overview of a movement that defied both the music underground and the LGBT mainstream community.

Through exclusive interviews with protagonists like Bruce LaBruce, G.B. Jones, Jayne County, Kathleen Hanna of Bikini Kill and Le Tigre, film director and author John Waters, Lynn Breedlove of Tribe 8, Jon Ginoli of Pansy Division, and many more, alongside a treasure trove of never-before-seen photographs and reprinted zines from the time, *Queercore* traces the history of a scene originally "fabricated" in the bedrooms and coffee shops of Toronto and San Francisco by a few young, queer punks to its emergence as a relevant and real revolution. *Queercore* is a down-to-details firsthand account of the movement explored by the people that lived it—from punk's early queer elements, to the moment that Toronto kids decided they needed to create a scene that didn't exist, to Pansy Division's infiltration of the mainstream, and the emergence of riot grrrl—as well as the clothes, zines, art, film, and music that made this movement an exciting middle finger to complacent gay and straight society. *Queercore* will stand as both a testament to radically gay politics and culture and an important reference for those who wish to better understand this explosive movement.

*"Finally, a book that centers on the wild, innovative, and fearless contributions queers made to punk rock, creating a punker-than-punk subculture beneath the subculture, queercore. Gossipy and inspiring, a historical document and a call to arms during a time when the entire planet could use a dose of queer, creative rage."*
—Michelle Tea, author of *Valencia*

## *Dead Kennedys: Fresh Fruit for Rotting Vegetables, The Early Years*

Alex Ogg with Illustrations by Winston Smith and Photographs by Ruby Ray

**ISBN: 978-160-486-489-2**
**$17.95 224 pages**

Dead Kennedys routinely top both critic and fan polls as the greatest punk band of their generation. Their debut full-length, *Fresh Fruit for Rotting Vegetables*, in particular, is regularly voted among the top albums in the genre. *Fresh Fruit* offered a perfect hybrid of humor and polemic strapped to a musical chassis that was as tetchy and inventive as Jello Biafra's withering broadsides. Those lyrics, cruel in their precision, were revelatory. But it wouldn't have worked if the underlying sonics were not such an uproarious rush, the paraffin to Biafra's naked flame.

Dead Kennedys' continuing influence is an extraordinary achievement for a band that had practically zero radio play and only released records on independent labels. They not only existed outside of the mainstream but were, as V. Vale of *Search and Destroy* noted, the first band of their stature to turn on and attack the music industry itself. The DKs set so much in motion. They were integral to the formulation of an alternative network that allowed bands on the first rung of the ladder to tour outside of their own backyard. They were instrumental in supporting the concept of all-ages shows and spurned the advances of corporate rock promoters and industry lapdogs. They legitimized the notion of an American punk band touring internationally while disseminating the true horror of their native country's foreign policies, effectively serving as anti-ambassadors on their travels.

The book uses dozens of first-hand interviews, photos, and original artwork to offer a new perspective on a group who would become mired in controversy almost from the get-go. It applauds the band's key role in transforming punk rhetoric, both polemical and musical, into something genuinely threatening—and enormously funny.

## *Silence Is No Reaction: Forty Years of Subhumans*

Ian Glasper

**ISBN: 978-162-963-550-7**
**979-888-744-000-2**
**$25.00 640 pages**

Formed in Wiltshire, England, in 1980, the Subhumans are rightly held in high regard as one of the best punk rock bands to ever hail from the UK.

Over the course of five timeless studio albums and just as many classic EPs, not to mention well over 1,000 gigs around the world, they have blended serious anarcho punk with a demented sense of humour and genuinely memorable tunes to create something quite unique and utterly compelling. For the first time ever, their whole story is told, straight from the recollections of every band member past and present, as well as a dizzying array of their closest friends and peers, with not a single stone left unturned. Bolstered with hundreds of flyers and exclusive photos, it's the definitive account of the much-loved band.

*"It's all here: the genesis of the band, the practising, the song-writing, the recordings, the gigs, the original split and the reformation . . . in fact everything you could possibly want to know about this very special band."*
—Tony Whatley of Suspect Device

*"Ian Glasper captures the emotion and excitement surrounding one of the most enduring punk bands on the planet. With an extensive—some might say forensic—narrative, this book really gets under the skin of a perennial favourite who have rarely put a foot wrong."*
—Nathan Haywire, *Louder Than War*

*"Subhumans have integrity in spades, and you can't buy that. They were important then and are important now."*
—Sean Forbes of Wat Tyler and Hard Skin

*"Subhumans are special both on and off stage. It's the passion that's evident onstage, with those beautifully constructed lyrics spat out with every breath—and that charged energy they generate, that sweeps through the crowd and leaves us feeling changed."*
—Ruth Elias of Hagar the Womb

## *The Day the Country Died: A History of Anarcho Punk 1980–1984*

Ian Glasper

**ISBN: 978-160-486-516-5**
**$24.95 496 pages**

*The Day the Country Died* features author, historian, and musician Ian Glasper (*Burning Britain*) exploring in minute detail the influential, esoteric, UK anarcho punk scene of the early Eighties.

If the colorful '80s punk bands captured in *Burning Britain* were loud, political, and uncompromising, those examined in *The Day the Country Died* were even more so, totally prepared to risk their liberty to communicate the ideals they believed in so passionately.

With Crass and Poison Girls opening the floodgates, the arrival of bands such as Zounds, Flux of Pink Indians, Conflict, Subhumans, Chumbawamba, Amebix, Rudimentary Peni, Antisect, Omega Tribe, and Icons of Filth heralded a brand new age of honesty and integrity in underground music. With a backdrop of Thatcher's Britain, punk music became self-sufficient and considerably more aggressive, blending a DIY ethos with activism to create the perfectly bleak soundtrack to the zeitgeist of a discontented British youth.

It was a time when punk stopped being merely a radical fashion statement, and became a force for real social change; a genuine revolutionary movement, driven by some of the most challenging noises ever committed to tape. Anarchy, as regards punk rock, no longer meant "cash from chaos." It meant "freedom, peace, and unity." Anarcho punk took the rebellion inherent in punk from the beginning to a whole new level of personal awareness.

All the scene's biggest names, and most of the smaller ones, are comprehensively covered with new, exclusive interviews and hundreds of previously unseen photographs.

## *The Fascist Groove Thing: A History of Thatcher's Britain in 21 Mixtapes*

Hugh Hodges with a Preface by Dick Lucas and Foreword by Boff Whalley

**ISBN: 978-162-963-884-3**
**$22.95 384 pages**

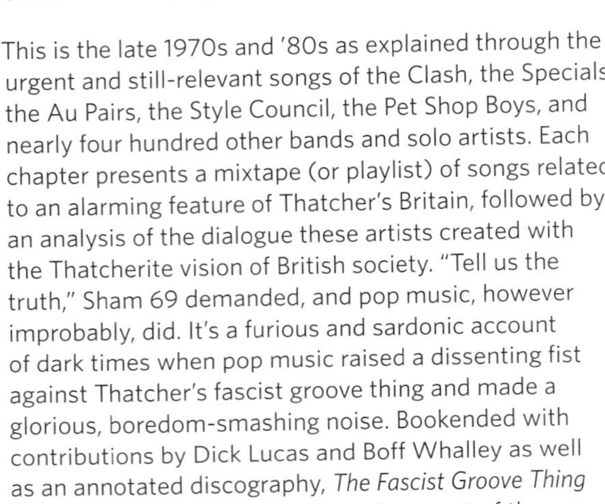

This is the late 1970s and '80s as explained through the urgent and still-relevant songs of the Clash, the Specials, the Au Pairs, the Style Council, the Pet Shop Boys, and nearly four hundred other bands and solo artists. Each chapter presents a mixtape (or playlist) of songs related to an alarming feature of Thatcher's Britain, followed by an analysis of the dialogue these artists created with the Thatcherite vision of British society. "Tell us the truth," Sham 69 demanded, and pop music, however improbably, did. It's a furious and sardonic account of dark times when pop music raised a dissenting fist against Thatcher's fascist groove thing and made a glorious, boredom-smashing noise. Bookended with contributions by Dick Lucas and Boff Whalley as well as an annotated discography, *The Fascist Groove Thing* presents an original and polemical account of the era.

*"It's not often that reading history books works best with a soundtrack playing simultaneously, but Hugh Hodges has succeeded in evoking both the noises and the feel of a tumultuous 1980s. Proving that pop music is the historian's friend, he has here recovered those who help us best make sense of a scary, precarious, and exciting world."*
—Matthew Worley, author of *No Future: Punk, Politics and British Youth Culture, 1976–1984*

*"Those who think the 1980s were camp and fun clearly didn't live them. The Thatcher/Reagan era was grim as fuck. This tells the real story from the underground."*
—Ian Brennan, author of *Muse-Sick* and *Silenced by Sound*

*"Very interesting and timely indeed."*
—Anne Clark, spoken-word poet, *The Smallest Act of Kindness*

## *The Fascist Groove Thing cassette*

Various Artists

**Catalog No: PMA 026-4**
**$10.99 63 mins, 50 secs**

This soundtrack compilation to Hugh Hodges's brilliant book *The Fascist Groove Thing: A History of Thatcher's Britain in 21 Mixtapes* features 20 tracks of classic punk, anarcho-punk and folk from Margaret Thatcher's reign and eventual demise (some quite rare). While intended as a companion to the book this mixtape works equally well on its own. It will help prove that while Thatcher's policies may have been utter crap, the music of this era that came out in response to her was anything but.

Tracklist:

A1. Crisis – UK '79 (Live 2019)
A2. Diagram Brothers – My Dinner (1981)
A3. Metro Youth – Brutalised (1982)
A4. Subhumans – Rats (1983)
A5. The Astronauts – Typically English Day (1983)
A6. A-Heads – Isolated (1983)
A7. Icons of Filth – Your Military (1983)
A8. Anti-System – Government Lies (1983)
A9. Passion Killers – Judging by Headlines (1984)
A10. Political Asylum – System of War (1985)
A11. Chumbawamba – Fitzwilliam (1985)
B1. Terminus – Propaganda War (1986)
B2. The Three Johns – Sold Down the River (1986)
B3. Hippy Slags – Sunlight on the Truncheons (1987)
B4. Oi Polloi – Nuclear Waste (1987)
B5. Culture Shock – Northern Ireland (1989)
B6. Wat Tyler – No ID (1989)
B7. Citizen Fish – Home Economics (1990)
B8. Robb Johnson and Pip Collings – Vic Williams (1992)
B9. Attila the Stockbroker's Barnstormer – Maggots 1, Maggie 0 (2012)